Unstructuring Chinese Society

Studies in Anthropology and History

Studies in Anthropology and History is a series which develops new theoretical perspectives, and combines comparative and ethnographic studies with historical research.

Edited by James Carrier, University of Durham, UK.

Associate editors: Nicholas Thomas, The Australian National University, Canberra and Emiko Ohnuki-Tierney, University of Wisconsin, USA.

This book is part of a series. The publisher will accept continuation orders which may be cancelled at any time and which provide for automatic billing and shipping of each title in the series upon publication. Please write for details.

Amsteldijk 166
1st Floor
1079 LH Amsterdam
The Netherlands

British Library Cataloguing in Publication Data

Chun, Allen
 Unstructuring Chinese society : the fictions of colonial
 practice and the changing realities of land in the new
 territories of Hong Kong. – (Studies in anthropology and
 history ; v. 27)
 1. Village communities – China – Hong Kong 2. Hong Kong
 (China) – Social life and customs
 I. Title
 307.7′62′095125

ISBN: 90-5702-450-0

Allen Chun

Unstructuring Chinese Society

The Fictions of Colonial Practice and the Changing Realities of 'Land' in the New Territories of Hong Kong

ho ap

harwood academic publishers
Australia • Canada • France • Germany • India • Japan
Luxembourg • Malaysia • The Netherlands • Russia
Singapore • Switzerland

To the memory of Wai Cheong Chun, Kit Yung Chun,
Morton H. Fried and David M. Schneider.
The fruits of their parental guidance live on.

Contents

Tables

Preface

This book is really about the virtues of patience. After I finished writing my dissertation, upon which the present manuscript is an expansion and recasting of several key chapters, I resisted several offers to immediately publish the book. For one thing, although not particularly evident in the dissertation itself, the final product turned out to be radically different from the study as initially proposed and carried out. I did not stray far from the core concerns that first prompted the proposed study. Instead, the solutions to my concerns increasingly led me farther away from the narrowly defined field where I had expected to find and isolate my problem. The larger and more complicated my problem became, the more unsure I became about my ability to unravel the various entanglements of culture, history and discourse that I apparently encountered, given also the gaps in archival and other data that were filled only much later. Moreover, these entanglements were not just exceptional peculiarities of my local case study but rather constitutive of deeper processes of state and unconscious social transformations. These processes and transformations problematized existing notions of colonialism, modernity and globalization, among other things, and the magnitude of these problems, insofar as they resonated in other venues as well, led me to take stock of the literature and rethink certain underlying propositions. The emergence of postcolonialism as a current of theoretical criticism over the past decade has invoked new interest in historical colonialism and the extensive ramifications of colonial experience on the changing fabric of local rural society. Far from being an open and shut case, this current of criticism has made it possible to rethink a whole complex of relations.

At the outset, the contribution of the late David M. Schneider was seminal in helping me not only to rethink certain problematic assumptions underlying the descent model but also to question the fictive qualities of lineage-village complexes in southeastern China. However, unbeknownst to either of us at the time, it was not just a matter of understanding kinship from the perspective of its symbolic or cultural definitions. While he was right in insisting that these cultural concepts were the appropriate point of departure for any such reinterpretation, it became apparent as the study went on that the basic frame of reference for understanding lineage organization as a local, social phenomenon rested less on the centrality of defining kinship relations, which were embedded in a complex of ideas pertaining to the person, family, social exchange and domestic worship, than on defining the Chinese village as a peculiar kind of cultural and social entity. Rather than being the natural extension of a lineage model in descent terms, the village community clearly embodied concepts and practices that had their own genealogy and through which kinship was radically reappropriated. Instead of blindly imposing the model in its entirety on empirical reality, which is what most anthropologists appear to have done, it was necessary to see both parts of the lineage-village as analytically distinct as a precondition for seeing how one entailed the other. Ironically, while the initial project was built with this objective in mind, the unpacking of cultural concepts pertaining to the family, household, domestic ritual and social exchange in relation to the village presented in this book can only be considered a point of departure for something that requires separate and systematic discussion later on.

In the process of understanding the New Territories village, it became clear that it had undergone tremendous change since colonial occupation, despite claims by anthropologists and historians alike that they were vestiges of traditional social organization and that the British were more Chinese than the Chinese themselves, in ways that obscured what those traditional relationships really were. The work of Bernard S. Cohn in nineteenth century India had long signalled underlying conflicts between a colonial regime and indigenous governance that led to the invention of caste, its archivalization of culture and overt codification of people and things that later became mistaken for 'tradition'. Through no fault of his own, I did not fully appreciate the significance of these insights until well after I stumbled upon the same phenomena in a Hong Kong context. For reasons that will become evident toward the end, land is the common interface that reveals the essential differences between the regime of colonial governmentality and traditional practice. Land has become the point of application not only for the colonial government's definition of the village and constituent community but more importantly for the regulation of local life in society as a whole. The conflicts that made manifest the differences between the imposition of a colonial (ultimately modern) system of social values and its native referent became effaced in writing, setting the scene for this book.

Map 1 Hong Kong

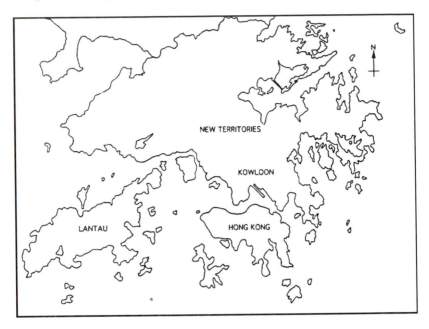

Map 2 China

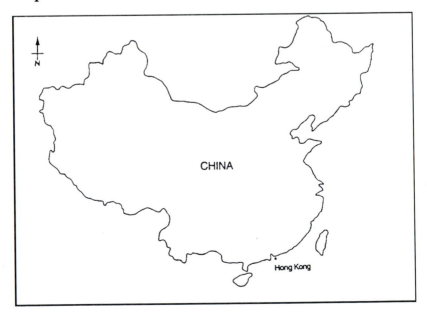

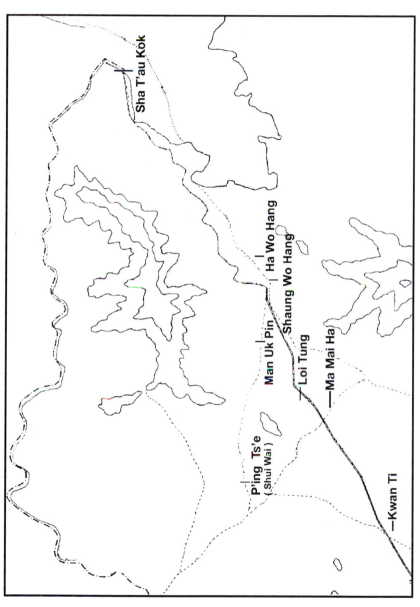

Map 3 Hong Kong and the New Territories

The Field of History in the Field

T he more things remain the same, the more they change.

The term "history" in our "postmodern" era has a double entendre. It refers, of course, to the facts and events of history as they happened and their underlying meanings. But the act of viewing and narrating history implicates the subjective interpretation of the analyst-cum-author as well. Thus, it is not enough to state that history is significant as it takes place, "as a matter of fact". Its significance changes also as a function of its relevance to the producer (author) and consumer (reader) of history. In this regard, the dictum "the more things remain the same, the more they change", which is itself a reversal of structuralist thinking, can be understood to refer to both the process of social change in the New Territories of Hong Kong and the way in which actors (once removed as a function of culture) then scholars (twice removed as a function of culture and history) have portrayed the significance of these changes. History in these two senses is intertwined, and it is the goal of this book to show how and why this has been the case.

This book has a history. It started out as a simple ethnographic field study of what I was told was a traditional village in a remote area of the northern New Territories of Hong Kong, a single lineage-village with a traceable genealogical history and an established pattern of relations with neighboring villages. Despite the drastic social, economic and political changes that had transformed the rural landscape elsewhere, especially in the postwar era, this village had remained for most part staunchly "traditional" by refusing to accept outsiders and to succumb to the various pressures of commoditization that saw the influx of new industries and high-rise settlements. This ethnography was supposed to be a story of how tradition thrived in a progressive society, presumably also as a vindication of the assorted anthropological

1

principles that held sacred the kin solidarity of the clan or lineage and its various underlying rationales. No sooner had I moved into the village then I noticed strange symptoms of this traditional way of life. Agriculture had been totally abandoned decades ago, most of the houses were unoccupied, and in many instances occupied by a single elderly caretaker. The residents, by their own admission, were composed of the elderly and the young. Those of working age who remained in the village were almost certainly unemployed. Needless to say, those who lived there and were not working in any capacity were almost certainly subsisting on remittances sent from householders working in the city or abroad.

There appeared to be an abundance of land, but this too turned out to be a fiction. People constantly complained about not having land to build houses, and the plight that afflicted both agricultural livelihood on the land as well as scarcity of housing land had similar roots in the nature of colonial land policy, especially during the postwar era, which was itself a response to, as well as manifestation of, even larger sociopolitical forces occurring at a global level. Moreover, the further I traced the historical roots of these events along with their underlying causes and motivations, the more it became clear that the source of many problems stemming from the government's attempt to define and administer land was still hopelessly entangled in the theory and practice of the New Territories Lease. But to invoke the nature of the Lease was to unleash an even larger Pandora's box of fictions and contradictory practices that lay at the heart of colonialism, moral regulation of the state and a changing global capitalism. Its relationship to the functioning of rural social organization centered on the government's unwavering belief that in the midst of all these radical global changes, they had governed the territory on the basis of indigenous custom, in accordance with the principle of the Lease. My effort to unravel all the historical, legal and cultural complexities underlying these dilemmas eventually took me far away from the field, where I started. This book then is a long answer to a simple field study, to show that the appearance of local, social phenomena, especially "traditional" ones, is far from "simple".

I could have stuck with my original field project for which I was properly trained to undertake. After all, a symbolic study of ancestor worship in a Hakka village in rural Hong Kong would still have important repercussions for a deeper anthropological and sinological understanding of Chinese kinship, domestic ritual and social organization. Moreover, local lineage organization exists, patrilineal inheritance of surname and property is alive and well, most villages can be seen as survivals of a single-surname ideal or multi-surname variation thereof, and the relationship of all above to land and ancestor worship still remains intact, if this is what concerns the field. The abundance of ethnographic monographs published in the New Territories during the postwar era alone attests to the popularity and viability of such studies. But to write in an ethnographic vacuum, as if to blind myself to what appear to be corrupting influences on the systemic if not holistic enterprise to which anthropologists hold dear in regard to "the field", would have unduly prejudiced my focus away from the larger context that had defined the setting for and enabled the ongoing existence of local society in the first place. Far from being a cut and dried matter, as can be evidenced by the authority of unilineal narratives of utilitarian progress and social well-being that have buttressed most prevailing social scientific theories of culture and society, our understanding even of "tradition" and the "native's point of view" is quite problematic.

Ironically, despite such anthropological classics as Potter's *Capitalism and the Chinese Peasant* (1968), one knows little or nothing about the nature or process of "capitalism", especially in a Hong Kong local context. The advent of postmodern writings have on the whole rightly shifted our attention away from modernization as economic progress to modernity. The advent of postcolonial theory in various incarnations has also problematized the existence of underlying regimes of power, but more importantly both have underscored the seminal importance of culture as point of social application and mediating force in the practice of power. Culture takes many forms, and in the context of the present study it will be apparent that the realm of culture is not just limited to symbolic notions of "land" but that the latter, by its association with cultural notions of family, household and village, entails a systematic practice of social life that is quite different from that posited by the ideologies of modernity and kinship theory. The colonial interregnum and its narratives of rules are instructive, insofar as they make manifest conflicts at the level of culture that in other circumstances probably would not be apparent.

The nature of Hong Kong's colonial experience is worthy of scrutiny not just for what it is, as a matter of *fact*, but also for how it represents itself, through *discourse*. It is probably not surprising thus that in retrospect both government and academic authorities have consistently denied the existence (or maybe just the relevance) of colonialism, as bluntly highlighted by Birch's *Hong Kong: The Colony That Never Was* (1991), in terms not unlike the way the exploitative character of capitalism was systematically written out of mainstream narratives of social and economic progress in Hong Kong. One may extend this observation to include the question of whether the "traditional" village in the New Territories of Hong Kong today is all that traditional. The way in which actor-authors constantly efface their own subjectivity in action (through claims of cultural objectivity) and writing (through rationalization of the facts) is part and parcel of this colonial *violence*.

In short, I am not simply advocating global ethnography, as a corrective to studies in the field, and historical anthropology, as an amendment to synchronic analyses of sociocultural systems, but more importantly a study of culture which views the latter as an integrated feature of institutional and local social systems of practice in an ongoing context of power. To say the least, colonialism is not the only relevant aspect of power in the context of a lineage-village, but it is certainly a sorely misunderstood dimension in the study of local society that begs further attention, particularly as a result of its deliberate and systematic effacement.

Behind every ethnography is a story, and mine is no exception. Moreover, the seamless character of most ethnographies tends to disguise the fact that much of its truly important data is obtained through a process of trivial conversation, drunken thoughts and outrageous bumbling. In my case, three serious errors of interpretation formed the basis for the study that followed. First of all, like most urbanites, I was struck by what appeared to be the freedom and spaciousness of living in the village, an illusion that disguised instead a locally perceived crisis of land scarcity engendered by an entangled complex of legal rules over land use and ownership. Secondly, I assumed that there was something privileged about this village, simply because it was an archetypical single-lineage village, a phenomenon made paradigmatic by anthropologists and historians of Chinese society. Thirdly, I assumed that there was a significant relationship between land and lineage that accented or magnified the social nature of the village. In all three cases, these errors were less invalidated by their factual inaccuracy per se than magnified by certain false projections of theory. However, discovering why theory is blatantly misleading is less difficult than understanding how things in fact really click.

On the surface of things, the perception of land scarcity was illustrated by the fact that villagers were not free to utilize and build on land as they pleased. The restrictions on land use were exacerbated by the fact that, in addition to the minute, often excessively fractured divisions of land, adjacent plots of land differed radically in value, sometimes over hundred-fold. Restrictions on land conversion and disproportionate land values impeded rational growth and development from a village point of view, but more importantly these legal impediments turned out to be the result of a long distorted history of land policy. The privileged nature of the single lineage-village was on the other hand the overall projection of descent principles that had its own genealogy of discourse in the anthropological literature. In brief, the constitution of a village was supposed to be a product of certain kin based rules which in turn had its own formal organizational logic. Appealing as such logic appears to be, I argue to the contrary that the conceptual relationships posited regarding the nature of family, household, lineage and village are seriously flawed and await assessment in new light. Finally, the relationship between land and lineage (or village), as witnessed by the long obsession with 'land-o-mania' in the anthropological and sinological literature, has no doubt been accentuated by the singular influence of Freedman's (1958) theory of Chinese lineage organization. Without denying the relevance and salience of land as a source of economic wealth and social livelihood, it suffices here for the moment to say that the utilitarian rationality attached to land by Freedman's theory does not explain under certain circumstances the secondary value that villagers attach to the land, especially in the face of the perceived sanctity of the community. Instead of being an independent variable of lineage and village growth, I argue that land is a socially dependent variable which is rather a function of community values (or the lack of them).

The kind of conceptual gap that had to be bridged between our own reality and that of the villagers can be exemplified by my initial efforts to rent a house to live in the village. The village that was recommended to me was in a remote, economically depressed region of the northern New Territories. Its residents had abandoned agriculture over a decade ago, and many migrated overseas or to the city to find a living. My inquiries about housing always met with the same kind of reply: "we don't usually rent to outsiders; besides, all houses in the village are lived in". After several futile attempts, I left the matter in the hands of liaison officers at District Office North, who then made inquiries on my behalf.

Several weeks later, I was notified by the District Officer that he was able to find me accommodations in the village I requested, free of rent and for however long I wished. The villager who extended the invitation was an elder residing in Sheung Wo Hang who, according to colleagues at the Chinese University of Hong Kong, was trying to cultivate a talking relationship with scholars there. So, there I was, helping him bridge a gap with the ivory tower. He received me cordially and said that the house belonged to his nephew, who had been living in the U.K. for several years along with his children. Although this house was built only 15 years ago, its owners built a new house a year ago in another part of the village, thus making the older house expendable. Moreover, the owner's son had recently returned from the U.K. to find work locally and was living in the new house. The elder then took me to visit the village headman, who welcomed my stay there.

Two weeks into my stay, everything began to fall apart. A colleague at the Chinese University left me a note saying that the village headman called early that morning. I was told that, contrary to expectation, I could only be allowed to stay in that village house for a week or so, and that having already overstayed it by a week, it was imperative that I vacate the premises as soon as possible. At the end of the note was a postscript, reminding that on behalf of the university I should make apologies for any inconvenience caused. I rushed back to the village and spoke to the elder who arranged my accommodation. He said that the village headman paid him a visit in the morning to talk about problems regarding use of the house. Apparently, the house's owner called his son, who lived in the family's new house, to say that they could not let the house out to a stranger for any long period of time. Since I was not at home, the village headman called my colleague at the university. Later on in the evening, the owner's son came personally to explain the situation to me. He apologized for the sudden change of circumstances and said that it would all right with him if I stayed in the house until new lodging was found. Early next morning, I asked the headman for advice on where to go. To my surprise, he expressed total ignorance of the matter and denied ever having talked to anyone at the university. Obviously, the elder, Mr. Li, lied.

Lies, alibis and deceptions without doubt have more of a place in detective mysteries. In this case, they not only shed light on why people bothered to make a fuss about renting a village house to an outsider but more importantly fleshed out certain distinct moral values of the community that I was supposedly studying, the implicit relationships that characteristically bound people to each other as well as the essence of what it meant to "live" in a village. As it turned out, the elder took the liberty of letting this house out and did not anticipate that his nephew, who had a house to spare, would object. The owner only found about it when his son casually mentioned the arrangement on the phone to his father. Faced with loss of face after the rejection, the elder had no recourse but to retract his offer as tactfully as he could, even to the point of pretending to speak as village headman.

The two weeks eviction notice stretched into two months, before a villager returning from the U.K. offered to let me stay in his house. Yet in retrospect, the most surprising thing about this affair was not the episode surrounding my initial attempt to find a place to live but rather my discovery not long after settling down that nearly half of the houses in the village were *vacant*, some for 10–20 years. But how could I reconcile this fact with statements made by everyone there that all the houses were "lived in"? Obviously, there was either a discrepancy in their definition of terms or a wider communication gap between us at a conceptual level.

Needless to say, the communication gap was much wider that could be seen at first glance. These simple incidences of misunderstanding about something that appears to be so basic or which people would automatically take for granted raises serious questions about the validity of certain judgments and speculations about the nature of social life made by bureaucrats and academics even further removed, most of whom enjoy the benefits of living in a sophisticated, cosmopolitan world characterized by simultaneous language translation and a high degree of cultural interchange. The problem of cultural (and theoretical) misunderstanding should have been compounded many times over in a past era where relations between the colonizers and colonized or rulers and ruled were separated even more as self and other. Many more cases of misunderstanding and conflict should have surfaced, contrary to the way inconsistencies of history have tended to be glossed over and written as unilineal narratives of ongoing social and political continuity.

It is possible thus to write an historical anthropology of the village in the New Territories of Hong Kong, but not without delving into the minds of people and behaviors of institutions at the local level on the one hand, and unpacking the events and machinations that have cumulatively given rise to the situation on the ground on the other. Yet despite the lofty epistemological goal, the methodological strategy for carrying out such an ethnohistory is more difficult than said. The process of unlocking "the native's point of view" involves in part stepping into a void where there can be no predetermined course or design, and in part stretching the limits of previous notions and assumptions, whose implicit influence one can never be sure of having shaken. In order to probe the changing meaning of land in a Hakka village of the northern New Territories, it was necessary to attempt to unpack in native terms the myriad concepts and practices that contribute to the meaning and functioning of diverse social institutions to which land is associated, namely ancestor worship, family, marriage, household, lineage and village. The primordial basis for reconstituting a native understanding of these social processes and local institutions is represented by the underlying cultural morphemes *zong, jia* and *qin.* This forms the main framework of discussion in Chapter Four.

The historical reconstitution of these institutions on the ground is a complex task that must view events, people, concepts and practices at the local level as embedded within a larger social, if not global, process. This process is not just the function of actions per se but more importantly perceptions and strategies that are culturally mediated and juxtaposed in a context of power. I argue first of all that many of the theories that anthropologists have used to make sense of local society are elaborate reifications of colonial encounters that have already taken place and become institutionalized in the codification and regulation of everyday life. These reifications are not simply mirror images of Eurocentric concepts that the colonial government put into practice in the administration of the territory but also deeper embodiments of disciplinary regimes that have as an ultimate goal a certain kind of moral regulation, social structuration or totalizing integration of local society in a traditional world where land, custom and village organization were largely immune to such hegemonic processes. In this regard, there are parallels here with British colonial experience elsewhere. This forms the main thesis of Chapter One.

The unique character of British colonialism in the late nineteenth and early twentieth centuries is epitomized in part by the principle of "indirect rule", which was amplified by the nature of the New Territories Lease and the government's repeated commitment to administer on the basis of indigenous custom. However, from the very beginning, this principle had already been complicated by conflicting interests dictated by colonial expediency and changing imperatives of state power. The record of indirect rule in this regard was mixed at best, but more importantly in the process of such rule the codifications and practices introduced an entangled web of codes and procedures that had merely the semblance of preserving custom. The system engendered by this entangled web became what was referred to later as "tradition". This forms the primary thrust of discussion in Chapter Two.

More than the politics of difference, colonialism must be seen as a moment in the sociological evolution of state power. In my opinion, this accounts for the eventual transformation of British colonial governmentality from a technology of power founded on the rule of law backed by the spectacle of force, to a disciplinary regime facilitated by the localization of the state apparatus, the appearance of all sorts of self-regulating grassroots organizations, village representative committees, rural cooperatives, etc., and the professionalization of the administrative system that essentially transferred authority from the person of the District Officer to a routine body of clerks and records, all effectively governed by the rule of law. This new mode of colonial rule intersected with the imperatives of modernity brought about not only by the structural evolution of the state but also by the vissitudes of market capitalism that made utilitarian survival a general way of life. This created strains in rural society not only by radically transforming the economic livelihood of indigenous villages, in some cases destroying agriculture altogether and in other cases replacing it with other forms of industry and new patterns of tenancy, but also by recasting in somewhat different light the ongoing dualism of colonizer and colonized interests in the practice of land policy. The ramifications of these ongoing conflicts manifested themselves differently in different regions, and this set of events provides the immediate background for the current state of village society seen in the New Territories. Far from being the norm, tradition has become a residual category. This forms the essential corpus of Chapter Three.

Finally, a note about romanization. Romanization is a convention, albeit an imperfect one, whose relevance is largely a function of intended audience. The sinological literature has generally followed the Pinyin system based on standard Mandarin (M). Those writing in the field of Hong Kong studies have preferred to romanize in Cantonese (C), the major dialect spoken there. In deference to local nuance, anthropologists have in principle tended to romanize in the actual dialect spoken in the field, which in my case was Hakka (H). For purposes of consistency, it probably would have been easier to be a purist by romanizing all terms in the same dialect. However, in consideration of a specific term's relevance to respective niches in academic discourse, I have opted instead to romanize according to level of specificity, especially since in many cases different sounding dialect terms are represented by the same Chinese character, from which they derive their essential meaning. Thus, it is assumed that Hakka is the most local, followed by Cantonese (which is considered by Hakka speakers in Hong Kong as the colloquial standard), then Mandarin (which is the dialect on which standard written Chinese is based). In practice, this means that the first romanization I will note in writing shall be the dialect term used in the text or actual context of speech. This will be followed in parentheses by the corresponding Cantonese or Mandarin terms, if

comparable or equivalent in meaning. Unmarked romanizations immediately following dialect terms should be taken to be Mandarin
pronunciation, unless they are terms that have appeared previously in
the book, thus do not require repeated explanation. I have been de-
cidedly ambivalent about place names. The popularization of Pinyin
on mainland China has in the long run even influenced Westerners to
adopt place names such as Beijing and Guangdong for formerly An-
glicized ones (Peking and Canton). The handover of Hong Kong to
China in 1997 should have sparked the same trend in romanization,
but this has failed to materialize. The most obvious case in point is the
continued reference to Hong Kong (instead of Xianggang) in the official
literature, although in certain contexts it is sometimes accompanied by
the suffix S.A.R. (Special Administrative Region). Thus, place names
in China, such as Shenzhen and Xinan county, are romanized in Pinyin,
while place names in Hong Kong and the New Territories remain
romanized in their usual Cantonese (for the sake of familiarity). Names
of local persons are generally in Cantonese.

Chapter One

Earthbound Anthropologies in the 'Structure' of Rural Chinese Society

There can be no such thing as a 'history' of rent, for this word fluctuates and dissolves before attempts to construe an essential meaning for it. A history of rent theory would further presuppose that an economic discourse exists as an eternity within which this category occupies a reserved space. But a theory of rent, a major component of a theory of distribution, cannot exist outside of the discourse which sets it to work; thus a history of rent theory has as much meaning as a history of medieval aircraft production, or an account of Elizabethan speedway racing. (Keith Tribe, *Land, Labour and Economic Discourse*)

LINEAGES OF THE ABSOLUTIST THEORY, OR THE POLITICS OF "SOCIAL STRUCTURE"

What you see is not what you get. Yet there was a time in anthropology, if not social sciences generally, when one was taught, to put it plainly, that the solution to all empirical questions of knowledge was simply to go out and "do it". If a sociologist wished to know the mind of society, he usually started by asking people. With enough opinions based on systematically designed surveys covering a typically diverse population, it would be possible to extrapolate an accurate or representative distribution of the whole. In a similar vein, anthropologists with intentions of understanding "the native's point of view" usually started by doing concrete fieldwork. The prime directive of talking with the natives and thinking like a native, not to mention seeing everything with one's own eyes, in essence placed a methodological premium on the visibly tangible, while at the same time devaluing the invisible and imaginative. Moreover, the foundation for empirical research was typically other empirical research. Survey and statistical analyses could always be compared with analyses in other places or times. Anthropologists on the other hand conventionally prepared for fieldwork research by reading other comparable ethnographies. However, in my opinion, the methodological basis for empirical analyses of these kinds resides less in the inherent concreteness of the speakable, thinkable and visible than in the notions of society implicitly invoked by these methods. Just as the validity of opinions is predicated by the axiomatic existence of a social consciousness as well as a technology capable of articulating individual consciences, then the validity of the fieldwork enterprise must likewise be predicated on the representative nature of local communities in a larger social field as well as a value-free technology for observing, selecting and making sense of ethnographic facts. The critiques by Clifford (1983) and others of ethnographic "authority" have already undermined the objectivity of the descriptive apparatus, yet few have successfully demystified the axiom of social structure that has been a fundamental if not ubiquitous feature of this "empiricism", too. It seems rather ironic that, in order to get what you see, you have to be convinced first of social structure's validity and reality in the "abstract". Why should one not question it?

When I first took up study in anthropology, kinship and social organization was considered a required course in the curriculum of the discipline. By the time I finished my formal professional training in anthropology, the significance of the field of kinship and its underlying theories had been so seriously undermined that few people bother now to teach it anymore. Nonetheless, the present work began as a field study of the cultural dimensions of kinship and social organization in a traditional Chinese village in the New Territories of Hong Kong, then eventually became an investigation into a process of colonial intervention that has in my view serious ramifications for how we understand customary practices and institutional patterns in Chinese local society as well as the ongoing dynamics of social change.

It is certainly not necessary to write a history of colonialism just to analyze the nature of Chinese local society, within which kinship constitutes one of many arbitrary phenomena. Despite criticism from within and outside the ethnographic enterprise, anthropology has increasingly diversified its "field" to incorporate the background of colonial pasts, presence of nation-states, advent of modernity, and intrusion of globalizing factors without having to make the entire world an object of scrutiny. Yet in this instance, these atypical excursions into the genealogies of colonialism and other unseen presences highlight perhaps the overall tendency of anthropologists in the China field to underestimate the disruptive effects of these interventions, while offering a different perspective on the nature of colonialism.

The transition from social organization to colonialism as the thematic focus of my study should not be read simply, however, as an arbitrary shift from kinship to politics as functionally distinct axes in the study of human society. One of the essential pillars of the theory of social structure, as it was articulated without doubt most eloquently by A.R. Radcliffe-Brown, was his assumption, largely gone unchallenged, that the reproduction and institutionalization of socially permanent bonds (epitomized best by relationships based on consanguinity) was a necessary precondition for the maintenance of a stable society. At its roots then, this theory constituted less a *scientific* statement about the objective nature of the world, and more accurately an argument in *political* terms about the viability of society as a functional entity. The relevance of social structure to the colonial experience of Hong Kong resides in the fact that a prime directive of colonial policy in the New Territories of Hong Kong was the need to administer society on the basis of local custom. The apparent need to identify an underlying social structure and ground the functioning of existing custom in relation to it as a primary precondition for maintaining the status quo, in effect put into practice a theory of society that came to be formulated more elegantly in abstract terms by A.R. Radcliffe-Brown several decades later. Far from being an accident, this coincidence of anthropology and history reflects in my opinion the commonality of *cultural* interface that guides the mind of both social structural theory and the colonial experience in general. The degree to which attempts by the colonial government to regulate local custom and Chinese tradition in accordance to what they viewed were objective or codified representations of customary law resulted in *conflict* with indigenous inhabitants, reflects in turn the concrete difference between these conceptions of custom on the one hand and native principles underlying those practices and institutions on the other. Given especially that these codes, definitions and assumptions have already been put into practice and even made "efficient" through the apparatuses of state power, evidence of a difference should indicate in the final analysis the implicit *violence* of what one would otherwise assume to be scientific or theoretical truths.

Much of the ethnographic and historical literature on Chinese kinship and social organization has focused so intensely on documenting the actual existence of large-scale lineage organization and its relationship to various aspects of local village life that one has virtually lost track of what exactly about the lineage accounts for its enormous staying power in both institutional and historical terms. To what degree is its organization a ramification of the natural staying power of descent relations, as kinship theorists have tried to make us believe, and to what extent does the Chinese lineage-village, as a complex of institutions involving the existence of kin relations, notions of locality, property devolution and ancestral practices, constitute a systemic presence in sociological terms? While explanations of phenomena in the field will continue to generate heated debate in sinological circles for years to come, it is important in the first instance to show how the *model* of social structure itself has evolved in the literature to the point where it has become a powerful construct in its own right that has enabled anthropologists and historians to make sense of customs, practices and institutions on the ground.

The road from the primordial conception of social structure in anthropology to the full-fledged study of descent groups throughout the world is a long, familiar tale reproduced in endless textbooks and courses on the subject. On the surface, at least, it is also one that traverses from one theoretical version to another and is reflected presumably in various ethnographic flavors. Nonetheless, it is useful to examine some of the major contributions to such thinking insofar as they reflect back upon the presuppositions of the model in epistemological terms. On the one hand, these presuppositions may simply represent the peculiar quirks of individual authors, influenced by any number of local factors that may have contributed to their creative faculty. On the other hand, I contend that these presuppositions may also represent cultural *truths* of a more fundamental (ultimately Eurocentric) nature, and that this has contributed not only to the longlasting appeal of such concepts to a broader community of thinkers but also to their unquestioned status in the actions of various colonial practitioners in relation to native others.

It goes without saying that lineage theory, which was the end distillation of various irreducible principles about kinship and descent groups, was a formal construct that preceded concrete ethnographic study rather than being the product of experience per se. Its inevitability in the field then was simply a consequence of the fact that it was driven by an internal logic. Much of its internal logic was forcefully demonstrated in Radcliffe-Brown's (1935) classic essay "Patrilineal and Matrilineal Succession". In this essay he attempted to lay out the reasoning for studying descent by arguing first of all that in order for society to perpetuate itself over time, there had to exist in society a set of rules definable in terms of rights of and duties that could guarantee definite and ongoing relations between persons. In *jural* terms, there was a need for rights *in personam* and rights *in rem*. His unusual emphasis upon rights *in rem*, defined as being in respect to certain people and things "as against the world", not only implied the existence of some out-of-the ordinary rights; more importantly, it implied the necessity of institutions which were constituted in a way that bound individuals to each other as though by some unambiguous and immutable law of nature. By virtue of having to impose duties in respect to a person (member) or thing (property) "as against the world" (i.e. on all other persons), the internal cohesion of such a group was thus a function of its own interrelatedness. In this regard, descent epitomized this jural rule, not only because its unambiguous, unchanging nature virtually guaranteed its continuity over time, but also because the exclusive character of property and boundedness of persons "as against the world" inherently tied considerations of social structure into an entire complex of obligations pertaining to the regulation of custom and community as a whole. In other words, it was not enough simply to postulate the existence of orderly jural rules like those based on descent. What made social structure so important was that it provided the basis upon which practices, beliefs and institutions could perpetuate themselves and become staple fixtures of society.

In short, Radcliffe-Brown understood social structure to be both a jural and morphological construction. His logical justification for society's *a priori* need to define jural rights in persons and things is general to his theory of social structure and is distinct from his assertion that kinship represents a most privileged form of social relationship that naturally varies in different societies. With regard to the latter, Radcliffe-Brown was one in a long line of anthropologists from the 19th century onward who recognized the highly developed existence of kinship systems in non-Western primitive societies. What distinguished him from his predecessors, however, was his attempt to view the operation of various functional components of society as being integrated in relation to or embedded within an abstract social structure, which was by nature a jural construction and constituted the objective basis of society as a whole.[1] More than just a series of classifications, the theory of social structure was a complex set of axiomatic assumptions, formal definitions and analytical tools for making sense of social institutions and practices as they existed on the ground.[2] Even more importantly, it was an *a priori* projection onto rather than an *a posteriori* rationalization of concrete experiential phenomena.

While acknowledging the contributions of Radcliffe-Brown's jural conception of social structure and its thematic centrality to the study of society, the work of Meyer Fortes generally emphasized the irreducibility of biological ties emanating from the family and the classificatory principles underlying descent itself that gave rise to diversity in social organization, making the functional study of social systems based upon the descent rule amenable to cross-cultural comparison. In combination with E.E. Evans-Pritchard's classic ethnographic account of the Nuer, the cumulative effect of these studies of descent groups or lineage systems seemed to contribute to the creation of "African models", but it was more importantly the synthesizing effect brought about by the thematic centrality of social structure that gave kinship and lineages a new role in the functional constitution of society.

The evolution of a "classic" ethnography centered initially in Africa can be seen as paralleling to a large degree the evolution of the anthropological literature on China, which also capitalized on the existence of similar lineage organizations and corresponding customs and practices. There are two concurrent developments in this overall evolution however, that must be distinguished. On the one hand, the operation of traditional Chinese institutions became "seen" now as functionally integrated by virtue of being tied to a general paradigm of social structure. At the same time, peculiarities of Chinese practices (as manifested in descent ideology, rules of inheritance, ties to locality and forms of social organization) also became incorporated into the eventual construction of a particularistic "Chinese" model.

In short, through an entire package of jural rules, primary relations coded in terms of descent and assumptions about the relevance of social interrelatedness to the functioning of belief systems, customary practices and other institutions, such a "kinship" model is less a mere set of definitional constructs pertaining to an exotic component of human societies than an ambitious set of propositions in epistemological terms about the natural constitution of society as a whole.

FROM EARTHBOUND KINSHIP TO THE CHINESE LINEAGE-VILLAGE

The phenomena of descent and lineage in China must be distinguished from the descent models or lineage theories that anthropologists and historians have deployed to make sense of the functioning of various customary practices, domestic organizations and socio-political institutions in a local Chinese context. Familism of all kinds appears to be a staple feature of Chinese life, a fact noted in textbook accounts, whether they be rooted in philosophical concepts like filial piety, or cast in ethnographic descriptions of earthbound kin communities. Moreover, most of what scholars know about the ideology and organization of Chinese descent groups in particular had already been spelled out systematically in a monograph by Hu Hsien-chin entitled (not surprisingly) *The Common Descent Group in China and Its Functions* (1948). Despite the timing of this book, which coincided with the appearance of classic ethnographies on African segmentary lineage systems, Hu was concerned simply with describing the multi-functionality of the *zu* (*tsu*), what she called the common descent group in China, in sociological and historical terms.

The state of the Chinese *zu* prior to the advent of lineage theory was in effect not unlike that of the Nuer before *The Nuer* (the book). Early ethnographies like those by Kulp (1925) and Fei (1939) in particular provided a wealth of factual data pertaining to the *zu* and other aspects of "Chinese familism and kinship". From these ethnographies and Hu's work, it is easy to distill certain unambiguous features of the *zu*, for example 1) the existence of definable descent-phrased rules regulating membership and succession within the *zu*, 2) the existence of clear-cut rules regarding the possession and transmission of a shared estate, and 3) a set of identifiable rites, beliefs and obligations pertaining to ancestor worship.

On the other hand, the transition from the empirical existence of descent and descent groups per se, richly documented in the social scientific literature with allusions to a much wider body of textual knowledge in classical Chinese, to a full-fledged model of descent that powerfully reshaped scholarly understanding in later years about the basic nature of Chinese society as a whole, really had to do with the development of a conceptual paradigm focused largely on the representation of the "single-lineage village" as the structural foundation of local Chinese society.

Seen against the background of Hu's textual analysis of the *zu*, the path breaking work by Freedman (1958, 1966) on lineage organization and society in southeastern China provided not just a new model of Chinese kinship; it was an ambitious attempt to offer a distinctive theory of Chinese society (as a structural entity) within which the *zu*, now called a lineage, played a seminal role. Or as Freedman (1958: v) succinctly defined his project, "unilineal kinship organization in a differentiated society and a centralized political system forms the main theme of the essay". The revolutionary transition from Hu to Freedman was one marked not necessarily by better scholarship but rather by the introduction of a different paradigm that saw diverse phenomena like agnatic village organization, corporate estates in land, genealogical segmentation, social stratification and a centralized polity as interdependent elements within a more encompassing functional system.

At a polemic level, Freedman's construction of this functional system was an explicit critique of Fortes' (1953) Africanist model of lineage organization in relation to decentralized political control, using obvious elements within a Chinese context to explain how kinship and the polity reinforced each other in sociological terms. Ironically, this part of the argument was by and large a failure. Far from showing how such institutions reinforced each other, except through the role of Janus-faced scholars-officials who as lineage elites and civil servants catered simultaneously to these respective interests, his elaborate rationale was a cover-up for a blatant failure to explain why one found lineage organization to be strongest in precisely those regions of China which were furthest removed from centralized political control and vice versa.[3] While the anti-Africanist dimension of his model has largely been forgotten by anthropologists and sinologists alike, his specific construction of the Chinese lineage on the other hand exerted enormous influence on prevailing notions of Chinese kinship that continued to reverberate throughout the rest of sinology. In essence, Freedman attempted to show that Chinese lineage organization, and the complex, differentiated society that emanated from it, had a certain structural foundation "on the ground". The logical consistency of his model was aided by the existence of established large-scale localized lineages and a widespread pattern of single-surname villages throughout southeastern China.[4]

It is not necessary here to spell out all the details of Freedman's complex thesis except to say that he placed crucial importance upon the role of a corporate estate in land as a key catalyst in the developmental process of lineage expansion, which then had important structural ramifications for social stratification, political power and local organization. In contrast perhaps to Hu, the singular importance placed upon landed property magnified the "representative" nature of the single lineage-village as the archetype at ground level of a functionally integrated and structured social system.[5] Thus, when succeeding generations of anthropologists and historians explicitly hailed the importance of Freedman's contributions to the study of Chinese kinship, they were really referring to the influence of a paradigm or set of analytical constructs that had given new *meaning* to existing phenomena than to new encyclopedic knowledge about kinship of the kind provided by Hu.[6]

As in the case of Radcliffe-Brown, one should emphasize that, as an *a priori* construction, the worth of the model put forth by Freedman resided in its internal consistency in analytical terms rather than the degree to which theory replicated empirical reality. In other words, it was a model meant not to explain patterns *of* social organization based upon the constitution of actual descent groups, since fieldwork had not even begun, but rather to explain the functional characteristics underlying patterns *for* social organization that accounted for the operation of descent groups in China, as he understood them, which had ramifications for other forms of socio-political organization. Or as he clearly declared at the outset:

> I must make it plain that while I attempt to remain faithful to the facts I have been able to adduce, the (analytical) picture I gradually build up inevitably departs from (empirical) reality by subsuming many variations under generalized heads. But if my picture of the localized lineage (as a sociological idealtype) in fact corresponds to no lineage (actual *zu*) which has ever existed in Fukien and Kwangtung, it is at least a summary of the characteristics of a great number of such lineages (*zu*). (Freedman 1958: xii, parenthetical enclosures mine)

In this regard, the first of Freedman's two core works, *Lineage Organization in Southeastern China* (1958), can be seen in essence as an analytical construction of the Chinese lineage as functional entity, based on existing documentary sources. Through deft use of ethnographic and village survey data, which reflected a direct relationship between *per capita* landholding and family size, he attempted to show how accumulation of property contributed to corporate solidarity within the *zu*. At higher levels of agnatic organization, accumulation of economic resources in general provided the basis for increasing ritual and social differentiation, which in turn became a fulcrum for establishing relationships to power and locality. The dynamic process that linked the growth of the lineage in demographic, economic, ritual and socio-political terms in effect made the *zu* a functional entity, with ties eventually to the rest of society. In short, the lineage model was a kind of reality.

Juxtaposed against empirical actuality, Freedman's "theory" then attempted to explain variability of organizational scale in localized descent groups, within a single conceptual framework. That lineage organization in this region displayed a great deal of diversity was already well known. A single descent group could in some cases spread over a cluster of neighboring villages while, in other instances, several kin groups would occupy distinct territorial niches within a single village.

Freedman's second of two volumes, *Chinese Lineage and Society: Kwangtung and Fukien* (1966), attempted to deal explicitly with the problem of local variation in descent groups, and it was really at this level that it sometimes became unclear as to whether the lineage "model" really referred to the construction of the *zu* as a functional entity or to the concrete manifestations of large-scale single lineage-villages that epitomized the lineage as sociological idealtype. Like popular usage of "African" models to highlight the classic existence of descent groups, Freedman's conflation of the single-lineage village to underscore the operation of the *zu* as functional entity led some in turn to substitute representation for reality.[7] In Taiwan, anthropologists immediately reacted to the widespread absence of single lineage-villages of the kind described by Freedman for southeastern China. This led Pasternak (1972), for example, to accent strategic access to resources like water and land, and other ethnographers to point to peculiarities in local historical development (Chuang 1973) and temple alliance networks (Hsu 1973, See 1973) as factors influencing the relative importance of territorial bonds over descent ties (Huang 1980, Wang 1981). In Hong Kong, while large-scale, single-lineage villages appeared to be a statistical norm (Baker 1968, Hayes 1977), social scientists were concerned too with explaining the evolution of multi-lineage villages as variations of the "model" (Lee 1981, Strauch 1983). It is perhaps at this point that looseness in the discourse now gives way to a cacophony of local voices and interpretations.

Taken together, his two monographs nonetheless contributed more than any other work to accent the conception of the single-lineage village as the essential framework upon which social organization in southeastern China was rooted. In economic terms, accumulation, control and transmission of the estate provided the means by which the lineage could grow and diversify in socio-political terms. In turn, largeness of scale and complexity of organization reinforced the importance of the lineage (as kinship phenomenon) as the social structural framework upon which other forms of local organization, the village in particular, were constituted.

Insofar as the lineage "model" constituted a reality in its own right by virtue of its inherent power to make meaningful phenomena that would otherwise simply "exist", it should also follow that at some point the constructed reality of the model built upon various layers of definitions, assumptions and projections is really more important than the surface manifestations themselves or the statistical frequency by which various correlations between phenomena can be inferred. Freedman was by no means the only one to offer a theory of Chinese lineage organization, but at a certain level of generality or shared consciousness he galvanized an entire field of sinological discourse that had ramifications far beyond the ethnographic domain per se. In this regard one should ask, what is this shared field of consciousness? To what extent do such underlying definitions, assumptions and projections reflect the epistemological mindset of the analytical observer rather than the various customs, traditions, practices and institutions that they are meant to explain?

I purposely draw parallels between Freedman's construction of the lineage-village and Radcliffe-Brown's jural-morphological construction of society to suggest that it is really at the level of logical relations within the model that meaning has been imposed upon social phenomena, even though the concrete examples raised are not exactly the same. Deconstructing the myth of the "single-lineage village" may be useful in the long run for field anthropologists concerned primarily with understanding the nature of Chinese local society, but one may ask, what is its specific relevance to Hong Kong's colonial experience? Likewise, in unmasking the process of colonial intervention that has in the long run irrevocably altered the functioning of "traditional" institutions and customary practices, leading either to their petrification in time or their eventual disintegration, one may ask, how does this directly affect our understanding of the specific kin-social organizations that anthropologists have focused much of their attention on, not only in Hong Kong but elsewhere as well? In this regard, I argue that the anthropologist's broader problematic concerns with the nature of Chinese kinship and social organization can be resolved partly by way of analogy.[8] In essence, if it can be shown how the colonial government's efforts to institutionalize in legal terms Chinese notions of land, customary practice and social organization in a Hong Kong context inevitably introduced certain "hidden injuries", which were perpetuated through maintenance of the system, as though in relation to a fixed structure, then by analogy one can also show how anthropologists have equally unwittingly through imposition of a lineage "model" projected similar (inherently cultural) assumptions and definitions onto our understanding of Chinese lineage organization. Although not colonial in a literal sense, the model ultimately reflects back on its own authorial subjectivity.

As in the case of Radcliffe-Brown, I argue that Freedman's attempt to view the *zu* as a functional entity imputes the existence of interrelatedness between the economic, social and political dimensions of the *zu* while at the same time grounds the functioning of diverse social institutions in reference to a fixed and unambiguous nodal point that is the localized lineage. How accurate the model is in reflecting the actual nature of phenomena on the ground is and will continue to be a point of debate, but it is necessary nonetheless to separate the conceptual underside of the model from empirical reality as a precondition for understanding the subjective nature of its mind. In this regard, there is little difference between the "mind" of the anthropologist, who through an act of interpretation and writing attempts to decode the behaviors of people or the operation of institutions, and the "mind" of colonial administrators and historical agents dealing with those same people and institutions, except for their relative positions in the context of power. In the following section, I shall attempt to show how the events constitutive of the British experience in Hong Kong were not just the products of material encounters but more precisely ongoing streams of consciousness mediated by culture. Insofar as the successful administration of the territory was predicated on the regulation of customary practices and traditional institutions, as they understood them, it might be feasible here also to view historical action as a kind of anthropology.

THE MIND OF BRITISH COLONIALISM IN CLOSE ENCOUNTERS OF THE THIRD KIND

It goes without saying that Hong Kong was a British colony, ceded in 1841 as a result of the Sino-British Opium War. The New Territories was leased from China to Britain in 1898 for 99 years as an extension of the colony for purposes of military defense. Hong Kong was no more than a barren isle when the British first occupied it. The New Territories was on the other hand a large stretch of land occupied by settled rural communities. Yet despite the literal facts, one must ask in what sense

Hong Kong constituted a "colony", in what sense the experiences that have shaped the nature of history and society there can be deemed "colonial", and in what sense the kind of "colonialism" indicative of Hong Kong's experience can be seen as a cultural project that contrasts with other colonial experiences, while at the same time reflecting certain more general or fundamental truths that lie at the core of an ongoing relationship between ideology and power.

Much important work on colonialism and culture has appeared recently in the historical and social scientific literature. Scholars writing from the general perspective of cultural studies have been correct to distance themselves from a previous generation of scholars that has for the most part focused on the economic and politically exploitative dimensions of colonialism. This is, of course, not to downplay the obvious effect of domination and destruction that has characterized colonial rule and that capitalized on the creation and maintenance of difference in racial and other terms, but instead to highlight the role of both explicit practices and underlying mentalities in legitimizing and normalizing the colonial project.

The relevance of colonialism to anthropology is, of course, nothing new. The classic collection of essays edited by Asad (1973) on the subject, made explicit what most anthropologists working in the first half of the 20th century already knew, namely that if it were not for colonial rule, anthropological studies of many non-Western societies would not have been possible. The physical presence of colonial authority probably not only invoked the use of anthropological knowledge in some cases as a tool of indirect rule but also served an indirect role in creating a form of knowledge that generally reflected the values of colonial pacification than of the local societies themselves. In this regard, the a priori fact of colonial pacification effectively helped to reify later structural-functional characterizations of a static, integrated society found everywhere. A more recent collection of essays edited by Stocking (1992) pursued this key relationship between the history of ethnographic writing and its colonial setting even further by arguing that the anthropologist was an unwitting agent in the maintenance and legitimation of colonial rule. As he (1992: 19) aptly noted, one must explain the paradox of why, despite its obvious background existence, "the colonial system was characteristically unmarked and invisible".

Whether one sees a strong degree of complicity between colonial rule and the construction of anthropological knowledge, or perceives coloniality in more passive terms, it is clear that the effacement of colonial presence in ethnographic writing itself makes the content of knowledge presented therein quite problematic. The power/knowledge relationship that situates the anthropologist in his colonial context of writing and practice is perhaps not unlike the situation that Said later describes for "Orientalism", but in my opinion instead of viewing colonialism as simply a backdrop for situating the nature of anthropological knowledge one must take it a step further to develop an *anthropology of the colonial experience.*

In this regard, numerous studies have thus pointed to the positive effects of diverse colluding factors like religion, language, history and ethnicity that have made the colonial project a quintessentially civilizing as well as routinizing process in ways that have managed also to contribute to the efficacy of rule. Yet by saying that colonialism is a cultural project, one can mean many things. Anthropological interest in the role of Christian missions has situated colonialism within a wider civilizing process while at the same time accenting the importance of symbolic systems in the political process as a whole.[9] Others have noted the strategic use of language in the construction of colonial power.[10] The emergence of discursive fields like historical writing and Orientalist writing can also be viewed as products of colonialism, whereby the meaningful construction of knowledge constitutes an integral part of an ongoing cultural struggle.[11] To these examples of culture, one might add other forms of narration and representation, like travel writing and art, as phenomena that emerge out of a colonial context.[12] The ethos and rationality of colonialism are not limited to the overt superstructural aspects of ideology and culture. They can also be abstracted from the system of colonial practice itself.

The collusion between colonialism and culture can be understood not only in terms of how colonialism may be constituted as a cultural project but also as a function of the way the colonial experience has given rise to the phenomenon of culture. There is a plethora of examples to illustrate what Clammer (1973) first saw as the colonial objectification of social structure in Fiji and what is referred to now in the literature commonly as "invention of tradition". Asad (1973:

115) has argued in turn that, in addition to glossing over the disruptive effects of colonial domination through recourse to descriptions of functional integration, the kind of cultural objectification implicit in ethnographic writing during postcolonial times actually reflected to a large extent a situation of "routine colonialism". As Cohn (1984) has noted, such forms of objectification are not just conceptualized but also become subject to census control and incessant statistical analysis. On the other hand, Dirks (1992b: 3) has asserted that modern notions of public culture, of the kind that usually invoke the systematic unity of language, race, geography and history, may have indeed been literal products of nationalism but were in essence really claims encouraged and facilitated by a preexisting history of colonialism.

Without denying the utility of the diverse notions of culture that have been invoked by recent writings on colonialism, I believe that there is another aspect of culture implicit in the practices themselves, a kind of *mentalité*, if you like, that can be seen as guiding the actions of agents and behaviors of social institutions that ultimately shed significant light on the nature and meaning of colonialism.

I argue that how one understands that culture (as *mentalité*) depends upon how one understands colonialism. Despite calls from certain quarters of literary criticism to rally around the general banner of "postcolonial" theory, quite rightly criticized by Gates (1991) as a kind of "critical Fanonism", I think that colonialism in this context has to be taken in the first instance quite literally as a historical phenomenon. Whether or not it is desirable for us in the final analysis to produce localized theories rather than general laws of colonialism, I believe it is necessary, methodologically speaking, to situate the colonial experience within its proper geo-historical context. There are many kinds of colonial experience, not only because different kinds of colonial agents inevitably bring along different kinds of (cultural and socio-political) baggage but also because, in each specific situation, colonialism inevitably changes as a result of interaction with local forces in ways that demand ongoing syntheses and shifting strategies. Each colonial experience is in other words a narrative in itself. But this does not mean on the other hand that such narratives should be understood only at the level of events. On the contrary, it is possible to understand these events by recourse to some interpretive framework by viewing action, discourse and practice in terms of their underlying motives and intentions and as a function of inherently cultural rules and assumptions.

I believe that many of the essentializing tendencies of postcolonial theory stem from a misleading preoccupation with explaining the politics of "difference". In this regard, racism has been conveniently viewed as a tool for making manifest a process of political domination and cultural construction of alien others which appears to be universal to colonial regimes everywhere. It is as though colonial institutions are themselves contingent upon such sentiments, cultural in origin, for their continued sustenance in socio-political terms. Noting that it is something of a paradox that racial differences between colonizer and colonized should become most prominent in precisely that period of the late 19th century when technologies of disciplinary power were deployed in the service of the colonial state, Chatterjee (1993: 10) extends this "rule of colonial difference" even further to explain the inner dynamics of anti-colonialism, nationalism and post-colonialism. To the contrary, I think that it is easier to show that racism or ideologies of racial difference are common to all cultures and are, if anything, analytically distinct from the formation of colonial regimes.[13] By neatly showing how "the *quality* and *intensity* of racism vary enormously in different colonial contexts and at different historical moments", Stoler (1989: 137) makes it possible to suggest that the polarization of racial and other differences are instead arbitrary signs or dependent variables of a socio-political institution whose nature is grounded in specific places and times.

The same criticism can be brought to bear against Said's *Orientalism*. To be sure, more attention has been drawn to the objectification of the other in the construction of hegemonic discourses than to the more important point that such discourses have been made possible by the prior existence of an "imperial contest". Yet while Said has been content largely to concentrate predominantly on texts of high colonialism and the production of metropolitan knowledge, he has much less to say about the institutional realities of colonialism that have given rise to the possibilities of discourse as well as those native realities that have been effectively obscured and objectified by both the discourses and practices of colonialism.

If one can accept the institutional realities of colonialism as an appropriate point of departure for understanding the underlying *mentalité* of (local) colonial regimes and the way it may differ from the *mentalité* of native institutions and practices, one must then necessarily ask, what kinds of colonialism are there, and how does the Hong Kong experience contrast with other examples in reference to both (cultural) origins and (historical) specificity? What is it about the underlying *mentalité* of Hong Kong's colonialism that sheds light on its cultural uniqueness and makes it relevant to anthropological misunderstandings of Chinese traditions?

At the risk of essentializing the nature of British colonialism in Hong Kong as a bounded category (*vis-a-vis* French colonialism or the experience of British colonies elsewhere and at other times), one must nonetheless admit that it shares certain features of colonial experience found elsewhere. Perhaps the most obvious was the implementation of what has been referred to in the literature as the policy of "indirect rule". Hong Kong society may have been built from scratch since its cession by China in 1841, but given the predominantly Chinese population that eventually settled there and in Kowloon, ceded in 1860, there was much more to suggest that the overall disposition of the place resembled that of other treaty ports in China than colonies like the Falkland Islands. This became even more so the case when the New Territories was "leased" in 1898. Even though in strict legal terms, Hong Kong (and Kowloon) was a colony in the outright sense of being permanently ceded, while the New Territories was a temporary lease where the colonial government simply assumed the role of manager-cum-taxlord, in practice, however, this distinction eventually became blurred and for all intents and purposes non-existent. In other words, the New Territories may have been in actuality an outright lease, where the colonial government attempted to administer the territory in accordance with native custom and tradition, but this policy of indirect rule was in principle no different from that which guided administrators in late 19th century Fiji, India and elsewhere. Having said this, however, one should also note, of course, that the faithfulness to which individual colonial administrators regulated society in accordance with local custom varied considerably, largely as a function of how strictly policy was carried out.[14] In the New Territories, one can honestly say that indirect rule was largely guided by purity of purpose but for complex reasons to be explained in the course of this study became subverted as a result of many other mitigating factors. Given then that colonial policy here was by initial intention guided by the principle of preserving traditional institutions on the basis of local custom, one must then ask to what extent did the colonial government accurately understand the nature and operation of traditional custom, and what were the consequences of "their" particular implementation of tradition upon the actual state of those beliefs and practices? While such questions have been posed already in the burgeoning literature on Fiji and India in particular, historians and anthropologists of Hong Kong have almost without exception taken the appearance of "traditional" custom and social organization at face value.[15]

The flip side of the colonial government's effort to administer society on the basis of local tradition was the emergence of modern institutions, most notably the state itself, that necessitated the disciplinary regulation of those same local social organizations and practices. In a Fijian context, Thomas (1990: 170) has argued that colonialism was in this regard a "contradictory" project that on the one hand encouraged non-intervention in the maintenance of a customary order yet on the other hand necessitated intervention to subordinate that order to the disciplinary designs of the state. Similarly, in his study of law in colonial India, Dirks (1986) has shown how legal efforts to codify and legitimize existing institutions led to subtle changes in rural society yet at the same time constituted the major failure of rural society to effect a complete and fundamental change. Contradictory as it may seem on the surface, I believe that the very aim to preserve tradition, which was a culturally arbitrary feature of late 19th century British colonial policy, was ironically part and parcel of the state's hegemonic and disciplinary designs. More than simply preserving tradition, it was the state's implicit aim to systematize and rationalize it, using the entire technology of modern objectification at its disposal (law, statistical knowledge, economic management) to make it optimally effective as a means of regulating it. At the heart of the colonial regime and its mandate or desire to rule then is the notion of governmentality (in a Foucaultian sense).

Chatterjee (1993: 26) has attempted to explain the essence of colonial rule largely as a function of its inherent project to perpetuate cultural difference and through continued imposition of categories that mark the duality of colonizer and colonized, like tradition and modernity. He notes that from a European point of view, colonial rule was usually never about the imposition of their own political institutions onto the other but the promotion of native self-government; it really aimed toward the preservation of local tradition instead of its destruction in the face of modernity. These claims that colonial rule was always about "something else", as if to deny the obvious fact of political domination, was according to him a persistent theme in the *rhetoric* of colonial rule (my emphasis). This has also coincided with his observation that the more nationalism (anti-colonialism) tried to contest colonial power in the outer or material domain of politics, the more it met with efforts by colonialists to harden the boundaries of cultural difference to keep the inner or spiritual domains of self and other separate and sovereign.

Scott (1994) has attempted to extend Chatterjee's ideas about the nature of colonial governmentality by showing how its intrinsic politics of cultural difference and reconstruction is really the evolution of a rule of modern power. The implicit contradiction that Chatterjee sees between the inner and outer domains of colonial politics becomes in Scott's terms a basic change in the nature of governmentality where modern power is characterized by its shift in "point of application" from the economy to the body social, which includes the various conditions of customary and disciplinary life routine invoked by terms like tradition and modernity.

There is indeed much one can say about the "rhetoric" of denial pointed out by Chatterjee as being fundamental to the contradictions of colonial rule. While the masking of domination is clearly an element of colonial governmentality that is intrinsic to the efficacy of any kind of hegemonic presence, in Gramscian terms, I argue that this deliberate process of cultural mystification is general to the emergence of state power rather than peculiar to the colonial regime. However, contrary to Scott, I understand the nature of the modern project inherent to late 19th century British colonialism to revolve around its *discursive content* and *practical instrumentality* rather than its point of application. Without denying that all of society becomes the site of power, much like the way anthropological views of a total and systemic society later become galvanized through reference to the conceptual interlocking of "social structure" and "function", what needs to be explained in my opinion is why tradition, which is a culturally *peculiar*, hence symbolically *arbitrary*, aspect of late 19th century British colonial *imagination*, suddenly becomes incorporated into the colonial state's project of modernity, then how the content of tradition becomes reconstructed and given new meaning in full light of the various technologies of legal codification, administrative practice and policing. It remains now to show how this field of discourse is defined, then spell out in what sense it entailed modern interventions through routines of state.

To reverse the Gramscian order of things, I argue then that the empire is basically a (cultural) fiction whose reality is intertwined with the process of state legitimation and methodologically put into practice by an entire technology of legal apparatuses and disciplinary institutions. Richards' (1994: 6) observation that the late 19th century British "imperial archive was a fantasy of knowledge" and that it was a "paper empire" united not by force but by "information" is quite germane in this regard. It was not so much that the need for information what was kept the empire unified in lieu of actual physical control but rather that the Victorian project of positive knowledge was something incorporated into the colonial project as a whole. Institutions like the British Museum, which served as monuments for the accumulation of artifacts and documents, was clearly one product of such an imagination. Similarly, the exhibitionary complex that viewed the entire world as taxonomy was quite rightly called by Mitchell (1988) a form of "colonizing".[16] As Cohn (1984) noted in his study of the census and social structure in colonial India, this process of objectification was part of the colonial government's need to know the nature of society as a prerequisite for administering it in its own terms. In broader terms, one can argue that this imagination of the universe as ordered taxonomy that had to be made visible through the accumulation of knowledge in order for it to be regulated systematically and efficaciously was a peculiar kind of world ethos or cultural vision that deeply influenced the conduct of government and by implication made all dimensions of social routine subject to what Corrigan (1990) aptly termed "moral regulation".[17] Rather than being peculiar to colonial governmentality per se, it was general to the governmentality of modern society in ways that became easily appropriated by the state. As Cohn (1988) phrased it,

the emergence of the state created its own forms of knowledge, necessitating the incessant accumulation of documentation in the genre of
reports, investigations, commissions, statistics, histories and archaeologies.
Such knowledge has usually complimented various imaginations of the
social invoked by myths of sacred origin, icons of national identity,
shared values, ethnic traditions and political thought.[18] This need to
know, document and imagine provided the basis for its capacity to
govern by defining and classifying spaces, making separations between
public and private, demarcating frontiers, standardizing language,
defining national identity and licensing the legitimacy of certain activities over others. It is thus part and parcel of the state's project to define
itself and rationalize its continued existence.

Smith's (1985) study of the instrumentality of records and reports in British imperial rule of law in 19th century India is an important
example of how various forms of knowledge coalesced to provide the
framework for a systemic technology of colonial governing. Records of
rights were prepared for every village-estate and formed the basis of land
administration. These were complemented by Settlement Reports,
Gazetteers, Census Reports and Reports on Customary Law that were
the authorized version of knowledge about Indian society. In effect, the
phraseology and functioning of the records converged with the production and utilization of knowledge in administration, the reports. The
relevance of social structure to the production of records and reports
in the process of colonial was predicated on the assumed existence of
a social morphology upon which the entire population was seen as
unambiguously constituted. As Smith (1985: 156) put it, "once society
had been broken down into a group of individuals, by means of censuses
and surveys, and pieced together again by means of statistics, it was no
longer necessary to delegate the function of government contractually
through privileged instruments of mediation, whether families or the
'little republics' of village communities. An individual's relation to the
State could be defined instead by his status". In this regard, according
to Smith, the British invented caste by institutionalizing it. It was not
until the mid-19th century that individual cultivators and proprietors
were listed in specimen papers with the names of their fathers, castes,
sub-castes and religion. Only with the emergence of caste in the village
records did colonial rule begin to be theorized and practiced in reference

to customs, rites and duties, instead of on the basis of self-regulating villages. The emergence of the census and statistics then galvanized the whole nature of colonial governmentality by providing the link through which a direct relation between the individual and the modern state could be nominally established. In the context of India, the notional Indian individual was stripped of the universality of his social roles in a "village community" and clothed instead by his status in a caste. In the context of an emerging modernity, the notion of social structure was not just a set of images, as though it could be objectively grafted onto any social landscape. Its existence implied the operation of customs, rites and duties and was in effect a Eurocentric projection that is often mistaken for the actual constitution of society itself.

In short, in order to govern efficaciously, it was necessary to "know", and the content of such knowledge was made possible by an ensemble of methodologies and practices that made visible the "structure" of society and put into functional operation the various components of social life. If colonial governmentality was part and parcel of the state's project, it also had to be to some extent intertwined with the very conduct of a modern, disciplinary society. In my opinion, law played an important role, not only in terms of its ability to objectify in reference to "value-free" codes and rules but also by virtue of its institutional link to power. Far from being an "objective" institution, as perceived by those in power, it should be the very source of conflict with "native" reality. As Dirks (1986) has noted for India, law was one of the reasons why the British failed to achieve a complete change of society (through the preservation of tradition) yet on the other hand explained why the (modern) changes that came about were actually achieved with so little major disruption. The dual consequence of legal rule is in my opinion ultimately the real source of contradiction that lies at the heart of British colonial governmentality.

In retrospect, it is possible to understand the experience of late 19th century British colonialism in Hong Kong as the realization in practice of a fundamental contradiction in the colonial state's effort to institutionalize the content of tradition using the methodology of a modern, disciplinary society. This interaction between colonizer and colonized was mediated through culture and played out in shifting contexts of power over time which can be read at the level of concrete events.

HONG KONG RURAL SOCIETY AT THE FULCRUM OF THEORY AND HISTORY

In sum, the following analysis takes as a point of departure the premise that anthropologists, historians and other social scientists do not understand well the nature of local Chinese society, whether it be in the New Territories of Hong Kong or elsewhere, and that this has to do with the poverty of epistemological and methodological apparatuses at our disposal for making sense of "native" social practices and institutions. There has been much significant work done both by anthropologists (especially Watson 1985) and historians (most notably Faure 1986) on the local social history of village communities in the New Territories. Most of this recent work has largely been an extension of more traditional concerns with the role of lineage institutions in shaping regional history. While one cannot deny the contribution of such local studies to our understanding of the underlying fabric of rural society there, the questions raised here address somewhat different issues in the study of local society. The New Territories of Hong Kong may be viewed on the one hand as a special case *vis-a-vis* China, Taiwan and other overseas Chinese communities in consideration of the effects of British colonial administration upon a primordial Chinese society. Yet on the other hand, if one were to accept at face value the literal meaning of "indirect rule" and the New Territories "lease", the Hong Kong case should actually represent an ideal setting for assessing the "real" nature of that tradition. Thus, what role can the colonial experience play in this scholarly endeavor to understand the nature and function of such institutions? I argue that in order to understand the evolution of rural Hong Kong society to the present day, one must effectively separate the epistemological assumptions and methodological practices that guided "indirect rule" from the nature of those social institutions it was meant to regulate. If "knowledge" of local tradition was the prerequisite for governing society in its own terms, one must in the first instance ask, what exactly did they "understand" and by what "means" was such knowledge made systematic in the institutional practice of normal life? More important than what people saw as "existing" beliefs, practices and institutions, I believe that, by making the perceptions and actions of actor-subjects an object of critical scrutiny, one can show in fact how the nature of indigenous society was irrevocably altered and by analogy how the functioning of these beliefs, practices and institutions was primordially different. Because interaction between colonizer and colonized was the basic framework within which understanding (misunderstanding) and action (conflict) took place, one must look at the events themselves, too, as the concrete venue or source for understanding differences at the level of cultural meaning.

At this point, it is perhaps important to recognize that, just as there are many kinds of anthropologies, there are many kinds of histories. France's (1969) monumental study of British land colonial policy and its consequences upon the construction of a Fijian "tradition" has shown that the development of British land policy in Fiji was itself a near century-long, ongoing discourse which only at the end became inscribed into law. Early encounters with traders, missionaries and other settlers had already introduced changing notions of boundedness, alienation, ownership and commoditization that had been associated with European concepts of property even before consular officials began to shape any systematic sanctioned policy. Under consular authority, shifts in the discourse were equally a function of the personal ethos of the Consul himself and the changing socio-political climate that enveloped the times. The legal codification of a tradition that unified diverse customs and compromised the interests of contending social classes and ethnic groups was really only the beginning of an convoluted situation that later was to have significant ramifications for economic development and notions of identity.[19]

By contrast, the experience of Hong Kong's New Territories has been less complicated in terms of historical narrative at the level of politically significant events and policy discourse or ideology. Except for events surrounding the initial occupation of the New Territories that contributed to the establishment of a land policy and a series of conflicts between the colonial government and indigenous inhabitants concerning land housing policy in the postwar era that precipitated a radical transformation in the constitution of rural society, it is difficult to conceive of social history in the New Territories as a sustained reflection on land. Nonetheless, the peculiar nature of these events on the ground reflect significant underlying trends or changes that must be properly viewed within a larger global context. While it is important to point out that the kinds of global forces which determined land policy in the initial era of colonialism were significantly different from those that influenced land policy during a postwar era of colonialism, one might also say that the concept and practice of colonialism had been changing, too.

There is a sense then in which the historical narrative unfolds not only at a conscious, decision-making level but also at an unconscious one as well. Both aspects of this narrative are important, since they constitute the source of cultural contradictions between concept and practice as well as between shifting definition of crucial concepts like "native" and "tradition" at an unconscious level. Ironically, it is at the point where the explicit domination of colonial rule becomes supplanted in the minds of agents in the system by notions of a benevolent paternalism and the invisible hand of modernity that the hardened identity of a colonialist "other" becomes most pronounced in the minds of indigenous inhabitants and that colonial policy becomes perceived in explicit terms by natives as a system of exploitation.

That "land" should be an explicit point of contention as well as an eventual entree into problems concerning the continuity of tradition, the viability of custom, the structure of society and the possibilities of change is most clearly understood perhaps in the context of Fiji and India, where it represented the focal point of an overall project to domesticate society. At a general level, it is evident that even the culturally peculiar phenomenon of late 19th century British colonialism shares many common elements of discourse in this regard. At this point, however, one must ask, in what sense do these discourses on land form a kind of "logic of the concrete" which is connected not simply to the apparent fiscal necessities of the colonial state but also to discourses pertaining to the welfare of the body social, the constitution of local organization and the functioning of customary practice?

Perhaps in order to deliberately anticipate the imminent, I argue that these various discourses of the concrete at some point inevitably reflect back upon the politics of social structure, because what the colonial state institutionally really put into practice in the course of history was a modern theory of structuration.[20] In this regard, Dirks' (1992a) study of the politicization of caste during mid to late 19th century India that subsequently made caste the locus of all information about Indian society is particularly germane. The central importance of caste as a kind of master symbol through which relationships to religion, status, custom and land could be meaningfully understood was what made caste the single most significant variable for explaining the nature of Indian society. What made caste eminently political on the other hand was that the domain of objective knowledge which was accumulated and structured on the basis of caste became the hegemonic tools for making society functionally integrated and politically ordered in everyday practice.

In the context of Hong Kong, what must be considered here is not just the accuracy of land demarcation in the initial administration of the New Territories but more importantly the effect of such demarcation in the overall process of social structuration, not just the hard and fast definitions of land use in the constitution of local communities but more importantly the way in which structuration of land categories has actually impinged upon existing rules of land use, and finally not just the process by which custom became legally codified but more importantly the effect of such customary law upon the archivalization of existing custom to the point of unnaturally stifling meaningful possibilities for change. It may well be that the New Territories today represents an exceptional case in the comparative study of Chinese communities, but it is only by portraying the colonial experience in cultural light and by making politically visible the underlying nature of our own cultural-cum-theoretical constructs that one can hope to begin to understand the nature of Chinese social institutions and existing local practices in any one place.

In the end analysis, if one can be sufficiently impressed that certain aspects of what one sees today as traditional custom and social organization in the New Territories of Hong Kong are in fact legal strictures systematically put into place by colonial rule and are not, as anthropologists arriving in the field often assume, the natural culmination of self-regulating sociological rules, then it will be easier to show how the social structural and utilitarian axioms built into the conception of the single-lineage village provide an equally misleading interpretation of the operation of kinship, locality and custom in a local village setting while reifying the nature of traditional social organization in a different sense. This purging of social structure in both senses will hopefully provide the basis for an alternative interpretation of these same institutions and practices as they exist on the ground.

Yet to put it differently, the fact that the social structure that was put into practice in a colonial context through legal codification and the technologies of the state's moral regulation seems to be the same social structure that anthropologists (are trained to) take for granted as the objective constitution of society should be no accident, for both are products of precisely the same cultural imagination that emerged in the late 19th century. As *mentalité*, it is a set of values and behaviors that without doubt permeated the actions of actors and motivations of institutions within the system and may have been articulated in various forms of discourse. Implemented with full force by the instruments of state power, it may well have been the reification of a situation of "routine colonialism" that began to proliferate in a later generation of anthropological writing. But it is more likely that, similar to the search for unilineal descent groups in the Holy Grail of lineage theory, the idea of social structure as refined by anthropological theorists was an inevitable permutation of Eurocentric social scientific principles that served as the model of social order for ethnographers in the field, whether or not they actually found it. In terms of phenomena on the ground, it is important to reiterate that the British did not invent lineages, customs or villages in a Chinese context and instead that, whatever existed in a local context, it codified and institutionalized practices and organizations according to its own (legal-cum-social structural) rules rather than those of existing values and customs in ways that had ramifications for later social change. Moreover, this *mentalité* cannot simply be read at face value and must be viewed in relation to an ongoing global situation, that defines the parameters within which various agents can be seen to make strategic choices as a function of their positionings within institutions. In other words, there exists an ongoing relationship between discourse and practice that is characteristic in part of this underlying *mentalité* of the system. The local context of power that pits colonizer and colonized is in essence a contest of opposing *mentalités* and not just opposing interests per se. In the context of a changing global situation, one can expect that the discourses and practices on both sides will change accordingly in ways that not only change the meanings of people's actions and intentions but also the identities and strategies of those people as well. All of these factors have a relevant as well as important bearing on the resulting events and those institutions so affected.

The works of Watson (1985) and Faure (1986) in particular have shown that the history of the lineage-village provides an equally relevant point of departure for understanding the nature of local society in the New Territories. However, despite the obvious focus on local history, both have tended to look at the nature of the village largely in light of its constitution as a lineage rather than as a moral community in its right. To be sure, both lineage (in loose sense of descent group) and village (as a territorial community) have long genealogies as separate concepts and institutions in Chinese history. For example, it is possible to trace the origins of lineage (*zu*) and the descent concept (*zong*) back to classical antiquity, but it is doubtful that the clans that existed in the era of *zongfa* ("rule of *zong*") resembled any in later imperial times. Similarly, villages (and its correlative notion of *xiang*) with symbolic ties to land and the social reproduction of an agricultural livelihood have probably existed in China since earliest recorded sedentary history, but there has been little evidence to show that one necessitates the other or that both should ideally co-exist. In fact, it is widely recognized by sinologists that the so-called lineage-village complex is a recent phenomenon of the last 300 years at best. The intertwined existence of the two in the present makes it difficult to ascertain what the respective contribution of each is to the whole. But contrary to the projections of lineage theory, it is not obvious why the territorial (village) community should be a natural extension of descent principles and why the growth of lineages should not be the product of appropriation or cultural accommodation by the village. We know, for instance, that the settlement pattern of villages in north China, where many anthropologists have commonly acknowledged that it is often difficult to tell where one village ends and another begins, is radically different from the bounded, sometimes walled enclosures of villages in south and central China. Why should this not be the appropriate point of departure for explaining the kin constitution of villages throughout China, to which one might add the impact of other customs?

Far from being a cut and dried affair, I argue that our present understanding in native (Chinese cultural) terms of basic institutions such as the village, lineage, household and family is superficial at best and that a deeper understanding in sociological terms of their existence and operation is clouded by the influence of lineage and kinship models that are themselves Eurocentric if not modern cultural constructions. Ideally then, one should view the constitution of local society in the New Territories today as the end product of two separate genealogies or histories, one being the regional evolution of village communities in their own terms and the other being the impact of colonial rule. In terms of their component parts (village, lineage, household and family), the relevance or importance of various institutions, such as descent, ancestor worship, social exchange and land, is vastly different. The difficulty of understanding the nature of "traditional" village communities lies in part in our misunderstanding of certain basic cultural morphemes of Chinese kinship, namely *zong*, *jia* and *qin*. In addition to showing how in Chinese cultural terms the village, lineage, household and family constitute different sociological phenomena that cannot just be viewed as different levels of "social organization", it is necessary to show also how the principles of *zong*, *jia* and *qin* operate in each case. If anything, it should be clear that land is a dependent variable that has different meanings in these different situations and not an independent variable, as has been suggested by Freedman's theory of Chinese lineage organization. The difficulty of understanding the impact of colonialism in the ongoing existence and functioning of villages in the New Territories lies on the other hand in the complex transformations, both in theory and practice, that it has undergone from Britain's initial occupation of the territory to the present. Nonetheless, methodologically speaking, land appears to be an appropriate point of departure for contrasting key differences between the ongoing evolution of traditional village communities in the New Territories (and their customary practices) and the colonial administration of the same. In each case, land represented a different point of application upon the body social. In the colonial context, kinship appeared to be an insignificant concern (at least in discursive terms), except for the often repeated commitment to respect and preserve local customary practice in this regard. But it should be clear that the way in which colonial policy was applied to land eventually had direct ramifications for the functioning and meaningful existence of village and household communities. In the final analysis, the colonial experience may prove not to have altered all the core aspects of the lineage-village, but it is certainly one way to highlight various distinctive features of its ongoing operation or sociological rationale in native, cultural terms that would not be so apparent otherwise.

The consequences of colonial land policy upon an increasingly convoluted situation on the ground not only have important ramifications for how one should view the functioning of indigenous social organization and local lifestyles but also can be used to rethink the peculiar transformations of the colonial experience in Hong Kong and the unusual nature of colonialism as a system of social practices, in cross-cultural perspective. This system of practices should not be confused with government agencies and policies in a narrow sense. It is true, for example, as Scott (1989: 39–80) has argued, that from the point of view of evolving political institutions, the organizational apparatus of the state in the 19th and early 20th centuries could hardly have been called a modern, rational institution by present-day standards. Its limited administration was maintained by meager financial resources for public expenditures, the police was corrupt and its relationship with the business community was often uneasy. Professionalization came only during the postwar era. Yet underlying this "minimal" if not impotent state, there was a systematicity of rule that was reflected in the nature of routine administration and the way these practices were ideologically coded to establish a certain kind of rational-ethical order. These practices as well as the ideological principles that informed them changed over time, and it is necessary how these changes affected the situation on the ground and the relationship between rulers and ruled invoked therein. Needless to say, the meaning of land begins to change as well as people's relationship to it, and the concrete events that take place ultimately reflect back on deeper globalizing changes in the operation of the colonial regime as a whole.

In the following chapters, I shall focus my attention first on the formulation of British colonial land policy in the context of local events, while examining at the same time its immediate effects upon the management of indigenous society in the New Territories. This will then serve as the basis for understanding later phases of colonial discourse and practice in the postwar era. Given our understanding of "modern" change in postwar Hong Kong, it will be possible thus to cast the plight of an exemplary "traditional" village in somewhat clearer light. In view of this history of colonialism as cultural narrative or process, one can turn to the concrete situation on the ground to suggest how the functioning of local organization, social relations and customary practice can be seen as a function of other concepts. At each phase of historical transformation and at every level of social interaction, it is important to trace the intertwined relationship between ongoing discourses and practices. Only by bringing colonialism out into the fore can one then question it.

NOTES

1   As Radcliffe-Brown (1950: 13) characterized it, a kin group comprises "a network of social relations which constitutes part of that total network of social relations which is the social structure".

2   In other words, it was the social structural paradigm that made meaningful the idea of descent and descent groups rather than ongoing refinements of the descent principle that made possible Radcliffe-Brown's theory of social structure.

3   As Hu (1948: 5) pointed out, "we have seen that the solidarity within the group and rivalry between strong tsu (zu) is not entirely compatible with a centralized form of political control... Hence the development of the tsu is inimical to the strengthening of centralized control". (tsu is the Wade-Giles romanization for zu)

4   One can contrast the high percentage of single-surname villages in central China (86.85% of a total of 1291 villages in western Jiangxi) reported by Hu (1948: 14) with the relatively low percentage (12.5%) of such villages in a typical county in north China reported by Niida (1952: 60–61), where the remaining 87.5% of villages were composed of 3–12 surnames.

5   For a fuller critique of the literature on Chinese lineages, see Chun (1996).

6   In this regard, Freedman's achievement was not just limited to kinship in the narrow sense of family organization (Cohen 1976) but extended more importantly to the study of previously unrelated phenomena like corporate estates (Potter 1970), agnatic villages (Baker 1968), rural economy (Potter 1968), local systems (Brim 1970), emigration (J.L. Watson 1975), ancestor worship (Ahern 1973) and militarization (Kuhn 1970), just to name a few prominent examples that explicitly acknowledged the power of kinship in the analysis of Chinese society.

7   For a clarification of the overlap between locality and descent, see Chun (1988).

8   I am not saying here that lineages or the forms of customary practice and social

organization found today in Hong Kong or elsewhere were the products of colonial intervention. I argue instead that the meaning and function of certain traditional customs and social institutions found in the New Territories today have already been distorted if not supplanted by cultural principles underlying colonial policy and administration that aimed to mirror native tradition. Similarly, as one looks at the concept and practice of Chinese ancestor worship, native definitions of social organization and their relationship to customary practice, one may find that they are inherently different from cultural principles that underlie the lineage model.

[9] Perhaps the most prominent and systematic of these studies is the recent work of Jean and John Comaroff (1991).

[10] Representative works here are those of Fabian (1986) and Viswanathan (1989). Fabian is interested particularly in showing how choice of language was a means to maintain hierarchical distance between colonizers and colonized, while on the other hand Viswanathan shows that literary study of English served technocratic, utilitarian and civilizing functions in the maintenance of colonial hegemony.

[11] The work of Said (1978) has spawned a minor cottage industry that does not need elaboration here. Likewise, colonialism has made the writing of history and resistance to imperial history (as in subaltern studies) important and inevitable enterprises in the process of political legitimation and public reconstruction.

[12] See especially the works of Pratt (1992) and Thomas (1994).

[13] The work of Burrow (1966) and Stocking (1968) alone sufficiently shows that even the Victorian concept of race has roots in ideologies and institutions quite independently of colonialism, although there can be no doubt that colonialism can be used to institutionally intensify racial differences, among many other things.

[14] France's (1969) brilliant study of the changing discourse of land policy in the construction of a Fijian tradition shows how such indirect rule was the cumulative result of individual interpretations of policy principles and native custom.

[15] In addition to the work of France (1969), Clammer (1973) has detailed the role of colonialism in inventing Fijian tradition on the basis of its perception of social organization and its synthesis of a unified set of customary laws. Similarly, Thomas has noted the contradictions of the state's non-intervention in "preserving" Fijian custom and its intervention in the disciplinary reordering of routine life in other regards. In the context of India, Dirks (1992a) has emphasized that caste was a political construction of the colonial state, paralleling earlier arguments put forth by Cohn (1984) regarding the objectification of social structure in the census.

[16] See Bennett (1988) and Stocking (1987) for different views of the evolution and function of museum archivalization and cultural classification in the Victorian era.

[17] According to Corrigan, this notion has roots in Durkheim's arguments about the obligatory nature of moral rules that are really at the heart of social norms.

[18] As Corrigan and Sayer (1985: 3) put it, "the state never stops talking".

[19] See Rutz (1987) for an account of how an invented tradition of land ownership eventually enabled Fijian chiefs to exploit capitalist interests in a way which was essentially contrary to the moral economy that was the object of preservation by colonial policy. Jolly's (1992) comparison of colonial practices in Fiji and Vanuatu shows how continuity and discontinuity of traditions have had radically different ramifications for the development of customary practices in general.

[20] The process of structuration referred to here should actually be taken to be synonymous with Foucault's description of the emergence of a disciplinary society. At this point, it should be obvious also that the structuration implicit to Foucault's account of disciplinary society coincides with Radcliffe-Brown's functional society.

CHAPTER TWO

The Changing Meaning of Colonial Policy on Land in the New Territories of Hong Kong

'T was brillig and the slithy toves
Did gyre and gimble in the wabe;
All mimsy were the borogroves,
And the mome raths outgrabe.
(from Lewis Carroll, "Jabberwocky")

THE MYTH OF THE NEW TERRITORIES "LEASE"

Territoriality seems to be an all too obvious aspect of colonialism. Although mercantilist theory favored the establishment of colonies by every possible means and viewed them as a mine of wealth, later economic theory considered them to be a drain on resources and a diversion to the force of the mother country. Yet insofar as it was linked to the imperatives of maintaining trade in an expanding world system, territorial acquisition and control in one form or another was clearly a factor in its continued existence well into the twentieth century, even though one should add that the proper articulation of what constituted these interests was always prone to conflicting and changing interpretation. It is commonly known, for instance, that the cession of Hong Kong to Britain at the end of the Opium War in 1841 (and Kowloon in 1860) was directly related to the defense of ongoing trade interests, but the Chinese government regarded this territorial concession as a loss of little or no significance. The island was quite literally a rock on the periphery of the Empire. It had no industry or agriculture to speak of, no major population settlement and represented no strategic threat to the defense of the Pearl River Delta, located several miles away, ultimately leading to Canton. This "victorious achievement" also failed to impress an irate Lord Palmerston, British Foreign Secretary at the time, who greeted news of the cession by referring to it as "a barren island with hardly a house upon it". The cession was apparently a diplomatic *faux pas* in an attempt to exact more important trade concessions from the Chinese government at other existing treaty ports. Captain Elliot, who was in charge of British efforts in Canton, was promptly recalled, and the following years saw a change of leadership in the Home Government and the signing of the Treaty of Nanking in 1842, with subsequent ratifications of it on June 26, 1843. Throughout this time, major trade issues remained unsettled from the perspective of the British, complicated now by the question of what to do with Hong Kong.

When the New Territories were leased to Britain by China in 1898 for 99 years for purposes of defending Hong Kong, it should have in theory been treated differently from Hong Kong and Kowloon, which were, strictly speaking, cessions in perpetuity. However, seen at the level of events, the meaning of the "lease" was anything but clear. After jubilation among British in Hong Kong subsided over the signing of the lease for the New Territories on June 9, 1898, referred to as the Convention of Peking, there were still many unresolved details as to the conditions of the lease, including the demarcation of the northern frontier, the operation of Chinese customs stations and military garrison at Kowloon City as well as the precise administrative setup to be adopted for the New Territory. The northern boundary was decided upon in March of the following year and accepted somewhat reluctantly by the British, since the Shenzhen River line ended up dividing the Shenzhen Valley and nearby market town of Shataukok in half. Nonetheless, this was the least pressing problem. There was still considerable confusion and debate on both sides over the juridical definition of the lease, from which all other issues, such as the continued presence of the Chinese military and customs station, were related. For several months after the signing of the treaty, the Viceroy at Canton administered the territory as though nothing really changed (Endacott 1958: 25).

The situation on the ground was even more confusing. Although boundaries of the New Territory had been mapped out in August 1898, the British did not take any actual steps to occupy it until March 1899.

This began with the building of a police station atop a hill overlooking Ping Shan, a large well-established clan community. Construction work was met by indignation and hostility on the part of indigenous villagers which quickly spread to neighboring communities, then escalated into large-scale armed resistance organized by the various local village alliances (*yeuk* (C), *yue* (M)), segments of which were commandeered by village leaders.[1] Notices were sent out to prepare and mobilize the local braves into a state of readiness, placards were distributed and posted on halls and other public edifices to warn of impending foreign aggression, and leaders assembled in the various *yeuk* to map out possible strategy.[2] Two weeks before the formal hoisting of the flag on April 17, contractors began erecting matsheds for the Hong Kong authorities on a hill adjoining the market town of Tai Po.[3] Work was repeatedly obstructed by villagers who claimed that the hill was private land and that the matsheds would disturb the geomantic disposition of the area. A detachment of Sikh policemen from Hong Kong along with Chinese soldiers stationed at Kowloon City were dispatched to the area to maintain order and guarantee resumption of construction. As expected, this military detachment was met by an angry mob demanding their withdrawal. That evening, several hundred men from one local *yeuk* organized an assault upon the detachment, eventually burning the matsheds and forcing the latter to retreat to an adjacent hill. Similar instances of fierce, armed resistance took place as the British stepped up military efforts. They sent reinforcements toward Tai Po market from the east, troops landed in the vicinity of Castle Peak Bay in the southwest, another detachment marched into the Lam Tsuen Valley toward the central plains, and still another force went up north to secure the market town of Shenzhen. The resistance collapsed in a matter of just few days after continued penetration by British troops, backed by naval artillery. In retrospect, after all the dust had settled, all parties involved agreed that the whole affair had been the result of an unfortunate misunderstanding. Apparently, the Chinese provincial government had failed to inform inhabitants of the territory that their land was handed over to Britain little over a year ago.[4]

To say that the inhabitants of the territory did not know of the forthcoming arrival of the British is an overstatement, however. The Governor of Hong Kong issued proclamations in several villages urging people to remain orderly, stressing that through cooperation with government and non-interference in local customs, the government endeavored to maintain the status quo, as was reflected below:

> . . . the most respected of your elders will be chosen to assist in the management of your village affairs, to secure peace and good order and the punishment of evil doers. I expect you to obey the laws that are made for your benefit, and all persons who break the law will be punished severely. It will be necessary for you to register without delay your titles for the land occupied by you, that the true owners may be known.[5]

As Groves (1969: 48) rightly pointed out, both the tone and content of official proclamations more often than not caused results that were contrary to intended aims. Instead of advocating non-interference with local practices on the land, they ironically appeared to advocate more stringent control over it, and instead of advocating enlightened self-government they made village elders feel like pawns within an autocratic system of administration. Or as Groves (*ibid.*) phrased it, "control over both land and political institutions appeared to be at risk". The first suspicion by colonial authorities of resistance was news of a gathering of elders in Ha Tsuen's ancestral temple on March 28, followed by similar discussions at Yuen Long on March 29, attended by representatives of the adjacent districts of Pat Heung, Shap Pat Heung, Ping Shan, Ha Tsuen and Castle Peak, and on March 31, which involved participation by leaders of Sheung Shui, Fanling, Tai Po, Ping Kong and San Tin. Uncertainty was sowed in some areas by dissemination of rumors by a Hong Kong based land syndicate that the colonial government was preparing to expropriate all privately owned land, allegedly to buy up land at low prices (Wesley-Smith 1980: 84). Anxieties escalated to a point where all aspects of everyday life were perceived to be under threat, as was exemplified by comments made at a village meeting in Ha Tsuen just prior to the outbreak of fighting:

> . . . that under English law a poll tax would be collected; that houses would be numbered and a charge made therefor; that fishing and woodcutting would be prohibited; that women and girls would be outraged; that births and deaths would be registered; that cattle and pigs would be destroyed; that police stations would be erected, which would ruin the Fung Shui of

the place. In short, that the evils that would arise would be so great that one could not bear to think of them.[6]

Thus, by the time violence first erupted with the burning of police matsheds at Tai Po, villagers of the territory had already organized an alliance called the Tai Ping Kung Kuk. Chinese naval forces arriving at Castle Peak to facilitate the handover few days prior to the formal hoisting of the British flag were repulsed by local village militia.[7] At the diplomatic level, fearing increased hostility toward the upcoming occupation of the territory, the Governor of Hong Kong Henry Blake met with Viceroy Tan Zhonglin to press for Chinese assurances of protection for work parties engaged in the construction of police matsheds and to put down local disturbances by punishing rebellious agitators. But the Viceroy appeared not to be interested in talking about such matters, preferring instead to force concessions from the British in regard to the operation of custom houses, noting: "this country is only leased: it is China, and there is nothing about Customs in the Convention". (Wesley-Smith 1980: 59). Nonetheless, he issued a decree discouraging disorder.

The disturbances that began at Ping Shan provided an appropriate rationale to expel Chinese official and military presence at Kowloon City and occupy the Shenzhen Valley north of the New Territory.[8] The colonial government demanded that Shenzhen be included within the new boundary and that customs stations be withdrawn immediately. On May 14, the Secretary of State Joseph Chamberlain ordered the occupation of Kowloon Walled City and Shenzhen. On May 16, the British flag was hoisted, and troops put into place.[9] Shenzhen was used largely as a bargaining chip to gain punitive compensation from the Chinese government for disturbances and was eventually relinquished to Chinese control in November, 1899.[10] As for the Walled City, the colonial government decided early on that it would not be returned to Chinese jurisdiction, being inconsistent with the defense of Hong Kong.[11] This was officially put into law by order in council of December 27, 1899, which stated that "the City of Kowloon shall be, and the same is hereby declared to be, for the term of the lease in the said Convention mentioned, part and parcel of Her Majesty's Colony of Hong Kong, in like manner and for all intent and purposes as if it had originally formed part of the said Colony."

The events surrounding the physical occupation of the territory exposed all the different interpretations of the lease on each side. As Wesley-Smith (1980: 90) pointed out, international leaseholds of the type imposed by the foreign powers in 1898 were inventions, ad-hoc improvisations adapted to the environment created by imperialist rivalry in the Far East. Their status and effect in international law had not been carefully worked out, and it was vital to colonial interests in Hong Kong that subsequent practice should affirm that the leased territory adjoining Kowloon had been transferred to Great Britain in the same manner as Kowloon itself and Hong Kong Island. The New Territories was not to be just another part of China administered by a Western power, but an extension of Hong Kong; the convention was to be seen as a treaty for the extension of established colonial boundaries, not just for the lease of territory. Thus, the Colonial Office declared from the outset that both countries would be administered in the same capacity and with the full powers of legal jurisdiction. This "new" interpretation of the "lease" was thus a post-hoc imposition upon the original convention, and while it did much to clear up whatever confusion the British initially had in their own minds about the status of the New Territory, it probably did nothing but widen the gap on both sides over most of the unresolved questions.[12]

In essence, Chinese officials still treated the leased territory as a lease in which British territorial rights as lessee (over the "topsoil") would not by definition conflict with Chinese overall claims of sovereignty as landlord (over the "subsoil"), including jurisdiction over its inhabitants.[13] This explained their insistence upon maintaining a military garrison, customs station, continued payment of land tax by residents to the provincial government, and sovereignty over the land and its people.[14] By this token, the Convention of Peking really did little to change their "business as usual" attitude toward the territory. The Chinese view of the lease was largely consistent with the assumption that sovereignty of both the land and its people were to remain intact during the entire period of its lease. The repeated assurances given by colonial authorities to the territory's inhabitants that their lifestyles would not disturbed in turn reinforced the impression that nothing had changed at all. Did it really matter then whether people were notified or not?

On the British side, the changing theory and practice of the lease reflected less its semantic meaning as borrowed place and was a function of a deeper notion of territoriality, which was itself embedded within a historically constituted vision of colonial-cum-global politics. It is too easy to reduce this "imperial contest" into a process of exploitation of colonized by colonizer. The strategies that prompted the British to treat the New Territories as a provisional cession or borrowed lease were a function of their "perception" of the colonial imperative that constituted the epistemological conditions of territorial rule. Defense of trade interests may be seen as an expression of the colonial imperative in strategic terms, but this, like an earlier mercantilism, was a historically specific notion that fit a certain global vision, as the priority of this and other notions inevitably changed under different strategic conditions and mutating global visions. More importantly, the dualism of colonizer and colonized presumes unchanging identities, as though fixed by race or ethnicity, that were immune to changing global imperatives and discourses of rule that appropriated the language of modernity, cosmopolitanism and democracy.

The contrasting conditions of the British leased territory at Weihaiwei in north China reveals the influence of different strategic considerations that affected semantic definition of the lease. Although the treaties that created the leases were almost identical, the administration of Weihaiwei was set up by an order-in-council issued under the terms of the Foreign Jurisdiction Act which recognized China's continued sovereignty and allowed residents to retain Chinese nationality. Chinese magistrates were allowed to co-exist with British administration in the Weihaiwei Walled City.[15] There was no consistent policy of land administration, quite unlike the way the British conducted extensive cadastral surveys in other colonies for the explicit purpose of collecting land tax, and administration of the territory in other regards was generally based upon a policy of non-interference that for the most part resisted any attempt to "progressively" introduce reform along Western lines, this being in part the result of Colonial Secretary Stewart Lockhart's respect for Chinese tradition.[16] Most peculiarly, there was no date on the lease, stipulating only that it would be held "for long a period as Port Arthur shall remain in the occupation of Russia".[17] In both cases, strategic concerns pertaining to defense and intercolonial rivalry remained of utmost priority, but the nature of local rule was determined by its intrinsic viability as a colony. Unlike the New Territories of Hong Kong, Weihaiwei was economically impoverished, its infrastructural connections to the interior remained primitive and difficult, and its position as a port competed poorly against those of neighboring colonial powers. This made systematic administration of the territory of the kind seen in the other colonies impractical, and the trade situation deteriorated to a point where it was a burden from a British point of view, leading to its return to China in 1930.

The global dimensions of colonial practice have important ramifications for how one views the nature of indirect rule, particularly at the local level, and its eventual mutation under changing global circumstances. In principle, after much strategic maneuvering, it was decided at top echelons of the colonial government that the territory would be administered as though it was a provisional cession rather than a lease per se, although the manner and degree to which British and Chinese elements defined colonial administrative practice was always a matter of ongoing interpretation and dispute between officials.[18] Yet functionally speaking, some aspects of legal administration were more prone to deliberate codification in British terms, for example in the area of civil and criminal law, while others were carried out with more sensitivity and respect for indigenous values and practices, this being the case for land tenure, social organization and ritual custom. The exclusion of customs pertaining to land from codification and regulation in British legal terms was clearly inscribed into Section 13 of the New Territories Ordinance: "In any proceedings in the High Court or District Court in relation to land in the New Territories, the court shall have power to recognize and enforce any Chinese custom or customary right affecting such land". Why the British went to great lengths to preserve indigenous authority with regard to land, while other aspects of social life were to be administered as though the territory was a provisional cession deserves serious and critical reflection. This was hardly unusual in light of similar policies carried out at this time in other colonies such as Fiji and India, and this strategy was not just a result of the arbitrary application of Anglo-Saxon law. It is clear that there were two aspects of coloniality that must be analytically distinguished. There was the domain of social life, pertaining to economy and the conduct of public life, that was subject to colonial domination and various civilizing processes, thus constituting part of colonialism's "cultural project". This domain of social life was distinct, however, from those private aspects of custom that were not meant to be a primary object of direct control but could have been used as a tool of domination in the civil or public sphere, hence indirect rule. Whether this separation of powers was ever carried out successfully in practice is one question. Whether the separation between the civil/public and customary domains of life was eventually maintained in actuality in light of later global/social transformations is another question to be addressed. I think there were failures in both regards.

But perhaps more significant than the debates at a level of conscious policy, the practice of local rule had to be understood also in terms of how the ethos of social order and the spectacle of political power necessitated a routine system of control. More than just legal codes and administrative practices, local rule invoked an underlying *mentalité* that guided the system as a whole. The latter constituted the means and ends of colonial rule. At one obvious level of generality, the colony as defined was an object of policing within changing utopian (trade based) visions of the "empire". At another level of generality, the land and its people were also objects of knowledge and structuration in a system of disciplinary control. Thus, territoriality was not simply about the routine administration of land policy nor exploitative conquest by imperial powers but a combination of the two seen at the level of a deeper *mentalité*. In this sense, coloniality reflected the intersection of an evolving global politics and an emerging sociology of state power.

The occupation of the New Territories following its lease in 1898 exemplifies the imagination of land and people which constituted the object of administrative control that was central to the late 19th century imperial archive. Simply stated, land demarcation and village surveys were not just prerequisite for the collection of tax revenue; they were the basis of effective and orderly local administration in all other respects. As time went on, the relevance and function of land in relation to the maintenance of the status quo may have changed, but the extent to which the colonial government regulated affairs of local society in reference to indigenous tradition reflected the importance generally of native knowledge to efficacy of rule.

It was in this sense that rational administration of land ultimately relied on the necessary collusion between social order and indigenous rule rather than its mutual separation, as indicated by the frequently invoked colonial imperatives regarding non-interference in matters of custom, especially pertaining to land. To be more precise, it could be said that there were aspects of land that the British perceived to be relevant to social order and other aspects that were considered, by virtue of their being customary, to be arbitrary and functionally insignificant.

The novelty to the Chinese of both a territorial imperialism that had roots in mercantilist economics and a structural conception of society that was based on the archivalization of knowledge cannot be underestimated, for this was precisely the root of conflict that was to disrupt the underlying constitution of local society in the long run. The need to acquire territory as a means of maintaining vested trade interests was for the most part already by the late 19th century a vestige of a dying mercantile capitalism. The territorial imperative was a criterion for defending trade interests in China, but only in the minds of the Europeans. The very "lease-qua-cession" or "cession-qua-lease" of the New Territories demonstrated that the Chinese government was willing to yield territory to the British in order to enhance the latter's sense of physical security, but from a Chinese perspective territoriality was never logically related to the amelioration of trade relationships that were already well-defined and generating immense profits for all involved.

At the local level, the British made repeated assurances in proclamations that local customs and ways of life would not be interfered with. However, from the perspective of the inhabitants themselves, the British ended up doing precisely the opposite, e.g. disrupting the local feng-shui, and imposing customs which the Chinese perceived to be foreign to their own way of life, such as levying poll taxes, house taxes, numbering houses, registering births and deaths, and erecting police stations.[19] This discrepancy in perception deserves further attention, because it reflects a problem of cultural substance that the colonial government repeatedly dismissed as cases of petty resistance rather than legitimate grievances, enabling these conflicts to deepen and become diffused throughout the fabric of society.[20]

In this regard, one might say that British and Chinese both differed as to their interpretation of the inherent functionality of various customs or at least did not share the same views as to which aspects of custom were subject to or immune from political control. Moreover, conflicts at the phenomenological level escalated to new heights as changing global imperatives complicated the ongoing equation.

It was almost as if, by turning Marx's version of Hegel back on his head, facts and personages in the history of Hong Kong's New Territories occurred twice, the first time as farce, the second as tragedy. The chaos and confusion at the level of events erupted in overt conflict between colonizer and colonized, which subsided over time, but the real injuries of colonial rule began with the creation of a system of structuration and control, predicated by the will to knowledge, maintained by a set of "value-free" codes and implemented "efficiently" by the entire apparatus of the state. Through the operation of colonial "land" policy, one can understand the nature of social organization and lifestyle affected by changes on the land in a way that reflects generally on changes occurring throughout society as a whole.

PAX BRITANNICA AND THE SILENT LAND REVOLUTION

Hong Kong and the New Territories constitute about 60% of the 600 sq. mi. of what used to be Xinan (San On (C)) County. For much of the 900 plus years since the region was first settled by Han Chinese, the New Territories have been occupied predominantly by what has loosely been referred to by local people as "The Five Great Clans" (*wu da zu*), the Tangs, Haus, Pangs, Lius and the Mans. Being historically the most established and longest settled surname groups in the territory, they gradually came to occupy the central plains and lowland valleys of the New Territories, clustered themselves into highly nucleated village settlements and walled cities (*wei*). According to clan genealogies, the Tangs were the first to take root (*kaiji*, literally "open a base") in Xinan County, then part of Baoan County (early Sung dynasty, 973 A.D.), followed by the Haus (1026 A.D.), Mans (late Sung, 1260 A.D.), Lius (late Yuan, mid-14th century), then the Pangs (early Ming, late 14th century).[21] By the Ming dynasty (15th–17th century), it appeared that Xinan County was on the whole well settled. In addition to the dominant, clan communities mentioned above, there were many other surname groups who entered this region at about this time in addition to a wide assortment of Han ethnic groups (Punti, Hakka, Hoklo, Tanka). In retrospect, the settlement history of Xinan County strongly suggests that the term "Five Great Clans" most likely originated during the late Ming, if not early Qing dynasty (the Pangs built their walled city at Fanling in 1573). Moreover, local clan accounts of their own glory years at the height of the Ming mirrors the evolution in other parts of China during the Ming and Qing dynasties of territorially well defined, highly nucleated single surname villages based upon large scale appropriation of land.

The period of coastal evacuation from 1662–69, referred to locally as *chianfu* (*ts'in fuk* (C)), an abbreviation for *chianhai* ("move from the coast") *fucun* ("return to the village"), was a set of events which abnormally disrupted the course of social developments that had been taking place in the region prior to this time. Qu Dajun (1700: vol. 2, 57), an early Qing scholar, characterized the evacuation by saying, "ever since Guangdong province has existed, as far as calamities involving life were concerned, there was none worse than this". By order of imperial edict, all inhabitants along the coast of south China within 50 *li* (Chinese miles), later 80 *li*, of the sea were moved inland from their villages as a tactic to prevent Ming loyalist pirates still rebellious to the Qing dynasty from provisioning themselves while harboring on land. This meant that about 90% of the population of Xinan County was moved inland during this period. The boundaries between affected and unaffected portions were literally marked off with a rope, sometimes dividing villages and even houses or rooms into halves (Sung 1938: 38, Hsieh 1931–32: 591). According to the Xinan County Gazetteer, only 3972 people returned at the end of the evacuation out of about 18,000 prior to it.[22]

Aside from the fact that many people died as a result of the evacuation, it appears that this experience did not radically alter the social situation within the region and may have even served to consolidate the existing structure of power among clan communities there. By sheer proportion of numbers, the smaller and less prosperous village communities along the coast probably suffered the most by giving already well established communities additional leverage to reconsolidate their position in the region. In any case, the position of The Five Great Clans did not appear to have diminished in the aftermath of the evacuation, and in following years a new influx of settlers, mostly Hakka agriculturalists, moved in to fill the gap (Lo 1963: 104).[23] The Xinan County Gazetteer of 1688, for instance, showed some 529 distinct villages divided into 7 *dou* (sub-county units), of which about 147 are identifiable on existing maps (Ng 1983: Map 7). The revised Gazetteer of 1819 listed about 857 villages in the area, of which 309 are identifiable on existing maps (Ng 1983: Map 8). This excluded the Tanka (boat people) who lived offshore.

In short, by the time the British took over what is now referred to as the New Territories, they inherited an already long established, well settled, highly stratified, ethnically diverse piece of real estate which, despite its physical remoteness from the core of Chinese civilization, was nonetheless clearly affected by changes in ideology and social organization occurring throughout the rest of Chinese society. Yet at the local level, one can also see from a brief turn of events such as the Coastal Evacuation of 1662–69 that pre-existing communities were for the most part abandoned, then reconstructed from scratch in its aftermath. Thus, the Five Great Clans probably refer not to those communities that dominated the territory, as though from antiquity, but more precisely to those surviving villages who managed to reconsolidate their strong position in the aftermath of the Coastal Evacuation. Whether these actualities affected what the British later perceived to be "custom", however, remains less clear.

The first priority for the new administration after the occupation of the New Territory was to prepare a Crown Rent Roll, which was to serve as the basis for collecting tax and administering affairs pertaining to land. Problems encountered in legally exchanging Chinese titles (red deed) for Crown leases, ascertaining the precise nature of landholdings and determining the real owner led to the creation of a Land Court, which was empowered by New Territories Ordinance 18 of 1900 to demarcate for all villages in the territory each individual plot of land as a basis for adjudicating any disputed claims of ownership. This survey entailed the work of special Indian surveyors, assisted by Chinese coolies, working continuously over a period of three years from June 1900 to June 1903. A map was drawn for each demarcation district, showing physical boundaries for each plot. Each unit of land, be it agricultural or residential, was numbered and registered in the name of a person or group that held a claim to the land and could furnish the proper deeds. Upon submission of the deeds, the colonial government issued in return a Crown Lease, literally "license" (*zhizhao*). These demarcation maps along with details of landownership provided the basis for the Block Crown Lease, a register compiled by lot number, and a Crown Rent Roll, which was the instrument of tax collection. It took another two years to get these land registers in order. All unclaimed land not registered in the above manner was duly declared property of the Crown.[24]

In his 1899 Report on the New Territories, published in 1900, J.H. Stewart Lockhart summarized the task of setting up a system of land registration when he said, "a perusal of this memorandum (on Chinese land tenure) will, I think, show that, though the Chinese system may be excellent in theory, it has not been well carried out in practice, with the result that the land question has proved one of great difficulty" (RNT 1900: 253). This remark is important, if not suggestive. For the British, the complexity of the Chinese land system in theory represented less of a obstacle than the laxity and failure of the Chinese government to properly "operationalize" the principles, which led to widespread abuse and confusion in the system. The British were initially frustrated by the Xinan County Land Registry, which recorded only deeds and not titles to land. These deeds never delineated exact land boundaries, people were often not able to document rights to land, and frequently two parties would claim ownership to what seemed to be the same piece of land (RNT 1900: 278). Moreover, it was discovered that large clans and wealthy landowners made it a practice to bribe corrupt land officials so as to underreport actual landholdings. Chinese also lacked the custom of making out wills, probates or other documents to verify succession to property, and it was rare to officially register customary transactions at the Land Registry. It was in reference to such irregularities and abuses that the colonial government set out to "operationalize" the land system on the basis of Chinese custom, in accordance with "the lease".

However, after land surveys got underway, other problems slowed up the progress of work. Reporting on the results of the Land Court from 1900–05, J.R. Wood cited several major problems (RLC 1905: 146). Excluding the more trivial problems like the language barrier between Indian surveyors and Chinese staff, general uncooperativeness of the peasants, especially during ritual and harvest seasons, and the problem of land belonging to landlords residing outside the leased territory, the British discovered first of all that large clans often claimed tracts of land for which they either had no documented proof or paid a small percentage of taxes (RNT 1901: 10). Secondly, peasant cultivators were often found exploiting plots of land on the less productive periphery of the village for which they had no titles and generally refused to register with the new government (RNT 1902: 559). Finally and most importantly, cases of dual ownership of land were found to be a common occurrence throughout the New Territories and became a point of dispute between actual peasant cultivators and taxlords, both of whom claimed to be the legitimate, registered owners. Gradually, it became apparent to the government that these disputed instances did not represent conflicting rights to the same piece of land but rights to distinct parts of the soil, namely the "surface" and "subsoil", and that much of the dispute arose out of the fact that the new government could only recognize a sole legitimate owner. The actual situation was complicated when one or the other side was unable to produce the proper red deeds (to the subsoil) or white deeds (to the surface) and where the colonial government was put in a situation of having to subjectively decide upon whom should be the real, legitimate tax-paying owner. The problem of dual ownership, taxlordism or perpetual lease ultimately frustrated the British for a long time and became the subject of intense discussion by later scholars (Nelson 1969, Kamm 1977 (1974), Hayes 1976, 1977).

With regard to the government's attempt to "operationalize" in legal terms Chinese customs relating to land, it is important to distinguish between the legal authority embodied within the person of the District Officer who, with the aid of native counsel, became the official interpreter of and final arbiter on matters of Chinese custom on the one hand and the legal authority reflected in the system of codes and practices which the British devised on the basis of Chinese custom.

Most District Officers in the service of the New Territories Administration seemed committed to upholding local custom in the operation of colonial policy, a point made by scholarly observers such as Nelson (1969: 33), Wesley-Smith (1979: 15) and Huang (1982: 56).[25] In many instances, of course, the system of legal codes and practices was able to "translate" in objective terms its customary referent. But as evidenced by the many disputes and litigation cases that later arose with regard to land, there were clearly many significant differences. In some instances, the government resolved the disputes by deliberating circumventing legal restrictions pertaining to the maintenance of custom as spelled out in the Convention, and in litigation cases the District Officer was sometimes forced to make a choice between arbitrating in favor of Chinese custom or the hard and fast rules the government adopted to administer custom. The fact that there was a difference and that this difference sometimes became a point of legal dispute between the government and the people or between two parties involved in litigation in turn shows that these differences cannot be dismissed as trivial.

In sum, the government was confronted with three kinds of problems: 1) the dilemma of perpetual lease or taxlordism, 2) problems arising out of the creation of land registration procedures for routines transactions such as inheritance, sale, and succession, and 3) rules pertaining to the adoption of Chinese categories of land tenure and taxation. In all three domains, the British generally understood quite well the descriptive and prescriptive nature of indigenous custom, which was meticulously researched in reference to texts and on advice of native counsel in the District Office Administration. However, they still had uneven degrees of success in faithfully executing a policy based on local custom. This had less to do with their objective understanding of these customs than with the degree to which they, in the Colonial Office or the District Office, could afford to sacrifice "bureaucratic expediency" and "legal rationality" for the sake of maintaining customary practice. Such decisions were pragmatic by definition insofar as they always involved the primacy of one set of competing values over another in reference to some implicit goal-orientation, and contrary to established scholarly opinion conflicts at the level of (conceptual) value were commonplace. In the end, I argue that the British in most cases opted against custom and that this became the root of profound conflict over the land, a conflict which has continued and escalated to the present day.

By far, the dilemma surrounding the nature of perpetual lease proved to be the most perplexing that the British had encountered in the initial stage of land registration work. At the surface level, they discovered that landlords and tenants claimed rights to different parts of the land, namely the "subsoil" (*digu*, literally "skeleton of the land") and "topsoil" (*dipi*, literally "the skin of the land").[26] Both rights were exclusive of each other in the sense that the landlord, as master of the subsoil, was responsible only for paying taxes on land to the government and that the tenant had full rights of cultivation to land as long as he paid rent in kind to the landlord under conditions mutually agreed upon. Hoang (1888: 136) succinctly described the nature of the land-lord-tenant, subsoil-topsoil relationship as follows:

> The 'soil' (i.e., subsoil) is commonly worth from 3–6 times as much as the 'surface' (i.e., topsoil); if they belong to different proprietors neither has the right to build a house or make a tomb on the land. He who possesses only the 'soil' cannot himself cultivate the land, but is required to lease the 'soil' to him who possesses the 'surface', and who has the right, unlimited in time, of leasing the 'soil', nor can he expel the lessee at his own will, except in the case where the tenant owes him for rent an amount equal to the value of the 'surface'. When the possessor of the 'surface' has contracted a debt of this kind, he is expelled from the cultivation of the land, and the 'surface' becomes the property of the owner of the 'soil'; then the latter may sell the 'surface' to another or may lease it with the 'soil'.

The contractual relationship between landlord and tenant under such an arrangement made it clear that both parties were entitled to different rights to the soil, each of which was exclusive of each other. These two kinds of rights were designated by two kinds of deeds, one red (*hongchi*), the other white (*baichi*). Moreover, the tenant was free to sublease the topsoil to another tenant without the consent of the landlord as well as to pass it on to his descendants; in many instances the landlord did not even know the precise location of the plot of land in question nor the name of the actual cultivator. Leases of this kind were usually drawn up for long periods of time, in many cases in perpetuity, hence the term "perpetual tenancy" or "perpetual lease". Contrary to expectation, the longer the period of the lease (typically the case of perpetual leases), as Rawski (1972: 19) first pointed out, the greater the degree of freedom exercised by the tenant over the land *vis-a-vis* the landlord. Economically, it provided the cultivator with an incentive to increase productivity given the guarantee of fixed rents for the entire duration of the lease (Kamm 1977: 63, Rawski 1972: 18), and politically it provided a high degree of autonomy in everyday affairs. It was the clear self-assertion and independence on the part of the tenant that was a result of the contractual nature of this "one-field, two-lord system" (*yitian liangzhu zhi*) that led Rawski (1972: 20) to conclude, "custom was on the side of tenant and not the landlord".[27]

This system of dual landownership probably originated as imperial grants of pristine but potentially cultivatable land to officials and monasteries. The earliest instances of such grants in Lantao Island and Kowloon date as far back as the twelfth century during the late Sung period.[28] The recipient of the first known grant was a *jinshi* degree holder, who was awarded the island of Lantao as a royal domainal grant (*fengyi*), presumably in recognition of his meritorious achievement as a county magistrate.[29] Large tracts of land conferred as a result of imperial favor or granted by provincial authorities for the explicit purpose of opening up pristine subsoil for surface cultivation by tenants and ultimately tax collection were a common fixture that continued up until the late 19th century. While it appears to have been a general pattern of land tenure relationship most frequently referred to in the historical literature, Palmer (1987: 13–17) argues that this form of subsoil-surface arrangement actually differed from two other kinds of dual landownership that were prevalent in south China in later imperial times. According to Palmer, the second type of subsoil-surface relationship was more rigidly tied to the existence of and management by localized patrilineages for the purpose of exploiting and maintaining control over areas of intensive cultivation. Under this scheme, the government granted land to local patrilineages to open up previously cultivated land in exchange for payment of land tax. Sometimes, newly cultivated land in marginal and reclaimed areas remained classified as waste land, in which case subsoil holders were able to evade full reportage of land taxes to the local government.[30] Finally, the third form of dual landownership represented a deliberate system of fraudulent land collection, according to Palmer, whereby large and influential patrilineages without actual rights of subsoil ownership browbeat tenants into accepting false claims over land. In these instances, perpetual leases served in actuality as hidden sales of land that managed not only to avoid paying the official conveyance tax but in some circumstances were used to circumvent kin customary rules usually prohibiting the sale of land to agnatic outsiders. This discrepancy between legal principle and actuality became quite wide by the late Qing period, leading to blatant cases of exploitation by established local lineages of immigrant settlers. Palmer attributes widespread abuses of dual landownership (in the third sense) to the chaotic circumstances surrounding the repopulation of coastal areas following the brief forced evacuation of the late 17th century and argues that the use of perpetual lease to disguise a ubiquitous pattern of unregistered sales was not peculiar to this region and common throughout south China during the later imperial era.[31] If custom was on the side of the tenant, as Rawski noted, then practice appeared to be on the side of the landlord. Or to put it another way, the conditions of the dual ownership arrangement facilitated the needs of different parties in different ways under given social conditions.

The practice of dual ownership, as it developed as a result of local struggles over territorial control in the aftermath of the brief period of coastal evacuation and its subsequent repopulation by newly immigrant settlers, forms an important background to British attempts to deal with the actual situation and incorporate the "system" into both legal policy and routine administration. In the absence of extensive historical data regarding the concrete nature of dual ownership practices in various parts of south China, it is difficult to assess to what degree customary practice reflected the official record of landownership, not to mention whether there was any systematicity to the way rules operated at the local level.

When the British took up the task of land registration, they were faced with the dilemma of how to administer perpetual leases and on what basis they would recognize which of the two parties was to be the sole registered owner. In contrast to all the other problems pertaining to land, the authorities spent a great deal of energy dealing with this particular problem. At the surface level, the debate was an attempt to resolve a rather obvious bureaucratic impossibility, namely that they could not recognize in legal-administrative terms a system of dual ownership of land. Since the whole purpose of land registration was tax collection, they could have simply, upon confirmation by all parties, regarded all landlords (whom they called taxlords), as owners of the land proper. But it was not as simple as that.

In the initial stage of demarcation work, the British were puzzled in many areas by claims of both landlords and tenants that they had been paying taxes on the land. After it became apparent that tenants were paying rent to the landlords and that landlords were supposed to have been paying tax to the government, the authorities discovered that this system of perpetual lease appeared to be in many instances a cover-up for widespread abuse within the system. On the basis of a copy of a Ming dynasty Register Book from Dongguan County, to which Xinan County belonged at that time, colonial land officers argued that the amount of land claimed by absentee landlord clans was in actuality much larger than the amount that they had been paying taxes on. How such a situation had actually developed and whether the authorities were correct in assessing the real degree of delinquency in tax payment, especially from a tax register more than 200 years old, are topics of debate, but the authorities concluded from this evidence that the landlords were most likely exploiting the system by wielding their influence and power to browbeat weaker groups, mostly recent immigrants, into acknowledging spurious claims to landownership. The need to address a possible social injustice took priority over the legal obligation to determine the nature of the situation. As Orme (RNT 1912: 1) pointed out in his Report on the New Territories for 1912,

> Before the New Territory was taken over, many Punti villages were living on their capital, on 'squeezes' from their neighbours, and on pay received from the government for collecting taxes. Under British rule, these sources of revenue soon failed, and the older families became impoverished: but their frugal neighbors, especially the Hakkas, released from their former exactions, then increased rapidly in numbers and riches at their expense.

It may have been, as Palmer suggests, that the massive influx of settlers and opening up of new and abandoned land after the Coastal Evacuation combined with the attempt by established patrilineages to reassert territorial control created a situation of discrepancy between actual landownership and official tax records, but it is more likely that the colonial government capitalized on the inconsistent nature of the records themselves to rectify the system as they saw fit, relying as it were upon a subjective interpretation of the facts to determine who the proper legitimate owner should be.[32] Thus, all instances where tenants had been paying rent to landlords were subject to re-evaluation. From the beginning, the landlords were in a losing position since, in many cases, they could not verify, even upon proof of deeds, the exact location of the plots of land they had claimed rights to.[33] The names of tenants they provided often turned out to be nicknames or those of persons deceased for one or more generations. This, along with constant delays on the part of the landlord in supplying information, frustrated land officers who wished to expedite matters. On the other hand, the tenant cultivators were in general much more cooperative with land officers in providing the specifics of landownership, and this also helped to sway the government in favor of registering landownership directly in the name of the actual cultivator (RNT 1900: 256).

Within the Colonial Secretariat, pressure to abolish perpetual lease in one form or another was even greater. For one thing, the drawing up of tax schedules could not proceed without a clear ruling on how perpetual lessors and lessees were to be treated, a situation that was complicated by conflicting claims over what constituted legitimate titles. The necessity to "consider claims by taxlords on their merits" was simultaneously juxtaposed against the desire to correct a gross social injustice (as the same land officer put it, "it is also clear that we must get rid of the taxlords throughout the N.T.").[34] Officials in the Secretariat simply opted for bureaucratic expediency by establishing as first principle that "if the perpetual lessor has either laid no claim, or a late claim, the perpetual lessor is out of court", noting that, even according to strict Chinese law, the title of taxlord is unsound.[35] Measures were proposed to allow the tenant to buy out the landlord over a period of time at a cost equivalent to the total value of the land or enable the government to compensate the landlord directly for the full value of the land. In proposing one of these schemes, Cecil Clementi, a member of the Land Court, argued, "I do not think that such a course will inflict hardship (on the landlord) for the fact of his granting a perpetual lease shows that he meant to part with the land. I expect that by this means the majority of perpetual lessors can rapidly be got rid of".[36] Colonial authorities finally opted to accept claims from landlords as legitimate only in cases where they could produce material proof in the form of registered land deeds. Only 14 taxlords in the entire New Territories were deemed by the government to be eligible for compensation, and they were granted a total of 252.3 acres (RNT 1912: 5). With trifling exceptions, tenant cultivators and shopkeepers were registered everywhere as owners.[37] Thus, in one fell stroke, British colonial rule quietly and swiftly brought about the first agrarian reform in China.

The report on the taxlord problem compiled by H.H.J. Gompertz, President of the Land Court, on January 4, 1904 and presented to the Governor spelled out in explicit detail the diverse aspects of the phenomenon that led to its eventual resolution by the Land Court.[38] It recognized on the one hand the various levels of subletting that actually took place on any piece of land and on the other hand the existence of both legitimate and fraudulent ownership by absentee landlords. Without determining to what extent the nature of actual ownership was influenced by its degree of subletting or exploitation, Gompertz opted for land registration in the name of actual cultivators, who were in any case able to supply the details of each specific plot. It was a solution that satisfied in practice the requirements of land taxation while at the same time eliminating in principle the role of taxlords as unnecessary middlemen. As Gompertz rationalized it, the government should not be bound by such an arrangement if it preferred to receive its tax directly.

Despite initial protest by some landlords and futile late claims by others, hostility regarding the resolution of the taxlord issue quickly died out. Most were unable to substantiate claims of ownership to the satisfaction of the government or the courts, while some could not shoulder the sudden impossible burden of tax payment imposed by the government. As Kamm (1977: 63) described for one case,

> When the British occupied Hong Kong Island, they found
> slightly less than 1500 mow under cultivation, of which 1000

were devoted to padi cultivation. The Tangs, in petition to various officials, were able to show claim to slightly more than 1100 mow from which they collected rent-values. A more extreme example is offered by the Tsing Yi estate. The Tangs laid claim to the whole island and the surrounding fisheries. In evidence to the Land Court, they cited rent payments of 40 piculs on 36 mow leased to perpetual tenants. The crown rent, levied by the British, would have amounted to $7.50. However, the surveyors found well over 1000 mow under cultivation, roughly valued at 228.10 crown rent. At the current price of $2.30 per picul, the Tang's rent-value equalled $92.00. The British administrators were of the opinion that the 40 piculs rent was indeed in respect of all cultivation on the island, and hence the Tangs should be held responsible for 'encroachments'. As can be imagined, the Tangs eventually lost interest in pursuing the claim.

Given the heavy handed manner in which the British finally resolved the problem of perpetual lease and taxlordism in general, it is difficult to justify the position that British colonial policy in the New Territories was predicated upon the aim of maintaining indigenous custom, despite the principle of indirect rule, or that it was adopted in the best interests of indigenous inhabitants. The system of perpetual lease probably had unambiguous customary rules whose practice was complicated by the disruptive consequences of the Coastal Evacuation and a power struggle at the local level between previously established communities and newly settled immigrants, which made it prone to corruption and abuse, but the colonial administration was clearly motivated by bureaucratic expediency and the need to rationalize the system according to its own sense of justice. If it in the process happened to serve the interests of the majority of indigenous inhabitants (i.e., the tenant cultivators), it was only by sheer accident. Certainly, the view from the top (Colonial Secretariat) was even more straightforward; it was an ideal opportunity to eradicate the existence of evil, exploitative taxlords. Thus in the final analysis, far from having rationalized in customary terms a system of land registration and taxation where the Chinese provincial government had not, as the British claimed, it more accurately rationalized the system according to its own values, rules and requirements and not according to custom, the end result being, of course, the abolition of that custom. As the Registrar-General perceptively remarked during discussions in the Colonial Secretariat over the possible handling of taxlordism,

> With the knowledge they (the taxlords) possessed, inaccurate as it was of their land and their tenants, they were able under Chinese rule to collect their rents. It cannot be said that it is due to their negligence that they find themselves unable now to obtain their rent under changed conditions. It is entirely due to the change of government.[39]

ON THE LEGALIZATION OF CUSTOM AND THE CUSTOMARIZATION OF LAW

In retrospect, the abolition of the dual landlord system may be seen as an extraordinary case of social change. Whether this first act of colonial pacification irrevocably upset the balance of local power by depriving established clan-villages of a staple source of revenue is a question that has been raised by historians and that will no doubt continue to be debated.[40] Nonetheless, like the subtle changes forced upon the original treaty, the rationalization of the event under the label of legalization is in my opinion an even more extraordinary act that has effectively diverted the attention of historians and social scientists who continually parrot the government's policy of non-interference in the administration of local society.[41]

Regarding land administration, the colonial administration felt it urgent to set up rigid procedures to register inheritance, succession and conveyances of sale in order to keep track of all changes in land-ownership.[42] The initial work of land demarcation and registration in the New Territories was then an important first step in maintaining an orderly system of land records. On the whole, the British were especially sensitive to Chinese customary laws pertaining to the devolution of property in land. However given the high proportion of land owned by ancestral estates (*tso* (C), *zu* (M)) in villages, the government conceded to Chinese custom one important aspect of English law, namely the Rule Against Perpetuities.[43] In order to accommodate the existence of such estates, special by-statutes were added to administrative procedures relating to land registration that were subsequently written into the New Territories Ordinance of 1910. They included the following:

1. (Section 15) Whenever land is held from the Crown under lease or other grant, agreement or license in the name of a clan, family or *tong*, such clan, family or *tong* shall appoint a manager to represent it . . . Every instrument relating to land held by a clan, family or *tong*, which is executed or signed by the registered manager thereof in the presence of the Land Officer and is attested by him, shall be effectual for all purposes as if it had been executed or signed by all the members of the said clan, family or *tong*.

2. (Section 17) The Land Officer, on ascertaining the name of the person who is entitled to land in succession to a deceased person (hereinafter called the successor), and on being satisfied than any estate duty which may be due has been paid, shall register the name of the successor, and upon such registration being effected the said land shall vest in the successor.

3. (Section 18) Whenever land is vested in a minor, it shall be lawful for the Land Officer to appoint some fit person to be a trustee . . . With the consent of the Land Officer a trustee many buy, sell, mortgage, lease or otherwise deal with or dispose of any property to the like extent as if he were the beneficial owner thereof.

The second of the above by-statutes did not exist in Chinese custom or law and was stipulated simply to ensure that persons actually registered transactions with the government. As for the other two stipulations relating to trusteeship, they enabled the government to accept the material existence of perpetuities such as ancestral estates in accordance with local custom. Yet more importantly, the institution of trusteeship in administrative terms transformed the perpetuity into the status of a legal person by making the trustee legally responsible for actions of the entire group. For all intents and purposes, these three amendments to land administration practice did not really modify colonial policy on the basis of local custom but instead had a converse effect, that of accommodating local custom into a system which recognized only the legal status of individuals. In other words, the fact that the trustee in his capacity as a legal person properly represented the group meant that by the same token the perpetuity had no legal existence per se. Nowhere in the New Territories Ordinance does one find any legal definition of a perpetuity, which is after all a matter of custom. The trustee may be constrained by custom insofar as the decision making process is concerned, but this is distinct analytically from the requirements of the legal transaction itself, which held the person of the trustee solely responsible. Nelson (1969: 23) clearly characterized this difference between legal procedure and its customary referent when he stated,

> The New Territories Ordinance, which lays down that a manager(s) shall be appointed for all property registered in the name of an ancestral trust, does not lay down the responsibilities of the manager to the other members of the *tso* (ancestral group). In fact, the ordinance stipulates that he shall be treated as sole owner of the property, subject only to the requirement that he give notice of any transactions relating to the property and the permission of the Land Officer for those transactions. . . . Any instrument relating to the *tso* shall, when signed by the manager, be 'as effectual for all purposes as if it had been executed and signed by all members' of the *tso*.

The process of accommodating custom within the law points to a seminal feature underlying the theory and practice of "indirect rule" in a colonial context. Far from being seamless and transparent, it was by definition an act of cultural translation that assumed moreover the *value-free* nature of legal codes and the objective status of law in the practice of custom. Even in theory, such translation was rarely perfect, but more importantly the very process of legalization dictated that the practice of custom conform to a set of procedures which was by nature modern. When backed by state power, the legal machinery thus institutionalized with a vengeance the absorption of custom into law and tradition into modernity.

The difference between legal reality and customary reality of social relations on the land becomes important especially when one begins to consider cases where there was an obvious conflict of interest between the two. During the period of British administration, it was not unusual to hear cases in the New Territories where individuals suddenly discovered that they were owners of land they never knew was in their possession or where persons were to their surprise summoned by district authorities to account for disputes on land which they claimed did not belong to them. First of all, the Chinese did not have a custom of memorializing in written form successions to property nor did they as a rule bother to register conveyances of sale with provincial authorities. Succession to property followed well defined rules that hardly necessitated formal wills, probates, etc., even in cases of unequal divisions of property where the conditions of such arrangements were spelled out orally among an audience of relevant individuals and witnesses and morally sanctioned by the group. With regard to other landed transactions, a written contract was sometimes drawn up and signed by each respective party, witnessed by trustworthy individuals and enforced by village authorities. As such practices continued in the colonial period, British official records of landownership sometimes did not accurately reflect the situation on the ground. Moreover, these discrepancies would not surface until an actual problem arose in reference to a plot of land that would in the process of deeper investigation uncover unregistered transactions that took place several generations ago.

Nelson (1969: 13) cites one case in point. About 60 years ago, a man handed over a field to another man in return for a debt he could not pay. The transaction was not registered, and the field was farmed by the recipient and his descendants for the next 30 years when the successor of the man who had given up the field suddenly discovered that he was its registered owner. He demanded its return. However, the District Officer decided in favor of the current occupant, on grounds that no one would give away a piece of land without good reason.

A similar incident involved the death of a man who left behind a wife, a concubine, an adopted son and another son each by his wife and his concubine, respectively (Nelson, 1969: 16). Upon this man's death, all the property was registered in the name of his eldest (adopted) son, who in the words of the deceased's wife's complaint to the District Officer, conspired with the deceased's brother and his concubine to sell the estate. The District Officer felt it was wrong for the eldest son to inherit the entire estate, and after consulting local counsel he ordered that all three sons be named equal successors, in accordance with custom. Concretely, he proposed that the estate be held jointly by the three sons, with the deceased's wife and concubine serving as trustees for the two younger sons, who were still minors. The disputants instead offered to divide the estate into three equal shares, registered separately in the names of the deceased's eldest son, wife and concubine. The District Officer did not object, assuming that any arrangement satisfactory to all parties involved was *ipso facto* in accordance with local custom.

The interesting thing about both these cases is that the District Officer used his position as final arbiter of the law to reinforce the rule of local custom. However, the more important point to be made is that he was able to do so only by simultaneously overruling the legal rules of evidence. One could not have it both ways, as it were, and this forced the District Officer in each case to sacrifice one in favor of the other. This decision by the District Officer to rectify the legal situation in favor of custom prompted Nelson (1969: 13) to remark that, in these and similar instances, the District Officer acted "in a manner more analogous to that of a traditional Chinese magistrate, setting aside the letter of the law in favour of what appeared to him a just settlement of a dispute".

The role of the District Officer in the early phase of colonial administration as final arbiter of the law enabled him, as a person, to uphold local custom when justified. But this merely exposed the fact that the legal procedural apparatus of land registration itself ironically ran counter to the very thing it was meant to systematically regulate in the first place. This became increasingly apparent in later years, after the District Officer's power to sit as magistrate in land cases was transferred to a professional judge and authority over all routine matters of land registration fell into the hands of low-level clerks. In another case cited by Nelson (1969: 13–14), two brothers two generations back during the pre-colonial era divided their father's property. The separate holdings were entered into the Block Crown Lease of 1905. At some later point, the two men exchanged a pair of lots but did not register the transaction. Each man had one son, who in turn produced single sons, the latter being the disputants in this case. Each of the descendants of the two brothers continued to work the fields of which they were unknowingly not the registered owners. In 1960, an outsider wanted to build a house on the field in question and was told by all the villagers that it belonged to brother Hung, who gladly rented the land to him for 20 years for a total rent of $600, paid in advance. No one suspected anything until the tenant built an illegal extension to the house, and brother Pei, who was unknowingly the legal owner of the land, was summoned to the District Office to explain the situation. Brother Pei then began to demand rent for the land, which the tenant, having already paid his rent to brother Hung, refused. Meanwhile, brother Hung, insisting that the field was his, refused to hand over the $600, and his position was backed up by all the elders in the village as well as by brother Pei's mother. Nonetheless, brother Pei refused to concede and demanded payment of rent or repossession of the land. The dispute continued between brother Pei and the tenant while brother Hung, keeping the $600, faded from the dispute. Although this case was never brought to court, Nelson argues that probably none of the third party testimony would have been admissible in a professional court of law and that brother Pei's insistence that the land was his simply because he was its registered owner would not have been challenged.

That this case between the two brothers was never brought to court was not unusual, especially in the postwar era. As Nelson (1969: 14) noted, the process in which Land Records kept by the District Office increasingly came to be the final arbiter of rights to land, even when the records conflicted with village testimony and village customary rights, was well underway during the prewar era as well. It also meant that the further back in generational time an error in registration was committed, the less chance that it would ever be rectified in the present.

Another case in point comes from the northern New Territories, where I did fieldwork. During the 1930s, a villager, referred to here as Au, bought a piece of land adjacent to his own from a clan brother, referred to here as Bei, living several doors down so the former could build an extension to his house. A document of sale was written up and properly witnessed, which transferred rights to the land for $500 from the old owner to the new owner in the name of a small ancestral trust (*tso*) in which Au was a sole surviving member. The sale was not registered with the Land Office. The villager Au passed away shortly after the war, leaving behind his mother, who became the new manager for the *tso*, two wives, one of whom was estranged, and two young sons, each of whom was born to a different mother. Around 1960, the elder son, who by now had made his fortune in England had a new house built in place of the old one. Also around this time, Au's mother died, leaving the management of the *tso* vacant, since no successor was registered in her place, although Au's second wife carried on managerial responsibility in the absence of her elder son, still in England, and her younger son, who was a minor.

Few decades later, the younger son, now aged 30 and preparing to emigrate to England along with his mother, decided to clean up affairs of the house, one of which was to register a new trustee for the *tso* to replace his grandmother who died over than 20 years ago. There were many problems even in this regard. He could not show proof of death, since death certificates were not issued at that time, the grand-mother's name was registered in the land records by her nickname, which was not the same as the official name later used in her identity card, and no one could remember the exact date of death except that it took place sometime before the harvest of the second crop of rice that year when so-and-so was so many years old. But all of these proved to be minor albeit irritating problems, for after the young man was made to go repeatedly to various agencies in the New Territories as well as the central registry of births and deaths in Hong Kong to search for substantive proof of the facts required and to make sure that all possible avenues had been exhausted, a formal notice was put up in the village for the usual 30 days and passed without objection, then a memorial to the Block Crown Lease was entered, after which the transaction became law. But in the process of registering this succession and check-ing the particulars of his *chap-chiu* (licensed record of landholding), the young man discovered that half of his house sat on land which did not belong to him. After being informed about the unregistered sale which took place a generation ago, he went to the District Land Registry armed with the available facts and documents to plead his case. The clerk promptly responded that they could not accept as legal private agreements made with respect to land and that the only way to resolve the problem was to have each respective party, armed with appropriate documentation and proof of identity come in and formally register the conveyance of sale anew, as it were. In any event, Bei, the one who by customary agreement originally sold the land to Au but on paper still remained the owner, was still alive, albeit aged well into his 80s. He was informed by Au's younger son of the discrepancy in land records and the need to rectify it. Although Bei admitted to the prior sale, he repeatedly excused himself when asked to go to the District Office. Eventually, he went there, but only to register a succession of his own property. On his way home, he "suddenly" remembered that the sale of land made to Au was formally registered with authorities during the Japanese occupation and that he had nothing to do with it anymore. An open and shut case.

As seen in the above cases, it is apparent that there were definite rules, procedures and contractual arrangements, written as well as oral, that served to regulate matters pertaining to custom. Participants within these arrangements were bound not only by protocol but more importantly by a set of values embodied within and constitutive of that network of social relationships they were meant to regulate. If the British in their capacity as colonial administrators perceived local custom to be "imperfectly executed", this merely proved that they and the system that they established were guided by a different set of values and prerogatives. To claim, as the colonial authorities did, that these customary institutions were not functionally operational misses the point that they were optimally operational within that relevant domain of social relationships they were meant to encompass and fully sanctioned by the force of those underlying rules that bound people to the group. One can now appreciate Nelson's comparison of the District Officer to the Chinese district magistrate's handling of customary matters by saying that the Chinese magistrate would have used the force of the law at his disposal to make the system conform to custom. The colonial government on the other hand devised a set of legal codes and procedures by which custom could conform to the system. By extension, one might also argue that, as a result of its creation of separate legal procedures, the government enabled and even encouraged some, such as the lucky recipients of land mentioned in the latter two cases, to exploit the system by giving them legitimate cause to maximize self-interested gains. Or as Nelson (1969: 14) neatly summed it up, ironically "the way is now open for unscrupulous villagers . . . to exploit the British

Records against village custom, where the former supports, and the latter is against, their own interests".

An exemplary case in point is a dispute over family property lodged with the District Office, South, and archived in the Public Records.[44] This case was first brought to the attention of the District Officer in February 27, 1952 and dragged on for a decade before arriving at a resolution on January 12, 1962 with a division of property between the three disputants. All three disputants were descendants of Lam Tung Loi; one was a son of the eldest (adopted) son of Tung Loi, named Lam Hin Wing; the second was a natural son of Tung Loi, named Lam Kit Kun; the third was a daughter of Tung Loi, named Lam Yee Kiu. After the death of the patriarch Tung Loi, his estate was registered in the names of all three successors as tenants in common in September 1949. The property was managed by Tung Loi's daughter, Yee Kiu, since the other two, Hin Wing and Kit Kun, were living abroad. A petition to divide the property was put forward to the District Office in February 1952 by Hin Wing sometime after his return to Hong Kong.

The petition to divide the property was the result of dissatisfaction by Hin Wing with Yee Kiu's management of the family estate and her unfair distribution of income from the property. He petitioned first to the Rural Committee to have the family estate divided, to which Yee Kiu agreed, conditional upon the return of Kit Kun from abroad. Kit Kun returned a year later, but instead of proceeding with the division, took control of the entire estate and its income, to the exclusion of the other parties. On April 2, 1953, Yee Kiu also petitioned the District Office to have the property divided, saying that she had dutifully carried out her duty as manager of the family estate and expended much money to repair the property, only to see it unilaterally expropriated by Kit Kun upon his return to Hong Kong. Last but not least, in a letter to the District Office on July 26, Kit Kun wrote that the dispute arose on the contrary out of financial ambiguities, that the manager, Yee Kiu, misappropriated funds set aside for repairing the property, most of which was remitted from abroad by him, and that his nephew, Hin Wing, was a useless unemployed opium addict who was a financial burden and squandered away much of the family earnings. As the sole natural son of the deceased, Tung Loi, and in his role as sole wage earner in the family, he felt that he was justified in taking control of the family estate, at least until certain grievances were rectified.

The attitude taken by the District Office in this matter was first of all to let the parties go home and try to arrive at an amicable agreement, then come back only in the event of failure. In September 1953, after having consulted with two of the disputants, Yee Kiu and Hin Wing, in the presence of members of the Rural Committee (Kit Kun failed to appear) and the District Officer, Austin Coates, wrote the respective parties to propose a division of property. In the next two months, the District Officer, acting on behalf of Yee Kiu and Hin Wing, and lawyers, acting on behalf of Kit Kun, exchanged a series of letters to settle what Kit Kun claimed to be misappropriations of past remittances sent by Kit Kun to Yee Kiu, manager of the family estate. Much of the haggling back and forth involved clarification of how remittances were actually redistributed and which expenses were accounted for by whom. First, Kit Kun requested that money spent by him for repairs on the estate be deducted from the final estate settlement, including 1) repairs on the estate for $1770, 2) estate duty of $720, 3) money paid to one Cham Chai Ping for redemption of a house in the amount of $2400, and 4) repairs effected on another house for $3688. Yee Kiu rebutted by arguing that 1) only $1200 of the $1770 was remitted by Kit Kun, 2) estate duty was correct, 3) the $2400 redemption was paid out of Yee Kiu's own money, and 4) in addition to the $3688 in repairs, this house was redeemed for $1400 by the wife of Hin Wing. Adjustments were made to the original figures claimed by Kit Kun, minus also the rents on the entire estate he had taken since having assumed managerial role upon his return to Hong Kong. This first round of accounting sparked a second round, in which Kit Kun listed in addition all living expenses he assumed for the maintenance of both his sister and nephew's dependants in his capacity as the family's primary wage earner. This invoked more rebuttals on both sides, until November 27, when the District Officer Austin Coates arrived at a blunt conclusion, the core of which stated as follows:

> The conflict in the various accounts and statements made by the brother and sister point only too clearly to the fact that this is a most unseemly dispute which cannot really be solved by people outside the family. The custom undoubtedly is that

money is remitted by family members abroad for the benefit of the whole family, to be spent as the senior member of the family at home thinks fit. The question of seniority in this case would go on age to Miss Lam Yee Kiu, and she has undoubtedly spent the money and managed the family affairs to the best of her ability. For Mr. Lam Kit Kun to return to Hong Kong and say that his money has been misspent raises a question to which there is no answer. Of the money spent over the years, what is Mr. Lam Kit Kun's money and what is not? All money received has quite clearly been pooled for the general use of the family and was not kept separate as money belonging to individuals for the use of individuals.

It was for this reason that, when I first came to know of this dispute, I declined to take into consideration anything to do with the money remitted by your client to his family, because I do not consider that according to Chinese custom his attitude towards the contribution he has made to the family's welfare is the correct one. As this correspondence clearly shows, to attempt to differentiate between his own money, the rent, the money from pig sales, and the money made by Miss Lam's sewing, is impossible.

There is no doubt nonetheless that Mr. Lam Kit Kun's contribution to the family has been very considerable. In fact, without his remittances it is difficult to see how the family would have had anything left in the world. But it is not possible at this date to divide into separate sections what has been treated for years as a single unit. Actually I am also strongly against dividing the house property, but if the family continues to insist on it, I fear that this may have to be done.

In reply to your letter of 28th September therefore, and to our subsequent exchange of letters concerning Mr. Lam Kit Kun's claims against his sister, I must give my considered view that according to the local custom Mr. Lam has no claims that can be financially defined, the repairs to house property etc. having been paid out of a common fund (to which he was of course the principal contributor). . . . The position as I now see it is this: that either your client may agree to equal division of the property with no conditions attached, or he may suggest some alternative for solving the dispute.

A monetary appraisal of all the properties was made, which formed part of Coates' judgment of June 2, 1954 concerning the division of property. This along with a summary of his understanding of the relevant aspects of the case, according to Chinese custom, were spelled out and resulted in the following concrete verdict:

> Lam Hin Wing, being the descendant of the senior branch of the family, shall receive the family house, Lots Nos. 75 and 76 (valued at $10,000 and at present non-productive of rent), on condition that during her lifetime Lam Yee Kiu shall be permitted to occupy as her dwelling the front portion of the upper floor.
>
> Lam Yee Kiu shall receive Lot No. 37 (a barber's shop valued at $4000) and shall during her lifetime enjoy the rents therefrom, on condition that she may not sell this property, nor dispose of it in any way, nor part with her right to the full rents from it.
>
> Lam Kit Kun shall receive the remaining properties, Lot No. 66 (a house valued at $4000), Lot No. 65 (a kitchen valued at $2000) and Lot No. 27 (2 small houses with a total value of $2000); and Agricultural Lot Nos. 1578, 1595 and 1597 (with a total value of $1300).
>
> It is agreed between the parties concerned that at the death of Lam Yee Kiu the barber's shop building and the land on which it stands shall be deemed as belonging in equal shares to Lam Hing Wing, or his heirs, and to Lam Kit Kun, or his heirs.

Kit Kun was dissatisfied with the judgment, which was legally non-binding, since the property was worth over HKD$10,000. Lo Cho Chi, an assistant to the District Officer, noted in correspondence to Coates on September 15, 1954 that:

> Lam Kit Kun has made no move and is not going to make any. He benefits from the deadlock, as he continues to receive rents from the ancestral properties, as if nothing has ever happened. The aggrieved party are Lam Yi Kiu and Lam Hin Wing as a matter of fact. Two months ago before your letter (of August 12, 1954), Lam Yi Kiu succeeded in persuading the barber to pay her one month's rent for the barber shop. After the receipt of the said letter, Lam Kit Kun jumped on the barber, threatening to take legal proceedings and warning him not to pay rent to anybody except him. Since then the barber has made no payments to Lam Yi Kiu, much to her disgust and disappointment. I have advised Lam Yi Kiu to bring the barber before you when you will explain to him that since she is one of the owners of the lot it will be quite in order to pay the rent to her.

A year later, on August 25, 1955, Kit Kun registered his complaint to the District Commissioner of the New Territories, listing ten grounds for appeal, the main points of which can be summarized as follows: 1) both Yee Kiu and Hin Wing registered the succession of his father's (Tung Loi) property without his knowledge or approval, since he was abroad. 2) He protested after the fact, but to no avail. 3) According to Chinese custom, women do not have a right of inheritance. 4) The money for house repairs was put up by himself, while all three of them had equal rights to reap the benefits of it, this being irrational. 5) He was the primary wage earner for the other two, who then squandered away his money. 6) The manager of the property in his absence could not satisfactorily account for the distribution of his remittances. 7) Being the sole natural son of the deceased, he should be sole successor to his father's property. 8) The original succession should be revoked.

Six years later, on November 21, 1961, the new lawyers for Kit Kun wrote the District Office to request the details of the original succession of property that resulted in the registration of the three disputants as owners in common. The new District Officer, B.V. Williams, confirmed that the succession was registered indeed in the names of the three people after the death of the patriarch, noting that "the usual notices were posted in Sai Kung Market, calling for objections, and when none were forthcoming, the property was registered in these three names by Memorial No.53294 of September 23, 1949". On January 10, 1962, after all three disputants were interviewed in the presence of Kit Kun's lawyer and the District Officer, a settlement was reached to divide the property, which basically resembled Coates' original judgment of June 2, 1954 along with some minor modifications.

The complexity of this case illuminates the various conflicts between legal process and customary practices and the ambiguities inherent in both that can be magnified as a result of interpersonal dispute. Kit Kun was perhaps correct to question the original succession of property registered with the District Office that transferred ownership to the deceased's children (or lines thereof). The procedure that required official notice to be put up in the village while calling for objections was a colonial invention that facilitated eventual registration

of land transactions with the Land Office, which should not be mistaken for customary practice, and assumed that, if custom was contrary
to the proposed transaction, someone would lodge an objection. Quite
clearly in this case, inheritance by the daughter Yee Kiu of the deceased's
property was contrary to custom. Kit Kun should have had legal
recourse to overturn the original registration of land succession, but this
simply underscored the fact that the legal-administrative apparatus was
based on its own system of values (and not that of custom), which at
a superficial level attempted to mirror custom and, when all else failed,
had to resort to a special section of the New Territories Ordinance,
enforced by executive authority of the District Officer. Regarding remittances to the estate, Kit Kun's unfortunate position as major wage
earner in the family meant that he had a moral obligation to provide
support for all other dependents, at least until the latter could fend for
themselves. How far this extended in terms of monetary support, either
for specific people or toward the maintenance of that collective estate,
was a matter of individual circumstance or negotiation rather than fixed
customary rule. The transmission of an estate to the next generation
did not include strictly speaking the obligation to maintain the estate
according to some state of functionality or desirability. One could have
sold part of the estate to upgrade the remaining estate without incurring
problems of individual or collective responsibility, as was the case here.
The fact that Kit Kun took it upon himself to use his remittances on
behalf of the estate without at the same time specifying the nature of
these contributions and future reciprocations made the task of defining
what everyone's moral obligations were unresolved. In effect, it was
perhaps true, as Coates concluded, that it was impossible or difficult
to determine under these (general) circumstances where the boundary
of personal or communal contributions to the family well-being lay.
Had the property been divided initially instead of held in common, the
nature of individual responsibility would have been easier to demarcate,
but this would have been a matter of mutual moral obligation that was
subject to negotiation, too. The role of the manager was equally
amorphous; it could only be assumed that he/she was supposed to act
on behalf of collective interests. Such customary flexibility contrasted
with the hard and fast authority that the colonial administration del-
egated to the legal person of the manager to act in all matters pertaining

to the estate. With regard to the adopted son's rights of inheritance to ancestral property, this was something that according to custom could have differed from one locale to another. Although not indicated exactly in the case records, if the adopted son of the deceased (the father of Hin Wing) was not a close agnate, and instead someone adopted from outside or through uxorilocal marriage (which in many places would be considered acceptable forms of customary practice), by strict imperial law he would not have a legitimate right to inherit property. In the final analysis, the settlement mediated by Coates, who divided the property between the two sons (or descendants) and made further provisions to support the unmarried daughter as long as she lived, appeared to be one based on custom. But more importantly, the fact that it happened to be a just resolution reflected his individual skill at weaving through the complex actualities instead of the accuracy of the legal system in translating the nature of custom.[45]

The gap between legal principle and customary practice was a contradiction built into a system that claimed to rule on the basis of local custom. Custom was not without its own imperfections and ambiguities, but when people were forced to negotiate within a space of law rather the usual confines of customary practice, conflicts inevitably erupted and could become exaggerated, though not necessarily snowballing into social proportions.[46] One final aspect of this interaction between East and West that deserves further attention was the colonial government's said commitment to preserve existing custom and not Chinese law per se. One should note that, when the British took over the New Territories, their interpretation of local custom was guided by sinological knowledge of the imperial codes. As Faure (1988) has shown for inheritance cases in the late imperial court, the magistrate normally ruled in favor of law (*fa*) instead of custom (*su*). That the British opted for local custom and endeavored to institutionalize that into something now called customary law was thus ironic not only in light of the above incommensurabilties of Chinese custom *vis-a-vis* English law but also for the resultant customary law's double removal from anything that existed in "traditional" imperial times.[47] In this sense, "customary law" was without doubt a British colonial invention. What must be reconciled here, however, is not simply the degree of fit between custom and law in terms of content but equally importantly as a mode of social practice. Liu Han (1988) has argued, for example, that custom first of all tended to be the product of broad based rules, which is at the same time its source of ambiguity in specific contexts, secondly could be the product of interpretation of elites speaking on behalf of others, thirdly were always prone to change, and fourthly subject to popular consensus. The flexibility of custom represented in certain instances the source of its legal indeterminateness and could in special circumstances precipitate conflicts of interest that in a customary context tended to be resolved by consensus within a familiar (rather than impersonal legal) domain. Its peculiarities in mode of social practice made custom amenable to changing conditions (in ways different from law), while in general effectively insulating its rule and operation from forms of governmentality that were incompatible with local moral authority and inherent norms of community. Perhaps unlike the radical reform precipitated by abolition of the dual landlord system, the legalization of custom produced hidden injuries whose symptoms remained dormant until inflamed. In the short run, law archived custom. In the long run, legalization was the basis of its modern transformation.

FROM POLITICS TO GOVERNMENT: THE NORMALIZATION OF TRADITION[48]

The British implementation of a traditional social system based on Chinese custom was a legal construction that should not be confused with whatever existed in the imperial past or customary present. Wesley-Smith (1980: 95) has argued that the colonial government's decision to administer matters pertaining to land according to Chinese indigenous custom, even to the point of assiduously following an alien and complicated system probably had to do with the non-expropriation clause of the New Territories Convention, which protected rights of inhabitants from confiscation of their property. Like the initial problem of whether the New Territories should be treated as a lease or provisional cession, it was so important to resolve the sovereign status of land that Section 15 was inscribed into the New Territories Ordinance stating, "all land in the New Territories is hereby declared to be the property of the Crown" for the duration of the lease. Although there was brief rebuttal that it contravened the non-expropriation clause of the Convention, the objection was overruled and the statute written into law. In strict legal terms, everyone was, by order of Section 15, duly expropriated of his land. Simply put, by establishing the authority to collect taxes, implementation of the statute then made legal what the government had already recognized in diplomatic practice.

In any case, the decision to administer land in accordance with local custom was not a necessary condition or strategic motive to circumvent the expropriation clause of the lease. Such a policy was standard procedure in other British colonies at the time. Just as the British decided from the turn of events to administer the territory as a provisional cession than as a lease per se, the sovereign status of land during the term of the lease was as meaningless as the notion of lease itself. To the contrary, land registration and taxation were predicated on the assumption that the legal apparatus was an objective process that did not interfere with the operation of existing practices and that Chinese custom was amenable to rational and efficient administration in this regard. The land survey eventually took years to complete and the taxlord problem was resolved with drastic consequences before land registration could even begin to take place. The diligence of the Land Court in disputing taxlord and other claims on the basis of Chinese law indicated that their determination to adjudicate according to custom was based more on positive application of the principles than conscious constraints of the Convention.

The colonial government's attempt to adopt Chinese categories of land as the basis of taxation showed how translation, even at a superficial level, produced incompatibilities at a basic conceptual level. In an appendix to Report on the New Territories for 1899, Lockhart attached a *précis* on Chinese customary law entitled "Memorandum on Land". This as well as excerpts from other Western scholarly sources provided the basis upon which the British appropriated Chinese notions of land taxation for their own use. First class land (*shangtian*) included land near villages in fertile valleys with good depth of soil and good water supply, producing two crops of rice annually. Second class land (*zhongtian*) was rated less fertile, was generally situated higher up the slopes of hills, did not have as good a water supply as first class and usually produced one crop of rice annually. Third class land (*xiatian*) was situated on even higher slopes and tended to be far removed from good water supply. It was thus more suitable for the cultivation of peanuts, sweet potatoes, millet and crops that did not require much water. In addition to these three classes, fish ponds were taxed at slightly higher rate than first class agricultural land, burial grounds were taxed a one time registration stamp fee, while house land was exempt from tax altogether. Land officers also noted that hills and waste land that were not yet put to productive use were usually claimed by nearby villages or powerful clans. Land along the seashore under water on the other hand was registered and taxed only when it was actually put into production (such as salt making). Finally, the notion of "crown land" among the Chinese that included large tracts of virgin land granted to families by imperial or provincial decree was vaguely defined and did not appear to be subject to land tax at all.

In view of the above, the colonial government modified the Chinese three-tiered land tax system as follows. First class land was to include choice padi land as well as first class house land. Second class land then included less fertile padi, dry cultivation and lesser quality house land. Third class land included residual categories of non-agricultural or minimally productive land and other waste land. Land not claimed by any party was duly declared "crown land". These hard and fast categories, strictly enforced by land registration, subsequently became "law".

In the process of "translation", the colonial authorities in effect rigidified the categories and imputed rules of usage that did not exist within the system. Two notable revisions of the Chinese three-class tax assessment scheme was taxation of house land and the interpretation of crown land as that residual category of all non-claimed land. Thirdly, the adoption of absolute fertility as the taxable value of land mirrored the Chinese emphasis on potential productivity (which considered agricultural and seashore land and fish ponds taxable yet exempted house lots and unused waste land), but the differences in practice became points of conflict over the years. To some degree, exemption of house land and uncultivated land from taxation in Chinese terms was related to the principle of productivity. The fact that rent from tenant cultivators was collected in kind was really a function of the productive value of land rather than its market value in an abstract sense. This was the reason why untenured land and land not exploited for its productive value as a mode of livelihood (notably village house land) were not considered taxable. In regard to seashore land, the Land Office generally renewed leases to salt pans on a yearly basis.[49] Reclamation of seashore land was a hotly disputed matter, as evidenced by one court case in 1905, which disallowed the claim of Tang Tsz U, a taxlord, to foreshore and waste land at Cheung Sha Wan.[50] However, rights to the seabed created instances that established the prevalence of Chinese law over the grant of a crown lease where there was no precedent in British law.[51]

In determining the productive value of land, absolute fertility was usually less important a consideration than the quality of tenants in maintaining the land. Ironically, from a Chinese perspective, sometimes the most expensive land was in fact the middle grade, which was not necessarily the most fertile (Rawski 1972: 21, cf. Yang 1925: 48–50). Chen Han-seng explained the logic of this as follows:

> The share rent does not . . . depend on the fertility of the soil alone but largely on the respective amount of labor power and fertilizer which the tenant puts into the land. In this particular district, the tenant of good land often supplies more means of production per mow than other tenants because such an investment is certain to pay. Improving the soil, he is actually in a better position to bargain with the landlord who cannot afford to lease his good land to tenants who cannot or will not keep up the fertility of the soil. It is for this reason that the landlord gets less rent from the tenant of the best land, paradoxical as this may seem, than he gets from the tenant of medium grade land. (Yang 1925: 50)

The most heated point of conflict between the government and indigenous villagers centered upon what the British called "crown land" and what inhabitants called the "people's land" (*mintian*). The next most hotly contested issue revolved around the government's decision to tax house land. In both cases, the underlying conflict was not just a dispute provoked by different definitions of land value but also something that threatened the fabric of the village community. The hard and fast rules used to demarcate existing house land in village spaces characterized by inherent freedom of use and mobility served in effect to petrify these spaces in time. The designation of all remaining land as Crown Land in turn limited future evolution of that village space by making improvements on existing lots impossible without intruding onto land subject to increasingly convoluted government control.

Matters pertaining to land classification provoked dissatisfaction not just over the nomenclature itself but also in the way they translated into higher taxes overall, producing a volatile situation that escalated and became intertwined with other policy dilemmas. In 1905, inhabitants protested against increases in Crown Rent, twice in the space of six years, as well as the imposition of a tax on houses and buildings. These were not just isolated incidences.[52] In one prominent case, 30 petitions were submitted by 296 villagers in protest to the government. The Colonial Secretary was of the general opinion that, judging from the background of the petitioners, this action appeared to represent agitation by a minority rather than dissatisfaction by the populace as a whole. Despite recommendations by the Registrar General Brewin to lower taxes, he defended the overall increases, adding that "these people who are obliged to be overtaxed can afford to offer a substantial fee".[53] It was then recommended not to increase overall rates as initially planned and to lower latrine rates. On the more important subject of a house and building tax, petitioners argued that this tax had never been imposed before and was thus unreasonable.[54] The Governor Matthew Nathan replied, noting that the novelty of a tax did not affect the validity of its imposition, which clearly contravened the colonial government's original policy of administering the land question according to indigenous custom.[55] Given the extent to which Chinese law was upheld in other matters, this stance was contradictory. Nonetheless, the Colonial Secretary defended and articulated the rationale in a memo to the Governor as follows:

> There is a house duty in England on inhabited houses occupied as farm house, public house, copper shop, shop warehouse, lodging house, and I think on house let in tenements or flats over certain amount. This is in addition to local rates. Unless we are to go on the principle that no taxes are to be levied in the New Territory other than such as were levied by the Chinese government, a house tax is a usual tax. All the other taxes mentioned are fair taxes.[56]

The objection was circumvented and the complainants mollified in part by a proclamation issued on July 11, 1906 which promised not to raise Crown Rents during the term of the lease. Such a promise not only deprived the government of large sums in revenue; it was also contrary to specific instructions given in 1899 by Chamberlain, the former Secretary of State, stating in effect that land tax must be subject to periodic revision. Even when Crown Leases were renewed in 1973 after the initial 75 year lease had expired, the Crown Rent remained unaltered with respect to most lots in the New Territories despite enormous increases in the value of the land. In short, in order to compensate for what appeared to be a legal contradiction of the Convention, the government made a financial concession. But in order to compensate for the obvious loss of revenue to be suffered in the course of succeeding years, they would have to make further revisions and restrictions in land policy and administration. All of this produced a vicious cycle, the end result being the increasing rigidification of those categories of land use which they first modified on the basis of custom then reimposed upon an indigenous way of life.

A corollary to the hard and fast rules the government used to classify land was their policy toward conversion of agricultural to building or other land. There was no Chinese law that prevented persons from using their land to build, if they wished. Early cases of land conversion tended to be handled routinely, conditional upon paying a higher tax.[57] In theory such conversions were permissible, but in practice a license had to be obtained from the government before one could build, and this was subject to growing restrictions. Given the urban expansion into New Kowloon in the early 20th century and elsewhere in the New Territories later on, the volume and desirability of conversions necessitated ever tighter regulation.

The 1920s was a period in which many of these pent-up frustrations came to a head. This decade was in a sense a continuation of physical growth from the previous decade. Refugees from mainland China continued in the aftermath of the 1911 Revolution to move into Hong Kong and Kowloon urban areas. Urban areas experienced a growth in light industries, and market towns came to be linked by the development of a transportation infrastructure spreading out from the city. A "List of Industries in the New Territories in 1918" compiled by the Captain Superintendent of the Police showed that 121 new industries out of a total of 148 had been established since 1898. A high proportion of the population in the New Territories was still agricultural by occupation (70% according to the 1911 census), but with cultivators from the mainland gradually filling up villages in the rural area, staple rice production became increasingly displaced by vegetable cultivation.

The physical movement of people to the territory accompanied by the growth of rural towns as well as urban-industrial expansion into the countryside created pressure on the land in a material sense. To resolve this problem, the government laid out diverse plans for development. Development dictated the levelling of hills, the raising of valleys and the diverting of waterways, but such work involved at the same time the resumption of large tracts of land in adjoining rural areas. The phenomenon of land resumption raised issues of legality as well as compensation. Legally speaking, resumption for the development of building land contravened the wording of the Convention, which stated that there should be no expropriation of land or expulsion of inhabitants and that if land was "required for public offices, fortifications, or the like official purposes, it shall be bought at a fair price".

On April 29, 1925, a petition was sent to the Secretary of State Amery from 671 residents in New Kowloon to protest the government's policy of resuming land for development purposes. It charged that land resumption for "official purposes" did not explicitly include things such as town development, thus inhabitants were being illegally expelled and their land forcibly expropriated. The problem had to do first of all with the wide powers of the Crown Lands Ordinance and secondly with the unfair rates of compensation, in which landowners were being reimbursed according to the value of agricultural land, even though following resumption the land was worth far more on the open market. In a memo to the Secretary of State Amery, the Governor R.E. Stubbs replied by rejecting claims that land resumption contravened the wording of the Convention then maintained that, with regard to compensation, full value was given. He added that this was a matter to be settled with the Chinese government rather than the petitioners. The Colonial Secretary Cecil Clementi also agreed, noting that expropriation actually meant "confiscation without compensation" and that the issue was rather a matter of compensation or "fair price".[58] Despite disagreement among

Land Officers over these attempts to circumvent the legality issue, the Colonial Office persevered and stood its ground by interpreting "like official purposes" loosely to mean those defined by the better interests of government that contributed to the overall benefit of the populace.[59]

. In effect, the government's efforts at resumption were legally stifled by a restriction in the wording of the Convention, a restriction whose objective was not to impede future growth and progress, strictly speaking, but to prevent unwanted expropriation of land and the expulsion of its inhabitants in the process. Forced expropriation for narrowly defined "official purposes" specified in the Convention thus had to be viewed in the context of the traditionally non-interventionist role of the imperial or provincial government in matters of development, which in turn accounted also for the laissez-faire definition of house land and its corresponding notions of village space. Yet despite the economic and demographic expansion that characterized this period, the constant fears of speculative elements among the local elite, who constituted the majority of petitioning "landholders", combined with skepticism expressed by officials that compensation at fair market value could not in the short run recoup the initial cost of land resumption for purposes of housing development indicated that, at least initially, the state did not play an active role in initiating large-scale planning. The government's policy of compensating land resumed for its full value as agricultural land and not for its potential value as building land was at first an attempt to prevent profiteering by the inhabitants.

But as time went on, the economics and politics of land resumption evolved in a way that enabled the government to compensate for a policy blunder made in 1906, when it froze rates of Crown Rent in response to native protests over the imposition of a tax on houses and the generally excessive taxes imposed by the British *vis-a-vis* the Chinese provincial government. While large-scale resumption and urban planning was a response to a social need to facilitate development in an orderly fashion, such planned development under the direction of government could be used to generate revenue to make up for the loss of land tax in real terms due to the freezing of Crown Rents. Recouping of such lost revenue through land resumption was made possible first of all by pocketing the difference between the cost of compensation paid to the indigenous villager for the expropriation of his land and the upgraded market price of the land after it had been developed. By this means, the government also profited in the long run by collecting higher taxes on land whose value was enhanced by resumption. With regard to compensation, boards of arbitration awarded compensation on cultivated land according to its value as agricultural land, although it was to be converted into higher priced land for building purposes and was worth far more than that on the open market. Such a policy of compensation was the government's interpretation of "a fair price".

The government's policy regarding land resumption and compensation was combined with new restrictions in 1923 on the conversion of agricultural land into building land. Previously, in converting agricultural land for building purposes, one only had to apply for approval from the District Land Office, after which one would simply pay a higher tax for the house land. To build on that land, a license had to be applied for at the Department of Public Works, which was responsible for enforcing all building guidelines and regulations. According to the new law, however, one would be required to pay a premium for converting land for house building purposes. The premium would be based upon current market value, and in effect the premium paid would make up the difference between the old Crown Rent value of the land and its real market value. In addition to the imposition of a premium on building land, further tax penalties were later imposed upon the renting of house land to outsiders, that is, those recent immigrants who were not descended from the original pre-1898 inhabitants of the territory. A premium was charged whenever house land was rented out to others (usually outsiders) and whenever an outsider erected a building on house land, whether for purposes of living there himself or renting it out (Liu 1977: 54). From the government's point of view, the intended goal of such legislation was probably to ensure that only indigenous villagers could enjoy the advantages of low Crown Rent and to prevent villagers from taking advantage of the government by selling or renting out land to outsiders at a profit to themselves. However, regardless of its presumably moral tenor, such legislation was still guided by an economic imperative.

The imposition of a premium upon the sale or rent of property to post-1898 settlers into the New Territories (outsiders) then created a double standard in the administration of land. Given the special status of indigenous custom that was built into the New Territories Ordinance, this distinction between indigenous and outsider served to concretize a category of self-proclaimed "primordial inhabitants" (*yuanzhumin*) whose rights to land and community became increasingly reified as a result of being tied to the government's preservation of tradition, which became in the long run increasingly lost in time. This tie to traditional rights rather than the content of custom itself became increasingly strategic in utilitarian rationalist terms as the widening disparity between unchanging Crown Rent and real market value of the land separated in tangible terms the benefits of the "haves" from "have nots". This disparaging gap between real and frozen land values also forced the government to adjust policy strategies to transcend its convoluted predicament.

In this regard, to say that both the imposition of a premium on building land and penalties to prevent others from profiting off unnaturally low Crown Rents transcended existing categories of land use is quite an understatement. The government quite deliberately resorted to such measures to recoup what it had considered to be justifiable revenue. However, such sanctions, aside from the fact that they were not based upon custom, were interpreted by inhabitants on the other hand as another act of coercion undertaken by the colonial government to unilaterally deprive the people of their customary rights to land and exploit them economically by exacting a premium on what was quite clearly their land.

In response to the new ordinance of 1923, indigenous villagers headed by a group called the "committee of six" (*liuren xiaozu*) voiced their opposition to the government. Their actions in general found support among leaders of the Chinese community. The "committee of six" then sent petitions to various high authorities, including the Governor R.E. Stubbs, the Land Officer at Tai Po, and an official of the Chinese government. In all of these petitions, the petitioners emphasized repeatedly that the imposition of a premium for purposes of building on village land (including "crown land") was a direct contravention of the non-expropriation clause in the Convention. A statement at the end of the fifth point of the petition to the Chinese representative phrased the point most explicitly as follows:[60]

Today, because people erect houses for their own use, they oppose payment of a premium to government; in essence, what this really means is that the property of the people (*minchan*) has been expropriated by the government (*ruguan*)! If it is not the case that the soil (*tian*) is the personal property of the people, that the price (*jia*) is that of the personal property of the people, that the surface of the land (*di*) is bought for payment of the price, then whereupon does one begin to talk about paying a premium (*bujia*)?

From a native's point of view, the imposition of a premium on building land was explicit proof that the land had been expropriated by the government. After all, there was no reason to pay a premium on one's own land unless the premium itself represented the cost of buying back the land from the government so that people could erect houses for their own use. This was invoked by the term *bujia*, which literally meant the making up of a difference (premium) to account for the actual price. More importantly, the Chinese lacked a distinction in Anglo-Saxon terms between private and communal land in the village. All land, regardless of whether it was physically occupied or not and whether claims of "ownership" over demarcated pieces of land could be documented with red deeds or not, constituted the "the personal property of the people" (*minchan*). Moreover, the British use of the term Block Crown Lease to describe their jurisdictional authority over land in the leased territory combined with the power invested within such authority to re-enter or confiscate private land in situations of non-conformity to legal guidelines, the latter of which (i.e., power of re-entry) did not even exist under Chinese rule, simply intensified fears held by indigenous villagers that all rights of ownership over land had been taken from them as well. Or as one writer later phrased it, "rights over land ultimately (literally 'eternally') belonged to the government. That whom the ordinary person thought of as being the owner (*yezhu*, literally, 'master of the estate') in reality was (now) a Block Crown Lessee (*guandi pi zuren*) (XJZW 1971c: 12)". Thus, from a native point of view, the expropriation of land was not just a threat made by government but more precisely a reality engendered by the imposition of a premium on "the people's land". Even the controversy over the strict definition of "official purposes" with regard to land resumption that heated up in government circles was a secondary matter in contrast. Continued rejections encountered by the "committee of six" contributed directly to the emergence of the Heung Yee Kuk (N.T. Rural Committee) as a spokesman for indigenous interests.

Finally in 1926, facing mounting opposition from indigenous villagers, the government rescinded the policy they initiated three years earlier by abolishing all premiums imposed upon building land in the village (Cheng 1978: 15). But this did not prevent future land policy from taking on new twists and turns. In short, these encounters intensified even more sharply the overall view that colonial land policy, with its adoption of increasingly Draconian measures, was growing more repressive and in a direction which was contrary to its original intent of governing "on the basis of custom". This fear was echoed by the Secretary of State Amery over the Governor's inflexible handling of the land resumption problem when he remarked, "it does appear that the views of the Hong Kong government as to the rights of the holders of the land under Chinese law have become less sympathetic as time progressed and the Convention and the promises made under it receded into the past".[61] Over time, the conflict became not just a difference of definition but more importantly the accumulated result of contradictions built into a system of administrative practice that would have serious ramifications for the viability of existing social lifestyles and notions of local community.

The history of British land policy in the New Territories of Hong Kong is as much a history of British colonialism as it is a history of rural society in the New Territories of Hong Kong, insofar as the latter has been affected by developments on the land. In the context of colonial history, the meaning and function of land are enveloped within narratives of territoriality both in relation to a changing global order within which colonial rule is a means to an end and in the construction of a peculiar ethical vision of society. At the global level, the process of indirect rule was an ongoing negotiation between Britain and China in terms of the "lease" as well as the attempted imposition of a rational order that shared similarities with colonial experiences elsewhere. The consequences of land policy upon a changing rural society as mediated by this colonial interface must not only be understood as a function of how well or not the colonial government succeeded in preserving the nature of "tradition" but more importantly in terms of how local society itself was unconsciously absorbed into an evolving societal order.[62] In the short run, the letter of the law may have archived a customary way of life, but in the long run legal overdetermination in my opinion hastened its eventual disintegration.

Seen at the level of events, things changed considerably without doubt from the initial occupation of the New Territories to various attempts to institutionalize a system of land registration and rural administration. The events themselves show that the intentions of the actors were often not all that clear. Even when they were clear, they resulted in many levels of cultural misunderstanding and unnecessary conflict. The constant changes of strategy that afflicted the British in the early days demonstrated that even the conception of the lease and other basic issues were not sharply defined or well thought out. In institutional terms, if there was a system, it came about mostly in the making, and not without heated resistance at times from indigenous inhabitants. The events thus reflect conflicts at the level of meaning rather than fact. It is possible to pause and analyze the underlying features that have given rise to this "clash of civilizations". To say the least, the government's understanding of "native" custom varied from case to case, with mixed results. But more importantly, the moral autonomy enjoyed by local custom and the flexible uses of land that tied the village to a privileged space of social livelihood conflicted with the processes of social structuration that forced its incorporation within a different globalizing system. Ironically, the policy of indirect rule involved in certain senses a deeper investment in the regulation of everyday life. In cases where legal codification mirrored the content of custom at face value, it changed nonetheless the way custom functioned in its social context. "The more things stay the same, the more they change". Yet in other cases where custom was altered to conform to legal conventions and statutes as a precondition for its efficient administration, this was seen on the other hand as a product of "rationalization" rather than a process of Eurocentric acculturation essentially no different from the kind of acculturation used to depict the adoption of a different language, clothing, or way of life. "The more things change, the more they stay the same". Thus far from preserving the existing "order", the process of indirect rule in institutional terms, backed by an evolving and increasingly disciplinary power of the state, first tied the fate of the local order to the social whole, then facilitated its transformation through "modernization". It was really within the context of modernization that preservation of tradition then took on a different meaning, while elevating colonial "rule" to even higher stages of refinement.

NOTES

1   See Liu Qunkuan (1995: 94–5) for transcripts of village proclamations warning of a British invasion and the need for urgent militia preparation and self-defense.

2   One such placard posted in Ping Shan said the following (from Correspondence (June 20, 1898 to August 20, 1900) Respecting the Extension of the Boundaries of the Colony, pp.138–39. Eastern no. 66. Colonial Office, London):

> We hate the English barbarians, who are about to enter our boundaries and take our land, and will cause us endless evil. Day and night we fear the approaching danger. Certainly people are dissatisfied at this and have determined to resist the barbarians. . . . On the one hand we shall be helping the (Chinese) government; on the other we shall be saving ourselves from future trouble. Let all our friends and relatives bring their firearms to the ground and do what they can to extirpate the traitors. Our ancestors will be pleased and so will our neighbors. This is our sincere wish.

Consult Correspondence Respecting the Extension of the Boundaries of the Colony, pp.190–219. Eastern no. 66. Colonial Office, London, for details pertaining to militia preparation in villages from Tai Po to Kamtin. It was initially thought that resistance spread from the county seat in Nantou, but this was later proved false (see Correspondence Respecting the Extension of the Boundaries of the Colony, Serials 112 and 224 in particular. Eastern no. 66. Colonial Office, London)).

3   At this time, the Governor of Hong Kong issued a proclamation to inhabitants of the Territory, which instead of appeasing local anxieties heightened fears that the British would confiscate land and threaten livelihoods (CO 129/290, April 7, 1899, N.T. Disturbances: Reports by C.S. Police Superintendent General).

4   Liu (1976: 83) notes that many villages spontaneously reacted to British entry by closing village gates as though to defend themselves against alien invaders.

5   Correspondence (June 20, 1898 to August 20, 1900) Respecting the Extension

of the Boundaries of the Colony, p.159. Eastern no. 66. Colonial Office, London.

6   Correspondence (June 20, 1898 to August 20, 1900) Respecting the Extension of the Boundaries of the Colony, p.261. Eastern no. 66. Colonial Office, London.

7   As hostility began to mount over the building of police matsheds overlooking strategic points, which in the process disrupted the geomantic disposition of the area, the Chinese government admittedly did little to dissuade or persuade the villagers in their intentions. By the time Chinese troops attempted to intervene in the impending skirmish that was about to take place over the construction of the matsheds, they were fired upon and repulsed by villagers who by this time were probably convinced that the provincial government was collaborating with the British to sell them out (Groves 1969: 48). The confusion of inhabitants in the more remote villages of the territory was perhaps even more heightened.

8   See FO 881/7226, Colonial Office to Foreign Office, April 18, 1899; FO 881/ 7226, Blake to Chamberlain cable, April 20, 1899; CO 129/291, Blake to Hamilton, April 22, 1899. Claiming complicity by Chinese officials to incite inhabitants in other areas to incite resistance in the New Territory, the colonial government demanded punitive reparations as well, which were refused by the Chinese side.

9   See CO 882/5, Chamberlain to Blake cable, May 14, 1899; FO 881/7226, Blake to Chamberlain, May 16, 1899; CO 882/5, Blake to Chamberlain, May 16, 1899.

10 FO 881/7280, Foreign Office to Colonial Office confidential letter, October 17, 1899; FO 881/7280, Colonial Office to Foreign Office letter, October 21, 1899.

11 FO 881/7226, Colonial Office to Foreign Office letter, June 21, 1899.

12 From the point of view of the Hong Kong government, the desire to administer the New Territories as part of the colony as a whole was greater than its intention to view it as a lease in a literal sense. As early as 1914, Governor Henry May recommended to the Secretary of State the desirability of converting the territory into a cession in perpetuity, a recommendation that was nonetheless dismissed as being untimely and impractical. See CO 129/323, May to Lyttleton, June 17, 1914.

13 The Chinese government repeatedly put forth the position that the leased territory had the same status as the trade concessions or "settlements" at the treaty ports. China never relinquished its right of sovereignty over the territory and its citizens. At the same time, this right of Chinese sovereignty was never accepted by the British, who managed to push it into the background and impose their own interpretation of the issues, an interpretation which was, of course, sanctioned by pure force. As late as the 1930s, the Chinese government continued to assert its "landlord" status, an instance of which involved the

granting of mining licenses in the territory and fishing licenses in the waters of the Colony. Dr. Philip Tyau, special delegate for foreign affairs for Guangdong and Guangxi argued that the Chinese government retained the power to grant licenses in these matters on grounds that the New Territories and Kowloon City were not part of the Colony proper of Hong Kong. As the British consul- general at Canton stated, "China has by no means forfeited all her rights *as ground landlord* in these territories and adjoining waters under the lease agreement" (CO 129/564, "Extract from Canton Intelligence Report for Half Year Ended 30th September, 1937"). The KMT's position on sovereignty over Hong Kong persisted even until after the war.

[14] The Viceroy expressed his views explicitly regarding collection of land tax in point 10 of an eleven point statement on Kowloon's extension by declaring, "land owned by Chinese subjects within the new settlement must pay the land tax to the Chinese authorities. Should British subjects purchase land, (ground) rent shall be paid in accordance with the Regulations prevailing at Shanghai." The British Consul at Canton Mansfield scribbled the word "nonsense" next to both items. See FO 228/1282, Enclosure No.2, July 17, 1898.

[15] See Atwell (1985: 1–63) for detailed discussion of the events and circumstances leading up to the acquisition of Weihaihei and the nature of its administration.

[16] After presiding over briefly over the administration of the New Territories, Stewart Lockhart was dispatched to Weihaiwei in north China to serve as Colonial Secretary. His overall policy of ruling in ways that accommodated to local practice was consistent with the external factors that discouraged the implementation of a British style of administration, the latter being the case in Hong Kong. As Airlie (1989: 123) characterized him, "Stewart Lockhart knew exactly how to behave. His manners, speech, and compliments when in the presence of senior Chinese officials were those of a mandarin, and thus he was accepted as an equal. The inequalities of power were brushed aside because of the equalities of manner and learning".

[17] This was the exact wording of the Convention for the Lease of Weihaiwei.

[18] A well-known incident exemplified differences between Hong Kong's Governor Henry Blake and the Colonial Secretary of the New Territories Stewart Lockhart. In retaliation for the murder of Tang Cheung-hing, one of the men appointed to post the Governor's proclamation on the day the flag was hoisted, Lockhart burnt down the houses belonging to the murderers, who had long escaped, then ordered the clansmen of the three murderers to contribute $1200 compensation to support Tang's widow. Blake censured Lockhart for his actions, saying that "I have no doubt that the burning of the houses was effective, but we have come to introduce British jurisprudence, not to adopt Chinese" (cf. Wesley-Smith 1980: 70). Lockhart on the other hand reiterated the rationale of his actions, saying that the crime was political, whose ultimate responsibility had to be borne by the clan as a whole.

[19] The reaction by Ping Shan villagers to the construction of the first police station was quite explicit:

It says that land, buildings, and customs will not be interfered with but will remain the same as before. Why should they therefore, when they first come into the leased area, wish to erect a police station on the hill behind our village? When has China ever erected a police station just where people live? The proclamation says that things will be as before. Are not these words untrue? (Correspondence Respecting the Extension of the Boundaries of the Colony, p.261. Eastern no. 66. Colonial Office, London)

[20] Most of the time, the colonial government preferred to believe that it was simply dealing with disorderly elements in society. As the Governor of Hong Kong Henry Blake remarked during the outbreak of resistance to the hoisting of the flag in Tai Po, "I am not disposed to attach much importance to this attack upon Mr. May and his party. Such a sudden access of militant irritability is not uncommon in Ireland and subsides as rapidly as it rises" (Correspondence (June 20, 1898 to August 20, 1900) Respecting the Extension of the Boundaries of the Colony, p.154. Eastern no. 66. Colonial Office, London).

[21] Hong Kong local historians differ on the dates depending on the sources used. For instance, Balfour (1970: 164) cites 1026 A.D. as the date of arrival of the Hau, whereas Siu Kwok-kin (1982a: 44) suggests early Ming (late 14th century). Siu also (1982a: 43) cites 1260 A.D. for the arrival of the Mans, while Baker (1966: 25) claims that they were the last of the Five Great Clans to settle in the region.

[22] Barnett (1957: 262–63) stated that 3667 persons were still living within the district in 1667 and claimed that only 1648 of those who left returned to their villages when the evacuation was rescinded in 1669. See Hayes (1974) for another account of these events in the Hong Kong area.

[23] The Hakkas not only took over villages that were permanently abandoned as a result of the evacuation but also opened up virgin areas, notably in the northern and eastern parts of the territory and the islands. Lo Hsiang-lin (1963: 4) posited that the rapid influx was facilitated by an edict drawn up by A-ke-min, Viceroy of Guangdong and Guangxi, during the early years of the Qianlong era (see zouyi no. 27, also reproduced in part in ZYWHZS, vol. 3: 65), that offered favorable terms to cultivate waste land as well as special civil service examination quotas for Hakkas (Ng 1983: 94). Nonetheless, the influx of Hakkas was, of course, part of a larger emigration of the dialect group as a whole from north China, the demographic and genealogical aspects of which are already well documented (Lo (1933) is the most authoritative general account; also see Siu Kwok-kin (1982b) for a genealogical reconstruction with special reference to Hakka groups in the Hong Kong region).

[24] The demarcation process and resolution of claims are described fully in the Reports of the Land Court (RLC 1902 and RLC 1905 in particular).

[25] As Nelson (1969: 33) noted, "until 1961 at least, the District Officer was able to act as a sort of super-charged Chinese magistrate: one might be forgiven for feeling that the British administrators had become more Chinese than the Ch'ing". In similar terms, Huang (1982: 66) attributed the success of British administration of Hong Kong to its "indirect rule" and "enlightened colonialism". As he put it,

> We should probably credit this 'enlightened colonialism' as the only reason why traditional Chinese kinship organization, land tenure system, and beliefs have been preserved in their authentic forms. . . . The presence of British rule, with its high efficiency and legalistic interpretation of 'traditional custom and laws', has as Nelson puts it, literally 'fossilized' Chinese society in the New Territories. I would contend that they have not only been fossilized, but also been pushed to their 'pure' and 'ideal' manner.

By pointing to the role of the District Officer, Nelson and Huang overlooked the fact that it was on the basis of legalistic constructs and codes of administrative practices that the British set about rationalizing the indigenous system and that this set of ideological constructs rather than the role of the administrator became eventually the more salient aspect of what they called "colonial administration".

[26] Other terms abound in the literature depending on locality such as *tiangu, tiangen* for "subsoil" and *tianmian, tianpi* for "topsoil" (Niida 1946: 129–30, 245, 248) or *liangtian* ("taxed land") and *zutian* ("rented land") (Hoang 1888: 135–36).

[27] Rawski (1972: 20) also notes that the landlord did not generally have the right to evict the tenant, even when payments were in arrears. Tenants were also free to sublet cultivation rights without notifying the subsoil owner.

[28] Sung Hok-p'ang (1936: 34) notes the grant of tracts of land to a Buddhist monastery in Dongguan county in 1169. Other cases of endowments originating in the twelfth century were noted in Colonial Secretary Office correspondence, namely CSO 436 ext., "Recovery of Rent in the N.T.", January 15, 1904 and CSO 5956 ext., "Claims in Survey District II", July 25, 1904.

[29] H.H.J. Gompertz, the President of the Land Court, in his recommendations on the problem of taxlords, referred to the Lantao grant as an instance of hereditary tax farming, noting that, although the Li family was unable to show actual land deeds to document this grant, they were able to point out a passage in the 1753 Guangzhou Gazetteer attesting to its historical facticity (CO 129/322, "Position of Taxlords in New Territory", pp.749–50). See also Siu Kwok-kin (1982c).

[30] Fu Yiling (1961: 25–43) notes that in most cases it was easier for tenants to deal directly with lineages than to register for permission to open new land with the magistrate, thus accounting for the small proportion of land actually taxed.

[31] Palmer (1987: 29) cites in particular the works of Xu Tiantai (1941: 61–63), Guo Songyi (1980: 116), Yang Guozhen (1981: 37–39) and Han Henggyu (1979: 39–45) for evidence of different uses of dual landownership in other regions of China.

[32] Bruce Shepherd, a Deputy Land Officer, noted in his memorandum of work in the Land Office that, in its first year, the number of petitions from inhabitants in the territory disputing matters relating to land totalled over 1000 (RLC 1900: 279).

[33] Lockhart's Memorandum on Land notes, "the greater part of the land claimed by clans was never registered and, as a rule, it appears that no land tax was ever paid on this land to the Government. The cultivators, who have paid rent for years to the clans, in view of the fact that the land had not been registered, were afraid to dispute the rights of ownership, as they anticipated it would result in the land being resumed by Government and they would thus be deprived of their right of cultivation." (RNT 1900, Appendix No.III)

[34] CSO 280/04, Clementi to Colonial Secretary minute, January 12, 1904. See also discussions in CSO 226 ext., "Taxlords in the N.T.", January 9, 1904.

[35] CSO 280/04 ext., Clementi to Colonial Secretary cover letter, January 12, 1904; CO 129/322, May to Lyttleton cover letter, May 20, 1904.

[36] CSO 280/04 ext., Land Court to Colonial Secretary, December 1, 1904.

[37] The most complete account of the taxlord settlement is recorded in CSO 6269, August 5, 1904. See also RLC 1901, p.372. CO 129/328, Nathan to Lyttleton, May 17, 1905, spells out more fully the reasons for denying compensation to taxlords. With regard to the Li family claim on Lantao, Cecil Clementi remarked in a letter to the Colonial Secretary, "there are no taxlords left in Lantao. They have either disappeared completely or become landlords" (CSO 3164 ext., April 20, 1904). Reference to taxlord claims in CSO and other files continued well into the 1920s.

[38] CO 129/322, May to Lyttleton cover letter, May 20, 1904.

[39] CSO 436/04 ext., Registrar-General to Colonial Secretary, April 24, 1904.

[40] Kamm (1977: 80) argues, for example, that the abolition of the dual landlord system essentially undermined the power of supra-village divisions such as *ju*, while Hayes (1976: 40–42) has tended to minimize the consequence of its abolition, noting that it traditionally favored the will of tenants over landlords, this being the case in regard to the Li family that owned most of Lantao (Hayes 1977: 50–52).

[41] See, for example, Hayes (1991: 99–107) for a representative view in this regard.

[42] There was a brief attempt in 1902 to introduce the Torrens System in the New Territories, an Ordinance that was repealed in 1903 without being implemented due to conflict with the New Territories Land Court Ordinance (Sihombing 1984). See also discussions on the Bill entitled The New Territories Titles Ordinance, in CSO 109, June 2, 1902, prompted by recommendations made first in RNT 1901.

[43] There are generally two kinds of ancestral trusts, *tso* and *tong* (C) (=*tang* (M)), found in the New Territories, both of which operated according to the same kinds of "familial" principles. The *tso* was strictly speaking a trust established by an ancestor for the benefit of his lineal descendants and in which members enjoyed *per stirpes* shares. A *tong* was a more flexible corporate group that had common propertied interests and that could incorporate kinsmen as well as comrades. It could also take on ancestral ritual functions, which would make it similar to a *tso*. An administrative guideline to the two was provided by J.W. Hayes in HKRS 511, Deposit 1, Serial 1, "*Tong* and *Tso* in the New Territories", December 19, 1962.

[44] N.T. Administration HKRS 116, Acc. 56, Deposit 1, Serial 88, "Land Dispute Among Lam Yee Kiu, Lam Kit Kun and Lam Hin Yau".

[45] It is interesting to note that when I discussed this case (as well as relevant material) in 1985 with Austin Coates, who after retiring from government service later became a prominent historian and novelist, he professed no memory of this particular family dispute, saying that he had to handle such cases "all the time".

[46] In regard to management practices of customary land trusts, Hayes (1988: 497) notes that some trusts allotted per stirpes shares and others per capita shares.

[47] As Wesley-Smith (1982: 12) put it, "it is ironic that the determined efforts of paternalistic British administrators to preserve an alien institution should, by their very success, have produced significant changes". Similarly, Emrys Evans (1971: 24) has noted that the constant tension between the Court's attempt to allow customary law to operate and its own desire to maintain administrative control totally altered the balance of interests under customary law.

[48] This is a reference to Miners' (1977: 203) section on Hong Kong local politics entitled "Not Democracy, But Politics", a criticism of remarks made by Halliday (1974: 101) and Rear (1971) that "there is no democracy in Hong Kong".

[49] See CSO 89 ext., "Report on Salt Industries in the N.T.", April 26, 1900 and CSO 106 ext., "Salt Pans, N.T.", May 23, 1902. Conversions of agricultural land into salt pans were assessed at a slightly higher rate (CSO 2176, March 22, 1907).

[50] CO 129/329, pp.91–94, July 28, 1905; also reported by the Land Court in 1903.

[51] See CO 129/305, Blake to Chamberlain, May 21, 1901 and *ibid.*, Chamberlain to Blake, July 4, 1901. This led to the Foreshores and Seabed Ordinance of 1901.

[52] The first recorded instance was in 1903, sparked by a petition from 18 elders in Shataukok. The government refused to alter its position, noting that "it should be clear that there is no promise taxes are to be same as that imposed by Chinese government" and that the residents interested in the petition were "quite well off" (CSO 9698 ext., Colonial Secretary to Governor letter, July 3, 1904). See also CSO 6990 ext., "Crown Rent, Petitions from the elders of the Tung Chung Village for reduction of . . .", December 9, 1905 and CSO 5510,

"Crown Rent wishes expressed by the N.T. elders . . .", which also protested against a fee on inheritance.

[53] CSO 3120/06, "New Territories 1) Crown Rent, 2) Land, 3) Licenses, submits petition from elders of the various districts respecting . . .".

[54] CO 129/338, Petitioners to Lyttleton, August 8, 1905.

[55] CO 129/335, Nathan to Elgin memo, Oct 23, 1906.

[56] CSO 3120/06, "New Territories 1) Crown Rent, 2) Land, 3) Licenses, submits petition from elders of the various districts respecting . . .", April 6, 1906.

[57] See CSO 807 ext., Colonial Secretary to Governor memo, May 1, 1906.

[58] CO 129/494, Clementi to Amery letter, September 1, 1926.

[59] In his letter to the Secretary of State L.S. Amery, the Governor Cecil Clementi concluded, "I suggest therefore that the Memorialists be told that they will receive full compensation for their agricultural holdings, as such, but that for the rest they must acquiesce in what is, after all, the law of the Colony enacted for the purpose of protecting the public community of which over 90% are like themselves of Chinese race" (CO 129/494, September 1, 1926).

[60] The entire memorial is reproduced in Liu (1977: 55–56).

[61] CO 129/489, Amery to Clementi letter, November 18, 1925.

[62] As the leased territory becomes incorporated into the socio-political life of the colony, the discursive canon of the lease thus becomes increasingly anachronistic.

CHAPTER THREE

The Changing Meaning of Land in Colonial Hong Kong

Economically, it maintains the interests of large corporations, allowing them to make use of cheap labour, without forcing them to make specific welfare provisions to protect labourers. Culturally, it promotes a pyramidal type of educational system to instill knowledge, mobilizes mass media to inculcate values that (induces one to) adapt to and passively accept social conditions, suppresses the development of one's traditional culture among the people, and on the dark side even indulges people with enticements of gambling, drugs and vice, lending opportunities to our oppressed brothers and sisters to give vent. In the process of rule, it cultivates a tiny group of indigenous elites. This kind of system is called in academic terms "the new colonial system". Painful reality tells us that today's Hong Kong is the only place in the world where both new and old colonial rule is generously practiced.[1] (portrayal of Hong Kong's social system, from an open letter issued by Hong Kong Alliance of Christian Churches during the Queen's visit to Hong Kong)

THE EVOLUTION OF A MARKET SOCIETY

One cannot write a history of land in the New Territories without trying to write at the same time a history of the society within which land is embedded. The embeddedness of land in its larger socio-political context is mediated through webs of meaning that invoke underlying social relations and strategic interests, which are themselves historically constituted and prone to change. A history of land may thus well be an impossible task or, stated positively, is at best a partial truth that reflects broader, more significant developments at the local and global levels.

The making of history begins with actors and events, and it is clear that the social interaction between colonial rulers and local inhabitants throughout much of the British pacification and administration of Hong Kong's New Territories was marked by different strategic interests and underlying values. The conflicts that arose initially from these encounters easily characterized the gap between these interests and values as culturally constituted, not to mention the fact that these interests were often themselves in flux and constantly mutating to suit changing situations. The global intentions and cultural rationales of these actions were not always conscious to the actors themselves, even as the events unfolded, and it is important in this regard to reconstruct the meaning of the events at least one step removed from the ongoing perceptions of the agents. Similarly, the notions of land and territoriality must be understood not just as taken-for-granted facts but also as objects of value, accumulation and control in different cultural universes. In the context of events, the struggle over land was a negotiation or conflict between these sets of interests or values as it was played out in various venues or sites of contestation, and it is only as a result of such struggles that one can see the emergence of the "system". In other words, far from being an a priori imposition of a given colonial "order", the land policy and system that eventually became codified as law and administered in practice for years to come was by definition the incorporation of arbitrary values, structural incompatibilities and legal inventions insofar as it reflected the sloppiness of the events that gave rise to it. Its neat social structural quality was then a function of its unambiguous codification as universal rule and the ruthless systematicity by which law was practiced in the norm of everyday life.

Seen from ground up, actors and events invoked global interests and values that engendered at a deeper level institutional interests and socially held values. As the times (or more precisely the geopolitical forces that influenced institutions at the time) changed, the meaning and function of land, the institutional system and social community within which they were embedded changed correspondingly. Already during the first half of the twentieth century, urban-industrial expansion from Kowloon and population increase within the territory and from China began to absorb the leased territory into the colony. Yet, the New Territories was still administered literally as a lease, legally distinct from Hong Kong and Kowloon. The colony remained intact, mostly because the power relationship between China and Britain in the larger global order remained stable until World War II.

With the contraction of the British empire worldwide and the emergence of fascism that led to Japanese imperialism and the fall of Hong Kong on Christmas Day 1941, the balance of power changed irrevocably. Ironically, in the midst of the immediate chaos following Japan's unconditional surrender in August 1945, the former Colonial Secretary Franklin Gimson unilaterally declared himself Acting Governor and representative of the King, even though authorization for this from the Home government was not issued until ten days later. Britain and China both argued over the right to accept Japan's surrender at Hong Kong. Finally, through intervention by the U.S., Cecil Harcourt, Rear-Admiral of the British Pacific Fleet, accepted Japan's surrender on behalf of Britain and Chiang Kai-shek as supreme commander of the China theater (Tsang 1988: 19–20). The ceremonial act by China and Britain to impose sovereignty over Hong Kong did not soften Chiang's efforts to recover Hong Kong from a downsized Britain, nor did it dampen Britain's overall ambition to regain its status as imperial power.[2] However, Chiang's losing war against communism on the mainland made occupation of Hong Kong untenable. On the other hand, London's desire to regain British possessions in East Asia at the end of World War II was simply a matter of prestige (Tsang 1988: 13, Chan 1990: 293). The threat of a communist regime on the mainland made territorial control of Hong Kong even more imperative, and Britain's rhetoric in this regard was increasingly met by subdued resistance by China (Chan 1990: 314). This and the need to reestablish a future commercial foothold in China became the rationale for diplomatically recognizing Beijing, while ironically the importance of trade with China in later years superceded the territorial primacy of holding onto Hong Kong per se (Tang 1994). Maintenance of the colonial status quo in turn received tacit support from the Chinese (PRC) side during the postwar period well into the early 1980s, largely in view of the role of Hong Kong as entrepot in China's economy.

Britain's military defeat in Hong Kong by Japan along with its diminished stature as imperial power in Asia, reflected by the precarious existence of Hong Kong under the shadow of China, changed the local complexion of colonial society in Hong Kong during the postwar era, or at least stripped it of its previous racial stratification and overt cultural arrogance. Vestiges of strict ethnic segregation began to wither away, as evidenced by the increasing residence of wealthy Chinese living on the Peak. Even the Hong Kong Club moved reluctantly to admit Chinese as members (Morris 1988: 261). It was in this context that the advent of a global free market capitalism institutionalized a new and different phase of colonialism.

Hong Kong may have been founded on trade, but despite its obvious role as trade entrepot throughout the 19th and early 20th centuries between China, South Asia and Europe, it was not until the postwar years that one could characterize Hong Kong as a society based on trade. The difference between a trading port and a society based on trade is not unlike the difference between a society where one finds the existence of markets and a full-scale self-regulating market society or one between capital and capitalism. Trade has been a social activity for most of human history, while societies based on trade are recent phenomena of a changing world system and a consequence of societal integration within that world system. This difference is no less irrelevant to our understanding of the transition of prewar Hong Kong society from one where market trade constituted a major social activity to one in which market activity as a thing in itself came to define the pattern for social action and the nature of society in the postwar period. Changing power relationships at a global level profoundly affected the nature of Hong Kong society, despite its legal status as a colony, by making its ongoing political survival prone to outside influences, stemming not only from British foreign policy and the global economy but also from the tensions of competing Chinese nationalisms. The effect of the global market in this regard was thus doublesided, on the one hand insuring Hong Kong's de facto autonomy, which served political interests of both Britain and China, while on the other hand setting in motion dynamics of societal transformation that fundamentally altered the nature of colonial governmentality.

It would be too easy to describe the nature of Hong Kong's emerging market society as "capitalistic" just as it would be equally simplistic to characterize the fact of British rule as "colonial".[3] It suffices for the moment to say that changes characteristic of postwar change in Hong Kong should not simply be attributed to material progress or introduction of Western ideas and institutions. Such socio-demographic trends were already underway in the prewar decades of the 20s and 30s.[4] Hong Kong had enjoyed a steady influx of immigrants from mainland China early on, who gradually made up the bulk of wage labor both in the urban areas and expanding industrial towns. In rural areas, immigrants were opening up land everywhere as vegetable cultivators on the periphery of settled villages, comprising 20.75% of the total population of the New Territories in 1931, up three-fold from 1911.[5] Increases in tenant cultivation slowly displaced traditional padi cultivation and were accompanied by a net outmigration of indigenous villagers to the urban-industrial areas to take up wage labor.[6] This trend continued in the postwar era.

Postwar Population Growth in Hong Kong, 1945–54

Year	Population	Natural Increase	Net In-Migration	Total Increase
1945	600,000	—	—	+300,000
1946	900,000	+14,000	+486,000	+500,000
1947	1,400,000	+29,000	+371,000	+400,000
1948	1,800,000	+34,000	+166,000	+200,000
1949	2,000,000	+38,000	+262,000	+300,000
1950	2,300,000	+42,000	−242,000	−200,000
1951	2,100,000	+48,000	+27,000	+75,000
1952	2,175,000	+53,000	+22,000	+75,000
1953	2,250,000	+57,000	−57,000	—
1954	2,250,000	+28,000	−28,000	—

Source: Hambro (1955: 148)

These trends were, however, accompanied by other changes which resulted from large-scale efforts to restructure the existing politico-economic framework of the colony. The government attempted to directly revitalize the social economy of the colony immediately after the war by creating government monopolies to control the distribution and marketing of agricultural goods, construction and centralized regulation of public works, and restructuring of the political administration at the local level. The influx of major industry caused a large displacement of people from the traditional urban and rural areas into the expanding industrial center of New Kowloon. The Communist Revolution in mainland China in 1949 brought about two important things that eventually became permanent features of the new postwar society, namely 1) an influx of capital, machinery and technology from Shanghai, which accounted for roughly two-thirds of total investment during the immediate postwar era (1948–50) and 2) a seemingly inexhaustible supply of cheap labor (Owen 1971). This immense influx of Chinese capital and labor contributed heavily to a twenty-fold increase in industrial undertakings (972 to 19,474) and an eleven-fold increase in employees (51,338 to 598,555) from 1947 to 1972 alone (England and Rear 1975: 25, citing Labor Department Reports).

With over 90% of Hong Kong manufactures headed for export, Hong Kong experienced a remarkable growth rate from 1950-70. Such material progress can be attributed firstly to the laissez-faire trade policies adopted by the government along with the minimal low tax rate on profits, which generally stimulated private industry. Laissez-faire monetarism along with tight-fisted control in other aspects of the public economy (including land) thus made up what Riedel (1972: 193) aptly termed the "microeconomic intervention" and "macroeconomic laissez-faire" of the Hong Kong government.[7] But more importantly, laissez-faire aspects of economic policy masked an equally salient feature of the operation of Hong Kong's market economy and its underlying value system, namely its nature as an exploitative system that benefitted the interests of entrepreneurial capitalists at the expense of labor (see table below).[8] Government policy thus promoted utilitarianism in the economy but in ways that undermined societal values of a prior "colonialism".

Two hidden "injuries" of the system are pertinent in this regard. First of all, much of the new industry in the postwar era was based upon a philosophy of short-term profit maximization along with low capital investment and intensive use of cheap labor. Presumably, this had to do with overall political uncertainty and the constant fear of Communist takeover, but much had to do as well with the generally labor repressive style of traditional Chinese industry. There was little job security associated with labor, and the wage system, whether it was based on hourly or piece rates, encouraged long hours and the recruitment of eligible family members, including women and children, into

Level of Real Average Daily Wages in Manufacturing, 1948–74

| Year | Average Daily Real Wages | | | Weighted Average | Real Wage |
	Unskilled	Semi-skilled	Skilled	Daily Real Wages	Index
1948	3.75	5.20	6.75	4.25	100
1949	3.35	4.64	6.03	3.79	89
1950	3.63	4.91	5.98	4.05	95
1951	3.35	4.53	5.71	3.75	88
1952	3.29	4.46	5.62	3.69	87
1953	3.27	4.42	5.58	3.66	86
1954	3.15	4.53	5.71	3.58	84
1955	3.25	4.67	5.89	3.67	86
1956	3.15	5.12	5.71	3.66	86
1957	3.52	4.69	7.42	3.93	92
1958	3.37	4.76	7.54	3.83	90
1959	3.13	4.96	9.19	3.77	89
1960	3.85	5.19	11.15	4.46	105
1961	3.82	5.15	11.07	4.42	104
1962	3.88	6.51	11.24	4.69	110
1963	5.42	8.37	11.06	6.18	145
1964	5.22	8.07	12.63	6.04	142
1965	6.01	7.89	13.21	6.66	157
1966	5.69	9.20	12.33	6.56	154
1967	6.17	8.96	12.66	6.90	162
1968	6.42	9.56	13.61	7.22	170
1969	6.28	9.30	12.90	7.03	165
1970	6.38	9.10	13.36	7.11	167
1971	6.48	9.64	13.09	7.25	171
1972	7.54	10.95	16.18	8.45	199
1973	7.93	10.84	14.57	8.63	203
1974	7.25	9.64	13.74	7.88	185

Source: Chow (1977:358)

the labor force (Salaff 1974, Walker 1972: 91–95).[9] Secondly, China played a significant role in subsidizing the market economy of Hong Kong through export of food and raw materials to Hong Kong.[10] Until 1972, the Chinese authorities pursued a consistent policy of pricing products sold to Hong Kong slightly below the prices of Hong Kong producers.[11] In light of the export orientation of Hong Kong manufactured goods, this meant, of course, that China served heavily to directly subsidize Hong Kong trade and economic growth, the chief beneficiaries of which were still the owners of capital. In the long run, this economic undercutting of Hong Kong food producers hastened the destruction of the latter's traditional rural economy and indigenous way of life that precipitated new land conflicts among inhabitants and *vis-a-vis* government.

China's Share in Supplying Food to Hong Kong, 1959–70 (million HK$)

Year	Local Production	% of Self Sufficiency	Food Imports From China	China's % of Imports	China's Share in Consumption
1959	258	20%	507	49%	39%
1960	290	20%	538	45%	37%
1961	319	21%	430	42%	28%
1962	320	19%	585	48%	35%
1963	321	18%	720	48%	40%
1964	193	15%	1003	51%	51%
1965	260	13%	1130	49%	56%
1966	263	12%	1242	45%	57%
1967	263	11%	1105	48%	46%
1968	334	13%	1218	50%	47%
1969	395	14%	1349	50%	47%
1970	—	—	1413	50%	—

Source: Wong (1972: 55)

The initial evolution of a market system in postwar Hong Kong had several major social consequences. First, it produced a widening discrepancy between the "haves", namely the owners of capital, and the "have-nots", which comprised wage-laborers and indigenous cultivators who had been experiencing a gradual decline in their own industry, especially in view of competition from China. Secondly, this ever-widening gap was driven by the same set of values that generally became the ethos of the new society, namely utilitarianism disguised both in the form of profit maximization and self-interested survivalism. Utilitarian values meant different things to different people within the system, and this created friction between new social elements that emerged in the postwar era. Finally, because this system was sanctioned by the social interventionist-cum-laissez-faire policy of the government, these global interventions not only corrupted preexisting values and lifestyles that effectively transformed the socio-economic landscape but in turn radically changed the nature of the indigenous side of the equation that was supposed to be the basis of the colonial government's practice of "indirect rule" in regard to local society.

On the land, many superficial changes took place over the first two decades that set the tone for deeper crises affecting the fabric of local society. Padi had always been the main crop in the New Territories up to the Japanese occupation period. In the first decade after the war, its continued importance was supported by fairly high prices, ranging from HK$55–80 per picul (Blackie 1954: 9). Surveys conducted by the Agriculture and Fisheries Department from 1956–68 from a peak of about 23,000 acres in 1956, amounting to 70% of the total agricultural land in the territory, padi cultivation began to decline gradually to a low of about 14,000 acres or 41% of total land in 1965. Its decline was countered by a corresponding increase in vegetable cultivation over the same time period from about 2200 acres (5%) to 8400 acres (25%) (Wong 1971: 18–19). At the same time, there was a many-fold increase in pig production (whose numbers rose from 8470 in 1946 to 429,000 in 1962) and poultry domestication (starting from scratch in 1946 and eventually becoming a HK$57 million industry in 1961) (Mason et al 1968). Local agriculture suffered a severe recession during 1964–67. Since then, it began to irreversibly decline, leading eventually to large-scale abandonment of agriculture in outlying villages, followed by massive outmigration to urban-industrial areas and overseas, and repopulation by outsider tenants in other villages.[12] Communities in poorer, more remote regions of the New Territories suffered most from depopulation and outmigration, predominantly to the U.K. and Holland, especially in the late 60s and into the 70s. Meanwhile, communities in the expanding urban-industrial zone encompassed by New Kowloon became development sites for large-scale satellite towns. Thus, regardless of whether pressure was due to competition from cheaper foodstuff originating in China or urban-industrial expansion, the gradual evolution of the global market system contributed directly to the decline of local agriculture as a major livelihood in the New Territories.

Different regions reacted in different ways to changing conditions, but progressive expansion and competitive decline were products of the same free market forces and utilitarian individualistic ethos.

In social-demographic terms, the single most important factor that affected relationships on the land and the nature of evolving communities in postwar New Territories was the changes in agricultural tenancy brought about by an influx of refugees from China after 1949.[13] In March 1950, there were growing reports of sharp increases in rents throughout the territory combined with threats of eviction of traditional tenants in deliberate scams to rent land to high paying occupants.[14] Complaints were most common in the northern districts of Fanling and Ping Shan, bordering China. The sudden increase in rents was precipitated specifically by an invasion of Shanghai entrepreneurs who had offered substantially higher rents to build chicken farms and other "northerners" seeking cheap country residences.[15] The government was taken by surprise by these complaints, acknowledging firstly that it was natural for rents to increase on land where vegetables are grown, as justified by higher profits earned by cultivators, then arguing that most tended to be isolated incidents that did not appear to affect the majority of landholdings in the territory.[16] As complaints to District Land Officers rose, it became clear that this crisis, exceptional perhaps only for the sudden manifold increases in rent and its immediate challenge to existing tenancy relationships, fractured relationships not only between landlord and tenant but more precisely along lines of indigenous versus immigrant (place) and landowning versus landless (class), long after the immediate crisis of tenancy died down. Thus in the postwar era, there emerged at least three different interest groups (indigenous elites, indigenous villagers and non-indigenous tenants), each of which was affected differently by developments on the "land". This inevitably complicated subsequent relationships between the (colonial) government and (native) inhabitants, insofar as the former continued to regard the latter as a homogenous entity, where rights and duties were defined by unambiguous "customs". Without doubt, money and greed precipitated a tenancy crisis, but on careful reading the crisis shed more important light on how elites, villagers and outsiders constituted their (customary) relationship to land, while at the same time exposing biases held by colonial officials in its mandate to rule.

In this regard, the question of how "real" the intentions of landlords were in threatening to evict and how much "rights" they had by custom to alter tenancy relationships is perhaps not as important as understanding "whose" interests the government valued in the process and knowing that custom was, contrary to being a fixed set of rules, always an ongoing negotiation between different interests. As the facts of the matter became increasingly evident, the government's position on tenancy appeared on the surface to reiterate the rule of local custom and advocate a middle ground that minimized conflict between landlords and tenant, but in the process exposed value judgments that exacerbated in the long run the widening gap between indigenous elites, indigenous villagers and non-indigenous tenants. Certain facts of the situation cannot be disputed, namely the sudden increase in rents caused by the leasing of land to rich immigrant entrepreneurs at inflated rates and its reverberations on existing tenancies as well as the normal absence of written contractual agreements between landlords and tenants that made any customary arrangement prone to renegotiation. K. Keen, District Commissioner of the New Territories, forwarded to the Colonial Secretary his recommendations, based primarily on the report of E.B. Teesdale, District Officer, Yuen Long, where most of the complaints stemmed, which discovered: 1) in no case was the tenant an indigenous (pre-1898) inhabitant of the New Territories, 2) the tenant appeared to be wealthy enough to absorb any rent increases, 3) the old tenancy agreement was due to expire or breached because of non-payment, 4) demands for rent increase appeared to be reasonable in light of the low rent in most cases and good profits made from vegetable farming, 5) landlords wished to reclaim land for their own use or to enable their own relatives in China to resettle in the territory and 6) the vast majority of padi land cultivated by other indigenous villagers did not appear to be affected at all.[17] Much of the testimony (gotten from landlords themselves) tended to downplay the ubiquity and severity of the situation. The government finally issued a statement to the press, excerpts of which were reported as follows:

> Some newspapers have recently carried reports to the effect that there have been many cases of landlords in the New Territories increasing rents of farm lands and evicting farmers who were unwilling or unable to pay exorbitant rentals . . . It is true that

some landlords have revised their rental upwards, but there is no evidence that the increased rentals demanded are exorbitant ... Many landlords want to take advantage of the good return on vegetable land by cultivating or managing their own fields, and there are some landowners who wish to settle on the land some of their relatives evacuated from China. Tenancy agreements concluded during or just after the Japanese occupation of the Colony are expiring or are due for revision. The vast majority of the padi land cultivated by native New Territories villagers is not affected by any of these changes. Careful investigations have failed to uncover a single case of "rack-renting" or of renting to a new tenant for a higher rent, concludes the statement.[18]

The issue in principle, however, involved their assessment of a "reasonable" increase in rent and the right of the landlord to evict existing tenants for purposes of reclaiming the land, both of which the government viewed as a matter of custom or mutual negotiation between the two parties. In this regard, the negotiability of customary arrangements was complicated by the fact that few of them were written down and that it was in fact unusual for a landlord to take back land for any reason. To the contrary, the tenant typically enjoyed a great deal of autonomy that included the right to sublet the land to others. Moreover, by cultivating the land, the tenant was maintaining the fertility of the land, and if the tenant gave back the land to the landlord, the landlord normally had to compensate the tenant for the value of the land that he invested in order to maintain its fertility. In any case, this was not the major point of contention for the government. On January 31, 1951, the Hong Kong Kowloon Chinese Farming and Agriculture Association petitioned the government on behalf of tenant plaintiffs, citing 31 cases of rental increase, 42 cases of repossession and 1 case of forced eviction and called for the enactment of legislation to protect tillers' rights. They were granted an audience by J. Barrow, District Commissioner, New Territories. The plaintiffs argued that they would not receive a fair hearing in the Rural Committee, which was made up of landed gentry. The District Commissioner countered by asking "to what point they claimed to represent, not only the immigrant vegetable growers of the fringes of Kowloon, and of Tsun Wan and other parts of the N.T., but the real indigenous N.T. population, who custom-

arily lived in villages. They said they spoke for all tenants, both immigrants and natives. But they saw my point".[19] Toward the end of the
meeting, the Association proposed motions to enact legislation to specify
conditions for eviction of tenants for various breaches of contract and
to set a cap on increases in rent to a fixed percentage over a period of
time. The proposals were then noted and later circulated to all Rural
Committees for their opinion.

The issue of whether or not to propose legislation was debated
internally without concrete results. T.G. Strangeways, Director of
Agriculture, Fisheries and Forestry, argued for some form of legislation
to protect tenant rights, noting that "protection is required for 'tenants'
irrespective of status within the Colony" and that many of these tenants
had been residing in the territory for over a decade.[20] He added that,
given the absence of any written law, tenants were dissatisfied with their
only recourse of appeal to the District Land Officer and his interpretation of "Chinese custom". His recommendations were seconded by
J. Cater, Registrar of Cooperatives, who suggested also that legal advice
be offered in response to tenant demands for written tenancy agreements.
However, actions in this regard were met with resistance by J. Barrow,
District Commissioner, New Territories, and E.G. Teesdale, who succeeded Barrow. Acting on a follow-up letter by the Hong Kong Kowloon
Chinese Farming and Agriculture Association on September 13, 1951,
Barrow noted that, regarding the question of custom, he could only
proceed on the basis of what could be agreed upon by the Rural Committees (made up of precisely those village elites who were favorable to
the landed gentry). He was also opposed to legislation for the New
Territories similar to the Landlord and Tenant Ordinance of Hong Kong,
because such cases were already satisfactorily handled by District Officers,
the proposed amendment would probably "stimulate a spate of more or
less artificial cases", and the Association was losing credibility in their
agitation over what he still regarded to be a small number of exaggerated
instances.[21] Teesdale was even firmer in his objection to the proposed
legislation. Claiming that the tenant has a great deal of security *vis-a-vis*
landlords, he argued then that "any interference with existing custom
regarding tenure and rents would adversely affect a very large number
of comparatively poor people, and would, one must suppose, be strongly
resisted".[22] On the subject of increased rent, he also noted that disputes

arose only with regard to vegetable land, where increased rent could be seen as justifiable recouping of higher income gained by tenants *vis-a-vis* padi land, concluding that in his experience "the landlord is more often the injured party and that the tenant has a sturdy disregard for the rights of property".[23] Due to this internal dissent and deadlock, no case for new legislation was made.

The tenants' grievances were raised again in November 1955, when Percy Chen, Chairman of the Hong Kong Chinese Reform Association, prepared to send a memorandum to Alan Lennox-Boyd, Secretary of State for the Colonies, during his visit to Hong Kong. Tenant protection was only one of several items on his memorandum. In essence, he argued that Chinese custom was unsatisfactory in dealing with injustices arising from landlord-tenant relations, since they could be terminated at any time, thus providing no legal protection for legitimate interests of the tenant. He summarized the main inadequacies of custom as follows:[24]

(1) Customary law seems to be ununiform even with so small a territory as the Leased Territory.

(2) Chinese customary law is difficult of ascertainment.

(3) Such Chinese customary law as can be ascertained is oppressive and unjust from the point of view of the tenant farmer, and therefore is completely out of accord with the times in which we live.

As in the earlier effort of the Hong Kong Kowloon Farming and Agricultural Association's attempt to address tenants' complaints, Chen's memorandum caused heated debate within the government. W.V. Dickinson, Registrar of Cooperatives, supported Chen's allegations of tenant hardship, citing numerous instances of tenure insecurity, and argued that the existence of such injustices overrided the need to follow custom. Regarding the ambiguity of custom itself, he warned of the biased interpretation of it by village elders, citing an aide-memoire from the prior District Commissioner himself as follows: "when you hear 'expert' evidence on local custom, and that evidence is given by men who belong patently to the landed class, you discount their evidence, and deserving consideration both as to vista into the past and as to respect for age, it is the evidence of 'haves'".[25] Obviously, it was evidence that the District Commissioner chose to disregard in deliberating on the topic when it first erupted. Dickinson then emphasized the personal rather than generally accepted nature of custom and suggested that in dealing with the matter one should avoid both rigid codification of any interpretation of custom. W.J. Blackie, Director of Agriculture, Fisheries and Forestry, largely concurred with Dickinson regarding the insecurity of tenure in those areas most seriously affected and suggested drawing up contracts similar to Crown land permits.[26]

People higher up for most part held dissenting opinions. K.M.A. Barnett, the new District Commissioner, New Territories, flatly dismissed Chen's criticism, saying "there is no substance in Mr. Chen's representations; that although Chinese customary law is not *uniform,* neither is it capricious, and the law for a given class of land in a given district is usually ascertained with ease; and that so far from being oppressive and unjust to the tenant farmer, the local customary law is sensible and fair; and that the situation has not changed since Mr. Teesdale's minute of 6th June, 1952, with most of which I agree . . . This 'no termination of tenancy' slogan—that is all it is—is repeated ad nauseam, in a manner completely reminiscent of the slogan adopted by another set of Mr. Chen's (Communist) friends (the Society of Plantations) during the Tramways strike: that no employer may discharge an employee by giving him notice. Both contentions are equally unfounded".[27] The Governor of Hong Kong, in his memorandum to the Secretary of State, reiterated that there appeared to be little substance in the allegations that tenants were being forced off the land by exorbitant rents and added, in concert with Barnett's memo, that "the (Hong Kong Chinese Reform) Association was persuaded to insert this criticism by the Communist dominated Society of Plantations which has taken up the question in the past with a slogan of 'No Termination of Tenancy', whatever the rights or wrongs of the particular case".[28]

Although short-lived, the conflict that pitted landlords against tenants that erupted in the early 50s is instructive on many levels. First of all, there was no doubt that the influx of outsider capital in the countryside disrupted the existing nature of tenancy relations, for whatever reason. While it is true that vegetable cultivation generated more income than padi, by virtue of multiple harvests and the embargo on foodstuffs from China in the first few years that necessitated self-sufficiency in the colony, the timing and concentration of affected areas were too coincidental to justify claims by landlords that they were simply getting a fair and overdue increase. Moreover, the government's insistence on relying on the rule of custom where custom itself was ambiguous, thus prone to abuse and conflict under conditions of external "disruption", was contradictory, to say the least. In theory, it absolved them of the complicated task of enacting legislation, but in practice it threw responsibility back onto the shoulders of District Land Officers, who were the final arbiters of "custom" in a court of law. In this regard, the usual practice of seeking the advice of the Rural Committee, made up largely of landed interests, in matters of custom, was akin to feeding the fire that ignited the conflict in the first place. But since they felt it proper to serve the interests of indigenous (pre-1898) villagers over those of later settlers, their position in substance resulted in the same conclusion: defense of the status quo. At a higher level, their concern about Communist influence clearly indicated that global Cold War political factors were not irrelevant at all to social developments "on the ground".[29] With regard to the conflicting inter-pretation of tenancy custom, it would appear that the events precipitated by an incipient capitalist market economy revealed the "traditional" character of tenancy relations as one based on a "moral economy". In essence, the traditional landlord-tenant relationship was mutually ben-eficial. It mattered little to a landlord who the tenant was, as long as someone continued to pay the rent, hence the autonomy and assumed perpetual nature of most relationships. In this regard, the capital influx of the early 50s was both corrupting and consistent with the nature of a traditional tenancy arrangement, *from the point of view of the landlord.* For the tenant, however, the stability of the arrangement was the most important aspect of the relationship, because it guaranteed a livelihood more than just a source of income. To be sure, the tenant's attitude toward land was more sedentary than that of the landlord, which can be easily exemplified by the diverse origins of postwar tenant cultivators in the New Territories, many of whom came directly from the city, but it was a profession that urban laborers deliberately sought in order to evade the uncertainties of the capitalist job market (Aijmer 1973). In the long run, the government's position on the crisis dualized the class interests of indigenous elites as opposed to outsider tenants even more by institutionalizing those social differences in the practice of colonial-cum-capitalist rule.

The plight of agricultural tenancy has been a relatively neglected topic in the anthropology of rural society in the New Territories (with exception of Aijmer's (1980, 1986) two important monographs). The life narratives of postwar tenants capture quite appropriately the vicissitudes of market society in the early postwar era, since many of them had urban backgrounds and turned to vegetable farming in order to escape the everyday struggles and constant volatility of the urban job market. One such tenant described both professions as a kind of "gambling" that differed fundamentally from the self-subsistence (*zijizizu*) lifestyle of the past (Lu 1975: 15–16). Due to the auction and distribution system regulated by agricultural cooperatives, cultivators bore a heavy brunt of earnings as well as losses in the marketing of their goods, which forced them to work hard hours to tread water. A rather different situation was portrayed by another villager who had been living in Yuen Long for over 30 years. He originally grew rice, but after his three sons emigrated to Holland five years ago he and his wife found the going rough. They hired two laborers to help in the planting and harvesting, but less than a year later both of them decided to find work in the factories rather than to tie their fortunes to the land. Since then, it was difficult to hire laborers. The only other alternative was to sell off part of the land, then fill up the rest of it by cultivating vegetables just to pass the time away (XN 1977b: 77). Such experiences were quite commonplace throughout the territory and contradicted opinions in official reports that cultivators were generally well off. In the marginal agricultural areas along the border with China and in remote villages of Saikung Peninsula, agriculture was abandoned wholesale and led to massive depopulation and emigration, first to Southeast Asia, then the U.K. and Europe, after immigration laws loosened up.

The vicissitudes of the market system in Hong Kong promoted utilitarian rationality (as both profit maximization and survivalism) as lifestyle and ethos, and this set of values did more than the fact of material inequality itself to corrupt preexisting social relationships and attitudes toward the land.[30] These changes in turn produced strange consequences for colonial policy. In sum, the government was increasingly put in the awkward position of being forced to protect the status of native custom against the aims of natives who became increasingly obsessed or corrupted by profit maximization and the "progressive" values of the new society.

LA TERRA TREMA, OR THE SHAKING OF EARTHBOUND COMPULSIONS

Recent social scientists writing on Chinese society have all in one form or another emphasized the "earthbound compulsion" or "attachment to the land" of the Chinese peasant without really making clear that they have been dealing with different aspects of land. For instance, Fei Xiaotong's early works on *Peasant Life in China* (1939) and *Earthbound China* (1945) have gone on at great length about the value of land in agriculture as an important source of material livelihood for the Chinese peasant. Material subsistence was the basis of his dependence on the land, as was reflected in his remark, "it is the hunger of the people that is the real issue in China" (Fei 1939: 282). For Gallin (1967), the peasant's attachment to the land was a more or less sentimental relationship that helped to explain his relative immobility and conservatism. This set of attitudes toward the land was less attributable to culturally specific values that the Chinese held toward it than to the sociological nature of Chinese agrarian society. Rance P.L. Lee (1981) noted "the fading of earthbound compulsion" in a village in the New Territories of Hong Kong, but of the diverse variables he actually touched on earthbound compulsion referred primarily to one's demographic residence. Aside from one's agricultural dependence on land as occupation, the fact of whether a village was residentially composed of agnates or a mixed community of "natives" and "outsiders" was taken to be the basic indicator of one's "earthbound compulsion". Finally, Freedman (1958, 1966) also talked about the relationship between land and lineages, but for him it was predicated on its value as a source of monetary wealth. Southeastern China, especially during the last three centuries, was marked by the widespread settlement of large-scale single-lineage villages, and the relationship between land and social organization was not specific to lineages but general to the continuity of a household based economy and the kin constitution of village communities.

To be sure, all these aspects of land were important to how villagers in the New Territories during the postwar era understood their particular "earthbound compulsion" and were relevant to the kinds of social change that took place. But each aspect of land invoked a different kind of rationality, and it is necessary to analytically distinguish between these notions of land in order to understand how indigenous inhabitants responded to material and other systemic constraints.

In short, the concept of "land" is best described as a complex of ideas. More than just "material livelihood", it represents a socially valued livelihood or "right to live" that was ideologically sanctioned by both Confucian and Taoist philosophy. This intrinsic value or sanction explains why the individual's attachment to land often transcended physical residence and resembled a kind of social rootedness. In fact, contrary to the myth of immobility and conservatism usually associated with the Chinese peasant, villagers often abandoned the land in traditional times and resettled when it was in their interest to do so. However, shifts of residence were consequences of other social imperatives which were quite distinct from the various cultural meanings of land. In the New Territories, the postwar decline of agriculture and pressure to shift to other modes of subsistence led to at least three kinds of adaptation or response to change. This included 1) the evolution of mixed residential communities from ethnically bounded and lineage villages, 2) wholesale abandonment of villages in the name of progress and 3) defense of the homogenous community in the face of increasing degradation. The diversity of changes "on the ground" was significant insofar as it reflected disturbances on the land as a source of both material and social livelihood, but its ramifications upon the nature of local community in the context of the New Territories were even more complex, insofar as they involved ongoing tensions in the nature of colonial governmentality in face of both external socio-political changes and negotiations with inhabitants whose interests continued to be phrased in terms of the legality of inalienable rights to custom. With regard to the latter, it is necessary to go beyond given dichotomies of foreign/indigenous and colonizer/colonized. Far from operating within a social vacuum, imperatives of rule and local notions of social community in the postwar era had to take into account the erosion of hard and fast cultural boundaries that were intrinsic to a previous colonial era, the systematic diffusion of a rule of law in the practice of local administration and the emergence of a global order that saw the inculcation of a market mentality as a principle of social survival. Even though the terms that dichotomized political relations between foreign colonizer and indigenous colonized remained unchanged in many respects, their underlying meaning had already undergone subtle change in ways that beg careful scrutiny.

The immediate issues that brought the land crisis to a head in the postwar era were invoked by the increased proliferation of squatter tenements that dotted the rural landscape following the exodus of refugees from the mainland and the renewed policy disputes regarding the conversion of agricultural to building land that was also an inevitable result of urban-industrial expansion and population growth in the existing villages. The status of unauthorized residential structures in the countryside caused by the influx of postwar refugees and debates over land conversion for purposes of village housebuilding analytically speaking arose out of the same policy dispute over land, but they reflected different social problems and were dealt with differently by the government. Due to protests from 1923–26 by indigenous inhabitants against the imposition in principle of any premium on building land in the village, the government eventually repealed initial legislation put into effect only three years earlier. As a result, villagers requiring additional land had to request conversions of agricultural into building land by applying for a Modifications of Tenancy Permit upon payment of increased Crown Rent made annually to the government. In practice, all such permits were subject to approval by the District Officer and in accordance with certain building regulations. In addition, Crown Land Licenses were issued so that domestic structures within an area of 400 sq.ft. could be erected on Crown Land. These licenses were issued on payment of a premium. In addition to the permanent structures built on Crown Land, however, many squatter huts were erected without Modification of Tenancy Permits or Crown Land Licenses. These "illegal" structures included watchmen's sheds, tenants' squatters and other farm related structures that frequently dotted the agricultural landscape. On legal grounds, there was little in the nature of these temporary structures to justify their tax exempt status as buildings *vis-a-vis* other permanent buildings, but there appeared to be little economic rationale at that time to resolve the problem of squatter buildings without incurring at the same time the wrath of inhabitants who viewed their necessity in other terms. Thus, although it was possible to apply for temporary permits to occupy land under the Summary Offenses

Ordinance, in the prewar period, authorities tended for the most part to look the other way in regard to the squatter situation.[31] In theory, premium free land conversion accommodated village expansion, but within limits.

Without doubt, the squatter situation and a need to accommodate increased village housing during the postwar era exacerbated tensions in all aspects of land policy. As early as 1950, a marked increase in unauthorized temporary structures of all kinds prompted the government to review prevailing policy and propose the application of the Hong Kong Building Ordinance of 1935 to the New Territories. Legally, the application of the Building Ordinance was an attempt to deal with the potentially uncontrollable situation of village expansion but without necessitating the cumbersome process of land re-entry under conventions of the Crown Lease.[32] This was eventually approved by Order of the Governor in Council on August 14, 1950. In practice, the Ordinance was used sparingly as a deterrent to the building of flagrantly illegal structures in the New Territories. It did not seek to remedy the building of squatter settlements that continued to proliferate. But in theory, regulation of buildings rather than land per se became increasingly incorporated into the government's handling of land policy, mirroring complex social situations.

Nonetheless, the crux of conflict between the government and inhabitants in the postwar era continued to revolve around the issue of land conversion. The immensity of the problem was signalled by J. Barrow, District Commissioner, in a memo sent to District Officers on March 5, 1951 that noted, among other things:

> 4. The most difficult questions are, of course, usually in connection with conversions, or sales. Here new District Officers are up against the bad old tradition whereby the Demarcator concerned quite uncritically reports the wishes of the owner or applicant, as the case may be, and the Land Bailiff sometimes passes these on to the District Officer with little or no attempt to see the question in perspective: too often the District Officer is presented with detailed suggestions for complying with the owner's or applicant's wishes. Being impressed with his duty as a public servant, he sometimes forgets his duty as *Public Trustee* for all land in his District.[33]

The wording of the memo is instructive, for it indicated that, contrary to being a cut and dried affair or unconditional right, land conversion was subject to many complex considerations that impinged on the District Officer's interpretation of "public welfare". This did not just involve the assessment of a fair value on the land but the worthy intentions of those behind the act. The directive behind policy was thus socially guided, not customarily bound per se. As Barrows warned:

> 10. Don't forget that many an application for land for "agriculture" is a thinly disguised attempt to acquire by private treaty land for building.
> 11. If a man comes along to you for land, don't consider it outside your scope to look into the question of whether he doesn't already own land, and if so, whether he is making proper use of it. You will often find that your speculator already has land, which he's just sitting on, not fulfilling the conditions of tenure.[34]

The debates within government over land conversion in actuality took place over a period of about ten years and eventually culminated in the establishment of the New Territories Small House Policy. Yet the entire course of debates was fraught with much internal division as well as heated dialogue with the Heung Yee Kuk (Rural Consultative Committee), who emerged as the main spokesmen for indigenous interests pertaining to land in the New Territories. The Heung Yee Kuk (*xiang yi ju*) was actually founded on April 23, 1926 as the corporate entity that survived an ad-hoc group called the *Zhujie Nunggongshangye yenjiu zhonghui* or Coalition for Agriculture, Industry and Commerce in the Leased Territory that was formed in 1923 to protest the colonial government's initial attempt to impose a premium on building land. In the postwar era, the Heung Yee Kuk, referred to simply as the Kuk, increasingly asserted itself as the public voice for indigenous inhabitants in dealings with the government, especially pertaining to land, even though that it was not officially recognized as an advisory committee until 1959.

Rumblings with regard to the issue of land conversion began to appear in 1949, prompted by local protests against the government's reimposition of a land premium in cases of agricultural land converted for building purposes. The chaos of war and Japanese occupation during

1941–45 disrupted more than just the flow of events. Many government records were destroyed, and the change of colonial administration meant that many practices started anew, that is, without reference to circumstances peculiar to the New Territories. A petition was sent by the Kuk on November 9, 1949 to the District Commissioner, New Territories, to protest the reimposition of a premium on land conversion, stating that this was one of the issues that led to native opposition in 1923, which was resolved by the decree of then Governor Cecil Clementi to abolish the imposition of land premiums in 1926. The petition then quoted from a recent letter written to the Kuk by the Village Representative of Sung Him Tong Village in Fanling an instance that appeared to exemplify the government's apparent change of policy, as follows:

> Mr. Wong Ying To, one of my villagers, is building a house on a parcel of land in On Lok Tsuen, which he bought many years ago. He has been told by the Land Bailiff, Tai Po, to pay $121 as conversion premium and $5 as formalities fee before carrying out the building work. We all understand that you (the Kuk) had, with much effort, once succeeded in persuading the Government to abolish the collection of conversion premium. We wonder why the Land Bailiff, Tai Po, has acted against the decision of the Government and ordered Mr. Wong to pay the conversion premium. I am writing to request you to take it up with the Government with a view of maintaining the previous decision.[35]

Not being able to find reference to Clementi's decree of 1926 in government records, J. Barrow, District Commissioner, initiated internal discussion regarding the viability of imposing premiums on land conversion, noting the following:

> Nowhere do I find reference to any premium payable upon this conversion, but the practice pre-war was to charge "conversion premium" only on lots other than "schedule lots" (of the original 1898 Block Crown Lease), the latter getting off without conversion premium. . . . Obviously, the intention originally must have been that we should not charge a countryman premium for building a simple peasant house on his land, and I have no intention of changing this practice. Post-war, however, there have been cases in which such people as Shanghai manufac-

turers have got permission to convert schedule agricultural lots which they have bought from N.T. owners. In such cases it has seemed wrong to me that the Crown should lose a conversion premium which the immigrants are well able to pay, and I have required them to pay conversion premium.[36]

Postwar amnesia withstanding, the divergent positions of the Kuk and the government in this matter are worth detailed scrutiny. For the Kuk, it seemed to be simply a matter of "law" that could be traced back to the decree of Clementi in 1926 that revoked a previous attempt to impose a premium on building land.[37] In the context of the events at that time, the imposition of a premium for land conversion was *in principle* inconsistent with Chinese conceptions of the free use of village land for cultivation and housing that made it exempt from government taxation or state intervention of any sort. This inconsistency was doubly relevant in the context of the *literal* definition of the lease that respected native customs on the land. The government's imposition of a premium was on the other hand consistent with their valuation of land in monetary terms and the principle that all land in the territory was in the first instance property of the Crown, subject hence to appropriate taxation. However, falling back on actual practice in the New Territories, Barrow's subsequent recommendation appeared to opt for a need to assess the complexities of the situation. From his comments, one can sense the existence of several variables that influenced the imposition or non-imposition of a premium. One was the distinction between Old Schedule Lots and lots acquired after the Block Crown Lease of 1898. Second was the distinction between land used for the building of simple traditional village houses and land acquired for other purposes that included extraordinary residential and commercial buildings. Third was the distinction between land owned by indigenous (pre-1898) villagers and land owned by later immigrants to the territory. While these distinctions overlapped in practice, it is important to note that, for Barrow, the principle of imposing a premium was one that should really be decided by conditions of actual (or potential) use that would reflect also the subsequent difference in land value. In any case, the times have changed. As he phrased the problem, "I have little doubt that if Sir Cecil had to make the decision to-day, he would agree that there is a vast difference between rural development by N.T. people and the aspect (hardly noticeable in his day) of urban or suburban development, whether by New Territories' people or others".[38] In this regard, the status of New Kowloon, which had been in theory part of the New Territories but which was in practice always administered in the prewar era more as an urban extension of Kowloon in matters pertaining to land, was symptomatic of the government's double standards.[39] In the final analysis, Barrow's general sentiment on the matter found added support from W. Aneurin Jones, Registrar General (the Land Officer), who argued,

> It would seem . . . that it has been accepted that no premium should be charged in the N.T. for agricultural land converted into building land, provided such land was granted under Land Court Judgements. I am sure, however, that this decision was never intended to cover land used for some of the speculations now proceeding in the N.T., and changed times and conditions demand changes in decisions. I recommend that the new order should stand — provided that we keep to the original intention, which would seem to be to permit a genuine N.T. resident to build a house for himself or his family on his native ground.[40]

Barrow's revised recommendations on land conversion were forwarded to the Kuk. The Kuk convened all its committee members to discuss the situation and sent to the succeeding District Commissioner, New Territories, K. Keen, a reply that, in addition to reiterating its objection to the imposition of a premium as an impediment to the right of villagers to freely utilize, transfer and build over their land, objected equally to its imposition for urban development land, stating:

> As to private lots in urban areas, they became private property long before the areas were defined as urban, and most of them have been inherited by the present owners from their predecessors. These lots are private and, we think, should be considered and treated the same as private farm land owned by ordinary villagers — all exempted from conversion premium payment — so that more houses would be built over them and local development and prosperity might be encouraged as what this Kuk and the N.T. people have been praying for day and night.[41]

Keen noted in the preface to the appended translation of the Kuk's letter that since the Block Crown Lease clearly stated that agricultural schedule lots cannot be converted to building land "without the previous license of His Majesty", the government was still free to set the conditions under which a license was to be granted. But the main point to him was not "are we legally entitled to charge conversion premium on schedule lots", but "ought we, from an administrative point of view, to do so"?[42] In an attempt to establish a guideline for what constituted grounds for the imposition of premium, the following list of cases was drawn up:

> a) any building in a Public Works Department (P.W.D.) lay-out area; b) any building in a town that is ripe for a P.W.D. lay-out but hasn't yet got it; c) a townee's villa in the country, wherever it may be; d) a hotel in the country, wherever it may be; e) a factory in the country, wherever it may be; and f) any building put up anywhere, even by a N.T. man, which is of a suburban type, i.e. goes farther than the grandest building normally put up by New Territories' people.[43]

Underlying the government's determination to impose a premium on land conversions for the sake of "rational development", there was tension between the Public Works officers who were responsible for setting up building guidelines in urban areas and District Administration officers who had to negotiate between the divergent interests of government and indigenous inhabitants. Those in Public Works advocated a system whereby agricultural land had to be surrendered in exchange for building land at equal monetary value, as was applied in the urban areas. District Officers on the other hand recognized this as an impractical option, noting the traditional reluctance of villagers to sacrifice four times the amount of land, not to mention the ongoing resistance to any premiums on land conversion. Internal discussions on this topic continued from 1952–54, until it was recognized that it was difficult to devise a uniform policy that had to take into account an entire range of situations from traditional village houses to small towns and all else in between. Perhaps the Deputy Colonial Secretary presaged the future most accurately, when he summarized the gap between views of District Administration and Public Works in a memorandum to the Colonial Secretary as follows:

> New Territories land, today, is clearly divisible into two sections: a) the land in and adjacent to the urban areas and b) the remainder of New Territories land. As regards (a) above,

you will see from the postscript to Mr. Walton's M.14 that
D.C.N.T. (Teesdale) is now coming round to the D.P.W.'s
(Forbes) view that the time has now come when he might hand
over to the D.P.W. responsibility for land in these urban areas.
This matter will be considered separately and if the changeover
takes place there will, of course, be no distinction between land
policy in these areas and in the urban area proper, and both
will be under the control of the D.P.W..[44]

On May 10, 1956, Ho Chuen-yiu, Chairman of Heung Yee
Kuk, petitioned the Governor of Hong Kong Alexander Grantham to
reconsider changes in land conversion policy. Citing a whole list of
ordinances and proclamations, such as by Governor Henry Blake in
1899 and Secretary of State Chamberlain in 1900 not to interfere with
local custom, to protect indigenous rights of land ownership, to guarantee the free conveyance, use and occupation of land, and not to
impose premiums on land conversion, Ho emphasized the continuity
of law in this matter to the present, before the government reimposed
premiums after the war in some cases and resumed land in exchange
for building land in others. Thus, "what is the difference between
measures like this and forcible expropriation of property", asked Ho?[45]
What was significant about Ho's petition, which replicated previous
petitions by the Kuk on the subject as well, was his insistence on the
inalienable right of inhabitants to use, transfer and develop on village
land. Yet at the same time, the kind of value-for-value exchange that
underlay the government's concept of land surrender or resumption for
building purposes appeared to be a non-issue.

In response to Ho's petition to the Governor, the new District
Commissioner, New Territories, K.M.A. Barnett, wrote a seven page
review of the government's land conversion policy which subsumed the
principle of imposing premium, the legal status of land in the New
Territories, the different developmental conditions posed by different
areas of the New Territories, and periods of economic growth or stag-
nation that influenced the degree of speculative interest in land conversion
by inhabitants.[46] In short, he cited five principles underlying government policy:

> a) the need for control; b) the need to finance the construction
> of streets, drains and other services contingent on urban de-

velopment; c) the need to honour our undertakings towards the country people; d) the need to encourage development in suitable areas; and e) the need to confiscate or at least tax the surplus value of the land.

After recognizing the difference between Old Schedule Lots in the original Block Crown Lease and new grant lots, which were post-1898 transactions, he stressed the need to distinguish five zones in varying degrees of development, namely:

> a) New Kowloon; b) areas expected to attract rapid urban development, . . . from Kowloon to Muk Wu and along the projected railway including the branch line to Shataukok; c) areas for which town plans or layouts have been prepared or are under discussion; d) areas (formerly) reserved for European residences; and e) all other areas, i.e. farming areas and villages.

He then demarcated five broad periods in New Territories land policy:

> a) the beginning, when the Land Registration Court was sitting, and ideas were very woolly; b) the period of optimism, when farmers were abandoning their land and it looked as if we could do what we liked — this period came to an end in the early 1920s; c) the slump, when nobody would buy land in the N.T. and all sorts of incentives were offered — this was at its worst after the Strike, but relics of the "incentives" still survive to plague us; d) the boom — 1950 to now. This has roughly, but not exactly, coincided with e) the attempt to apply Socialist theory.

What all this amounted to in practice was a situation where different areas were assessed differently: a) in New Kowloon, as in Hong Kong, land conversion needed approval by Public Works, that resulted in payment of a premium and adjustment in Crown Rent; b) areas in the New Territories, where free conversion was allowed only for traditional village houses and premium was assessed on new grant lots at an amount equal to the difference in value of the land. His explanation of the practice of free conversion for village houses was not based on respect of the treaty but reflected rather the fact that land auctions of village land, especially in times of economic slump, rarely exceeded the upset price, thus premium was waived.

In consideration of the above, Barnett concluded by recommending a policy that was already practiced in urban areas, where payment of premium would be replaced by a system of surrendering agricultural land in exchange for building land of equal value. However, in order to encourage land conversion given these zones of differential development, he suggested discounting the premium for some zones, that resulted in a complicated scale of differential calculus as follows:

> a) for Old Schedule Lots in farming areas for building of village house only: FREE conversion; b) for Old Schedule Lots in farming areas for building of non-village houses (if allowed): premium at HALF DIFFERENCE; c) for Old Schedule Lots in areas for which town layouts have been prepared and areas (formerly) reserved for European residences: FLAT RATE PREMIUM based on developments costs, or if this cannot be ascertained then HALF DIFFERENCE; d) for new grant lots in all zones: FULL DIFFERENCE, except where we particularly desire to encourage some development by announcing that conversions applied for by a certain date will be at HALF DIFFERENCE; and e) surrender of land only for streets and lanes.

The final item of his memo stated, "I think it would be better in the reply (to the Heung Yee Kuk petition) to avoid all mention of the Peking Convention and other irrelevancies". His last words articulated rather explicitly, at least in internal discussions, the fictional attachment the government actually had toward "indirect rule", especially in "changing times", despite rhetoric to the contrary.

Barnett's memo prompted a longer eight page memo by W. Aneurin Jones, Registrar General (Land Officer).[47] His comparison of the original ordinances referred to in the Kuk's petition produced several insightful observations, one of which involved the Kuk's contention that government proclamations repeatedly protected customary rights to land. In one such instance, Jones noted that the following definition of "customary land" and "customary landholder" appeared in Section 2 of the same "New Territories Ordinance 1902" not cited by the Kuk:

> a) 'Customary land' means land as to which a claim has been allowed by the Land Court constituted under Ordinance No.18 of 1900 or land expressly granted to be held from the Crown

under local customary tenure: but shall not include land as to which a Crown lease has been issued.

c) 'Customary landholder' means any claimant whose claim to land has been allowed by the Land Court constituted under Ordinance No.18 of 1900 and every person to whom land is expressly granted to be held from the Crown under local customary tenure and includes any person deriving title by transfer or transmission from such claimant or grantee from the Crown but shall not be deemed to include any person who shall have surrendered his rights to the Crown under Section 22 of this Ordinance nor any person deriving title through such person. (see Section 22 below)

22. It shall be lawful for any customary landholder to notify to the Registrar his desire to surrender his rights in his customary land to the Crown: and to receive in exchange a Crown lease. . . . such land shall from the date of the issue of such Crown lease be exempt from the provisions of this Ordinance and shall become subject to the general law in force in the Colony with regard to land held upon lease from the Crown.

From Section 22 of the Ordinance, it is clear that the difference between Old Schedule Lots and new grant lots was not simply one of being pre- and post-1898. In terms of the Ordinance, any act of conveyance resulting in the relinquishing or transfer of ownership of land made the land subject to conditions of the Crown lease, which may include the imposition of premium and increased taxation. Not only was this unknowingly (by indigenous definition) tantamount to expropriation by the state (insofar as its conditions of use now became subject to the general law in the Colony), but this should be interpreted more precisely to mean that, from a British legal point of view, the principle of the Lease that guaranteed customary rights to land was merely a concession or exception to the general rule that land was *by nature* property of the state. In principle, this was in direct conflict with Chinese imperial law that granted village land its basic *autonomy*, hence freedom from taxation and other conditions of use. This difference of principle was not just a superficial one, for it easily explained the intensity of resistance that villagers showed toward any kind of state control over land, including the rights of potential profit to be gained from any future development. In this regard, Barnett's final suggestion to disregard promises of the New Territories treaty as being irrelevant reflected a serious misunderstanding of the gravity of the conflict at hand. Jones continued to point out that, although Old Schedule Lots clearly noted restrictions on conversion except with license and consent of His Majesty, this clause "made *no* mention or reference to payment of any *premium*". Thus, this came back to the fundamental issue of whether the Crown, which under the terms of the Lease had no right to impose conditions limiting the customary rights of New Territories landholders, could legally charge conversion premium. In Jones' strict opinion, the government had perhaps gone beyond its legal powers, thus he found it difficult to agree with the opinion of the District Commissioner "that the Convention of Peking, the Blake proclamation, etc., are irrelevant and have no bearing at all on the matter of conversion" and could not form a definite opinion on the general question of whether the government was justified in charging conversion premium. Concretely, however, he urged that the government go no further with the District Commissioner's policy recommendation to require an applicant for land conversion to surrender agricultural land in exchange for the grant of a smaller building lot, which might be easily misconstrued by inhabitants as expropriation by the state.

In a meeting with members of the Kuk, namely a) Ho Chuen-yiu, Chairman, b) Tang Pui-king, Vice-Chairman, c) Ma Sai-on, d) Chan Yat-san, and e) Pang Fu-wah, District Commissioner Barnett noted in his confidential memo that a) and c) were "moderates", d) and e) were "leftists" and b) a "rightist". Testing their opinions on the propositions of 1) premium as reimbursement of capital works, 2) premium as partial surrender of the enhanced value, 3) premium as full surrender of the enhanced value and 4) surrender of land, Barnett remarked that "the 'left' stuck out all the time for no premium of any kind, which I called reactionary, and the 'moderates' spoke in support of the principles behind 1) and could see points in 2) as being simpler to calculate but wouldn't hear of 3) or 4)".[48] A follow-up meeting with the Kuk three weeks later on the other hand led to more productive results, in which "the 'left' had shifted their ground and no longer demanded free conversion, only conversion at low rates of premium. All, however, rejected 3) and 4), and even the 'moderates' contended that 'the greater part' of the enhanced value should accrue to the owner". He thus concluded that nothing in the treaty prevented the imposition of a premium on land conversion and that progress in meetings with the Kuk showed that their acceptance of it was inevitable.

The reply of the Kuk to Barnett's proposals, after consultations with other members of the Kuk, was, however, contrary to these expectations. The Kuk's deliberations "came to the unanimous conclusion that for private land in the New Territories, customary or traditional, there has never been any distinction between agriculture and building; any land could be used freely without restrictions".[49] The impasse created by the Kuk's reassertion of principles caused the government to embark on a more radical solution to the problem. A meeting was convened on February 4, 1957 and attended by the Colonial Secretary, Secretary of Chinese Affairs, Director of Public Works, District Commissioner of the New Territories, Attorney General and Registrar General. It was agreed first of all that there were no legal considerations that prevented the government from imposing terms for the conversion of land from agricultural to building status. In short, it maintained that 1) there were many practical difficulties in applying a flat-rate premium equitably, 2) there was no point in distinguishing between postwar and prewar new grant lots, 3) for new grant lots, the basic terms should be surrender and regrant, with option for cash conversion, 4) for Old Schedule Lots, free conversion could continue for genuine village houses anywhere, and 5) for other development in Old Schedule Lots, lessees would be given right of cash conversion or offer of surrender and exchange.[50] In sum, these resembled Barnett's original proposals.

A blunt letter was then written by E.B. David, Colonial Secretary, to the Chairman of the Kuk, stating that formal views of the Kuk were sought on three points put forward by the District Commissioner, and in its reply the Kuk instead put forth a claim that by custom or tradition there has never been any distinction drawn between agricultural and building land, at which point David cited various government ordinances to the contrary. In conclusion, he regretted that since the Kuk was "not prepared to continue the discussions which led up to the District Commissioner's letter of October 9, the government will now formulate its future policy in this matter without further delay and an announcement will be made as soon as possible. . . . I am to add with reference to your letter of January 24 that in the circumstances outlined above His Excellency the Governor does not consider that any useful purpose would be served by according an interview".[51]

The government's rebuttal to the Kuk's petition to the Governor muted all response by the Kuk for over a year, during which time the government continued to internally debate the details of a definitive land conversion policy, arguing over relative rates of premium and the merits of a surrender and exchange system *vis-a-vis* a cash conversion scheme. On all these issues, they were influenced on the one hand by the impracticality of cash conversions in New Kowloon and emerging new towns in the New Territories, such as Tsuen Wan, where land surrender in the long run facilitated planned development, and the undesirability of invoking criticisms of forced expropriation of land, especially in cases of Old Schedule Lots. As a result, the wording of policy tended to be unavoidably ambivalent and its practice in many areas was often inconsistent, as evidenced by statements such as "lessees of O.S. lots will not be required to surrender any land on conversion unless and until it became clear that such surrender is essential to permit planned layout to be implemented".[52] By this time, it appeared that the rift between the Kuk and government was deadlocked, with no negotiable settlement in sight.[53]

Policy deliberations continued after change of a new District Commissioner, D.R. Holmes, in 1958, which brought about further amendments. He first argued that, in layout areas, it would be unreasonable for owners, even of Old Schedule Lots, not to surrender more land than they get back, second that the value of land surrendered for streets and public purpose be deducted from any premium payable and third that Old Schedule and new grant lots be treated without distinction and more with reference to precise building specifications of what was to constitute a village house. The gist of his revised conversion policy can be itemized as follows:

> a) Conversion will be in accordance with general development policy in that area; b) owners of Old Schedule lots not in layout areas will not be required to surrender land but could do so if wished; c) in cases of cash conversion, the premium paid should be the full difference between the agricultural and building value of the land, deducting the value of land surrendered; d) in areas of rapid development, the District Commissioner may be authorized to charge less than full premium; and d) houses not exceeding 15 ft. height and 700 sq.ft. area on Old Schedule lots are permitted without premium.[54]

A formal and amended land administration policy went to the Executive Council in June 1960 for legislative approval. The details of the revised package aside, it is interesting to note that the principle of the issue on the government's side had changed considerably from the time the New Territories administration was forced to rethink its policy after the postwar resumption of colonial rule to the time the formal policy was submitted in 1960. Largely in ignorance of the peculiar situation of the Lease's effect on previous developments, the government's blanket imposition of premium on land conversion initially and its subsequent clarification based on a distinction between new grant lots and the exceptional status of Old Schedule Lots were evidence of its position that all land in the territory was really property of the state (or effectively at its disposal), quite contrary to indigenous notions that village land was exempt from such regulation, either as a corollary of the Lease or its traditional autonomy in Qing imperial terms. The principle of imposing a premium was in this sense both a function of the (modern) authority of the state as well as the peculiarly interventionist role that the British colonial authorities played in the broad regulation of society. This intervention at the macro-social level complimented rather than conflicted with its market mentality at the micro-economic level. The utilitarian rationale to place the tax burdens of development largely onto the shoulder of those speculative forces that presumably drove the New Territories land situation in the postwar era may have been the apparent philosophy guiding the government's land conversion policy, but this was a consequence and not the cause of the broad regulatory interests of the state to carry out its modernist project as a whole. This project of modernity was reflected also in the gradual devolution of the colonial government's political infrastructure in the postwar era that witnessed the development of administrative institutions at the grassroots level and incorporation of Chinese within a previously ethnically stratified authority structure, in addition to an increasing emphasis on economistic rationality in all areas of social life. However, the evolution of "indirect rule" in *these* (rationally calculating and normative disciplinary) senses that contributed to the illusion of a non-interventionist (non-authoritarian) state in the postwar era contrasted with a position that had in other dimensions of its land policy already contravened its initial principle of ruling on the basis of local practice. The times may have changed, but it was clear that the status of pre-1898 lots was already treated as a concession to rather than point of departure for prevailing policy. The decision to mute a system of land surrender and exchange, which was actually the approach favored at the outset by those in Public Works charged with the task of town planning, was of course made in consideration of protests by the Kuk that surrender of land constituted forced expropriation by the government. Holmes' later shift of emphasis to concede indigenous rights to build a traditional village house, irrespective of the status of such private land, combined with the need to impose premiums or preferably a voluntary system to enforce the state's role in regulating land development may have been the culmination of varied schemes on the issue but represented a subtle metamorphosis in the government's perception of indirect rule that led to a widening dualism in "traditional" and "modern" paths to development. On the one hand, it guaranteed inhabitants their right to build a "traditional" house that was consistent with their private ownership of land but upheld the interests of the government to define any course of development that fell outside the scope of these definitions. By shifting the basis of tradition away from the dualism of pre/ post-1898 that effectively archived indigenous in contrast to colonial, it now archived tradition and modern in relation to its symbolic facade.

THE MEANING OF PROGRESS ON THE LAND

In most of the notable disputes involving indigenous rights to land in the New Territories, the Heung Yee Kuk appeared to play a major role in voicing their views, especially in confrontation with the government. Yet on the other hand, the government, from its internal correspondence, tended to view the Kuk consistently less as the indigenous voice of the people than as the representative voice of an indigenous elite with vested interests. Their opinionated view of the Kuk no doubt had much to do their refusal to recognize the Kuk as an official advisory group representing the inhabitants as a whole, and it often colored their interpretation of the Kuk's intentions and actions. The representative nature of the Kuk as an indigenous voice must be carefully scrutinized, for it inevitably affects our deeper understanding of the Kuk's changing perspectives over time. But contrary to the government's simple critiques of the Kuk as a singularly elitist group with vested interests, it can be shown that the institutional transformation of the Kuk was complex, reflecting not only internal tensions between different factions but also different interpretations of native interests based on their position in the region and the "world". The internal dialectic within the Kuk has an important bearing on the ongoing dialectic between the Kuk and the government over changing land policy and the way events on the land eventually impact on other social changes.

As described in its founding constitution of 1926, the scope of the activities of Heung Yee Kuk included 1) support of local charitable work, 2) instigation of local reforms, 3) commitment to improve the livelihood of villagers and 4) provision of a forum for local grievances.[55] Despite its origins as a voluntary association (it also operated a primary school in Tai Po), the role of the Kuk as spokesman for native interests appeared to be transformed more by the changing institutional context within which it was set. In other words, it was the structure of regional representation defined by succeeding colonial administrations that galvanized its eventual role as de facto interlocutor in relation to the government and altered its statement of purpose to include improvement in the welfare of the overall region, defense of local customs and protection of the rights of indigenous inhabitants. In the prewar period, the Kuk's relation with District Officers was generally amicable and infrequent. During the Japanese occupation of World War II, a territory wide system of village representatives was instituted to act as local network to assist Japanese district administration. After the resumption of British colonial administration, the system of village representatives was expanded and organized to form 27 rural committees. Although these rural committee had no statutory powers, it provided a grassroots liaison network that facilitated the government's overall restructuring of local administration in the postwar era. Scott (1980: 98), for instance, noted the government's shift in priorities from a previous emphasis upon "law and order" to a distinct trend toward increased functional specialization in local administration, especially with respect to its dealings with local groups. But in addition to the establishment of more accessible contact within the populace through a system of village representation and professionalization of the administrative apparatus that effectively transferred authority from the person of the District Officer to a routine system of clerks and records, this local restructuring also had the explicit aim of enabling the government to more tightly and efficiently regulate matters than had been possible in the past. Thus, the government established rural committees and vegetable cooperatives to develop grassroot political and economic institutions, but registration of these institutions was strictly enforced in order to supervise and control them, given the turbulent, unpredictable Cold War climate. It was in light of this restructured system of village representation that the Kuk began to expand its role as a regional organization. Village representatives formed an electoral college to elect a body of Kuk Councillors, who in turn elected a group of Executive Councillors, made up of a Chairman, Vice-Chairmen and Executive Secretaries.[56] It was during this time that the Kuk began to be seen as a higher order council that appeared to represent a broad base of village heads and rural committees.[57]

The mid-1950s witnessed intense factionalism within the Kuk between the conservative elements, who came mostly from the established lineage communities such as Kam Tin and Yuen Long on the one hand, and the progressive elements, who came mostly from urbanizing areas such as Tsuen Wan and Tuen Mun. This factionalism culminated in the election of the Kuk's Executive Councillors in 1957. The conservative faction challenged the ex-officio status of Kuk Councillors and Executive Councillors that made up the governing body of the Kuk and that had been recently dominated by members in the rapidly growing urban constituencies. Those in the progressive camp threatened to boycott the elections. Nonetheless, the proposed amendments were passed, which enabled the conservatives to win a majority of the seats in the resulting elections of August 15 and 28. This victory was, however, short-lived, when the government introduced and passed legislation called the Heung Yee Kuk Bill on November 25, which essentially granted official advisory status to the Kuk but restored by force of ordinance the rules of selection that enabled former ex-officio Councillors of the Kuk to retain their status on the Kuk's Executive governing body. Equipped with this legal instrument, the New Territories Administration occupied the premises of the Kuk on December 11, 1959 for the purpose of undertaking "immediate and extensive repairs" (Kuan and Lau 1979: 22). Then in early 1960, under the supervision of the District Commissioner, new elections were held that swept a majority of progressives back into office and irrevocably altered the Kuk's ideological position on land.

The government, as it turned out, played a crucial role in determining the course of events. It was hardly neutral, given the decade of conflict that pitted the Kuk against the government's attempts to forge a new land conversion policy and the generally anti-development sentiments that blocked government efforts at land resumption for new towns and public works such as the Tai Lam Chung Reservoir. Threatened with possible ouster by conservative members in February 1957 over the proposed abolition of ex-officio status for already elected Kuk officials, the supporters of the progressive faction held secret meetings with K.M.A. Barnett, District Commissioner, who supported the creation of a new Kuk under the name of Heung Ching Kuk (Council for Rural Administration) (Lee 1984: 174). On July 12, 1957, in response to the government's newly enacted Registration of Societies Ordinance (which aimed to regulate Chinese associations in light of 1956 leftist riots in Kowloon), the Kuk, dominated by the conservative faction, voted against compliance with registration. This refusal to comply, combined with the decision by Rural Committees in the progressive areas such as Tsuen Wan to comply with the new Ordinance and apply under the special category of exempted registration, prompted the government to formally withdraw official recognition of the Kuk on the eve of elections on August 15, 1957. Whether the government just concluded that the Kuk had lost its respectability as spokesmen for the people, thus deserved not to be officially recognized, or tried to bring down the Kuk as a precondition for reconstituting it, became clear with the submission of the Heung Yee Kuk Bill to the Executive Council on October 27, 1959, the intentions of which was made clear by the Colonial Secretary in his first reading of the Bill as follows:

> The present Bill seeks to set up the Kuk as a statutory advisory body on New Territories affairs and to establish, consolidate and indeed to broaden its representative position. . . . The immediate occasion for the introduction of this Bill arises from a dispute, or conflict. . . . Matters finally developed into a dispute between one of the two factions on the one hand and government on the other. The point at issue was a very simple

one: those who had by then assumed control of the Kuk maintained that the government ought to treat that body as being authoritatively representative of New Territories opinion but should at same time in no way concern itself with the question how Kuk officials were elected — that is to say, with the Kuk's constitution — or with the question whether the Kuk was truly representative. Such a proposition cannot really command any support.[58]

As Chiu (1997: 27) viewed it, "essentially, the government's point was that it had to be satisfied with the composition of the HYK before it could be recognized as the representative of rural opinions". Monthly intelligence reports compiled by the Hong Kong Police Special Branch regularly kept tabs on the backgrounds of important rural committee chairmen and meetings of the Kuk, noting in particular anti-government activities and dangerous political leanings of various members.[59] The passage of the Heung Yee Kuk Bill in 1960 brought back into power a faction of the Kuk that the government considered was more sympathetic to its aims. Its aim was not to dissolve the Kuk but to coopt it. Whether the government actually coopted indigenous interests to its side as a result or just managed to replace one indigenous faction with another one, albeit a more desirable one, is a question that deserves deeper scrutiny. Yet without doubt, it ushered a new phase of relations.

Politics aside, the history of the Kuk's confrontation with the government over land in the New Territories reflects the changing meaning of "progress" that was inscribed by complex changes in society not only in the New Territories but more importantly in global terms. The changing values attached to the land were synonymous with values embedded in the newly evolving postwar society, and it was within this socio-historical context of competing values that the Kuk and the government represented the agents of specialized interests and goals. In the prewar period, the issues involved the nature of indigenous custom, law and order, and the politics of interaction that eventually resulted in the adoption of a system of values which was to guide the administration in matters pertaining to land. The postwar era provided a different social setting for the ongoing confrontation between the government and indigenous people. The change in the government's own global priorities was accompanied by a corresponding change in the social imperatives that guided indigenous interests. This is another way of saying that changes in what constituted "colonial" and "indigenous" interests simply cast the nature of that political confrontation in very different light from what existed in a previous era. Add to that the collusion of political forces that on the one hand witnessed the government playing "divide and rule" tactics and indigenous factions fraught with internal tensions that affected their ultimate relationship to its other, and it is clear that attempts to view this in dualistic terms becomes too simplistic. In short, conflict between "colonizer" and "colonized" continues, but it is necessary to read these relationships in terms of ongoing changes in cultural value in order to understand in deeper terms the significance of resulting social transformations.

More than just colonizer versus colonized, there were at least four different parties; more than British versus Chinese or modern versus traditional, each party was influenced not only by cultural, ideological and class factors but also by its positionality within this emerging global order. The world that the government confronted was not just one of ruling a colonial other but also realizing a rational-modern social project that balanced utilitarian imperatives of market efficiency on the one hand and hegemonic imperatives of ordering society through structuration. Structural disciplining was a useful tool of local surveillance in light of Cold War tensions that constantly threatened to destabilize Hong Kong in the early postwar era but also complemented modernizing processes transforming society as a whole in ways that eventually transcended Cold War politics per se. In legal terms, the trend toward functional professionalization within New Territories administration routinized the rule of law by replacing the authority of the District Officer with an impersonal bureaucracy of clerks and records. Attempts to increase channels of communication at the local level reformed the system of political representation and brought about the creation of self-regulating agricultural cooperatives, but these mechanisms of indirect rule produced in the end a more efficient technology of social control. The government's role in developing new towns and transforming the social landscape on land was in this regard an obvious aspect of a broader rationalizing ethos that had already penetrated many levels of local life.

At the other end, the Kuk and its conservative supporters probably never ceased to look upon the colonial authorities as red-haired
barbarians (*hungmao fan*) and alien usurpers who never corrected the
social injustices caused as a result of the imposition of their policies.
This stereotype was an exaggeration of the actual situation but one that
was no less extreme than the characterization of the Kuk by the government as a tool of wealthy, landed interests in local society. At a deeper
level, such name calling was indicative of a still unresolved gap between
the two sides on fundamental issues. The Kuk for its part continued
with staunch vehemence to defend what they thought were interests
of the indigenous people, but this did not preclude nor exclude the
possibility that these interests and their system of values were already
changing in response to changing conditions.[60]

The emergence of a progressive faction within the Kuk that later
dominated the course of Kuk policy on land represents a new factor
that challenges prevailing notions of indigenous interests, while casting
the relationship between inhabitants and government in different light.
Yet even in view of its pro-development stance *vis-a-vis* more conservative members in the Kuk, it is somewhat premature to say that its
interests coincided with the government, with whom it colluded briefly
to insure its own survival. One can say with much certainty that, in
contrast to the conviction of the Kuk's conservative members to defend
their customary rights as legally protected by terms of the Lease, the
progressive faction recognized the changed political priorities in the
postwar era and social conditions characteristic of their own living
environment more than their counterparts residing in the more remote
agricultural hinterland as a point of departure for their strategy in
dealing with the government. Whether these interests reflected those
of a privileged elite rather than of the "populace-at-large" is another
question altogether.

From the point of view of the populace-at-large, there was little
doubt that postwar urban industrialization brought about material
prosperity. But contrary to the descriptions of such "progress" generously offered in official and scholarly accounts, progress of this kind
for people on the land was unevenly distributed and brought about
a serious discrepancy between ideal expectations (defined by the possibilities of progress) and their actual realization. One's perception
of relative progress or poverty within a system of unequal means to

egalitarian ends was inextricably linked to one's pragmatic assessment of one's interests and goal-orientations as a whole, and this relative positionality within a situation of power produced a diversity of indigenous attitudes toward the land and its community.

There should be no reason to believe that the pro-development stance of the progressive faction of the Kuk *vis-a-vis* their conservative colleagues automatically endeared them to the government's position. Despite the nasty political infighting, the progressive faction differed less on matters of principle than in its strategy of battling with the government to gain rights over land. In fact, it is fair to say that the intensity of the confrontation became heightened after the change of regime. A perusal of the Kuk's later publications and petitions to the government reflected to some extent a sense of changing indigenous values toward the land. In many of these publications, reports and letters, dealing explicitly with problems of land in the New Territories, reference was almost invariably made initially to the legal status of the people's land in light of the government's interpretation of the New Territories Block Crown Lease, the non-expropriation clause in the Convention, and the attempt to impose premiums on house land in 1923.[61] Such publications reiterated from the Kuk's point of view that problems of the present had roots in the past and that these differences of principle remained important obstacles. But unlike the past, the Kuk did not allow these differences of principle to obstruct their goal of attaining tangible concessions in other areas. In essence, the rhetorical or ideological confrontation provided a bargaining position from which to maximize favorable conditions for building and development. By accepting the reality of the government's power to control land use and regulate development, the Kuk began to focus more on gaining advantages in areas of policy that were negotiable. Thus, in practice, it continued to defend the rights of natives, whatever they were, even though these rights were sometimes by nature contrary to custom. Concretely this involved bickering over the details of proposed rates of compensation for resumed land, disagreement over housebuilding specifications, appeals to adjust premium rates, legal restrictions on temporary structures and discussion of rules to benefit those without land. In short, while native rights to land were invoked to protest government actions with respect to the legality of things such as land re-entry and the applicability of new land policies to indigenous inhabitants of the territory, the nature of rights per se gradually became less of an issue than simply as political leverage to gain the respect of the Kuk's opinion in matters pertaining to land.

As part of its land conversion policy, the government devised the Letters B system on July 1, 1960 so that landowners could opt for full cash compensation (at a rate of about HK$1 per sq.ft. or of a sum roughly equivalent to 20 years rent) or exchange their agricultural land for building land at a later date using Letters B as an I.O.U. at a ratio of 5: 2 (agricultural land surrendered: building land acquired). Letters B were transferrable and could be sold to brokers or developers who would then accumulate them in hopes of exchanging them for large plots of land. As speculative fever rose, the market value of Letters rose accordingly.[62] In one case, villagers were offered $8 per sq.ft. by developers in 1975 when official cash compensation was $2.50. Market price later rose to $200 (Hayes 1991: 114). With both population and rural development growing during the 1970s, it became apparent that the system was unworkable. The cash compensation rate, although multiplied many times the original figure (average of HK$17 in 1976, see XXN 1977c: 106–09), was still a mere fraction of the value of land sold at government auctions, the sum of which, after taxes and income, constituted the government's second largest source of revenue. Moreover, the government was still lagging far behind in providing building land to those who exchanged their agricultural land.

The growing crisis of land insolvency heightened anxiety among affected residents, and the Kuk served as a forum for local discontent. The Kuk responded essentially by insisting again on fair value for Letters B issued for land resumed to reflect market value and by demanding a time limit for fulfilling promises of land made by the government under terms of Letters B.[63] Meanwhile, all during this period, disputes from cases of land compensation leading to arbitration were becoming increasingly endemic as far as the government was concerned, and a large majority of cases pertaining to land handled by the Kuk (14 of 23 cited, for example, in a two-year progress report in XXN 1974–76: 60–72) directly involved land compensation or disputes arising out of village land resumption.[64]

A new compromise was reached in April 1978, when the government agreed to review compensation rates at six month intervals. Moreover, the Letters B system was amended to allow villagers to exchange their fields half for cash and half for promissory notes. Nonetheless, the land debt on the government's side continued to grow at a rate of 5 million sq.ft. per year (FEER 1982a: 54). Much of the backlog resulted from the villagers' eagerness to cash in on the investment value of their land during the rapidly rising price of land on the open market in the late 70s. However, when land values began to cool in 1981 along with rising interest rates, letter values dropped correspondingly by as much as 40%, and most landowners affected by resumption began turning to cash compensation instead. Thus, when the government scrapped the Letters B system in 1982, it came as a relief both to the government, which had been looking for a way to resolve its land debt crisis, and the Kuk, which foresaw a weakening of its own interests in light of a downturn in the property market (FEER 1982c: 72).

In short, the demise of the Letters B system, devised initially as a means of resolving issues pertaining to land that divided both the government and the indigenous population brought to light the aims and values which motivated the agents involved. The establishment of the Letters B system provided a practical means by which the government could forego the large cost of initially buying up land for future development, while answering the Kuk's demand for a satisfactory compensation scheme for landowners affected by compulsory land resumption for urban-industrial or residential purposes. From the government's point of view, the system was designed also to give inhabitants an opportunity to protect their right to the land if they wished to (hence, the land for land exchange) while at the same time letting them contribute to development on the land and sharing in the overall profits. On the other hand, the Kuk's bargaining strategies, particularly with regard to the legitimacy of the non-expropriation clause of the Convention, clearly underscored the fact that, for them, the problem was a matter of "fair price" and that what was in the prewar era a legally non-negotiable contravention of local custom was now negotiable in economic terms. The demographic pressure which escalated the price of land during this period further intensified the speculative energy of landowners who wished to "play the market". In the end, contrary to the assumption held by the government that people were basically unwilling to part with land (meaning that they would be more amenable to some kind of exchange in kind than in cash as compensation for "forced expulsion"), the whole turn of events, especially toward the end of the 1970s, proved that people were not only quite willing to dispose of the land but moreover enthusiastically went along with the 5: 2 compensation scheme precisely for the profits that it would bring on the open market. Or as the Secretary for the Environment, foreseeing an end to the Letters B system two years later, remarked, "everybody wants to do better than the chap who surrendered his land before, but he's not going to be able to" (FEER 1980b: 66). In the end, the realization that there was simply not enough land to go around under the 5: 2 exchange scheme (since only 3/5 of all land could actually be developed) may have been a major factor that contributed to the abolition of the Letters B system, yet on the other hand less problems would have arisen had the government simply decided to pay everyone off, which was what everyone wanted in the first place. Thus, as the people's traditional appeal to custom was being subverted by self-interested profit maximization, the government, by attempting to make what "appeared" to be on the basis of custom a fair exchange, suffered most in terms which had little or nothing to do with custom.

Like the problem of land resumption, the pressure of population growth and the need to accommodate a changing urban-industrial society brought open attention to the plight of indigenous rural housing. The problem not only involved the need to provide better and more adequate housing under conditions of land scarcity, which was how most writers on the subject understood the problem (see Han 1978, Jones 1978, Hadland 1978). The problem of rural housing and building land in the New Territories was one that originated out of the government's creation of a Block Crown Lease and attempt to construct a system of legal practice based on custom to regulate matters of land ownership and usage.

As a result of mass immigration into the New Territories during the 1950s, the housing situation approached chaotic proportions. For the government, the squatter situation on the land became rampant, while unrestricted health and building conditions in light of rural expansion proved to be a major concern. A study conducted in 1971 estimated that there were over 70,000 waiver structures in residential use in addition to many other temporary industrial and commercial structures, often located in densely populated, poorly accessed areas (NTA 1972a). A survey conducted by the Medical and Health Department in July and August, 1972 of some 3836 rural houses reported primitive facilities and unsafe living conditions (PMOH 1972). Meanwhile, villagers complained to the contrary that government regulations with regard to housebuilding unjustifiably restricted land use and prevented the building of new houses. The heated debates that ensued between the government and the Kuk over these matters led to the establishment and implementation of the government's Small House Policy in 1972.

According to the terms of the Small House Policy, each indigenous villager was entitled to build for himself one small house in his village during his lifetime. Concessionary grant included any Free Building License, Restricted Auction Sale, Private Treaty Grant to a villager at two-thirds of the full market value, premium free modification for the construction of a small house, and any grant given under concessionary terms. The house would be allowed to cover a maximum area of 700 sq.ft. and could not exceed 25 ft. or three stories in height. As a general rule, application for a small house would only be allowed in recognized pre-1898 villages within a distance of 300 ft. from the edge of the last village type house built before the implementation of the Small House Policy on December 1, 1972. Crown Rent of $20 would be charged for the building lot, and in the case of a Free Building License there would be no premium for converting agricultural land (NTA 1972b).

Along with the concessionary grants made to indigenous villagers under the Small House Policy, two amendments were made to existing land policy. First of all, Modifications of Tenancy for the construction of domestic houses on private agricultural land was replaced in favor of the issuance of building licenses. In practice, what this meant was that, with the exception of Free Building Licenses granted to indigenous villagers under conditions of the Small House Policy for the conversion of private agricultural land into building land, such conversions became in principle (as a general rule of practice) prohibited. Instead, a license could be issued for building a house on Crown Land not to exceed 700 sq.ft. in total area and 25 ft. in height. Premium under these circumstances would be charged at full market value, assessed on an area basis and reviewed annually. The issue of such a building license was similar to a Modification of Tenancy except that it would be subject to resumption or re-entry on breach of covenant. A second amendment of existing land policy was to issue leases of Crown Land by Private Treaty for village houses in cases where there had been a (temporary) structure on Crown Land Permit for ten years or more. It would be subject to building regulations imposed on other houses under the new policy, and a premium would be charged at full market value, assessed on an area basis and reviewed annually. The latter amendment was designed explicitly to deal with the squatter situation.[65]

The significance of the new land policy in view of legal issues and customary rights to the land was enormous. The government in effect conceded to indigenous inhabitants their inalienable right to the land by granting them essentially cost free (premium free) a piece of building land subject to the limitation that each indigenous male villager would be entitled to only one such piece of land in his lifetime. For the villager, acceptance of this concession made by the government meant at the same time that he would be sacrificing his future rights in theory to all Crown Land in the village, land which had previously been referred to as "the personal property of the people". Secondly, for the squatter, at least those who satisfied the ten-year minimum occupancy requirement, the revision of land policy that allowed him to purchase Crown Land by Private Treaty for building purposes where he was previously "invisibly" erecting a temporary structure on the land implied moreover that the problem of squatter occupancy had become a definable phenomenon (in hard and fast legal terms) for which there was now a practical basis for eradication (see, for instance, XXG 1976b: xiv–xv).

The aforementioned legal implications of the government's new Small House Policy may not have been immediately apparent to the respective parties, but it appeared that the subsequent turn of events ran counter to whatever expectations the government had when they instituted the new policy. While the concessionary grants of building land were made to indigenous villagers in order to guarantee their inalienable customary right to live on the land, a principle that had been vehemently fought over in the prewar period ever since colonial occupation of the New Territories, villagers responded by doing to the land what was least expected of them. They sold it to the highest bidder. Out of 8390 people who were issued about 6 million sq.ft. in land grants in the first ten years of the new policy (with 7230 still on the waiting list), many ended up making a profit of HK$500,000 to 1 million per house. In the first five years, abuses became apparent. Applications were submitted by villagers living abroad who had no intention of returning to Hong Kong but who were still defined as indigenous villagers (male descendants of pre-1898 villagers). In one typical case, villagers made a total of HK$500,000 on 10 houses, and the developer made HK$80 million on resale. As village houses were not subject to Hong Kong Building Ordinance regulations, each three-story house was built and sold as three self-contained flats (FEER 1982b: 55).[66]

The policy was further amended, requiring villagers to pay the government a premium based on current market value, if they sold the house. But as property values continued to escalate toward the end of the 1970s, and premiums, although reviewed periodically, continued to lag behind actual market price, selling and profit-taking continued to be the trend. This forced the government to clamp down harder on fraudulent applications and further restrict eligibility for such grants. The government, to say the least, was embarrassed. But this did not stop the Kuk from pushing forward even harder on behalf of indigenous interests. In outlining its grievances with regard to Small House Policy in a major assessment of land problems in the New Territories, the Kuk continued to argue for a relaxation of the various building restrictions, e.g., on building height, extensions of buildings, permissible distances from public structures, and applicability of the policy to non-indigenous villagers (XN 1977f: 459–65). But attention to such petty details clearly represented concerns that were in theory secondary to the underlying legal issues invoked by the Small House Policy. While the offer of concessionary land grants represented a major concession in deed by the government to villagers' customary rights to land, it was still a minor sacrifice for what was in theory the principal issue, namely the government's right to (the remainder of) village land as property of the Crown (through imposition of a full premium upon Crown Land Licenses). The fact that the Kuk neglected to challenge this at all in the end represented perhaps an even greater concession on their part of "indigenous rights".

The events that resulted from the government's efforts to put into practice a land policy that could satisfy its objective of determining the course of rational social development on the one hand and mollify the Kuk's demands on the other to honor indigenous rights to land produced a diverse spectrum of reactions that was a clear function of one's relative positionality in a situation of power defined and exacerbated by pressures of the market system. For the average landowner, the decision to sell out was less a consequence of rational free choice than the end product of social changes that long ago destroyed traditional values of livelihood and pre-existing notions of community. The radical destruction of that lifestyle devalued the land to an extent that made commoditization an acceptable if not desirable life-choice. This made the conservatives' appeal to customary rights to land that was a staple of the Kuk's rhetorical fight with the government an even more anachronistic stance in a modern world system. For the government, the stipulations of the Lease ceased long ago to be a central policy concern, but the constant recourse to broken treaties and defense of custom by the Kuk forced all parties to negotiate with careful reference to these terms. Ironically, the Kuk's battle with the government on policy lines eventually evolved into a sophisticated war of words fought on many fronts that appealed not only to custom but also to anti-colonialism, human rights and comparisons to laws in other countries. By muting internal dissent over principles and taking a pragmatic approach, the Kuk reached a compromise with the government in 1971 to 1) liberalize restrictions on the building of private houses, 2) come up with a more equitable premium scheme for various areas, 3) review the government's right of re-entry on Old Schedule lots and 4) develop a more systematic policy toward areas falling within development layouts, eventually leading to the creation of the New Territories Small House Policy in 1972. These negotiated agendas were a far cry from the incompatible positions that dichotomized both Kuk and government on land issues early on. The Kuk's position on land later expanded to a broad ranging appeal for social reforms, which included a joint opinion by three well-known Hong Kong lawyers, S.V. Gittins, H. Litton and Winston Poon, defending the legality of various Ordinances protecting customary rights to land.[67] So in 1981, when Chairman of the Kuk Chan Yat-san gave a speech entitled "The British Government should keep up with the times in the administration of the New Territories", it looked as if the tables had turned.[68]

VARIATIONS ON THE THEME OF "THE LANDED COMMUNITY"

It is impossible to describe the diversity of changes that village communities in the New Territories have undergone in the postwar era. While anthropologists and historians have noted the transformation of many "traditional" single-lineage villages into multi-surname and even multi-ethnic ones, they have understood this process primarily as a function of the dissolution of a kinship ideal that had been subject to the onslaught of various "external" forces, mostly demographic pressure and market commoditization. As for the refugee situation that witnessed a large influx of tenant cultivators throughout the New Territories and the changeover to new types of agriculture and industry, the material pressures were apparent, but the extent to which outside elements were accommodated in any place depended on the existing situation of power, which was subject not only to local negotiations over the economic conditions of tenure but also community consent and the nature of state intervention. In the case of market commoditization, its immediate effects on village life were of course economic, but the ways in which people adapted to forced changes in livelihood were also a function of the way these pressures were perceived as threats to the viability of the community as a social entity. In both cases, these conflicts engendered by material dislocations pointed first of all to the existence of underlying conceptions and values in relation to land that were really inseparable from indigenous notions of the village community. Moreover, different communities absorbed outside forces in different ways, and it is equally important to explain the nature of that diversity, not just as a variation of a kinship ideal.

Within this spectrum of traditionally homogenous to totally heterogenous village organization, there were single-lineage villages that defiantly rejected all outsiders and others that accommodated them only on the periphery of the core community. In regard to mixed village communities, there were some that freely absorbed outsiders in addition to those that simply sold out to the highest bidder. In each case, perceived positionality or accessibility within a context of political and economic capital in my opinion influenced to a large degree how communities gauged their own viability in the world, which then provided the basis upon which individuals made rational, calculating choices. There was freedom, within limits.

Aijmer's (1986) monograph on a community of tenant squatters living on the periphery of indigenous villages which were themselves on the verge of making way for the development of a new satellite town described in great detail various tensions that underlay relations between settled villagers and immigrant tenants on the one hand and the overall plight of traditional inhabitants caught by the inevitability of modern social disruption on the other. In general, Aijmer showed that the relationship that indigenous villagers had toward land differed from that of immigrant migrants. There were several types of village clusters, some being nucleated settlements surrounded by fields and others being settlements situated on the rim of the fields where agricultural land met the hill slopes. Nonetheless, most villages tended to be closed kin communities that were generally hostile to the incursion of outsiders living therein. Many rented out houses in the villages to urban commuters and laborers, but selling property within the core village was usually frowned upon. The settled villagers had in general deep attachments to the land and were reluctant to part with it except under extraordinary conditions. Immigrant cultivators on the other hand were diasporic creatures who had no real fixed attachment to the land and tended to view it as a commodity. In addition to being physically scattered, there were no common foci to cement tenants together as a community. At the time of Aijmer's field study, plans to build the new town center at Shatin that would displace the villages and fields under his observation were already well underway. For those immigrants who rented the land and were at most temporary fixtures, their attitude was usually one of nonchalance and fate, contrasting clearly with that of indigenous villagers whose land would be resumed and whose futures would be transformed.

In terms of rights to land, the relationship between village land-owners and tenants was based on inequality, and this inequality became more accentuated by debates over policy that revolved around issues that were forced to privilege the legal primacy of indigenous rights. Moreover, voting rights in Rural Committees were limited to people who resided in the area for ten or more years, which often forced tenants to approach the District Office directly to air their grievances. In an atmosphere of Cold War conflict that saw polarization along ideological lines, Aijmer argued that one's relationship to land still remained a primary cleavage.

In his article entitled "The Fading of Earthbound Compulsion in a Chinese Village", Rance P.L. Lee (1981) described a village in the process of transition from a single clan community to a mixed community and tried to show how this process broadly reflected changes occurring throughout the New Territories. The influx of outsiders into the formerly single-clan community began immediately after the war with 9% of the immigrants coming during 1945–49, another 29% during 1949–58, and the remaining 62% from 1959–69. Immigration of outsiders from the city and refugees from China was combined with outmigration of indigenous villagers to urban-industrial areas and abroad, with the bulk of emigrants leaving during 1959–69. The entire process of resettlement within the village followed the gradual decline of agriculture as a mode of livelihood which had generally been taking place throughout the territory. Many opted to emigrate to Europe to seek different employment, while others turned to wage labor in the urban-industrial sector. Despite the occupational shift away from agriculture, the natal ties of those indigenous villagers who left to take up employment elsewhere remained unchanged. Few indigenous families left the village by abandoning ties altogether. Despite living and working elsewhere, emigrants continued to send remittances to relatives there, and they rented their houses and fields out to outsiders living there, keeping intact their hopes of eventually returning to the village.[69]

Although Lee viewed such population displacement as an example of the disruptive consequences of social change in an indigenous community, it appeared on the contrary that the only clear manifestation of social disruption was the abandonment of agriculture as a material livelihood. The fact that emigrants from the village, despite their physical absence, maintained their traditional natal ties to the land in other senses showed that "their earthbound compulsion" had been strengthened in the process. By renting out houses to outsiders, they managed to accommodate external elements (as tenants) while at the same time not sacrificing the cohesion of the natal community. Tai Po Tau on the eastern coast of the New Territories was representative of superficial changes taking place in the postwar period. The kind of response that villagers adopted here could be characterized as traditional, and it is clear that the process of transformation itself was one of positive change or adaptation to new (albeit disruptive) global social conditions.

In contrast to Lee's example of Tai Po Tau, villages in the Fanling area of the northern New Territories had a somewhat different postwar history. Partly because of its promixity to China, Fanling and Yuen Long were deeply affected by the influx of refugees in the late 1940s. According to the 1961 Census, Fanling in general had the highest rate of changeover from long-term tenancy to short-term agricultural tenancy contracts in the New Territories and witnessed a high rate of displacement of traditional agriculture by animal domestication. The stretch of villages from Fanling's market town along the arterial Shataukok Road leading to the remote mountainous villages close to the border with China is interesting. Unlike the large established lineage-villages in other areas, most of the villages along this arterial stretch were small to medium size population communities of varied origins. Unlike the more insulated villages in the mountainous Shataukok area, they accommodated the influx of outsiders but in diverse ways that require detailed scrutiny. It is through this diversity of experience that one can begin to sense the possible range of meanings and values attached to land and community.

Kwan Tei is a medium size village not far from the market town of Luen Wo Hui. The original village of Kwan Tei has a history of several hundred years and is made up of four different surname groups who share a single ancestral temple-cum-village hall. The settlement history of its inhabitants appears to be rather undistinguished, as there is no written genealogy for any of these surname groups. Nonetheless, the four groups have cohabited the village quite amicably to a degree where intermarriage between groups was generally practiced. Like most other villages in the area, the main livelihood up until World War II was padi cultivation. The area was not particularly well endowed in terms of water resources in comparison to the more fertile valleys elsewhere, and there was barely enough land for people to eke out a subsistence. Life during the Japanese occupation was even rougher. Many villagers migrated to Southeast Asia in the early 20th century to seek work, and the collapse of rice cultivation in the New Territories in the early postwar era led to more outmigration to Europe. Thus, Kwan Tei in general readily accepted the massive influx of postwar refugees, mostly as short-term vegetable cultivators. The population of tenants expanded so much that separate communities formed on the outskirts of the village, each occupied by different ethnic constituencies. Few if any of these outsiders settled in the original village of Kwan Tei. Instead, a cluster of settlements extended along the periphery and became known as Kwan Tei North Village. Refugee settlers came in waves and eventually formed in time residential niches based on place of origin. The big enclaves in Kwan Tei North were made up of people originally from Dongguan and Shun De (in Guangdong Province). Even in the process of expansion, the original inhabitants were unable to keep track of the actual tenants cultivating the land. Most built squatter huts in the fields, and because landlord-tenant relationships were not close, sometimes tenants changed hands without the landlords' knowledge. Kwan Tei was also the site of a large vegetable cooperative and home to several pig and poultry farms.

In terms of community, one might argue whether Kwan Tei is one village (as it exists in name) or many. Due to the chain migration over the postwar years that has resulted into the development of residential niches inhabited by people of the same region, community feeling has become in large part ethnically based. The separateness of each ethnic enclave is reflected also in ritual life. While many other villages participating in the annual celebration of the goddess Tianhou in the Tianhou Temple at Ping Che Village usually have one flower float association (*huapao hui*) to represent the entire village, Kwan Tei is typically represented by many, each representing a separate ethnic-residential community. Despite the affiliation along such lines, relations between different communities are amicable.

The example of Kwan Tei is representative of both traditional and modern influences in the accommodation of outsiders and small industries that contributed to the postwar evolution of the village. Dilution of the surname village was not a necessary feature of the modernizing process. The economic deprivation suffered during the early postwar era made the village amenable to the renting of land to outside cultivators and industries but did not disrupt the livelihood or residential pattern in the core village. The introduction of vegetable cultivation prompted the switch to short-term tenant relationships based on cash rent, but in other respects the nature of the landlord-tenant relationship itself was not unusual in customary terms. Thus, there were elements, both internal and external, that allowed the village to develop in complexity but without necessarily leading to any radical or dysfunctional change. Changes on the land followed changes in the community.

The village of Ma Mei Ha is located further on along Shataukok Road in the direction of the Chinese border. Its original settlers were Hakka agriculturalists who previously broke off over a hundred years ago from the village of Wo Hang in the adjoining region of Shataukok bordering China. The villagers of Ma Mei Ha were land poor peasants and rented the land from absentee landlords in the Shenzhen valley. They were beneficiaries of the British demarcation of the Block Crown Lease by claiming ownership of the land, as proprietors of topsoil, against the claims of absentee owners of the subsoil. Thus in contrast to more established villages in the territory, most of the land that they owned belonged to individuals instead of being inherited from prior generations as ancestral endowment. Still, even with this land, there was not enough land for everyone in the village, and many people supplemented their income by working elsewhere. There were also some who rented land from the village's ancestral trusts for personal cultivation. Like Kwan Tei, Ma Mei Ha was also profoundly affected by the influx of refugees in the late 1940s. On the whole, however, Ma Mei Ha villagers absorbed tenant cultivators into the community, most of whom became vegetable cultivators. At the same time, many of Ma Mei Ha's indigenous villagers migrated to England (and Holland), when traditional padi cultivation became economically untenable. The agricultural cooperative in the village had been run largely by these outsider cultivators until the land was resumed for other purposes. Indigenous inhabitants of the village characterize their relationship with tenants as amicable, without any record of prior conflicts. When villagers speak of their own village and its actual inhabitants, they tend to describe it as a heterogenous community, despite its origin as a single-surname village. This contrasts sharply with Kwan Tei.

Due to outmigration by indigenous villagers of Ma Mei Ha, outsider tenants actually constitute a demographic majority of the village population. Nonetheless, on ritual occasions, both indigenous and outsider villagers participate as a single community. During the annual celebration of the goddess Tianhou's birthday at Ping Che, Ma Mei Ha is represented by two flower float associations. But unlike Kwan Tei, one is the traditional association linked with the establishment of the "Alliance of Six Villages" to which Ma Mei Ha belonged and the other is a modern association which native and outsider villagers can join without discrimination.

The village of Loi Tung is situated further along Shataukok Road away from Ma Mei Ha and in the direction of the Chinese border. It is separated by a hill from the villages in the adjacent district of Shataukok (settled almost entirely by Hakka cultivators, named after the market town of Shataukok) that straddles the border of China. The indigenous inhabitants of Loi Tung are members of a distant branch of the Deng lineage of Kam Tin. When they first settled in Loi Tung over two centuries ago, they cohabited the village with another group surnamed Lai. Eventually, however, the Lais moved and left the Dengs as the sole inhabitants of the village. Economically, the villagers of Loi Tung tended to be better off than its smaller neighboring villages, because of a relative abundance of ancestral trust land, which could be rotated among kinsmen in need of agricultural land. But they were not considered a large village community, thus formed an alliance with three other neighboring villages (literally called "the alliance of four") for purposes of regional self-defense. For much of the 19th century, feuds between neighboring alliances were commonplace, sometimes ending in deaths. As for local economy, up until World War II, most villagers were engaged in padi cultivation, with exception of two short-lived brick factories. Rice cultivation suffered tremendously after the war, forcing villagers to emigrate to Europe and Southeast Asia (in some cases, as far as New Guinea). Despite the massive influx of mainland refugees, Loi Tung did not absorb outsider tenants until the 1960s, when it had already suffered from outmigration and remaining villagers were in need of outside labor. By that time, some of the villagers had already shifted to vegetable cultivation, and occasional labor was sought in neighboring villages and from elsewhere. Outsider tenants whom they rented land to for vegetable cultivation lived outside the indigenous village, referred to now as Loi Tung North, in contrast to Loi Tung East, where the tenants aggregated their own community. Relations between indigenous villagers and outsider tenants are termed amicable, but indigenous villagers have been firm in maintaining the sanctity of the core village community, despite the fact that many of the houses have been vacated by kinsmen who migrated overseas, some of whom still own land and continue to collect rent. Tenancy contracts tended to vary from short to long term. It was not unusual for those who enjoyed amicable relations with their landlords not to sign written contracts, as long as they paid their rent, and the average contract in Loi Tung tended to be over ten years, but there were also instances of three and five year contracts, whose rental amount could be renegotiated with each separate contract. The agricultural cooperative in Loi Tung has also been operated mostly by outsider tenants.

In the domain of ritual activity, Loi Tung is represented by two flower float associations at the annual celebration of goddess Tianhou's birthday at Ping Che. Like the example of Ma Mei Ha, one is a traditional association affiliated with the original establishment of "the Alliance of Four" to which Loi Tung belonged. This association itself was founded by and based in the neighboring village of Man Uk Pin. Its membership is quite small, and its primary bond of solidarity tends to be more with the symbolic unity of this village alliance than with the cult of Tianhou per se, whose worship has been used as a communal focus. On the other hand, a second flower float association is a recent organization consisting only of outsider tenants of Loi Tung and their friends who live elsewhere (including Hong Kong and Kowloon) and join the annual Tianhou celebration primarily for purposes of cult worship. Membership in this latter association is over 400, which exceeds the population of Loi Tung itself. Thus, the two ritual associations reflect the identity and sense of community that differentiates the indigenous from outsider villagers. In the case of both Loi Tung and Ma Mei Ha, the acceptance of outsider tenants into the social community-at-large did not affect other kin and ritual relationships that characterized the existing nature of their village as single-lineage community. In the case of Loi Tung, hierarchy between indigenous and outsider was clearly marked by the latter's physical exclusion from residence in the indigenous village. Even as the indigenous village of Loi Tung suffered gradual depopulation, lack of numbers did not diminish their ability to deal with tenancy relationships on the land. Their traditional agnatic and ritual activities also ran parallel with those run by outsider tenants. In Ma Mei Ha, there appeared to be greater acceptance of a heterogenous living community, and although it had always been a land poor village, the existence of tenancy relationships on the land did not, strictly speaking, interfere within the social constituency of Ma Mei Ha indigenous villagers as an agnatic or other community. The diversity of experience in these villages showed the possibility of different strategies for assimilating the same complex variables.

Communal identity and social interaction at the regional level are reflected in the changing functions of the Tianhou temple cult at Ping Che that was once at the heart of a village alliance system locally known as *luk yeuk* (C) (=*liuyue*) or "the alliance of six". Today, the festival is celebrated yearly on Goddess Tianhou's birthday by over thirty parade float associations (*fa-pao hui*) representing resident constituencies in nearby villages and religious pilgrims from elsewhere. In name at least, this was a continuation of a festival that traditionally linked six clusters of villages in the Ping Che area through mutual self-defense and social welfare.

According to village elders, the Tianhou Temple at Ping Che was originally built about 150 years ago as Sam Heung Temple in the small village of Shui Lau Hang at the foot of a hill called Wo King Shan. Despite the popularity of Tianhou among fishermen, villagers here note that, as agriculturalists, they had a constant need for (irrigational) water that led them to pray to Tianhou. In addition to the general material wealth and overall spiritual well-being that has been attributed to their worship of Tianhou, stories also abound concerning the efficacy of Tianhou in an increase in fertility and size of population. In this sense, worship of Tianhou by people of this area was predicated less by a belief in the efficacy in general of Tianhou than by the efficacy of this particular goddess at this particular temple.

With exception of Ping Yeung, settled by Hakkas surnamed Chen, villages in this region up until the mid-19th century had been small in population, some occupied by as few as 8–10 households.[70] As small village communities, they were constantly harassed by villagers in neighboring Wong Bui Ling, surnamed Zhang. There were three major segments in the Zhang clan at Wong Bui Ling, the third segment of which was said to be the most hostile. One major locus of conflict with villages on the other side of the Shenzhen River was a monopoly which Wong Bui Ling exercised that ferried passengers to and from Shenzhen market. All of the boats were owned by people in Wong Bui Ling, and other villagers were forced to pay a toll to cross the river. When villagers in the Ping Che region, who depended on frequent transportation to the market, attempted to build a bridge to bypass the toll at Shenzhen, they were met by fierce resistance and constant harassment by the people of Wong Bui Ling. As a result of these incidents, 14 villages in the Ping Che region south of the Shenzhen River formed "The Alliance of Six". Luk Yeuk was itself a consolidation of six smaller alliances, each linking neighboring villages. As a self-defense network, it mirrored the late appearance of regional alliances in the New Territories, none of which had a history of more than 150 years (see Faure (1986: 126)). Three battles were fought with Wong Bui Ling. Villagers founded an association (*shengping she*) to commemorate the peace brought about in the end and set aside land in the villages of Lin Tong and Sze Ling Ha, which it used for communal ritual purposes. The names of those martyrs who died in battle were inscribed on a plaque in the Tianhou Temple.

Villagers maintained that the Tianhou goddess was responsible for their victory over Wong Bui Ling, which further attested to the spiritual efficacy (*ling*) of the goddess (at this temple). They then decided to rebuild the temple and move it to its present site at Ping Che, where it has stood from the middle of the 19th century. The rebuilding of the temple, the installation of the martyrs' tablet into the new temple and the ritual celebrations that later came about which linked the villages of Luk Yeuk to the temple thus established the basis of a regional alliance system that set the pattern of communal consciousness and intervillage relations.

The ritualization of this village alliance system in the form of a Tianhou temple cult began with the annual celebration of Tianhou's Birthday (23rd day of the 3rd month of the lunar year) by Luk Yeuk villagers at Ping Che.[71] As far as present villagers can remember, large-scale celebration of Tianhou's Birthday has taken place annually without interruption there for just over a century. Three essential features of the celebration have remained constant: 1) the site at Ping Che's Tianhou's temple, 2) the organization of groups called *fa-pao hui* (C), each representing each member village and 3) annual pilgrimage linking members of the *hui* (the local community) to the temple (and its patron god).

The temple was opened up one week prior to Tianhou's Birthday (it is closed to the public otherwise). Activities tended to be modest in style and ritualistic in tone. The *fa-pao* itself was just a shrine of the Tianhou goddess fixed atop a four-cornered table (*bat-wei toi* (C)) that was adorned with various religious icons. A contest was held to determine which *hui* had the right to take back whose *fa-pao* by firing rockets into the air. Youths from each village scrambled to pick up these rockets that were fired into the middle of an open arena (*cheung-pao* (C)). Such competitions often resulted in fighting, because the goddess images (*pao-dam* (C)) were considered to be valuable prizes. Aside from this contest, there was little other organized or sponsored activity, except for an occasional puppet theater.

In the "traditional" era, Luk Yeuk's regional temple alliance was composed of 19 member villages. The temple cult and its village alliance were inseparable in the sense that one gave rise to the other. The cult was not open to non-member villages, thus its scope as a pure religious sect devoted to disciples of the goddess was limited. All of this changed during the postwar era. The colonial policy of non-interference in local custom enabled the temple cult to continue. Pacification of the territory altered perhaps the kind of situation that gave rise to local defense alliances, and the open border with China enabled social intercourse with villages in the Shenzhen valley to go on as usual. After 1949, the closing of its border with the mainland cut off 4 of the 19 villages making up the *yeuk*. More importantly, however, influx of refugee settlers along with emigration of indigenous villagers in ensuing decades changed the balance of resident composition and socio-political complexion. The global forces that touched off complex changes in the nature of land and community also contributed to the transformation of the village-temple alliance system into a cult of religious celebration that nominally tied together all adjoining inhabitants of the villages as well as Tianhou pilgrims elsewhere in the form of a commercially motivated public festival or local carnival. In 1961, after a period of sparse participation on Tianhou's Birthday, a managing committee was set up, and it decided to throw open Tianhou's celebration to the general public. Non-indigenous villagers in the neighborhood of Ping Che began to form *fa-pao hui* groups, and the number of regular *fa-pao hui* eventually doubled. On the average, only 1/4 of these hui represented indigenous villagers, 1/2 represented agricultural cooperatives, crop-watching associations, regional associations (*tung-heung hui* (C)) and kung-fu youth clubs, in addition to (non-indigenous) tenant communities, in the immediate vicinity. The remaining 1/4 came from villages outside the original Luk Yeuk region; some were religious pilgrims from the city, but none expressed any special affiliation with Ping Che. Thus, the territorial consciousness that had been associated with the village temple alliance cult during the traditional past was now displaced by a different kind of public sphere and spiritual communion.

Each *fa-pao hui* constructed a *fa-pao* or decorated float bearing the image of the patron goddess that was presented to and displayed in front to the Tianhou Temple on the morning of her birthday. After the procession of *fa-pao* by *hui*, the *fa-pao* were deposited together in an open arena, after which a contest was held to determine which *fa-pao* each *hui* would take home (one could not bring home one's own *fa-pao*). By taking home the *fa-pao*, one was obliged to return the following year to offer another *fa-pao* on Tianhou's Birthday. Each *hui* then held a dinner feast at which time various pieces of the *fa-pao* were auctioned off to the highest bidder, in the form of a pledge to be fulfilled the following year.

Theater performances by professional Cantonese opera troupes held in a makeshift theater tent (*hei-pong* (C)) during the five days of the festival became a new and permanent attraction of the celebration. Somber religious celebration and light popular entertainment became parallel events in this public celebration. Rural Committees played an important role in organizing these celebrations by seeking commercial sponsorship and holding official banquets for public functionaries and celebrities. In terms of entrepreneurial management, each *fa-pao hui* contributed an annual registration fee to the Committee called "incense-oil money" (*heung-you chin* (C)), while sales of theater tickets and private donations made up the other operating costs. In terms of ritual display, the modest decorations of the Tianhou shrine (*bat-wai toi* (C)) that made up *fa-pao* in the past were gradually replaced by extravagant, highly decorated floats made by professional shops in Hong Kong that dwarfed a simple picture of Tianhou in the center, heightening the heuristic edification of the moment. As most people casually admitted, they were there just "to have a good time" (*go hing ha* (C)). Ritual effervescence was the message of the day that made this event both publicly appealing and commercially viable.

The transformation of the Tianhou cult at Ping Che reflects at one level the changing cultural spaces that have not only contributed to a new commercial and public sphere in a way that contrasted radically with the closed and hierarchical regional "social structure" of the past. At another level, it reflects the emergence and accommodation of inherently heterogeneous communities engendered by new politico-economic relations to the land. The kinds of social and ritual integration found there without doubt contrast also with territorial communities elsewhere.

In sum, the brief glimpses of changing village composition and relationships to land in the villages of Kwan Tei, Ma Mei Ha and Loi Tung can be understood to reflect less the result of changes in Fanling District in particular than of the diversity of strategies that villagers utilized to accommodate insider and outsider communities in light of the complexity of indigenous origins and the broad pattern of global influences and displacements. It is simplistic to say, as anthropologists and historians have previously argued, that these changes in composition follow primarily as a functions of variations in a kinship ideal. In any one case, change may be the result of a complex variety of influences, any of which can be perceived differently by different people. In contrast to the experience of villages in other areas, such as Shatin and Tai Po Tau, the relative proximity to urban influences no doubt presents yet another factor. But more importantly, in each case, notions of land and community are polysemic; in practice both reinforce each other. The landed community is not just a customary entity but an ongoing social institution.

As social institution, the village and its intrinsic notion of community must actually be understood in reference to a complex of variables. Postwar changes in the colonial administration of land directly affected the viability of social livelihood in relation to land as well as the integrity of the territorial community itself, but these changes had to be assessed in the specific context of an emerging market system that had been transforming the fabric of society as a whole. The changes in the nature of the landed community were analytically distinct from the nature of kin relations within the lineage community itself, which in many instances remained constant, as members migrated overseas and continued to maintain ties with their natal village. In this regard, there were no doubt kinsmen whose natal ties dissolved over time, but this was not just the function of any one dominant factor. From a larger viewpoint, the diversity of response to material changes seen over a broad spectrum of rural society in the New Territories attested firmly to the diversity of strategies that people at different positions of (geographic and politico-economic) power used to survive under conditions of fierce, competitive change. To say the least, changes on the land (in its many senses) responded in the first and final analysis to peculiar socio-political conditions taken in its entirety that were fundamentally different from a prior "colonial" era and all other eras as well.

In retrospect, it is possible to view these underlying socio-political conditions in the New Territories purely as a product of transformations in the marketplace or as a function of rising population and corresponding land values that led people to inevitably adopt a drastic change of lifestyle. Events at this level of individual concrete actions provided the staple substance for unilineal narratives of progress that have become a common framework for later histories and anthropologies of Hong Kong society. Yet contrary to illusions that people "made" their own history, it is clear that global political and economic conditions during the early postwar era created a market situation in which choices were limited at best. It is perhaps more accurate to say that the political strife of the Cold War and the government's dual-edged policy of macrosocial interventionism-cum-microeconomic utilitarianism created tensions in society that exacerbated the anachronistic status of the New Territories in a changing Hong Kong while at the same time drawing the fate of people and communities into a common life struggle whose survival was based on the fiction of individual maximization and the reality of class/ethnic exploitation. In the various conflicts over land policy, it was obvious that the debate over the nature of "rational" land development was a process that inherently assimilated the fate of the leased territory into the colony as a whole in ways that dualized essentially incompatible elements of customary practice and state regulation. The socially disruptive consequences of the government's attempt to regulate categories of land use in the context of urban and village development were not dissimilar to the effect on enclosures in 17th century England prior to the advent of a market capitalist system.[72] The imposition of alien categories on the land perhaps set the tone for a primordial "clash of civilizations" that dualized self and other, but the experience of the postwar era was a crisis of processual incorporation in which the expansion and institutionalization of state modernity first disciplined then in turn radicalized diverse life-trajectories on the land. Not everyone chose to "sell out"; many "traditional" villages resisted any impetus to change, and there was a wide range of permutation between these two extremes. More importantly, all of this was a product of the same "great transformation", in Polanyi's (1944) terms. The fictions that drove the dynamics of an emerging market society had important consequences not only for ushering in modernity but reifying tradition as well.

NOTES

[1]   A similar mocking letter was written by *Chishi niandai* (The 70s) to the Queen, addressed "Dear Mrs. Mountbatten", not blaming her for evils done in her name:

> ... nor was it you who have decided that the people of HK should remain colonized and have no say in things which vitally affect them for years to come. Or who refused to grant compulsory primary education to children, thus blatantly vio-

lating inalienable human rights. Or who implemented a most inadequate resettlement programme transplanting people from one slum to another slum. Or who greedily sent back to the Bank of England annual financial surplus of Hong Kong without giving due consideration to the dire need for improvements in social welfare and health services. Or who allowed the bus companies to raise fares and to penalise the poor for the sake of the rich. ... Come to Hong Kong some time. But only as an ordinary private world citizen and not as Queen. And we would make you really welcome. No VIP planes, no red carpets, no sycophantic official receptions. But we would make you really welcome — as we would do all world citizens in the spirit of brotherhood of human kind. (Walker 1972: 24)

2 Instability of the postwar situation and the need to eliminate corruption and graft in the current administration were cited as major reasons for the colonial government to resume sovereignty over Hong Kong (CO 537/1662, "Hong Kong Administration"). The Chinese government made explicit requests for the return of the New Territories and the general abolition of extraterritoriality, while the British held that Chinese jurisdiction was inconsistent with military requirements (CO 537/1656 and CO 537/1657, "Future of the New Territories", parts 1–2; also CO 537/4800, "Status of the New Territories"). Even the status of Kowloon Walled City became a topic of renewed debate that sparked protests both in Hong Kong and Kowloon (CO 537/3706, "Future Policy: Kowloon Walled City"; CO 537/3709, "Kowloon Walled City: Canton Incident"). Needless to say, the British prevailed.

3 There are subtle differences between Marxist and Polanyiist approaches to the problem, and it is important to emphasize that this social transformation refers first to qualitative (systemic) rather than just quantitative (material) changes. Whether or not one agrees with Cooper's (1982: 25) argument that Hong Kong was "a veritable proving ground for Marxist theory where the enterprising student of Marxist political economy can literally watch chapters of *Capital* unfold before his eyes", this should not detract from the spirit of his critique. At issue then is a conception of society embedded in representations of Hong Kong as "John Stuart Mill's other island" (Smith 1966) or in Rabushka's (1976, 1979) classic utilitarian depiction of Hong Kong as the epitome of free-market principles (following Milton Friedman). That they and other social scientists of Hong Kong accent the material aspects of Hong Kong's growth at the expense of other features reflects less their "objective" description of that development and more their "subjective" assessment of the significant or relevant dimensions of social change and societal values. At a local level, it is also somewhat surprising that, despite the title of Potter's (1968) book, one gets little insight into what capitalism is, even in a rural context.

4   For an account of prewar industrialization in Hong Kong, see Leeming (1975).

5   Blackie's (1954: 10) report on agriculture noted that in 1937 the New Territories produced only 20% of the vegetable requirement of a population of about 800,000, which increased drastically to 60% in 1970, feeding a population of over 2,250,000.

6   A 23 pp. "Report on the Possibilities of Agricultural Extension in the Colony" was submitted to the government in 1940 that outlined the status of various rural industries in different parts of the New Territories at the end of the prewar era. In contrast, for a demographic account of postwar migration to Hong Kong, see Davis (1964). Data by Hong Kong Census and Statistics Department for 1947–67 showed that land for padi cultivation was replaced by vegetable cultivation almost acre for acre. The latter was usually rented to immigrant tenants on a short-term cash basis. From 1958–67, area for vegetable cultivation rose from 3000 to 9000 acres, while padi land decreased from 23,000 to 14,500 acres (HKCSD 1969: 72).

7   In this regard, Krause's (1988: S61) characterization of Hong Kong's minimalist government policy is misleading. Its "positive non-intervention" must be viewed in response to global political factors and not just in terms of fiscal non-regulation. Chan (1983) has also avoided depicting Hong Kong as a stereotypical laissez-faire economy, yet his "laissez-faire colonialism" was not free of stereotyping either.

8   This table (Chow 1977: 358) shows that while laborers enjoyed a definite rise in real wages in the postwar era, it did not occur until after the initial "boom period". Chen (1984) also notes that wages increases have been rather moderate. Between 1965–73, real wages increased 4.9% per year, while labor productivity increased 5.1% per year. From 1973–79, the discrepancy between annual real wage increase (2.1%) and annual labor productivity increase (5.7%) widened ostensibly.

9   A group called the Hong Kong Research Project (HKRP 1974: 25–26) summarized neatly this dual aspect of Hong Kong's economic growth in the following terms:

> One finds that during Hong Kong's period of fastest growth and greatest prosperity that the Colony had by far the highest level of utilisation of plants in the textile industry in Asia: in 1965 looms were employed the equivalent of 24 hours a day for 360 days in the year. No other country approached even 75% of this figure. That in 1968 Hong Kong workers had the longest working day and the longest working week of city dwellers in Southeast Asia: 58% worked 7 days a week, and 52% worked 10 hours or more a day. There is no legal limit on the hours worked by males over 18. When the government introduced a regulation making four days rest a month com-

pulsory (these four days include Sundays, not in addition to them) many workers signed agreements with employers to forfeit holidays in order to keep up their income to the minimum necessary to live.

[10] As Wong (1972: 52–3) aptly put it, "China's uninterrupted cheap food supply to Hong Kong had played the role of subsidizing Hong Kong's export-propelled type of economic growth. . . . China's creditability in the Hong Kong food market can be explained in terms of economic pragmatism rather than 'altruistic' attitude."

[11] Wong's (1972: 55) table shows the extent to which Hong Kong was dependent on food imports from China. One should note, too, the absence of 1948–58 figures.

[12] See SCMP June 28, 1965, "Farming for Living in N.T. on the Wane".

[13] C.T. Wong (1964: 66) of the Agricultural and Forestry Department notes that no official record has statistically calculated the proportion of tenancy in rural Hong Kong, but "practical investigation and observation indicates that more than 70% of our farmers belong to the tenant class, sub-tenant or part-owner class".

[14] This problem was first brought to public attention on March 2, 1950 in a South China Morning Post article entitled "Landlords' Demands on Farmer: Double Rent or Quit". Most of those affected were vegetable growers and immigrant settlers.

[15] Tenants both on padi land traditionally paying rent in kind and on vegetable plots cultivating cash crops seemed to be equally affected, sometimes facing yearly hikes of up to 3–4 times previous rent (see "NT Farmers Demand Gov't Action to End Land Rent Racket", Sunday Herald, March 19, 1950). Thus the crisis centered on the right of landlords to arbitrarily raise rents and to forcibly evict tenants, who customarily (by verbal arrangement) enjoyed rights of continued cultivation ("The Rent Racket in the New Territories: Dozens of Farmers in Ping Shan Area Affected", SCMP March 19, 1950).

[16] K. Keen, District Commissioner of the New Territories, summarized the official position in "Farmers' Complaints: Press Reports Said to Be Alarmist" (see SCMP March 24, 1950) by downplaying the crisis generally.

[17] HKRS 337, Deposit 1 Serial 2807, "Agricultural Land in the Colony: 1) Dispute between Landlords and Tenants on . . . 2) Question of Application of Landlords and Tenants Ordinance to . . .", Enclosure 16/1, March 31, 1950.

[18] Reproduced in South China Morning Post, April 20, 1950.

[19] HKRS 337, Deposit 1 Serial 2807, "Agricultural Land in the Colony: 1) Dispute between Landlords and Tenants on. . . 2) Question of Application of Landlords and Tenants Ordinance to. . .", Enclosure 32, March 21, 1951.

[20] HKRS 337, Deposit 1 Serial 2807, "Agricultural Land in the Colony: 1) Dispute between Landlords and Tenants on. . . 2) Question of Application of Landlords

and Tenants Ordinance to. . .", Correspondence of March 9, 1951 (T.G. Strangeways) and March 15, 1951 (J. Cater).

[21] HKRS 337, Deposit 1 Serial 2807, "Agricultural Land in the Colony: 1) Dispute between Landlords and Tenants on. . . 2) Question of Application of Landlords and Tenants Ordinance to. . .", Correspondence of November 30, 1951.

[22] HKRS 337, Deposit 1 Serial 2807, "Agricultural Land in the Colony: 1) Dispute between Landlords and Tenants on. . . 2) Question of Application of Landlords and Tenants Ordinance to. . .", Correspondence of May 12, 1952.

[23] HKRS 337, Deposit 1 Serial 2807, "Agricultural Land in the Colony: 1) Dispute between Landlords and Tenants on. . . 2) Question of Application of Landlords and Tenants Ordinance to. . .", Correspondence of June 6, 1952.

[24] HKRS 337, Deposit 1 Serial 2807, "Agricultural Land in the Colony: 1) Dispute between Landlords and Tenants on. . . 2) Question of Application of Landlords and Tenants Ordinance to. . .", Enclosure 60, November 1955.

[25] HKRS 337, Deposit 1 Serial 2807, "Agricultural Land in the Colony: 1) Dispute between Landlords and Tenants on. . . 2) Question of Application of Landlords and Tenants Ordinance to. . .", Enclosure 63, November 28, 1955.

[26] HKRS 337, Deposit 1 Serial 2807, "Agricultural Land in the Colony: 1) Dispute between Landlords and Tenants on. . . 2) Question of Application of Landlords and Tenants Ordinance to. . .", Enclosure 64, December 1, 1955.

[27] HKRS 337, Deposit 1 Serial 2807, "Agricultural Land in the Colony: 1) Dispute between Landlords and Tenants on. . . 2) Question of Application of Landlords and Tenants Ordinance to. . .", Enclosure 65, June 1, 1956.

[28] HKRS 337, Deposit 1 Serial 2807, "Agricultural Land in the Colony: 1) Dispute between Landlords and Tenants on. . . 2) Question of Application of Landlords and Tenants Ordinance to. . .", Enclosure 66, January 27, 1956.

[29] The Hong Kong and Kowloon Chinese Farming and Agriculture Association, which first represented the tenants in their grievances, was founded under left-wing leadership but was later dissolved by the government in the early 50s as a threat to political security (Aijmer 1986: 244–45).

[30] Aijmer's (1972: 202) argument that "indigenous villagers were able to remain in their traditional rice world by giving up rice cultivation" and that "change in land use in the New Territories was no simple process generated by maximization of profits" is a gross mischaracterization. On the other hand, Lau's (1981) study of "utilitarian familism" superficially reflected the nature of change in traditional Chinese kin relations in urban Hong Kong to some extent but failed to note that, while utilitarian values facilitated one's adaptation to a market based society, they served in the end to disrupt other preexisting social relationships and institutions.

[31] This, of course, did not prevent the local land officer from collecting his "tea money" (e.g., Aijmer 1973: 66, 1975: 563).

[32] Internally, this proposal was debated by those in the upper echelons of the District Commissioner's Office and Colonial Secretary's Office on the one hand, who wished an expedient way of eradicating illegal building structures, and those

in Public Works and the Land Offices on the other, who viewed it as a burden on understaffed services (see HKRS 337, Dep.4, Ser.191, "Unauthorized Structures in the New Territories", Correspondence of January 26 to July 31, 1950).

[33] CSO 4865/06, "Notes on Land for Use by District Offices", October 30, 1950.

[34] CSO 4865/06, "Notes on Land for Use by District Offices", October 30, 1950.

[35] HKRS 163, 1/2805, "'Conversion' of Agricultural Land in the New Territories to Building Status", Attachment 6, November 9, 1949.

[36] HKRS 163, 1/2805, "'Conversion' of Agricultural Land in the New Territories to Building Status", Attachment 1, January 15, 1949.

[37] The various petitions sent by the Kuk to the government to protest land policy in the past were reproduced in a pamphlet circulated by the Kuk entitled *Xinjie nungdi zhuan wudi wenti youguan wenxian* (Materials pertaining to the problem of conversion of agricultural to house land in the New Territories), printed in May 1956. Documents included a petition written to Shouson Chou and two Chinese representatives in December 1923, a petition written to the Land Officer, Tai Po, in 1923, a petition written to the Governor in November 1923, a petition written to Clementi in 1924, a collective letter on behalf of all New Territories landowners written to the British Foreign Office in 1925 urging the abolition of the Hong Kong government's New Territories land policy, and a petition written to the Governor on May 10, 1956 protesting the government's policy of land conversion premiums.

[38] HKRS 163, 1/2805, "'Conversion' of Agricultural Land in the New Territories to Building Status", Barrow to Colonial Secretary, November 14, 1949.

[39] "Notes for Use in the District Office, New Territories" (CSO 4865/1906), that were widely circulated among Land Officers during the early administration of the territory, contained the following passage regarding the status of New Kowloon:

> In New Kowloon a premium to be assessed by the Director of Public Works is chargeable for conversion of agricultural holdings (vide CSO 5012/1907; 2018/1908). Outside New Kowloon no premium is charged on conversion of land granted under the Land Court Judgments; but when agricultural land bought at public auction is converted, in addition to the increased Crown rent, a difference between the premium paid and the premium required on sale of the same land for building will be charged (CSO 807/06).

[40] HKRS 163, 1/2805, "'Conversion' of Agricultural Land in the New Territories to Building Status", Jones to Colonial Secretary, September 8, 1950.

[41] HKRS 163, 1/2805, "'Conversion' of Agricultural Land in the New Territories to Building Status", Attachment 8/1, Heung Yee Kuk to Keen, August 14, 1950.

[42] HKRS 163, 1/2805, "'Conversion' of Agricultural Land in the New Territories to Building Status", Keen to Colonial Secretary, September 12, 1950.

43 HKRS 163, 1/2805, "'Conversion' of Agricultural Land in the New Territories to Building Status", Barrow to Colonial Secretary, November 22, 1950.

44 HKRS 163, 1/2805, "'Conversion' of Agricultural Land in the New Territories to Building Status", D.C.S. to Colonial Secretary, March 16, 1954.

45 HKRS 163, 1/2805, "'Conversion' of Agricultural Land in the New Territories to Building Status", Attachment 47/2, Ho to Grantham, May 10, 1956.

46 HKRS 163, 1/2805, "'Conversion' of Agricultural Land in the New Territories to Building Status", Attachment 56, Barnett to Colonial Secretary, July 3, 1956.

47 HKRS 163, 1/2805, "'Conversion' of Agricultural Land in the New Territories to Building Status", Attachment 56, Jones to Colonial Secretary, August 22, 1956.

48 HKRS 163, 1/2805, "'Conversion' of Agricultural Land in the New Territories to Building Status", Attachment 71, Barnett to Colonial Secretary, September 20, 1956.

49 HKRS 163, 1/2805, "'Conversion' of Agricultural Land in the New Territories to Building Status", Attachment 85/1, Kuk to Barnett, December 21, 1956.

50 HKRS 163, 1/2805, "'Conversion' of Agricultural Land in the New Territories to Building Status", Attachment 92/1, Record of Meeting, February 4, 1957.

51 HKRS 163, 1/2805, "'Conversion' of Agricultural Land in the New Territories to Building Status", Attachment 95, David to Kuk, February 16, 1957.

52 HKRS 163, 1/2805, "'Conversion' of Agricultural Land in the New Territories to Building Status", Colonial Secretary to P.R.O., January 4, 1958.

53 In its reply to the Colonial Secretary's letter of February 16, the Kuk claimed that the three points put forward by Barnett were unilateral and personal views, then reiterated the same four points in its petition that the Colonial Secretary had apparently failed to answer. See HKRS 163, 1/2805, "'Conversion' of Agricultural Land in the New Territories to Building Status", Attachment 133, July 17, 1958.

54 HKRS 163, 1/2805, "'Conversion' of Agricultural Land in the New Territories to Building Status", Attachment 147, Holmes to Colonial Secretary, March 20, 1959.

55 Excerpted from *New Territories Heung Yee Kuk Special Issue* (1980–81), p.46.

56 A detailed listing of the Kuk's rules, including procedures for electing members to its governing body of Executive Councillors is reproduced in *Xinjie gailan* (New Territories General Report) of 1954, Volume 1, pp.121–22.

57 See Lam (1986: 1–14) for a concise history of the Heung Yee Kuk organization.

58 CO 1030/1333, "Heung Yee Kuk", Executive Council Proceedings, undated.

59 Excerpts of secret reports were included in CO 1030/1333, "Heung Yee Kuk".

60 The scope of who constituted indigenous people can be questioned as well. The government increasingly restricted "indigenous" to mean pre-1898 inhabitants and their descendants, mostly as a result of being forced by terms of the treaty to give concessions to inhabitants of the leased territory. For the conservative inhabitants of (established) communities in the New Territories, "indigenous" generally meant pre-1898 inhabitants as well, but this was a function more of their fear of being overrun by outsiders. As late as 1965, the inclusion of two

"non-natives" in the Executive Committee of the Heung Yee Kuk caused dissent among many members who called for the addition of a clause in the New Territories Ordinance to exclude outsiders (SCMP April 14, 1965, "Non-Natives in Heung Yee Kuk Opposed").

[61] See, for example, XXG 1976b: xiv–xv, XXN 1966–67a: 26, XXN 1966–67b: 39, XZ 1971a: 2–3, XZ 1971c: 12, XN 1970–71a: 7–9, XN 1970–71b: 145, XN 1970–71c: 1–2, XN 1976: 54–56, XN 1977a: 50–56, XN 1977e: 464–65, XN 1977f: 464, XN 1977g: 457–58, ZB 1979: 3, ZB 1989. For detailed historical analysis, see Liu (1976, 1977).

[62] As expected, the Kuk objected to the terms of the Letters B system. A petition was sent by the Tsuen Wan Rural Committee, maintaining that genuine residents, not speculators, should reap the benefits of growth in the area. Moreover, small farmers were most disadvantaged, since they generally could not meet the 5: 2 land conversion ratio, which forced them reluctantly to sell the land (SCMP September 6, 1963, "Government Petitioned by Tsuen Wan Rural Committee").

[63] See XXG 1976a: x–xii, XXG 1976c: xvii, XXN 1964–66b, XN 1977f: 461–62, XN 1978a: 36, XN 1978b: 38, XN 1980–81: 59–60, and XN 1982: 49–50.

[64] There were also disputes pertaining to inequities of reimbursement arising out of forced relocation in cases of town development. In Shatin, most of the 28 shop operators who paid $50/mo. in rent in an old market complex facing demolition were reluctant to move to a new block in Lek Yuen, where rent was $1700/mo. and when the government only offered $16,000 in compensation for relocation to new shop outlets that cost $40,000 (SCMP June 17, 1976, "Angry Scenes at Shatin").

[65] Leading up to official passage of the Small House Policy, the Kuk voiced its protest over many of the details, as exemplified by one petition that demanded the following: 1) regarding village houses, a) building area should be increased from 700 to 100 sq.ft., b) villagers should be eligible to build their own house at age 17, not 21, c) builders should be allowed to build up to 25 ft. without approval by the Department of Public Works; 2) villagers should not be required to pay conversion premium when building their own houses; 3) reasonable compensation should be given for land resumed for public projects, the present rates being "nominal" and below market value; 4) villagers should be allowed to develop land designated by government for town planning in accordance with official plans, arguing that they are unable to make good use of land, because plans are made 10 years in advance (SCMP March 3, 1972, "Kuk in Plan for Protest March"). The nitpicking of these complaints showed that matters of detail often outweighed those of principle.

[66] Wolf's (1959: 209) remarks on the effect of utilitarian logic in maximizing labor productivity in the hacienda system are quite relevant in this regard:

> On the hacienda, personal motives were harnessed to maintain the regime of labor. Given the appropriate conditions, men make peons of themselves.

[67] These documents and relevant correspondence with the government appeared in a Heung Yee Kuk publication entitled *The New Territories Community of Hong Kong under Colonial Administration*, printed privately in 1977.

[68] This speech, given on February 17, 1981, was on careful reading really a subtle challenge to the colonial government's authority to unilaterally define social policy in the New Territories. The threat of land expropriation that led the Kuk initially to oppose land resumption now became an issue of "fair price". The principle of free land conversion that prompted the Kuk initially to oppose any imposition of premiums was now replaced by politicking on building and legal specifications on village houses and rights of participation in the government's policy toward land development. In a petition of April 23, 1977, the Kuk's focus then shifted to the need for increased democratic representation, epitomized by 1) sharing of political rights, 2) sharing of development profit, 3) sharing of development opportunities, and 4) sharing of public services. These were rights basic to all free societies.

[69] Aijmer's (1975: 568) conclusion that "as an outsider in a village you can rent either a house or a piece of agricultural land but cannot have both" exaggerates the more important point to be made, namely that residence and agriculture, in both analytical and native terms, entailed distinct concepts pertaining to land. Moreover, regardless of whether one can live off (till) the land and/or live (reside) on it too, the tenant still stands in a hierarchical relationship *vis-a-vis* the other villagers, which has little to do with land, in either of the two senses.

[70] The Xinan Gazetteer of 1688 notes the existence of two villages, Tan Chuk Hang and Shan Kai Wat. In 1819, this was expanded to include Ping Yeung, Lee Uk Tsuen, Lo Fang, Kwan Tei, Heung Yuen and Heung Sai. (Ng 1983, Maps 7–8)

[71] On this occasion, rites of propitiation (*da-jiu* (C) =*jianjiao*) were also held once every ten years by villagers of the *yeuk*. Each member household contributed $2 toward ritual expenses. Male villagers aged 16 and above joined in a communal feast to eat a meal of stewed pork mixed with salted vegetables and bean curd (*ham-choi* (C)). The *da-jiu* was discontinued during the depression of the 1930s.

[72] Polanyi's (1944: 34) observation in this regard is both astute and germane:

> An official document of 1607 prepared for the use of the Lords of the Realm set out the problem of change in one powerful phrase: 'The poor man shall be satisfied in his end: Habitation; and the gentleman not hindered in his desire: Improvement'. This formula appears to take for granted the essence of purely economic progress, which is to achieve improvement at the price of social dislocation. But it also hints at the tragic necessity by which the poor man clings to his hovel, doomed by the rich man's desire for a public improvement which profits him privately.

CHAPTER FOUR

The Meaning of Tradition in a Progressive Society

D<i>englong shengjia; mingfeng fenghui.</i>
The fame of ascending the dragon's gate (scholarly success);
the reputation of the calling of the phoenix (good fortune)
(from two ceremonial placards hung in front of the
gate of the main ancestral hall, Wo Hang Village)

REINTERPRETING THE CULTURAL LOGIC OF KINSHIP IN LOCALITY AND HISTORY

The history of a Chinese lineage-village is not just the result of juxtaposing descent principles and territorial conditions, nor is it the aggregate history of its component social parts, namely households and higher order kin groups. Yet most of the ethnographic and local historical analyses in the prevailing literature have usually been written in one or the other genre. Anthropologists, beginning with theories of kinship, have admirably gone beyond synchronic structural accounts of local society by viewing both lineage and village in historical light. Historians on the other hand have supplemented their microsocial accounts of rural life by aligning it in reference to the rise and fall of great lineages. In both cases, few have questioned the concepts of kinship and locality upon which most such ethno-historical accounts have based their understanding of "traditional" village society leading up to the present day. What constitutes tradition for anthropologists and historians of local Chinese society is an important issue that must be confronted directly before one can then assess the impact of colonial change upon these local institutions, whose policies were predicated also on the maintenance of tradition.

The confluence of anthropology and history in a Chinese context appears to be attributable less to the structural-functionalist model that Maurice Freedman adopted from Radcliffe-Brown's notion of social structure and Fortes' concept of descent that formed the common framework of anthropological debates on kinship in general, as outlined at the outset, and more to the transition from Freedman's first monograph (1958), which spelled out the paradigmatic relationship between lineage organization and the existence of a complex functionally integrated society, to his second monograph (1966), which focused on the direct relationship between descent group ideology and the stability of territorial (village) organization. This relationship between sociologically concrete (local level) descent groups and actual (residential) village composition was what merged the interests of anthropologists and historians in their study of local Chinese society and brought together the eventual confluence between kinship models and historical approaches.[1] In effect, variation in descent group organization became in this sense also a key barometer of territorial solidarity in a village context. Along this axis of descent-cum-village organization, familial households and higher order lineages were seen as different levels of the same kind of domestic organization or kin bonding. What then was archetypically traditional in such an understanding of Chinese kinship was the strength or existence of the descent bond and the political or economic importance attached to it. To say the least, this characterization of traditional Chinese kin organization and its territorial manifestations has dominated the large majority of subsequent research on local society in the New Territories of Hong Kong, if not elsewhere in Taiwan and mainland China, to such a degree that most writings on modernization, colonization and globalization view their impact on tradition almost exclusively in terms of a variation of an implicit patrilineal or lineage-village ideal.

In contrast, I hope to show that our misunderstanding of land, village and kinship in the New Territories of Hong Kong is in part a consequence of our poor understanding of the kinship and local principles that are constitutive of family, household, lineage and village. This fundamental misunderstanding has further ramifications for our current misunderstanding of the colonial experience in that same context of local society. In this regard, native concepts of *zong* (common ancestral tie), *jia* (familial incorporation) and *qin* (kin relativity) constitute three core principles that underlie and crosscut the functioning of household families, higher order agnatic clusters and residential villages in ways that shed a clearer light on the legal codification, systemic routinization and disciplinary ordering of tradition and traditional social organization in the New Territories. More than an invention of tradition, its institutionalization by the state has sown the seeds for the destruction of that traditional lifestyle, despite appearances to the contrary.

The unambiguous existence of patrilineal ideology and descent group based residential villages in China have appeared to give credence to descent theory and its applicability to a Chinese context. However, it is necessary first of all to show how descent in its classical functionalist interpretation differs from the notions of *zong, jia* and *qin,* which constitute the basic morphemes of Chinese kin relations, then show how they apply to a characteristically unique understanding of Chinese domestic organization in terms of *zongzu* (clan, lineage), *jiazu* (family) and *jiating* (household), not to mention the village as an aggregation of households having ties to land. This reformulation of the problem, no matter how elementary it appears to be, has in my opinion important ramifications for sorting out in a local context what maintenance of "custom", "indigenous" rights to the land and nature of the "traditional" village really refer to as a precondition for understanding the effects of "colonialism" and "modernity" that claim to have defended those value systems.

It is curious to point out that Chinese anthropologists considered the idea of "descent" different enough from native terms to render it as *shixi* ("generation line"). Although many of the usual Chinese characters used to designate agnatic relationships and groups would simply be translated into English as descent, it is perhaps more accurate to say that many of these native terms have connotations or deeper symbolic associations that go beyond the geometric notion of generation line. In other words, more than simply descent, they invoke implicit associations with other concepts or institutions not easily rendered by any single word. Apart from the usual dictionary definitions, I argue that Chinese domestic groups (which encompass all levels of family and ancestral organization) are representable by the basic morphemes *zong, jia* and *qin,* that more importantly reflect core notions of "ritual transmission", "social incorporation" and "kin relativity", respectively, and engender processes essential to the continued (d)evolution of all domestic groups.

It is strange also, given the heightened attention devoted by anthropologists to the statistical distribution of single versus multiple lineage villages in China, that no one has bothered to make deeper sense of the obvious fact that in China there is no "descent" group which is at the same time an "ancestral" group, that is to say, a group of people whose identity and ties to shared substance are defined primarily in reference to a set of ritual obligations or practices. This devaluation of symbolic concepts is of course largely due to the embeddedness of functionalist notions of descent to a theory of social structure but also reflects a failure to take seriously the power of such a priori concepts in explaining the nature and function of existing social institutions. In essence, *zong* (which literally means "shrine") does not just indicate a relationship between ascendant and descendant through transmission of rites and property; it is a process of transmission that necessitates worshipping a common shrine or ancestor as the basic condition for its continued existence. Being of the same *zong* (*tongzong*) presupposes partaking of a common *qi* (breath), which among Chinese is transmitted exclusively through males. But while the core obligation to continue the line falls on those share a common *qi* (as though of the same "blood"), it is really the act of worship itself (through various religious associations pertaining to the life of the soul) that sustains the existence of any group predicated on *zong* (such as a *zongzu*). In this sense, accumulation of property is not really the means to a self-sustaining end, as might be the case of a typical corporation; it is always in the first instance a means for maintaining the continuity of worship. The latter prerogative sets serious limitations on the exchangeability and alienability of land as communal kin property, which should be a basic concern for understanding the nature of a "lineage". The inalienability of land in the context of a lineage is not exactly the same as the fixed attachment of a village to its land, although both notions of boundedness overlap in practice.

The specific association of *zong* with ritual transmission is important also for what it is not. There is nothing in the notion of *zong* or institutions based on *zong* that stipulates any intrinsic or necessary relation between lineages (descent) and villages (residence). Of course, lineage-villages do exist, but this is another way of saying that their existence cannot possibly be the consequence of a descent principle (native notion of *zong*) per se. In fact, it shall be argued later that the lineage-village was a recent historical creation that was in large part galvanized by a basic redefinition of the village and the role of common worship groups (i.e. lineages) in consolidating the solidarity of the territorial community. Needless to say, the implicit conjunction of descent and locality in the form of lineage-villages should be the first and foremost illusion that underlies the misguided perceptions of the "traditional" village put forth by anthropologists and historians of China.

The term *jia* is frequently translated as "family", but as a concept in itself its core meaning is very different from consainguineal notions of kinship and is reproduced in various social groupings based on it (such as household and lineage). Unlike *zong*, which accents filiation through continuity of worship, *jia* suggests a different kind of commonality that is not necessarily kin based. Its use in word-compounds such as *jiazu* ("family"), *jiating* ("household") *jiaxiang* ("hometown") and *guojia* ("nation") indicates a homogeneity based upon a common life situation that is at the same time presentist or horizontally inclusive instead of historically or vertically all-encompassing. Moreover, its degree of boundedness is subjective or speaker defined. The term *jiazu* (family) can be used to denote a uterine family in strict terms or a flexible aggregate of people, "expandable to infinity, really to an extent that all under heaven is a family", as Fei Xiaotong (1947: 42) put it.[2] In other words, flexibility of incorporation is more a characteristic of *jia* as basic morpheme, and its emphasis on a presentist, situational definition of commonality contrasts it with the focus of *zong* on continuity of ritual obligation. In this sense, *jia* really denotes "division through inclusion" and is most aptly represented by the parallel concepts of *fang* ("segment") and *tang* ("house"). The words *fang* and *tang* are, literally speaking, "the side room" and "parlor" of a house. They can both be used to denote a family, but clearly from different angles. *Fenfang* ("division into segments") and *tongtang* ("being of the same house") symbolize parallel processes of the domestic cycle that in semantic terms are not interchangeable (i.e., it would be incorrect to say *fentang* or *tongfang*). The system of exchange relations plays an equally important role as descent concepts per se in establishing *jia* identity and maintaining kin solidarity. This is an aspect of the Chinese family that has been relatively neglected by anthropologists and views family formation instead as the manifestation of affinal gift exchange beginning with marriage, sustained through child birth and culminating in affinal obligations at death. Finally, a clear sense of corporateness is associated with *jia*, but the defining criteria that makes *jiazu* families, *jiaxiang* villages and *guojia* nations in this regard, namely as concrete social organizations, does not derive from the notion of *jia* itself but the functional characteristics of its attached entity. These characteristics will be spelled out at length accordingly in a later context. Their relevance to lineage should be obvious.

The notion of *qin* (kin relativity) contrasts with *zong* and *jia* in that it does not engender social organization in a strict functionalist sense, nonetheless its relevance to a sociological understanding of families, households and villages in a local Chinese context cannot be underestimated. It is easy to distill the idea of *qin* directly from its common usage in the term *qinqi* ("relatives" or kindred), from which relative intimacy and closeness is simply a function of kin distance. More than just a barometer of kin distance, the importance of *qin* should be gauged in relation more to the nature of the phenomenon being engendered. *Qin* appears to find paradigmatic expression in the context of *wufu* ("the five mourning grades"), which is not just the folk principle by which ritual obligations are specified for different categories of kinsmen in a purely local or customary context. Ritual specifications for *wufu* have also been the object of intense debate in nearly every dynastic compilation on *li* (ritual propriety). The notions of hierarchical relativity encoded in *wufu* find similar expression in the constitution of households, villages and agnatic groups, insofar as the scope and identity of such kin groups, contrary to most hard and fast sociological-cum-jural definitions, tend to be in essence the products of flexible and subjective definition. Even the egocentricity of kindred or relatives in an everyday sense are not, strictly speaking, irrelevant considerations in explaining the scope of the agnatic bond in a village context. In other words, one should not assume the epistemological priority of the agnatic principle as an index of social solidarity, even in the obvious context of a "single-lineage village". That ties to kindred can override agnatic ties in a typical lineage village, even in matters pertaining to land and property, underscores to the contrary the necessity of spelling out the different institutional contexts within which *qin* operates. To say the least, the notion of kin relativity exists in a genealogical understanding of lineage or family denoted by the aggregation and segmentation of generational units. The same principle of relativity can become on the other hand an inclusive tie of imagined closeness and social solidarity that binds affinal relatives together as "one's own people", while effectively transcending agnatic boundaries. This is evident not only in an egocentric conception of familial relations and household autonomy but also in the processes that determine agnatic unity and segmentation in a larger territorial or regional context, at the level of local village histories.

Taken in sum, the notions of *zong*, *jia* and *qin* shed a unique light on what may be understood as the constitution of families, a history of households and the evolution of lineage-village organization in the south China region.[3] If anything, they should show in what sense *zongzu* (or ancestral worship groups based on the ritual continuity of *zong* and aggregative (*tang*) and segmentary (*fang*) processes of *jia*), *jiazu* (or families constituted through symbolic and material exchange), and *jiating* (or domestic groups that through underlying assertions of shared livelihood choose to become distinct residential units) all represent entities that, in addition to being constituted in different cultural terms, are partial and salient dimensions of what has already been sanctified in the anthropological and historical literature on China as the lineage-village. It is clear also that the one's understanding of the "traditional" ethnographic landscape should not be limited to the existence of single-lineage villages, agnatic relationships to land, or fixed juridical notions of native "custom" pertaining to any of the above. I would argue that our prevailing anthropological understanding of the basic ethnographic institutions are debatable to begin with and that this has without doubt corrupted prevailing scholarly (not to mention colonial) interpretations of that indigenous tradition. Yet before asking how the notions of *zong*, *jia* and *qin* contribute to the existence and operation of domestic groups in a local Chinese context of the New Territories that in turn then becomes the site of colonial contestation, one must first of all explain in what ways the history of human settlement in the Xinan region in the 18th to 19th centuries has contributed to the systematic evolution of a pattern of village organization in which large-scale lineage cults have played a significant localizing if not socially galvanizing role, secondly articulate how and why these particular dimensions of agnatic organization and practice have been appropriated in the service of village identity and unity in ways that differ from a symbolic and customary constitution of *jiazu* and *jiating* per se. Finally, one must examine the symbolic constitution of the village or *jiaxiang* itself to see in what ways inherent notions of village space and social community intertwine with notions of domestic organization while on the hand overlapping with explicit notions of land as territoriality and property. Only then can one begin to elucidate the cultural crises that were precipitated by the emergence of coloniality and modernity and their socio-political consequences.

WO HANG, A VILLAGE THAT ONCE WAS

Without doubt, the most unambiguous account of the history of Wo Hang (=Ho Keng (M)), as settled by members of a descent group surnamed Li who now constitute the sole inhabitants of the village, is from an unpublished genealogy compiled recently by one of its elders. From the perspective of their genealogy, the Lis of Wo Hang are a people like no other. It describes a line of uninterrupted patrilineal descent originating from the Legendary Age of the Five Rulers (Wu Di). Their primordial ancestor bore the *shi* surname of Tao Gao and was born in the latter half of the reign of Tang Yao Di (c.2300 B.C.). During the succeeding reign of Yu Yao Di, he was bestowed the title of *Shishi* and granted a feudal dominion in Liuliguan, now in Yunnan province. The second generation ancestor bore the *shi* surname of Bo I and was given the title of *Dashi* during the reign of Yu Wang in the Xia dynasty. Two generations passed without any meritorious commentary. Its fifth generation ancestor Cheng Gung was bestowed the title of *xiang* by the Xia Emperor Shao Kang and granted a dominion in Lungxi called Lishupo, now in Gansu province. It was from this place that the *xing* surname of Li originated, and from that point on succeeding generations all bore the *xing* surname of Li.

In sum, 82 generations in an unbroken line followed in the aftermath of this apical ancestor. During the Han dynasty, its 50th generation ancestor Li Yangxun migrated to Xizhuo in Sichuan province, and a title bestowed to 66th generation ancestor Haigong by Emperor Gaozu of the Tang dynasty was followed by further migration to Lungxi, then called Nancheng, in present-day Shensi province. The descendants of the 82nd generation ancestor at some time during the reign of the Sung Emperor Xiaozong (c.1100) began a gradual migration southward as part of a larger movement of Hakkas (literally "guest people") from the central plains of China toward the southeastern provinces. All told, five generations passed after they first settled or "opened a base" (*kaiji*) in Fujian province. Descendants of the fifth generation during the reign of Emperor Taizu in the Yuan dynasty (c.1240) moved southward to settle in Changlo county of Guangdong province. Another six generations passed before descendants settled in Yungan county of Guangdong. Four succeeding generations settled in Bolo county of Guangdong during the latter half of the 17th century or after the lifting of the massive Coastal Evacuation. Like other Hakka agriculturalists, the Lis moved southward to occupy virgin land in a remote mountainous region of the New Territories. Over ten generations of people have passed since Li ancestors first settled in the village of Wo Hang.

Several aspects of the Li genealogy of Wo Hang deserve mention as a source of information for local social history. While anthropologists and historians alike routinely invoke local genealogies as a natural point of departure for an account of a village, they usually begin with their genealogical record insofar as it relates to the region specifically, as though to appropriate its objective data for purposes of reconstituting an ethnohistorical account, and tend to omit serious references to any earlier genealogical history, as though to suggest that it eventually becomes difficult to verify the facticity of events so recorded, especially as it extends into the realm of "mythical" history. Whether a genealogy is a "traditional" account of a village or its inhabitants in the literal sense of being "a regime (*tong*) that has been transmitted (*chuan*) and perpetuated in a continuum" is questionable as well. Most sinologists know that clan genealogies are generally reconstructed histories that cannot be taken as primary sources for study of the "past". Nonetheless, by relegating "the rest" of a genealogy to mythical history, they more importantly neglect to take into account the inherent subjectivity of the author's intention in reconstructing such history, thus underestimate its importance as writing genre to the sociopolitical designs of the village that it serviced and sought to extol. The proliferation of written genealogies (with all its mythical dimensions) that began recently only in the Ming dynasty is a relevant prerequisite for the emergence of large-scale lineage villages no more than 300 years ago during the Qing dynasty and is thus a significant factor in the cultural constitution of the village that has apparently appropriated agnatic principles and organization as a constituent part of the lineage-village.[4] In other words, what needs more careful exposition in this regard is not just the objective social history of Wo Hang as a typical rural village but more importantly its transformation from village to *jiaxiang* for a narrowly defined community of Li settlers and in which the various dimensions of agnatic ideology and practice (including written genealogies) become strategic tools for galvanizing local identity and social solidarity. As an inherently subjective source of data, it would appear that as a genre genealogies offer a useful avenue for understanding the nature of the agnatic community as the inhabitants themselves perceive it.

As a subjective account, the genealogy is thus something that by deliberate design selectively excludes reference to peripheral others or presents an inherently egocentric view of the world. This is especially relevant to our understanding of Wo Hang as a lineage community and the nature of the latter as a sociological or even traditional entity, since apparently it was not always a homogenous village.

Genealogical accounts of older more established village communities in what was then called Xinan county has for the most part molded the picture of a region dominated by "the great five clans" (*wudazu*) of the New Territories, but the lifting of the Coastal Evacuation during the early Qing dynasty that brought about new settlers changed the local sociopolitical landscape considerably in ways that have only recently become the subject of serious research. A comparison of maps from the 1688 and 1819 versions of the Xinan county gazetteer illustrates the changing pattern of settlement throughout the territory. By 1688, much of the plains and valleys had been occupied. By 1819, village settlement extended outward to less accessible hilly areas and virgin stretches of land along the coast. According to the 1688 gazetteer, there were only two villages in the area of what now comprises Shataukok (=Shatoujiao (M)) district, namely Man Uk Pin (=Wanwubian (M)) and Ma Tseuk Ling (=Maqueling (M)). Wo Hang existed but was not recognized.

Man Uk Pin and Ma Tseuk Ling were small agricultural settlements, each occupied by groups of people comprising several surnames. The initial inhabitants of Man Uk Pin were all Hakka villagers composed of four different surnames. Sometime later, two of the surname groups moved to settle in another part of the territory. Their absence was eventually filled by other immigrant cultivators of unrelated surnames, and this situation more or less continued unchanged until the present century. Ma Tseuk Ling was another agricultural community founded in the immediate aftermath of the Coastal Evacuation. From the beginning, it was inhabited by Hakka cultivators comprising 8 different surnames. Like Man Uk Pin, each of the surname groups occupied a distinct niche within the residential confines of the village, although in most other regards villagers of different surnames were members of a single village community where distinctions based upon agnation per se were irrelevant or were of little importance in the regulation of everyday affairs. Plots of agricultural land were clearly demarcated on land surrounding the residential nuclear village and tended to be located near one's own house, but for the most part land belonging to members of one surname group was often found interspersed with land belonging to other villagers and vice versa.

The settlement of the Shataukok region in essence followed the reclamation of land opened up by the recession of the sea along the coast. In this regard, the inhabitants of Ma Tseuk Ling, presumably with the assistance of nearby villagers, played an active role in the settlement of its locality by building a dike to block inundation by the sea of lowlying land in the area. According to present villagers living in the area, the building of the dike allowed inhabitants in nearby villages (such as Wo Hang) to settle into villages and onto agricultural land opened up as a result. Due to its hilly terrain, generally poor soil, and relative inaccessibility to established villages and markets in the plains area, Shataukok was one of the last areas in the territory to be cleared for settlement. These factors contributed also to the fact that it was the only region of the territory during the pre-modern era that was so predominantly Hakka. According to the first census conducted by the British, a full 100% of the villages there claimed to be Hakka (RNT 1899: 203).

With regard to Wo Hang, the present inhabitants of the village state that they are all lineal descendants of a common ancestor who settled there in the mid-17th century, but this was not always the case. When ancestors of the present Li inhabitants first migrated into the region from nearby Nantou, then across the Shenzhen valley, the village was occupied by Hakka cultivators bearing surnames of Deng, Zeng and Ho and living in neighboring hamlets. Wo Hang was named literally for the padi stream which ran from the top of an adjacent mountain and through the valley, where most of the rice padi and other crops were grown. The Dengs were the most populous surname group there at that time, and as in other villages there the four surname groups coexisted quite harmoniously in general.

Shortly after the Lis constructed an ancestral hall in Lau Wai (old walled city), however, the other surname residents claimed that the geomantic disposition of the village had been irrevocably damaged. The Li ancestral hall, by customary standards, was a strange sight. It was a long rectangular edifice partitioned into a parlor which led to a large inner gate, an open-air atrium, and another roofed parlor housing the ancestral tablets. The ancestral hall proper was located in the middle of a row of residential houses. In principle, no buildings should be built in front of the ancestral hall, which would affect the geomantic fortunes of those concerned. While there was no building per se obstructing the Li ancestral hall, the wall that enclosed the complex and its courtyard blocked the entrance to the ancestral hall, and instead of designing the main entrance to the complex to lead directly into the main parlor of the hall, the door to the complex protruded from the side.

The other surname groups were probably not affected by the architectural peculiarities of the Li ancestral hall per se, since its disposition could only affect the fate of the Lis. However, the Dengs protested against the construction of the Li ancestral complex, because it was situated in front of their own ancestral hall and in effect obstructed the geomantic fortune of the Dengs. It is unsure whether accusations of permanently damaged geomantic fortune were raised at the time the Li ancestral hall was constructed, or after the occurrence of calamities that pointed to geomantic misfortune as a probable cause. Nonetheless, as time passed, the Hos living in the village dwindled over passing generations to zero, the Zengs moved to Yau Ma Tong near present-day Kowloon, and the Dengs settled into the nearby village of Kong Ha (=Gangxia (M)), then Ma Mei Ha. For a while after the Dengs moved out, they returned yearly to Wo Hang on ritual occasions to present offerings at their ancestral hall, but when another ancestral hall was built in their new village, they ceased to return thereafter. They abandoned cultivation of their remaining land in Wo Hang, and their houses were left to deteriorate.[5]

Strength in numbers and the advantage of being first on the block may have given villagers of Man Uk Pin, Ma Tseuk Ling and Kong Ha a privileged position in determining the course of local affairs, but in actuality these villages never played an influential role in the history of Shataukok. From the beginning, the Lis of Wo Hang and the Chens of nearby Luk Keng (=Lujing (M)) appeared to play dominant roles in local affairs. In most cases, wealth did not come directly from the land but was made by individuals who made their fortune elsewhere through successful enterprise and meritorious achievement.[6] Much of this individually acquired wealth, especially in cases in the region where a sizable fortune had been made, was usually reinvested into the purchase of agricultural land outside one's village, which was then rented to tenant cultivators for a set percentage of crops harvested. Many such individuals created ancestral estates after they died, and benefits of the estate were shared communally by descendants whose shareholding rights to the estate were counted on a *per stirpes* basis. Throughout Shataukok, as in much of southeastern China, property of lesser size tended to be divided up among sons upon the death of an individual. Rights *in rem* were same for both individually owned property and ancestral trusts, the only significant difference between the two being *per capita* size. More importantly, one can see from these examples that conversion of individual wealth into land represented not so much a transformation of capital for capital's sake (by generating profit through land rent) but rather a transformation of ephemeral wealth into permanent wealth (or permanent medium for generating wealth in the form of rent in kind). Through transmission of land, either as divisible or indivisible property, one was in effect transmitting a way of life that bound the livelihood of the group to the land.

As was later reflected in the 1905 Block Crown Lease, much of the village agricultural land owned by absentee landlords in the Shataukok area belonged to several Wo Hang ancestral estates. The extent of absentee landownership by Wo Hang ancestral estates on the other hand rarely ventured beyond the Shataukok or *Sup Yeuk* (= *Shiyue* (M)) region. *Sup Yeuk* was an alliance of ten (clusters of) villages that centered on the market town of Shataukok. In actuality, it included several tens of villages, many of whom were located just north of what is now the Sino-British border. Due to the fact that Wo Hang ancestral estates also owned up to an estimated 80% of the land in and around Shataukok market town, which was founded around the same time as the alliance, it appeared that Wo Hang was for many years a dominant figure in the local structure of power.

However, the appearance of power, its reasons for being and the kind of kin or village solidarity entailed by it must be qualified. The process by which Wo Hang came to attain the position of power that it did in Shataukok had less to do with its capacity as a lineage-village than with the achievements of individuals. From the perspective of insiders, wealth mobilized by the ancestral estate was, of course, by definition communal insofar as it was equally shared and enjoyed by its respective members. However, from the point of view of an outsider, such wealth was simply private by nature since it was for all intents and purposes mobilized for self-interested gains. To the tenant villager cultivating land owned by absentee landlords like those from Wo Hang, the land was always referred to as belonging to Wo Hang (as a whole) regardless of whether the land in question was actually owned by an ancestral estate or individual. Yet in precisely such instances, the absentee control and ownership of land was paradoxically less communal, in the sense that it represented property of that entire village, than private, insofar as it was acquired and mobilized for purely utilitarian purposes.[7]

The above distinctions are important for understanding where the nexus of land, kinship, and social solidarity lay in the context of competition for economic control, social prestige and political power, as typified in the case of the Shataukok region. Wo Hang's rise to power in the region, at a surface level, closely resembled the process described by Freedman where individual accumulation of land became the stepping stone for status and power within a wider socio-political framework. The attainment of status and power was without doubt utilitarian (self-interested) in motivation, but on the other hand there is no basis for believing that material achievement per se contributed in any way to the increasing social solidarity of Wo Hang, either as a kin group or village. In fact, there is no reason to believe that the internal solidarity found in Wo Hang as a result of their wealth, status, and power was any different from that found in any other village, large, small, single-surname or multiple-surname. Communal wealth was shared and mobilized by lineages according to rules (of agnation, common worship, etc.) which defined that segment as a segment "against the world". If in actuality individual wealth and power held by various corporate segments in the village contributed to the overall position of the village or kin group as a whole, it could only be due to preexisting social rules which bound members of the whole together and not to the process of economic accumulation itself, which was by nature utilitarian and self-interested.

In this sense, one can also see that utilitarian accumulation of wealth and power did not at all reflect the values upheld by the kin group or village as a whole, as depicted in the words of the placard hung at the entrance to Wo Hang's ancestral hall (quoted at the beginning of this chapter). Scholarly achievement and the reputation which resulted were no doubt gained at the expense of others "against the world", but unlike utilitarian accumulation they were values that were embedded in a cultural logic that ultimately contributed to social harmony.

Within a larger regional framework, one can probably concur with villagers of Wo Hang when they blandly state that there appeared to be little to mark the experience of their village as different or distinct from any other. In effect, the nature of the village and village life was subject to the same set of conditions which influenced other villages and other villagers. On the whole, after the initial years of mass immigration into the territory during the latter half of the 17th century, the settlement pattern of incoming villagers, at least in the Shataukok region, stabilized and remained largely unchanged for the next two centuries. For the most part, relations between villages and between neighboring village alliances were peaceful. Feuds were sporadic and tended to be forgotten with the passing of time. Villagers, whether they belonged to single-surname or multiple-surname communities, were sensitive to incursions by strangers, but this was less due to their innate feelings of suspicion than to feelings of vulnerability as "against the world". Some village elders also remarked that, during the 19th century, it was not unusual, for example, for peasants to take a gun with them to the fields. Not surprisingly, the staple production of villages in the Shataukok region was rice, which was sold at periodic markets at Shataukok and occasionally transported to the larger market town of Shenzhen a half day's walk away. Rice marketed at Shataukok also found its way to Hong Kong and other places in the vicinity. By the 19th century, however, local padi production began to decline as a result of competition from cheaper rice imported from abroad, especially Thailand. While other traditionally rice producing areas in Guangdong province began to switch to other more profitable enterprises, such as mulberry cultivation (for silk), the Xinan region and poorer areas like Shataukok in particular were generally slow to make any fundamental transition until well into the twentieth century.[8]

By virtue of its remoteness from centers of socio-economic activity and its relative poverty of natural resources, the Shataukok region was usually the first to suffer from deteriorating economic conditions in the marketplace (competition from imported rice during the 19th century) but on the other hand also the last to respond in a positive way to changing conditions. It has been easy to explain such resistance to change by pointing to the backwardness and conservatism of the peasant, but judging from the experiences of villages throughout the territory as a whole as well as those of successful individuals, it would be more accurate to say that those initially bestowed with the means were always among the first to take up an entrepreneurial attitude. On the other hand, those less bestowed with such resources were usually less inclined on the whole to take such risks. Faced with the greater possibility or risk of losing in entirety (what remained of) their means of livelihood, most people usually took one of two roads, 1) complete abandonment of their livelihood in favor of a radically different one or 2) further intensification of existing means to the ends combined with increasing deterioration of that way of life. In short, these strategies were indicative of the way in which villages in the Shataukok area as well as poorer inhabitants of any village responded on the whole to changing conditions in the 20th century. Such pragmatic considerations also affected their defense of particular underlying value systems.

In retrospect, the history of Wo Hang as a village must be seen first of all in the context of developments in the region as a whole. The transition from its existence as a physical agglomeration of households to a social community where its members identified to it in some ritualized or institutionalized way is a subtle one that was not just the product of set jural definitions of a village or lineage. There was a fine line (or was it geomantic fate?) that separated the development of Wo Hang as a multi-surname or single-surname village. Moreover, these events or conditions were distinct from the circumstances (achievements of few successful individuals) that made the village an influential force in the Shataukok area as a whole, which in turn were distinct from the kinds of processes that led to the later growth of ancestral estates in Wo Hang. In the end, there can be little doubt that the sociopolitical prestige of Wo Hang in the immediate area was significant, but both in theory and practice there was little to substantiate the existence of any direct relationship between the development of lineages and the village, at least in the way posited by Freedman's model or in revisions made by anthropologists and historians. Likewise, the kind of fierce arrogance attributed to Wo Hang by its own villagers was simply a product of the times, not agnatic pride per se.

THE STRUCTURE AND PRACTICE OF LOCAL LEVEL ANCESTRAL WORSHIP GROUPS

The conceptual unity of the *zu* manifests itself in various ways. It is both the unity of here and there, then and now. That is to say, its existence as a group of people thrives upon the fact that its membership includes those living locally and away as well as the living and deceased. In this sense, the inclusion of these dimensions to an understanding of the *zu* is somewhat antithetical to structural-functionalist theories of lineage that inherently privilege the "localized descent group". Of course, the existence of localized descent groups can be distinguished from its larger entity, but its relevance for those living in the here and now must be viewed in reference to the whole rather apart from it, as though sociologically *sui generis*. Secondly, the existence of such localized descent groups must also be viewed in the framework of the village, within which it performs specific functions. Previous scholars have apparently misinterpreted the "ritualizing" and "localizing" influences of the localized descent group by assuming that its a priori constitution as a "lineage" makes it *ipso facto* a function of descent rules. However, there is nothing in the symbolic constitution or ritual practice of the *zu* that necessitates its being locally concentrated (in contrast to territorially dispersed) or segmentally organized in order for ancestor worship to be efficacious. On the other hand, these local and segmentary manifestations of the *zu* have played an important function in galvanizing village solidarity, and it is really in reference to the resurgence of the village as sociological entity that one must regard the role of localized lineages.

The nomenclature of local level ancestor worship groups varies according to region. In the New Territories, both Cantonese and Hakka conventionally use the terms *tso* (C) and *tong* (C) to designate local ancestral groups holding a common estate. These terms differ from *zu* or *zongzu* in the sense that they appear to be established by and composed *of* people in the "here and now". This does not mean to say, however, that they are created *for* the people of the "here and now". It is largely in reference to *tso* and *tong* and not *zu* per se that anthropologists and historians of China have focused their attention on lineage. Yet despite their local existence, the estate that they control need not be localized or territorially limited. A *tso* or *tong* can in principle survive quite well despite the physical separation of its members or territorial dispersion of its estate, which explains its adaptability in a modern era of corporate management. Secondly, despite its management as a corporate entity, both *tso* and *tong* still exist primarily for purposes of common worship, which suggests serious limitations in the mutabilility of the estate after its creation that distinguishes it from modern corporations. In other words, there are no descent groups in China that are not at the same time ancestor cults, and this is a source of its limited sociological concreteness.[9] Thirdly, unlike the clear-cut distinctions made by anthropologists between "estate" and "corporation", both *tso* and *tong* are not really distinguishable in such terms. They can just as easily refer to a group of people or the propertied estate shared by that group of people. This ambivalence of meaning is a consequence of a symbolic equivalence between "common living" and "common budget" or the assumption that the sharing of an estate and a fixed livelihood is what makes a family a communal entity.

Thus, although such local ancestral groups are by anthropological standard not "localized" enough in a territorial sense, not "secular" enough in a sociological sense, and not distinct enough as a "corporation" or "estate", it should nonetheless be clear that the kinds of models used to explain "localized descent groups" are quite inappropriate and if anything distort our understanding of these institutions. Whether the localized lineage deserves the privileged status accorded to it (*vis-a-vis* the family, ancestral rites or other phenomena) in the theoretical literature is another matter altogether that awaits reassessment of all the basic variables.

By definition, the *tso* or *tong* is a group based upon common worship, and the system of values embedded in the rites and obligations of ancestral worship defines rights of membership to the group, while regulating the redistribution of goods and benefits among its members. The basic difference between *tso* and *tong* appears to be one of naming. *tso* (C) is the *zu* (M) of *zuxian* ("ancestor", not to be confused with the *zu* of *zongzu*). The name of a local ancestral group usually takes the form of the name of the ancestor being memorialized followed by the noun *tso*. The person so named by the *tso* is not just the founder of that trust; he creates it primarily for the future livelihood of his lineal descendants. A *tso* so conceived is basically a gift prestation that should be reciprocated by ritual veneration. In this regard, there is no difference between *tso* and *tong*. The name of the ancestor memorialized by a *tso*, however, is always his adult name or *daming* (genealogical name), which is a three character name consisting of his surname, a generational name and personal name. A *tong* (=*tang* (M)) on the other hand always uses the "*tong* name" (*tong-hou* (C)) of the ancestor, which is different from his genealogical name. The *tong* name may not usually be known to others but is always used in an honorific sense to designate, for example,

"The House of . . .". The creation of a lineage hall seems rare in the case of a *tong*, despite its literal meaning as "hall".

Other instances show further nuances between *tso* and *tong*. For example, the first Wo Hang Li ancestor, Li Duck-wa, was succeeded by one son, who in turn gave birth to three sons. The first Li ancestor was on the whole poor and left little in the way of an estate. It was not until the second and third generation that the Lis accumulated enough wealth to construct an ancestral hall. The hall was built by Li Kin-lam, the second generation ancestor, and named after his three sons in the third generation, each of whom shared the generation name Jit, thus given the name Sam Jit Tong (*tong* of the three Jits). Why the hall was not named after the first or second generation ancestor rather than the three brothers was not obvious from its choice of name, since the people of Wo Hang consider Sam Jit Tong their major ancestral hall, that is to say, of all the Lis in Wo Hang beginning with the first local ancestor. Moreover, the ancestors of the first few generations, including those of the previous two generations from their last village prior to settlement in Wo Hang, had their spirit tablets placed inside Sam Jit Tong, and the sign at the entrance to the hall stated *Lishi zongzi* (Li Surname Ancestral Hall). It appeared in this instance that its name Sam Jit *tong* accentuated the fact that the hall was built by the three brothers instead of its original ancestor, and it was perhaps only a fact of coincidence that Sam Jit Tong was synonymous with the whole lineage, since the three Jits also represented (by virtue of genealogical segmentation) the three major segments or *fong* (C) (=*fang*) of the lineage. Had the hall been built by descendants of the fourth, fifth or later generations, the possibility that this hall would have been called "*tong* of the thirteen Chius" or "*tong* of the twenty-five Tings" would appear rather remote. Nonetheless, the hall itself would in any case have been called a *tong* and under conditions where the use of *tso* and *tong* might have been equally valid, it would appear that *tong* more aptly described situations that transcended the overt meaning of *tso* as an estate that was literally or strictly speaking passed down after the death of an ancestor as an act of remembrance.

With regard to the latter, one should mention that there were in Wo Hang several *tong* established and held in common by brothers. In each case, the *tong* was essentially a landowning group with no ancestral house to mark it as a *tong*, yet the estate held by these brothers was distinct from the *tso* which they directly inherited from their father and in which they each had an equal share. The fact that *tso* and *tong* can be separate entities despite their similar membership as a group, points to a potentially more important distinction between the two terms. The conditions of its founding withstanding, there is nothing in the nature of a *tong* that requires it be to an ancestral group per se. It can be a purely capitalist corporation created by a group of persons (in this case, brothers) whose purpose is not expressly for ancestral worship. It is only after this group is succeeded and its estate inherited that the *tong* becomes subject to the rules and obligations of ancestor worship, and it is only after transmission that descendants of the group tend to view the *tso* and the *tong* at the level of practice as one and the same.

In Wo Hang, the three primary *fong* (segments) are known by its *tso* name, which commemorates each of the three third-generation ancestors, and its *tong* name, which is composed of a two-character expression designating the number of brothers in the following gen-eration and a self-styled marker. Each of the three *fong* has an ancestral house, and people usually refer to members of these *fong* and their estate by their *tong* name. There is no distinction between the *tso* and *tong* estate in these three cases, but there are cases where the estate of a particular *tso* and *tong* (of the same group of people) is different. In theory, the estate of a *tong*, which includes the ancestral hall and a landed estate, may be named separately from that of the *tso*. In practice, however, the accounting is usually handled by the same trustee and for all intents and purposes as part of the same account. From the point of view of its members, both *tso* and *tong* are worshipped as one and the same. In the context of worship, all that matters is the fact that a source of livelihood has been passed down as a prestation from above, an act that must be reciprocated in like terms. The personal attributes of the particular ancestor and the origins of that estate are of no relevance whatsoever to the worship per se.

From this perspective, one can begin to understand how com-mon worship determines who owns what, when, where and how. The guiding principles in this regard are the downward transmission of the *zong* and commonality of *qi* which link father to son and brothers to brothers. It is on the basis of these principles that both rules of membership to an ancestral group as well as rights of access to a common estate are seen as logically constituted. The transmission of *zong* from ascendant to descendant in effect represents the transmission of values, rites and obligations pertaining to worship at an ancestral shrine as the means by which the separation between generations may be bridged. The *zong* here is not so much the *zong* of the classical Zhou principle "ancestral origin moves in an upward direction; *zong* changes in a downward direction", but rather the *zong* of *chuanzong jiedai* ("to transmit the *zong* to link the generations"), a widely known metaphor used to mean "to maintain continuity of the (ancestral) line". Unlike the hierarchical, relativizing, hence changing nature of the Zhou concept of *zong*, the modern notion of *zong* is universal to the father-son relationship. It is through transmission of *zong* that a common surname is transmitted, hence the equivalence of *xing* and *zong* (*tongxing, tongzong*). *Qi* also expresses the sharing of common substance between father and son. This amorphous sharing of *qi* through a common father then links common livelihood, common subsistence and rights to a common estate.

The principles of *zong* and *qi* provide a clear basis for defining in a Chinese context the criteria of membership essential to Radcliffe-Brown's definition of a "corporation", and genealogical evidence without doubt confirms the effectiveness of these principles as a means of defining individual kin identity within the whole. However, when the picture produced by the various *tso* (and *tong*) is fit it onto a genealogical grid, the resulting picture of "group structure" and "group affiliation" is rather different from Radcliffe-Brown's principles of corporate kin identity.

The disposition of the various *tso* within the first few generations of Lis in Wo Hang illustrates the situation more clearly. The first Li ancestor to settle in Wo Hang and founder of the branch of the greater Li *zu* there, Li Duk-wa, died and left a small estate. He was survived by one son, Li Kin-lam, who built a Li family hall (*li jiaci*) in Canton and began construction of the Li main ancestral hall in Wo Hang, which was named Sam Jit Tong after his three sons. Moreover, he built a charitable tomb (*ichong*) in which he deposited the bones of unknown, unnamed individuals scattered throughout the area, and this tomb also came to be worshipped by the Wo Hang Lis during its annual sweeping of ancestral graves. Although there was no *tso* in the name of Kin-lam, the estate bearing the name Sam Jit Tong included numerous pieces of land located throughout Shataukok.

Kin-lam was succeeded by his three sons, Jit-kwai, Jit-wing and Jit-fong. The descendants of the first and third sons remained in the upper village, called Sheung Wo Hang, and descendants of the second son settled in the lower valley after the construction of a dike to prevent the flooding of sea water into the area. The village was named Ha Wo Hang (lower Wo Hang). The ancestral estate of the second son was known by the names of Li Jit-wing Tso and Ng Kwai Tong ("Tong of the Five Posterities"), the latter named after his five sons. This estate included property in land as well as an ancestral hall used exclusively by members of the second *fong* that housed spirit tablets of the first and second generation ancestors (as in the main ancestral hall) along with all the ancestors of the second *fong* up until the third and fourth generations. The first and third *fong* had no ancestral hall (*citang*), but they each had an ancestral house (*tso-uk* (C), =*zuwu*), which was used for communal purposes. Like the estate of the second *fong*, those of the first and third *fong* were also known by *tso* and *tong* names. Li Jit-kwai Tso (first *fong*) was also known as Ng Fook Tong ("Tong of the Five Happinesses"), named after the five sons of Jit-kwai. Similarly, Li Jit-fong Tso (third *fong*) was also known as Sam Yu Tong ("Tong of the Three Abundances"), named after the three sons of Jit-fong. All three *fong* had sizable estates with which they were able to finance ritual functions and allow for regular rotation of agricultural land for personal cultivation by individual families on a per stirpes basis.

The fourth generation was survived by 13 (5+5+3) descendants, each having the generation name of Chiu. Only 10 of the 13 ancestors in this generation had *tso* or communal property registered in their name. While the remaining three were all survived by succeeding generations, property transmitted was divided up among the sons rather than kept as a shared whole. This seemed to be a pattern in following generations, as about half of the descendants in the fifth generation (generational name of Ting) had *tso* registered in their names, the remainder being transmitted or divided up as private property (*see-yan chan-yip* (C), =*siren chanye*). Thus, four of the five fourth generation ancestors in Ng Fook Tong had registered *tso*, in contrast to 3 of 5 in Ng Kwai Tong and 3 of 3 in Sam Yu Tong. Moreover, 13 ancestors of the fourth generation formed a *tso* called Pak Hing Tso ("Tso of the Hundred Prosperities"). In sociological terms, its scope was identical with that of Sam Jit Tong in that it included all surviving descendants of the three *fong* of Wo Hang, but its estate and the peculiarities of its creation made it separate. Pak Hing Tso had no communal house, and its estate was relatively small. But it did provide for a selected group of elders from lower and upper Wo Hang to congregate once a year to feast and discuss matters of mutual concern.

The three fourth generation ancestors who made up Sam Yu Tong present an unusual situation. Here, each of the three brothers, Chiu-tung, Chiu-leung and Chiu-ju had a separate *tso* which was shared by his respective descendants. One of the three, Chiu-leung, built his own ancestral house called Pui Man Tong, which was used by his descendants for ritual purposes. Pui Man Tong owned on paper other pieces of property, including the ancestral house itself and several plots of land, rental income from which was used to guarantee maintenance of the house. In practice, both Pui Man Tong and Chiu-leung Tso worshipped as a single group, and the actual management of the *tso* and the *tong* was handled for all intents and purposes as a single entity. Apart from the above, descendants of two of the three brothers, Chiu-leung and Chiu-tung, shared in another communal estate called Yi Hop Tso ("Tso of the Two Combined"). It was not clear from members of this *tso* why or how this *tso* was created, especially to the exclusion of the third ancestor, but all that mattered from their point of view was that this was something which was passed down for the benefit of descendants in those succeeding generations. Yi Hop Tso had no communal house, and its property in land, which was small as well, was rotated for personal use among member families on a *per stirpes* basis.

The above description of the various *tso* in the early genealogical history of the Wo Hang Lis has important ramifications for the forms of social organization so engendered, the specifics of ancestral worship, the kind of group consciousness invoked therein as well as the meaning and function of lineage segmentation. At face value, however, there appears to be a discrepancy between the kind of social organization defined on the basis of *zong* and *qi* on the one hand and that defined by the juxtaposition of *tso* over the same genealogical grid on the other. Part of this discrepancy can be resolved first of all by seeing that there is nothing intrinsic to the principles of *zong* and *qi* that explains why a *tso* or communal estate is passed down as a whole or divided up among one's descendants. From the point of view of *zong* and *qi,* communal and private property are the same because they entail the same rules of transmission (from father to son), shareholdership (equal division among brothers), and ancestral worship regardless of whether the estate itself is kept whole or divided up. On the other hand, the rules that engender the creation of a *tso* or its displacement on a genealogical grid tell us nothing about the rules that (ancestrally) relate individuals to each other or the rules that define one's share in an estate. In other words, the rules that define the existence of a *tso* (as opposed to privately owned estates) have nothing to do with the rules that define the nature of "corporations" and "estates" in sociological terms nor can they explain the existence of that set of values, concepts and practices pertaining to *zong, qi* or ancestor worship. The overlap of *tso* and *tong* over a genealogical grid and the arbitrariness of both communal and private estates already attest to these points. This begs the question, namely what privileges the creation of communal (*tso*) over private estates (*see-yan chan-yip*)? The answer is *per capita* size.

This then brings us back to Freedman's essential theory of Chinese lineage organization. Indigenous villagers say quite plainly that the major criteria for keeping an estate communally intact for one's descendants instead of dividing it definitively is simply a matter of relative wealth and internal domestic harmony. Where there is relative abundance, largesse prevails, and chances are good that the estate may be transmitted as a *tso.* Where there is relative scarcity, there is a stronger tendency for sons to request their own share instead of sharing rights to a common estate.[10] In both cases, domestic conflict between brothers (or their wives) may lead to division of a family estate regardless of conditions of wealth. Moreover, the chances of dividing an estate upon the death of a family head are much greater before than after the *tso* is passed down for more than a generation. In the former, division is permissible upon request by any one of the sons, whereas in the latter agreement by all parties need to be observed and respected.

While economic conditions can easily account for the conditions under which communal estates are formed or not, this in itself cannot justify the assumptions and assertions built into Freedman's model of the localized lineage as a corporate kin group constituted on the basis of primitive accumulation. Part of the illusion which leads one to believe that bigger lineages evolve from smaller ones and that power and prestige oriented groups develop out of economically based ones resides in the creation of the *tso* itself. In its creation, the *tso* is essentially the act of one man willing his property to his descendants. The wealth that makes up the estate is a product of private accumulation, but aggregation and accumulation of the *tso* rarely goes beyond this point. With exception of clear-cut cases like Pak Hing Tso and Yi Hop Tso, instances of aggregation of two or more units into higher order segments are in fact unusual, ethnographically as well as historically, in addition to being logically inconsistent with the downward principle of *zong* transmission and even the principle of utilitarian maximization, where self-interest would be better served by creating one's own communal trust instead of diluting the wealth (at a higher level) among more people. Moreover, Pak Hing Tso and Yi Hop Tso were also relatively small estates whose reason for being could not have been for purposes of land accumulation alone, especially in the context of larger and other structurally overlapping *tso*. Even in the case of the three major *fong*, Ng Fook Tong, Ng Kwai Tong, and Sam Yu Tong, there is little evidence to show that these estates were the end product of continued accumulation over generational time. From 1905 to the present, the Block Crown Lease shows no instances of increase in absolute size for any of Wo Hang's *tso* landholdings. Contrary to Freedman's model, each passing generation led to (economically) asymmetric segmentation, one produced not by ongoing accumulation but rather ongoing transmission as a result of the creation of *tso* by some and division of family property by others. Yet in light of such (non-aggregative) transmission in phylogenetic terms, one sees also that increasing segmentation in the lineage leads instead to decreasing *per capita* concentration of wealth within each respective *tso* over time. Thus, segmentation has been a gradual process of diminishing returns, both in theory and in fact.

In sum, one can now integrate our discussion of the *tso* and its relationship to the segmentary process on the one hand with the conditions of socio-economic competition at the regional level on the other. As mentioned previously, at least in the eyes of neighboring villages, Wo Hang had earned the dubious reputation of being the seat of regional power, power which has in fact been grounded in the extensive landholdings controlled by large ancestral estates (*tso*) throughout the Shataukok region. But as has been argued above, little of this had anything to do with the organizational attributes of the *tso* or village as a whole. The *tso* were founded by one or a few persons and passed down according to well-defined rules of transmission to later generations. Moreover, given that few if any of these *tso* had ever in fact increased the size of its estate or merged with other existing *tso*, one can say that the wealth of the *tso* in any case was less attributable to the size of the estate or its structural attributes than to the wealth of the individual(s) who contributed to its establishment and survival. In other words, even the degree to which certain *tso* in a village could be seen to wield economic control over a region should expect to tell us nothing about the structure of *tso* within a particular local community or the nature of its overall social (kin) organization. The latter is in fact a consequence of those customary rules and preexisting conditions that define local level kinship as well as the village context that frames its reason for being.

The creation of an ancestral hall, which was for Freedman the criterion that symbolized segmentation at a higher agnatic level, deserves further scrutiny also. The building of an ancestral house (*tso-uk*) was neither a necessary nor common feature of a *tso* or *tong* at any level. Moreover, the building of an ancestral hall (*citang*) appeared to be an even rarer occurrence in the sense that it was unusual to find more than one such hall for any surname group in an entire village, which suggests on the other hand that it probably served more as a visible symbol for village unity than agnatic solidarity per se. While it may be too facile to say that the ancestral hall is in this regard more a product of the village than a descent group per se, it is clear that the *citang* itself is a recent historical phenomenon that had succeeded the official family shrines (*jiamiao*) that were prevalent during the Ming dynasty. Whether the form of the hall was a function of changes in the nature of the village or in the practice of communal worship is a complex topic in its own right that requires separate attention.[11] It suffices here to say that the formation of a village community was hardly a product of agnatic principles alone.

THE LIVING AND THE DEAD IN THE FRAMEWORK OF LOCAL WORSHIP

From the perspective of ego looking outward, ancestor worship is very much a personal affair. The list of persons whom one worships is in essence a reflection of who one is, since each list is as different as each ego. Those who are literate are sometimes able to recite the names of each ancestor beginning from generation one to the present. Those who are less literate, illiterate or basically uncaring commemorates each ancestor by reference to where his gravestone lies, when he is worshipped and with whom one goes to worship him. Chinese usually sweep the ancestral graves once or twice a year. The Cantonese of Hong Kong regularly make this pilgrimage around Qing Ming (third month, 12th day of lunar year), while the Hakka do it prior to Chong Yang (ninth month, ninth day of lunar year). Wo Hang villagers worship their close ancestors on Qing Ming but save communal worship for Chong Yang, and apical ancestors have set days on which descendants sweep their graves and present offerings to prevent conflict with other ancestors.

In Wo Hang, most pilgrimages to the grave are conducted in the month preceding Chong Yang. For any family, there are "personal" ancestors whom one will worship independently of other families in addition to "communal" ancestors whom one will worship along with other families as members of a common *tso*. Participation in communal worship of the various *tso* reflects in at least one sense one's genealogical position *vis-a-vis* other segments in a wider agnatic framework. Personal worship of ancestors on the other hand refers to those ancestors who did not leave behind property in the form of a *tso*. In these cases, property passed down to succeeding generations almost certainly had been equally divided by sons.

The principle underlying annual worship at the ancestral grave is that the living are part of a larger world that includes the dead. The dead are spiritually present and can always influence the course of the living. Their needs must be attended to like other living beings, thus attests to their relevance to the social world and the operation of social institutions. They need food, clothing and other materials (or representations thereof) without which they would become "hungry ghosts". If their needs are not satisfied, they can cast a malevolent influence among the living present. Ritual efficacy is sensitive to quantity and intensity of sacrificial offerings. These are in turn reflections of social intentionality.

The question of who worships whom, what, where and how reflects to some degree the kinds of values that are relevant to the nature of ancestor worship and the kinds of social relationships engendered by the latter. One family that I came to know quite well returned to Wo Hang not long after having lived in the U.K. for over seven years. The present head of the family is an old woman in her 60s. She is the second of two wives of her husband, who passed away at the age of 48 around 1955. The first wife ran away from the village in 1945 and has never since returned to the village. The family also includes two sons, one from each of the two wives. The eldest son in the family is now in his late forties, married and has several children. In the early 1960s, he emigrated to the U.K. to make a living. As time passed, his business began to prosper. He then brought over his wife and started raising a family before settling there. Despite having emigrated, he built a house in the village soon after making his newly earned money and occasionally returned to visit his natal village. The second son, who was fifteen years younger than his brother, was single and had for over the last five years been working and studying in the U.K. before deciding most recently to return to Hong Kong to live.

The members of this family belong to the third *fong* in the village, Sam Yu Tong. In terms of constituency, Sam Yu Tong outnumbers the other two *tong* in the village, and its members have in general been the first to emigrate on a large scale to the U.K. in the early 1960s. This family belongs to one of three *tso* that divides the third *fong* called Li Chiu-tung Tso. By their own admission, members of Li Chiu-tung Tso consider themselves to be the least fortuitous of the three *tso* in this third *fong*. Their numbers are few, and relative to their village brothers they have tended to be less successful both here and abroad. Within Li Chiu-tung Tso, this family, whom I shall call after its deceased head of the family Li Fo-sang, claims membership to one other *tso*, Li Yam-iu Tso. Li Yam-iu is the grandfather of Li Fo-sang. He had two sons, one of whom died without being survived by any direct descendant. The remaining son was succeeded by one son, namely Li Fo-sang. The living descendants of Li Yam-iu thus include only this one family.

In the context of ancestral worship at the grave, the family of Li Fo-sang has many ancestors to worship, some to be worshipped communally (in conjunction with others) and some separately. The remains of Li Fo-sang are kept in a burial urn and housed in a communal grave house established by and registered in the name of Li Yam-iu Tso. There are 18 urns housed in this communal burial house, 9 male and 9 female. The names of the deceased were originally written onto slips of paper and kept in place by each urn cover, but they have long since become unreadable. Not even the present descendants clearly recollect the actual names of the deceased, with exception of the more recent ones. Communal graves are common among the Hakka, in contrast to the Cantonese. But contrary to what Pasternak (1979) has suggested with regard to the fortune maximizing geomantic disposition of Hakka communal graves, the Hakka here attach no real importance to communal graves *vis-a-vis* individual ones. It is a simple matter of preference.

In the case of the Li Yam-iu communal grave, it houses the remains of Li Yam-iu (and his wife) along with those of his lineal descendants (and their wives). In addition, it also houses the remains of several of Li Yam-iu's direct ascendants who were initially buried separately then reburied by Li Yam-iu within the said house. Li Yam-iu was an only son, and those ascendants reburied in the present house were quite unlikely to have been worshipped by other villagers. The family of Li Fo-sang is the only family in the village that presents offerings at this grave, which is another way of saying that the members of this family are the only living descendants of whatever ancestors are represented by the 18 burial urns deposited in the grave. The fact that Li Yam-iu had taken the bones of his predecessors and reburied them together was viewed by his descendants to be an act of benevolence that coincidentally facilitated ancestral worship by succeeding generations.

Worship at this communal grave tended to be simple in style, and the kind of sacrificial offerings made here was no different than that made by the family at its other grave sites. The trip to the ancestral grave was usually made right after an early breakfast consisting of boiled greens, boiled chicken, steamed fish, clear broth and noodles. Accompanying the group were the members of this one family who were the only living descendants of Li Yam-iu Tso and some neighbors who volunteered to help clear the grave site. In all, the group included the wife of the deceased Li Fo-sang, her second son, an elderly woman who lived next door and a young male villager who was also a close relative of the family. As tends usually to be the case among the Hakka, the women ended up doing most of the hard work by clearing away the grass around the communal grave, while the son and his village brother did some light work, then for the most part sat idly.

After the grass had been cut and debris cleared away, the women then set up the sacrificial offerings and other utensils. In addition to the grave site itself, a small tutelary shrine (earth god) was located nearby to the right, which acted as a kind of guardian spirit (*mong-shek* (C), =*wangshi*), literally "lookout stone". Old slips of brown paper that were placed on top of a tutelary shrine and pressed into place between the jar and lid of each burial urn the year before were replaced by new slips of "blood paper" (*hit-ji* (C), =*xiezhi*), stained by fresh cock's blood.

Sacrificial offerings were placed in front of each altar. One plate containing a slice of boiled pork was placed in front of the tutelary shrine along with two lit candles. Directly in front of the grave housing the 18 burial urns, several candles and incense sticks were stuck into the ground. A slice of boiled pork and a plate containing assorted fruits and sweets were then arranged, followed by three cups of tea and wine. While the food and incense were all being set up, the old woman (wife of Li Fo-sang) began to speak kindly to the ancestors, announcing the nature of the occasion, who had come to visit, then beseeching them with offerings.

The son and his village brother then threw onto the ground in the vicinity of the grave site strips of plain white paper, each of which was perforated to form a circular design. These strips of paper, called *kai-ji* (C) (=*qizhi*), represented an unmarked form of money used to bribe the ghosts. A number of other things were then burnt as sacrifice to the ancestors. This included printed "hell money" (*ming-ji* (C), =*mingzhi*) and other square-shaped sheets of gold and silver money as well as paper clothing, one set for each ancestor. Each set of clothing consisted of an imperial gown, a pair of shoes and a hat. Also thrown into the fire were bundles of rough paper labelled on the front with a small piece of paper inscribed with the word *shou* (longevity). After everything had been burnt, everyone, including non-family members, offered a prayer to the ancestors. The son prayed for good luck in finding a job, his village brother prayed for luck in the next week's lottery, and the old woman prayed that the young man have luck in finding a wife and settling down. The group then rested a while, eating some of the fruits and sweets just offered, then collected their things and went home. Those who went to the grave were invited to eat a large afternoon meal consisting of an assortment of meat and vegetables. The boiled pork was cut and stewed with salted vegetables (*ham-choi* (H), =*xiantsai*), a typical Hakka dish, then served during this meal.

In addition to worship at the Li Yam-iu communal grave, the family of Li Fo-sang also made pilgrimages to two other ancestral graves at other sites, both of which were not considered to be communal graves, that is to say, registered in the name of a *tso*. One of the two was located on a hill near Tai Po market town, a long distance from Wo Hang that included a 30 minute ride from the base of the hill. On foot, it would have taken an entire day to get from Wo Hang to the final destination. As in the previous case, the party included members of the family and several helpers. But because the family had not made this pilgrimage for over seven years, they had to ask elders in the small village at the foot of the hill for probable directions. The hike up the hill took much longer than usual, because thick bushes had blocked up passages leading to the now abandoned terrace fields once used by villagers below. From the terraces, they travelled along a footpath that ran parallel to a ravine for 20 minutes before climbing straight up the face of the hill at some designated point to a small plateau. Then they got lost again. After several minutes of searching for a directional marker and calling out to the ancestor for help, they found the right path that led them directly to the gravesite.

The grave housed the remains of a single ancestor by the name of Li To-tai. From the generational name To, we know that he was an 8th generation Wo Hang Li ancestor, one generation above Li Yam-iu. Unfortunately, the members of the family did not know precisely who Li To-tai was except to say that they were not sure why Li Yam-iu did not rebury the remains of this ancestor within the Yam-iu communal grave near Wo Hang. But being an ancestor of the great-grandfather's generation from the perspective of the deceased Li Fo-sang, it appears likely that Li To-tai died sometime in the late 19th century. There is no record of him in the Block Crown Lease for Wo Hang, and the family has no record of landholdings in his name. Because the family has no personal recollection of him, one cannot say for sure whether he was married or was succeeded by children, naturally born or adopted. All one knows is that he is recognized by the family to be an ancestor, a fact affirmed by the provision of property to insure worship. One might say that the fact of his being worshipped seems to be the only proper definition of who an ancestor is. After all, not all of the ancestors worshipped by the family of Li Fo-sang were lineal descendants, and this did not seem to be an irrelevant concern.

One remaining ancestral site must be mentioned. It is located in the village of Kowloon Hang, a large village adjoining Tai Po Road halfway between Fanling and Tai Po market town and a 20 minute drive from Wo Hang. According to the wife of Li Fo-sang, the remains of two ancestors (one male and one female) were buried in an unmarked grave located next to a tree sitting on a villager's private house lot. She had been to this site previously on several occasions, each time accompanying her mother-in-law. All she knew about the ancestors was that they were "of many generations ago". The grave site bore no name, much less any sign of being other than (forgive the expression) "a hole in the ground". During our trip to this grave site, the occupant of this land was not home. The family continued to conduct all the ritual preparations, lighting four candles and burning two sets of paper clothing to indicate that there were two ancestors being worshipped there. After the food and other utensils were collected, the family departed as peacefully as they had arrived. The occupants of the land were not at home, so I was not able to assess their opinion of having outsiders presenting grave offerings there.

An accounting is now in order. The Li Fo-sang family made pilgrimages to three ancestral graves containing the remains of 21 individuals, 11 male and 10 female. Mathematically speaking, these individuals should have accounted for ascendants of 11 generations. However, this already far exceeded the number of genealogically possible descendants. The family worships Wo Hang ancestors of the first four generations communally with other Wo Hang villagers. The first two, of which there is only one in each generation, are worshipped by members of both upper and lower villages of Wo Hang. The family of Li Fo-sang worship Li Jit-fong, one of three ancestors in the third generation and Li Chiu-leung, one of the three sons of Li Jit-fong in the fourth generation. Each of these ancestors (and their wives) are worshipped by many families on days prearranged by themselves. This leaves unaccounted generations 5 through 11 (that of Li Fo-sang), a total of 7 generations of ascendants. Who then are the other 4 "ancestors" (and wives) worshipped in addition to the 7 (possible) lineal ascendants?

One of the four is Li San-him, one of the two sons of Li Yam-iu. Unlike his brother Li San-kwai, who was succeeded by his son Li Fo-sang, Li San-him died during the war without being survived by any descendant. Both he and his wife's remains are buried in Li Yam-iu's communal grave. He owned some agricultural land in the village and shared ownership of a house with his brother. Upon his death, his property was, according to custom, claimed and inherited by his nearest agnate, either his brother or nephew, and the family of Li Fo-sang continues to pay Crown Rent to this day on that property, which is still registered in his (the deceased's) name. Two other possible non-lineal ascendants are Li To-tai and the other ancestor worshipped by the family in an unmarked grave in Kowloon Hang. Given the genealogical amnesia of the current surviving members of the family, one can never be certain as to the precise identity of these ancestors.

What is certain, however, is that if any of these latter two do turn out to be lineal descendants, one is still faced with the problem of how to account for the other unknown non-lineal ascendants who continue to be considered by the family as "ancestors" and are worshipped as such. In the case of the latter two, property seems to be an irrelevant consideration. The family holds no interest in estates other than that formerly belonging to Li San-him, Li San-kwai, Li Yam-iu Tso and the larger *tso* in the village. Money for the worship of the other two individuals came from family expenses. Of course, the property could have been once owned by these bygone individuals and subsequently amalgamated into other estates or divided up among other kinsmen, but there is little conscious indication among present descendants that property was any kind of precondition for worship. In the case of Li San-him, the fact of his being worshipped as an ancestor by the family of Li Fo-sang had less to do with his having property to give than with his being a close relation to an agnate who was willing to undertake the burden of worship in the absence of a direct descendant. The fate of his property was not subject to negotiation or "competition for scarce resources" by distant kinsmen or outsiders, as Fried would have it. It simply followed from whom the immediate burden of ancestor worship fell upon. In the case of Wo Hang or even in those anomalous cases reported by Ahern and Wolf in Taiwan of outsiders having given land upon death to individuals in return for being worshipped as "ancestors" in the afterlife, there is no evidence to show that the immediate recipient of ancestral obligations (and property) was anyone *other* than the deceased's closest relation.[12]

At this point, it would be fruitless even to speculate about whom the fourth mystery non-lineal ascendant was, although it appears most likely that he was a close agnate in the distant past who was not survived by a direct ascendant. Such speculation, moreover, would be interesting only if one can assume that each of the 7 lineal ascendants and spouses from generations 5–11 was represented among the ancestors buried in the communal grave of Li Yam-iu. On the other hand, the genealogical amnesia of many of the worshippers apparently shows that lack of demonstratable descent in no way really marred the efficacy of ancestral worship as a meaningful set of acts in itself. The intention to and the (symbolic) necessity of worship seemed to constitute sufficient grounds for the continuity of the practice as a whole. In sum, one might say that the concerns of the dead are probably not reflections of the living but instead the other way around. The very existence of ancestor worship is evidence of the fact that the concerns of the dead essentially dominate concerns of the present, and if ancestor worship is what defines (agnatic) kinship in a Chinese context, then there appears to

be no justification for looking at kinship as an autonomous phenomenon divorced from these larger concerns.

In short, it is much harder to explain ancestor worship from the
perspective of descent than it is to explain descent relationships from
ancestral practices and obligations. The above examples show, if anything, that ancestor worship is not restricted to genealogical relations.
Worship here is at the bottom line an act of remembrance and memorializing. In the context of the spiritual world, offerings made to the
deceased placate restless or evil souls. It is perhaps less important to ask
what the genealogical relation of worshipped to worshipper is than to
assert that whomever provided for the establishment of the gravesite
wished, through the transmission of an estate, to guarantee the material
basis for ongoing worship. One can only assume that in the absence
of a direct relationship, the responsibility for taking for the soul of the
deceased would be the closest relation. Nonetheless, the presence of
non-lineal or non-agnatic ancestors does not appear to diminish the
efficacy of worship, descent groups or lineage halls, for that matter.

ZONG, JIA AND *QIN* IN THE CONTEXT OF THE VILLAGE: A PRIMARY SYNTHESIS

So much attention has been given by scholars of local Chinese
society on showing the diverse ramifications of lineage ideology and
organization in village life that few have bothered to problematize the
nature of the Chinese village as a cultural-historical phenomenon in its
own right. In essence, the village is not just a territorial aggregation of
households but a moral community whose ties to people and land must
be viewed in terms of its own cultural rules. As can be seen in the
settlement history of Wo Hang, there is perhaps a fine line that separates
the physical existence of a settlement and a community that marks its
conscious identity as such through a complex repertoire of acts and
symbols. The conditions by which people eventually coalesce as a
community are in the first instance the consequence of the overall socio-
political climate of the region or the times and not a refraction of agnatic
principles per se. In this regard, one can easily contrast the nucleated
settlements found in southeastern China with the dispersed territorial
pattern of villages found in the north as exemplary of these different

socio-political influences, where agnatic principles are generally the same. On the other hand, one cannot neglect the various aspects of lineage ideology and organization that have become standard features of villages such as Wo Hang. The writing of the clan genealogy that inscribes the settled existence of the group through its apical ancestor as well as the establishment of the ancestral hall are all obvious features that mark the presence of this sedentary community, but these accoutrements are themselves cultural constructions of only the past 200–300 years. During the Ming dynasty (1368–1644), family shrines (*jiamiao*) and acts of genealogical writing were phenomena restricted to literati elites who wished to preserve official pedigree and were different from the ubiquitous existence of ancestral halls and genealogies in most villages during the subsequent Qing dynasty. While it is clear that the latter has added new features to the substance of lineage organization, it can be argued instead that it has contributed considerably more to the functional constitution of the village than the practice of ancestor worship per se. Thus, the notion of the apical ancestor as inscribed in clan genealogies gave the agnatic settlement a clear sense of sociological groundedness that did not exist in the past, and the ancestral hall, far from being just an end result of segmentation, represented par excellence a public fulcrum for village activity and solidarity rather than merely an effective focus for ancestral worship. Both primarily enhanced the existence of the village as a social institution, and it was in the context of this redefined village that such agnatic institutions took on a *localized* rather than purely religious function.

Rather than being primordially an agnatic group or a cluster of them, the village is thus from the perspective of its constituent community a *jiaxiang* (home, literally "family-country"), which is effective regardless of how that community is constituted in kin or other terms. As will be shown in a later context, the concept of *jiaxiang* and its respective notions of kin relativity better explain how people relate to each other and to the land in ways that tend to be distorted by the social structural boundedness implicit in models of "descent". The subjective belonging inherent in one's attachment to a *jiaxiang* is a flexible one that can be affected by various factors and is moreover analytically distinct from the rites and obligations engendered by ancestral worship. Indeed, when one begins to look at the practice of local level ancestral worship groups in the context of *zong, jia* and *qin,* one can see extensions and permutations of certain basic principles. The social structural overlap between many *tso* and *tang* in practice suggest that their reasons for being are largely a function of the conditions of their creation and that these conditions in turn limit its possibilities for structural change and expansion as an economic enterprise in purely capitalist terms. In the case of Wo Hang, many villagers in the early generations acquired their wealth through commerce, which contributed eventually without doubt to their major presence in the Shataukok market. They transformed their wealth into ancestral estates, which provided the basis for the ongoing prosperity of their descendants. Few continued to expand and evolve into "corporations" that were managed for the sake of perpetually generating wealth. Moreover, the practice of rent rotation by its members suggests that these estates were intended to benefit the subsistence of its descendants as individual families. One is also hard pressed to explain why the existence of wealth per se did not lead to increasing segmentation (agnatic aggregation) and incessant establishment of ancestral halls in a village, as posited by Freedman's model. It is clear instead that landed estates and ancestral halls were created for very different purposes.

Our "local" knowledge of agnatic village communities in southeastern China is limited largely by the scope of our "field" of historical and regional vision. Over a much larger historical and sociological framework, I have argued elsewhere that lineage-village organization was a complex and peculiar interplay of intellectual, political and regional forces that runs counter to the principles that Freedman had argued logically culminated in higher-order agnatic organization (see Chun 1996b). In short, patrilineal inheritance, corporate kin property and systematic ancestor worship have concurrently existed in China for several millenia without producing full-scale lineages of the kind venerated by descent theory. The gradual evolution of a gravesite based ancestral worship, the invention of genealogies to memorialize the origins of territorially based kin communities and the explicit popularization of charitable estates all contributed to the formation of a universalized, locality based and socially egalitarian notion of kin communities that contrasted with the officially stratified, shrine worship based and socially exclusive ancestral worship corporations that had been staple features of village kinship up through the Ming dynasty. However, these latter developments could not have coalesced effectively into full-scale localized lineages (centered on public ancestral halls) without the parallel transformation of the village or a newly galvanized sense of community focused on it. The disruptive consequences of the Coastal Evacuation during the early Qing era should cast doubt on whether the structure of local communities in the New Territories up until the 20th century is a basic continuation of a model of its "Five Great Clans" or a radical departure from it. Similarly, the effects of the silent land revolution brought about by Pax Britannica's breakup of wealthy lineage estates and their claims as absentee landlord over large tracts of territory granted by imperial decree or other means is difficult to qualify. Nonetheless, it should inject caution into emphasizing the role of descent organization in defining the nature of the village when their renewed importance has clearly been consequences of changes in local organization. While postwar land policy has not directly threatened the relationship between land and lineage, in contrast to aspects of village land and residential space, it is clear from the vantage point of the postwar land crisis that considerations of ancestral trusts and lineage identity, which have invoked concern (by scholars) over the fate of the homogenous kin village, are locally irrelevant.

THE *JIA* IN THE PASSAGE OF RITES

No matter from what perspective one looks at it, the *jia* always seems to be a unit of something. Arthur P. Wolf (1970: 57), for instance, distinguished three components of the Chinese "family": 1) the *ke* (Taiwanese for *jia*), the basic unit of subsistence whose existence is symbolized by a separate stove, 2) the "descent line" within which the family can be seen as a constituent part of the lineage-at-large, and 3) the "uterine family", which he and Margery Wolf (1972) regarded to be the basic unit of biological procreation and reproduction. Although not noted explicitly by Wolf, these three dimensions of "family" that he "sees" as existing in a Chinese context refer more to Chinese manifestations of Eurocentric notions of family than to the multiplicity of institutions invoked by primordial notions of *jia*.

As a unit of "descent", the notion of "family" being referred to there is really *jiazu*. Strictly speaking, these properties of "descent" that Wolf seems to "see" in the notion of *jiazu* should more accurately be attributed to the concept of *zu* as in *zongzu* rather than *jia* itself. Thus, the continuity of a *jia* within such a line is largely similar to the continuity of values constitutive of a *zongzu*, namely that of *zong*, *qi*, *xing* and various obligations of ancestor worship inherent therein. In this regard, continuity of worship per se provides the logical or symbolic basis on which the *jiazu* can be seen as a unit within the whole of a particular *zongzu*.

As a unit of economic subsistence and social livelihood, the Chinese "family" being referred to there is more accurately captured by the notion of *jiating* (M). Insofar as the expression *jiating* can be rendered into local dialect, it appears to share with written usage of the term the essential meaning of a group of people who share a common *ting* (court). This is certainly the case with the Cantonese usage of *ga-ting* and to some extent the Hakka expression *ka-tin*. Hakka also talk in terms of *vuk-ka* (*wujia* (M)), which is similar to *jiating* and what Wolf renders in Taiwanese to be *ke* in the sense that it refers to a group of people who identify with a place of permanent residence or home. The notion of residence implied by the word *vuk* (=*wu* (M) or "house") of *vuk-ka* should not be confused with physical residence by census definition and can presumably include other members of the *ka* (=*jia* (M)) who for purposes of study or work live elsewhere and consider the *vuk* as their "home" or "residential base". Thus, in comparing conceptions such as *jiazu*, *jiating* and *vuk-ka*, one is dealing with the distinctive features of seminal concepts embodied in *zu*, *ting* and *vuk* that Chinese use to mark different kinds of social relationships or institutions involving a particular group of people. In the case of *vuk-ka*, one should expect then that the meaning of *vuk-ka* in the context of the abovementioned concerns centers specifically upon the notion of a common *vuk* and that complex of values, rites and obligations associated with it.

This leaves the notion of "the uterine family". Etymologically speaking, *jia* is composed of "a pig under a roof", which would at least explain the importance of pig sacrifice in almost all domestic rites. Shao Chün-p'u (1935), however, argues instead that the ancient ideograph for "pig" (*shi*) was often confused with the word *hai*, which according to Yen Zhangfu's commentary to *Shuo Wen* meant "a man and a woman".[13] Nonetheless, as a unit of reproduction, the symbolic and ritual meanings associated with *jia* are more complex than its biological and etymological associations and has important ramifications for how one should understand the various social institutions engendered by it. First of all, only through relations of exchange between *jia* in a context of marriage can one then meaningfully talk about *chengjia* (establishing a *jia*). Ritual relations of exchange mirror the life cycle of a (new) *jia*, which begins with marriage and construction of a house, is followed by birthdays, continues with the birth and marriage of sons, then culminates in the death of the *jiazhang* (family head). In this regard, exchange augments the notion of *jia* by tying together procreation, descent and shared livelihood in ways that not only underscore the significance of *zong*, *jia* and *qin* but also have bearing on an "indigenous" interpretation of lineage and village in southeastern China. Needless to say, an understanding of *jia* in the context of exchange and reproduction should be directly relevant to a further understanding of the various social institutions associated with *jia*, especially *jiating*, *jiazu* and *jiaxiang*.

In his essay on gift-giving, Marcel Mauss' interest in exchange was really motivated by an interest in explaining social solidarity. Exchange relations were socially solidary ones insofar as they were based upon the same kinds of ethical, moral values that society itself was based upon. Much the same can be said about the relations of exchange that are constitutive of *jia*. The efficacy of Mauss' ideas becomes most clearly manifested when exchange exists as a regularized system of acts. This regularity does not really refer to the regularity of a staple set of rites, like marriage exchange, but rather its regularity in the passage of rites. Marriage thus initiates a continuous, regularized series of exchanges between certain groups of people, exchanges which contribute to the very life process of the *jia*.

The following is a record of rites compiled on the basis of an account given by an elderly Hakka woman born into a family of wealthy background. Although the customs described are not typical of those actually practiced throughout the territory, which cover a wide diversity, the complexities noted therein manifest systematic features of the exchange relationship and its ritual expressions.

The informant is one of four daughters born to a family of merchants. Since there were no sons born in their family, a son was adopted from a close agnatic kinsman. The informant's husband was born into a small family of modest means and consisting of one older brother and sister. After her marriage, our informant brought up three sons and two daughters, each of whom in turn raised a family. At the time of her marriage, our informant was aged 17 and her husband 21. As in most other traditional marriages, this one was arranged by the parents of the two spouses through the services of an intermediary (*mui-po* (C,H), =*meiren* (M)). Upon mutual arrangement, the couple was engaged, when parents, relatives and friends of the groom were invited to the bride's house to "take a look at the bride" (*kon shin-nyong* (H), =*kan xinniang*). Any number of interested persons could go as long as there was an even number of people. At this time, brideswealth (*tin-kim* (H), =*dingjin*) was given to the bride's parents along with an abundance of gifts. They included a pair of red ancestral candles (*tsu-tsuk* (H) (*zuzu*)), one big and one small, two bunches of "ancestral incense" (*tsu-heong* (H) (*zuxiang*)), one side of raw pork, two bottles of wine, one or two pairs of live chickens, duck eggs, and bridal cakes. In addition, a red envelope containing a token amount of money called *tsia-mui tsien* (H) ("sister money") and marked as such on the cover, was given by the groom's family to sisters of the bride. In return, the family of the bride prepared token gifts to give to the groom's family and returned a portion of the gifts so that the guests would not return home emptyhanded. A portion of the bridal cakes was also returned, and a set of clothes each was given to the groom's parents as well as some incidental gifts for the groom. Of the pair of ancestral candles given, the bride's family kept the large candle to burn and returned the smaller one.[14] All other gifts were collected by the bride's family for personal consumption, while the betrothal cakes were divided among relatives and friends.

On the wedding day, the groom was accompanied by his village brothers to the bride's village. His arrival was announced by the sound of gongs, ushered in by two lantern bearers and flanked by dancing unicorns. On this day, more gifts were presented to the bride's family. They included a whole freshly killed pig, several live chickens, bridal cakes, two bunches of ancestral incense, a pair of ancestral candles, one big and one small, wine, duck eggs, a box of dried shrimp, and a box of abalone.[15] Of these, two chickens were given by the groom's family to the bride's grandmother and designated "grandmother's food" (*ah-po tsoi* (H)). A slab of lean pork was given to the bride's mother and called "stomach sore meat" (*du-tung nyuk* (H)), in memory of the time when the bride's mother gave birth to her daughter. On the other hand, the bride's family returned half of the chickens given by the groom's family and made other presentations of clothing to the groom's family. Depending upon family custom, a pair of shoes or a complete set of clothes would be given to the groom's parents and relatives (particularly FaBr, FaBrWi, FaSi, FaSiHu, FaFa, FaMo). The clothes might include a cap, several bundles of silk and other woven cloth, a pair of shoes and socks, a cloth belt or sash, a pair of fans, and a cloth pouch. Other things might be given also, such as a container of tobacco, rice cakes, and a box of sweets. After the bride's arrival to her new home and before going to her husband's ancestral hall to pay respects to ancestral spirits of the groom's family, the bride poured tea to parents and relatives of the groom who came to the wedding, essentially the same people to whom she brought gifts. Each of those relatives were seated in a row, and the groom's sister assisted the bride in pouring tea. In return, each relative gave an envelope containing good luck money, which the bride put into her cloth pouch along with her other coins.

Our informant also mentioned that, among many families, these prestations made on the day of the wedding were instead made on the occasion in which the two families came together to choose the day of the wedding (bau-nyit (H) (baore)). On the day of the wedding, the mother's brother of the bride undertook a major ceremonial role in giving the bride away. He was the one who offered incense at the ancestral hall of the bride's family to proclaim the departure of the bride from her natal village.[16] In the absence of mother's brother, mother's father's brother's son (MoFaBrSo) or other close male relative representing the mother's *zu* could act as substitute. On the groom's side, the groom's father's brother or a comparable male relative took ceremonial responsibility for guiding the groom and his family through the prescribed rites at the ancestral hall. These rites included a visit to the family's ancestral hall on the night before the wedding as well as another visit to the ancestral hall on the afternoon of the wedding by the bride and groom.

On the night of the wedding, the families of the bride and groom celebrated the event separately in their respective villages. After the departure of the bride from her natal village, the bride's family invited close friends and relatives to a communal dinner. The family of the groom did likewise, and the only outsiders present from the bride's natal village were village sisters who chose to accompany the bride on the road to the groom's village. Relatives and friends of the bride's family gave monetary gifts on occasion of the bride's departure (*qujia*). Other kinds of gifts given included jewelry and other ornamentation. Relatives on the groom's side gave monetary gifts to the groom's family on occasion of the bride's reception (*quqin*) also, but when nonmonetary gifts were given, they comprised a box of rice, sweets, a bottle of wine, a side of pork, fish and a pair of chickens.

Twelve days after the wedding, the bride returned to her natal home along with her husband. They brought with them token gifts in the form of sweets or cakes. After a short stay, during which they were invited to tea and engaged in lively conversation, they were each given a set of gifts by the family of the bride, which they took back to their new home. This set of gifts included two sticks of sugar cane, a pair of chickens, one male and one female, and a pot of glutinous rice. The sugar cane was kept for personal consumption, the chickens were bred to raise more chickens, and the glutinous rice was distributed among relatives.

In exchange terms, the marriage appears to be a simple matter between the *jia* of the groom and that of the bride. In this exchange, the *fuzu* (father's *zu*) of the groom and the *muzu* (mother's *zu*) of the bride played important ceremonial roles. On the side of the groom, the burden of responsibility rested largely upon relatives on the father's side, which included the groom's parents, grandparents (FaFa, FaMo) then uncles and aunts (FaBr, FaBrWi, FaSi and FaSiWi). Father's brother or similar person undertook the major ceremonial role of conducting the ancestral rites for the family, and father's sister assisted in preparations for the wedding. Each of these relatives received gifts of clothing (or shoes) given by the bride's family, and each was served tea by the bride on the afternoon of her arrival at her husband's village. The bride was given away by mother's brother; he or someone in that capacity was responsible for lighting the incense at the ancestral hall for the bride's family. Mother's brother was also invited on the day when both sides came together to decide the day of the wedding (*baore*). Of the gifts of food given by the groom's family, certain of these gifts were explicitly given to the bride's mother and bride's mother's mother. Within each respective camp, that is to say, in the separate celebrations held by families of the groom and the bride, there was no real distinction between *fuzu* (father's relatives) and *muzu* (mother's relatives). In other words, relatives of the bride on both father's and mother's side were invited as equals by the bride's family to join in the feast on the wedding day after the departure of the bride from her natal village. Those who came or were asked to come donated money or material gifts to the family. Both father's and mother's relatives on the groom's side were invited on the wedding day. Foremost among mother's relatives were mother's parents, brothers and sisters. At dinner, they would sit among other close relatives at tables closest to the bride and groom, while friends and distant relatives would sit at tables toward the outside.

The birth of a son was an important ceremonial occasion in the relationship between "affines". What was once the bride's family (*nüjia*, the female side) now became *waijia* ("external *jia*") from the perspective of the husband's family as ego (*benjia, benzu*). From the perspective of the husband, his wife's relatives were now referred to as *qizu* ("wife's *zu*"), and from the perspective of their children those same relatives became *muzu* (mother's *zu*) or *mufang qinqi* (mother's relatives). On the 12th day following the birth of a son, a pot containing a pair of chickens boiled in wine broth was presented both to wife's parents and wife's grandparents (MoMo) by members of the husband's family to signal the successful birth of a son. In return, the recipients gave back the head, tail and legs of the chicken (keeping the meat, returning the whole) so that the donors did not go home emptyhanded. This chicken was eaten by mothers to recover from delivery and regain lost blood.

The child's first full month's birthday was observed by inviting relatives and friends to a communal dinner. Relatives on the wife's side were also invited, the most notable of them being the parents and grandparents (MoFa, MoMo) of the wife, mother's brother, and mother's brother's wife. They brought with them gifts of clothing that included shirts, diapers, socks, cloth and cap. Other relatives gave similar gifts or money. Friends and distant relatives gave money enclosed in red envelopes. Sometime after the newborn son's first month's birthday, his mother would bring him back to her natal home. During this visit, relatives and friends of the wife's family were invited to see the baby, and small monetary gifts were presented to the mother in the name of the baby. Upon leaving her natal family to return to her husband's family, the wife would bring back with her certain gifts given by her parents. These included two sticks of sugar cane, a pair of chickens, one male and one female, and a pot of glutinous rice. The sugar cane was meant for personal consumption, the chickens were used to raise food for the family, and the glutinous rice was distributed to friends and relatives on the husband's side.

On the occasion of the child's first four months' birthday and first year's birthday, relatives, especially the parents and grandparents of the wife, would give more gifts of clothing and money. At four months, the child was given a pair of pants and other clothing, while at age one he was given a new set of clothing and money. To celebrate the child's first full year's birthday, the parents of the child would invite a large number of relatives on the wife's and husband's side as well as other close friends, during which gifts were presented. This event is equal in significance to that held on the first full month's birthday. Following the first full year's birthday, personal birthdays were celebrated every ten years (at ages 11, 21, etc.). While relatives on the father's side continued to celebrate these personal birthdays, relatives on the mother's side did not have any other ritual obligations in this regard. In the case of a second or third son born in the family, there was less of a ritual obligation than in the case of a first-born son, presumably since continuity of family *zong* had already been established. A pot of chicken boiled with rice wine may or may not be given to relatives on the wife's side, and wife's relatives, like other relatives and friends, would most likely offer monetary gifts. The birth of a daughter in the family also followed likewise, although in general money contributed to the family would usually be less than for a newborn son.

When the married couple and their children decided to move to a new house and live apart from their parents, this was also considered to be the making of a new *jia*, albeit in the sense of a house. Depending largely upon the fate of family fortune, the building of a separate house might be due entirely to the efforts of the younger couple or the gift of a *jiazhang* who intended to make similar provisions for each of his sons. Relatives on the wife's side were expected to present gifts to the couple to celebrate the establishment of the new house. They usually included household items such as cooking utensils or dinnerware by wife's brothers, sisters, parents, mother's brothers, mother's sisters as well as grandparents, and in some cases pieces of furniture and related accessories might be donated.

The raising of the main roof beam (*shang-leung* (H) *(shangliang)*) in the new house was an important symbolic act that also shed light on the meaning of *jia* as house. The center beam which runs beneath the top of the roof was considered the foundation of the house, and it was only after the beam was put up that the house formally came into existence. People held rites to mark the occasion, and every house beam was decorated in some manner. Among the Hakka, at the very least, a long strip of red cloth about a foot wide would be placed over the center part of the beam. Red is a felicitous color (in contrast to white, the color of mourning), and a much longer piece of red cloth would be seen draped over the front door of the house and over the main gate of the ancestral hall on the day of the wedding. In the informant's case, a small round mirror was also tacked to the red cloth similar to that which was hung over the top of the front door of the house. Of Taoist origin, it was meant to repel evil spirits (*bixie*). On each side of the cloth hung a red painted rice measure (*tau*) filled with rice. Next, a red foot-long ruler was hung from a string, and further to the side, small agricultural tools similarly were hung and tied to the roof beam. Our informant explained that the red cloth and pouches of rice hung from the beam signified "a hundred sons and a thousand grandsons" (*baizi qiansun*). It is clear from the kinds of objects hung from the roof beam and the relevance of the roof beam to the structure of the house that they symbolized the essence of the house and by implication the nature of the *jia*.

Not incidentally, all these objects had a direct relationship to the symbolic meaning of marriage. For instance, the red cloth was not dissimilar to the cloth that draped the door of the house and ancestral hall on the day of a wedding. On the bride's side, the red cloth was tied into a bundle and hung from the side of her house door. Upon leaving her natal village, the cloth was unwound and wrapped diagonally across the length of the bride's red wedding dress. Although it might be taken off on her arrival at her husband's village, she had to wear it again when she paid respects at her husband's ancestral hall on that afternoon. Likewise, the round mirror and red ruler were objects that hung visibly on a bride's wedding dress. The ruler was literally used to make clothing for the family. Rice signified abundance for a family blessed with many sons, and the agricultural tools stressed the importance of productivity on the land as a basis of social livelihood. There were variations on the theme of roof beam decorations. Some roof beams could have paper lanterns or cloth pouches containing coins (symbolizing wealth) hung from the top; others would paint the roof beam completely red instead of hanging a red cloth and might write the words "a hundred sons a thousand grandsons" on the beam. The Cantonese also hung the same kinds of symbolic representations from the roof beam, although the objects used differed somewhat.[17]

The process of aging is a universal feature of van Gennep's description of the individual life cycle. In the case of the *jia*, the participation of wife's relatives appears to be an important feature in the life cycle of the *jia*. This is most evident in the event of birthdays. In the case of this informant, as was the custom among many Hakkas, the wife's relatives honored newlyweds by presenting them with gifts and money on their first birthday after the marriage. A set of clothes and a monetary gift enclosed in a red envelope were given to the recipient. Outside of this, birthdays were celebrated once every ten years. Befitting this ten-year cycle, a major celebration was held for the individual by members of his family. A male individual in his early years would expect to be honored by his own parents; in later years one with grown up children would expect to be honored by his sons.

In the case of the informant's recently wed groom, his first major birthday after his marriage came at age 31. On this occasion, his parents made it a point to invite, in addition to relatives on the husband's side, members of the wife's *zu*, the most important of them being mother's brothers (*jiufu*) (or mother's brother's parallel cousin). Other relatives on the wife's side, such as wife's brothers and sisters, parents and grandparents, were also invited. On his birthday, the husband would be given gifts of clothing. Parents of the husband on the other hand could not by custom accept gifts given by wife's mother's brother, who might give money and a set of clothes. If money was accepted, the parents of the husband would make a return gift of money which was double that originally given. As for gifts given by other relatives on the wife's side, a token monetary gift would be reciprocated.

The birthday of a male head of household would be celebrated in much the same manner every ten years. The situation for the woman of the house, that is to say, the wife of the male *jiazhang*, would be slightly different, because they are no "affinal" relatives to speak of in her case. Having been married out of her own *jia* and into that of her husband (the term *chujia* literally means crossing over from the woman's (own) *jia*), a wife in effect was part of her husband's *jia*. Her husband's relatives thus became her own relatives (*ji-ga-nyin* (H)). That which her husband refers to as *qizu* (wife's *zu* or relatives) on the other hand still remained for the wife her own people (*ji-ga-nyin*) and not "outside relatives" (*ngoi-ka*), as her husband's family would call them. Thus on the occasion of the informant's 31st, 51st and succeeding birthdays, relatives from both the husband's as well as wife's side came. The same amount of gifts were given as in the case of her husband's birthday, except that instead of clothes relatives would offer presents of personal ornamentation, jewelry and money. Despite the presence of the same relatives on the wife's birthday and the offerings of similar kinds of gifts, the wife's birthday lacked the explicit relevance to relations of marriage exchange that one found in the case of her husband's birthday, this being a consequence of a married woman's peculiar status *vis-a-vis* her relatives. The same followed in the case of children's birthdays in the family. Both husband's relatives and wife's relatives participated with the same degree of ceremonial reverence observed in the case of the birthdays of the older generation. However, from the perspective of the child, one would be dealing strictly speaking with "one's own people" (i.e., "father's relatives" (*fuzu*) and "mother's relatives" (*muzu*)), that is to say, *ji-ga-nyin* and not *ngoi-ka*.

Death is the end of the life cycle. In the case of the *jiazhang* (family head), his death meant in essence the death of the *jia* and its succession by separate *jia*, each headed by a son, his wife and children. More so than in the case of marriage, a funeral was the one occasion where relatives from all sides were expected to participate and pay homage. Chinese regarded it a matter of personal dignity that a person should die at home in the presence of close relatives and that his remains be buried in his *jiaxiang* or home village.[18] The importance of being at home and among close relatives underscored the practice of *wufu* (five mourning grades) and overlapped in this regard with general notions of kin relativity (*qinqi*).

In short, one can in the context of death see continuing elements of social exchange that enhanced the meaning and life process of a *jia*. In this regard, one would be dealing only with the death of a male head of family, because, as in the case of birthdays, it was only with reference to a married male that one could talk about a distinction in symbolic terms between "ego's (husband's) relatives" (*benjia*) and "outside (wife's) relatives" (*ngoi-ka* (H) (*waijia*)), a distinction which did not exist from the perspective of the wife or children as ego. As in birthdays, relatives on both husband's and wife's side were expected to be present or participate in the funeral, but *waijia* nonetheless enjoyed a special status that was clearly expressed by their obligation to give and the obligation of the *benjia* to receive and repay. First of all, the *waijia* was not included among the circle of mourners, hence fell outside the framework of relative kin, as defined by the *wufu*. Moreover, when they paid their respects to the deceased, they did so usually as a group, and they were received by mourners as honored guests at the funeral. Secondly, like other relatives, they were expected to give monetary gifts to the family of the deceased. However, unlike the others, their gifts were not supposed to be accepted; if they were, the recipients had to at a later date reciprocate the gifts by giving back an amount equal to twice that originally given, a situation similar to that found on birthdays. This held true not only for wife's mother's brother (*jiufu*) but for any other relative within the classificatory group *jiu* (i.e., males and females associated with the wife's *zu*). This exchange of courtesies and gifts between "ego's relatives" and "outside relatives" at the funeral was the last formal affiliation between *benjia* and *waijia*, and it also symbolically coincided with the dissolution of the *jia*.

SEPARATE *VUK-KA*, SMALL *KA-TIN*

The Hakka expression *vuk-ka* (literally *jiawu*) is a difficult term to render into standard Chinese, much less English. Made up of the characters *ka* (*jia* or "family") and *vuk* (*wu* or "house"), it is a synonym compound that can be taken to mean a certain group of people (*ka*) sharing a dwelling (*vuk*), that is to say, a *vuk* occupied by persons related to each other as part of a *ka*. A *vuk* is, simply stated, a house or physical dwelling where people reside. The addition of the suffix *ka* to the compound *vuk-ka* implies that the *vuk* is not a random group of persons under a roof. Nonetheless, a *vuk-ka* does not specify how its occupants should be related exactly in kin terms but rather that its members, whoever they are, are bound by primordial values intrinsic to a *ka*, namely common livelihood (*tongjü*), common budget (*gongcai*) and common worship (*xianghuo*). Thus, a residential dwelling inhabited by a group of students could without doubt be called a *vuk* but definitely not a *vuk-ka* or even a *ka-tin* (*jiating* (M)). On the other hand, a similar dwelling occupied by a widow, her children, her mother, her husband's unmarried brother and her husband's divorced sister could conceivably be called a *vuk-ka* or *ka-tin* even despite the fact that this represents an unorthodox and unlikely combination by strict "social structural" rules of what should constitute a "family".

If one rendered the term *vuk-ka* into its equivalent in Mandarin, the closest approximation would be *jiating* or simply *jia*, given that *jia* in both Mandarin and Hakka can designate both a home or its occupants. However, in Hakka the literal term for *jiating* (*ka-tin*) also exists. While they share the same overall meaning, there are nonetheless nuances between the two. Like its Mandarin counterpart, *ka-tin* assumes that members of the *ka* in question reside with reference to some dwelling or literally a common *tin* (=*ting*, "court"). Moreover, most people tend to agree that *ka-tin* is more likely to refer to the "people" than its "house", while *vuk-ka* is the other way around. That is to say, a small or large *ka-tin* in Hakka, as in other dialects, means that there is a small or large number of people living in that *ka*. A small or large *vuk-ka* on the other hand refers to the size of a dwelling being occupied by that *ka*, and if there is the added connotation of containing a large number of people as well, this is probably a coincidence of fact only.

Perhaps another way of stating the difference would be to say that while the term *ka-tin* refers unambiguously to a group of people living in a given dwelling, it does not literally specify the nature of that dwelling except for the assumption of a common *tin*. Moreover, the term *ka* does not specify the actual composition or number of occupants in question. *Vuk-ka* on the other hand is similar to *ka-tin* in that one is dealing in both cases with a group of people sharing some common living situation. Unlike *ka-tin*, however, *vuk-ka* specifies a concrete relationship to some fixed dwelling, namely *vuk*. If the notion of a *vuk-ka* seems unambiguous among Wo Hang villagers, it can be attributed to the clarity of *vuk*. With regard to *vuk-ka* and *ka-tin*, there are two important issues that need elaboration, namely first of all the meaning of the *vuk-ka* as symbolically defined in local practice and secondly the dynamics of residence among members of a *ka* living in the same *vuk*. These two are quite distinct, and this distinction is crucial to understanding how the principles of a *vuk-ka* and by extension *ka-tin* in symbolic terms are logically different from those posited in the prevailing literature on "Chinese family size".

Rather than starting directly from what the composition and size of *ka-tin* is like in Wo Hang, I think it is more appropriate to describe what the *vuk-ka* is like, then show how it sheds light upon the nature of *ka-tin* composition in time and space as well as upon settlement patterns in the village at a broader level. The village is, of course, a community of *vuk-ka*, and while this is not to say that the village is *only* a community of *vuk-ka*, one can nonetheless in the process of describing the *vuk-ka* within this larger pattern of settlement begin to sort out the interrelationships between various concepts like *zong*, *jia* and *qin*, which have been effectively confused in anthropological analyses of the "single-lineage village".

Like many of the other villages in the New Territories, most of the *vuk* in Wo Hang tend to be clustered together in a residential area apart from the fields in the adjoining valley. Within this residential area, the *vuk* are rectangular in shape usually and built tightly next to each other in long rows which, depending upon the landscape, may be juxtaposed parallel to each other to form a closely knit community of dwellings. This compact pattern of village residential settlement per se probably has more to do with peculiarities of the region and conditions affecting the changing sociopolitical climate of the region as a whole than with ethnic traits, since it is indicative of most Cantonese and Hakka villages in the New Territories. While many villages are surrounded by walled enclosures and appropriately called *wai* (C) (*wei*, "walled city"), the compact features of the other villages in the region combined with the stark appearance of tiny one foot square sized windows in each house partitioned by steel matrices reflect the overall atmosphere of insecurity.

Within the environs of Wo Hang, most of the living and working space in the village can be named. Major blocks or subdivisions in the residential part of the village have names, and smaller niches within each subdivision can be referred to by name as well. Similarly, the surrounding fields are subdivided into major sections, each bearing a name. Each plot of cultivated field usually has a name which is given to it by the owner to distinguish the various pieces of land he has under cultivation. With exception of the more well-known or unusual plots of land, not every piece of land will be known by name to each villager. Since the village of Sheung Wo Hang is enclosed within a valley on three sides by adjacent hills, the surrounding hillsides can also be subdivided into named places. While not every nook and cranny of land has a name, certain plateaus, various hillsides facing the village, and places with geographical peculiarities are named as well.

Place names in the village have origins that either attest to some event in the past or particularity of the location itself. In Wo Hang, at least from the point of view of an outside observer, there seemed to be three major residential clusters, each separated by a natural divider such as a stream or large stretch of flat land. From a native point of view, only one of the three had any name, namely Lau Wai (old walled city). The other two clusters had no specific designation, except when referring to a smaller tract of land. Lau Wai was the oldest settlement established by the first generations of Dengs and Lis to live in the area. In the initial phase of settlement in the village, there were at least two other residential niches, one directly facing Lau Wai on an adjacent hillside called Ho Uk Che, another called Wang Weng Pai, and a third located in a remote part of the valley called Wo Ping Chai. Ho Uk Che was settled by people surnamed Ho, Wang Weng Pai by people surnamed Zeng, and both Lau Wai and Wo Ping Chai were occupied by those of the surname Deng prior to the arrival of the Lis into the village. With exception of Lau Wai, where the Lis lived, all the other inhabitants moved out to different villages in the region, and their settlements eventually became abandoned.

After emigration of the Dengs from Wo Hang to the present village of Kong Ha, the Lis continued to spread out of Lau Wai and into the present residential areas next to the old city. Most of the houses in Lau Wai were seen as belonging to specific blocks, namely Mun Liu Chai ("entranceway"), Chu Tong ("ancestral hall"), Mun Liu Ha ("lower entranceway"), Deng Vuk Kok ("Deng's Corner") and Tai Su Fong ("the school"). The remaining residential areas of the village are more neatly subdivided into blocks. The central cluster of houses in Wo Hang that was situated near the present entrance to the village, flanked to the southwest by Lau Wai and to the northeast by a third cluster of houses, was divided into five blocks bearing names such as Tai Mun Liu ("main entranceway"), Ha Mun Piang ("lower plain"), Tiu Kok ("top corner"), San Ding ("hilltop") and Tai Che Mun ("big plateau"). The third remaining residential cluster of houses also appeared to be neatly divided into blocks bearing names such as Wo Tong Tiu ("padi terrace top"), Su Fong Chai ("old schoolroom"), Sin Vuk Hong ("new house lane"), Lieng Gien ("hill slope") and Ti Mui Sak ("land tail rock") all the place names above are Hakka. Most of the latter names appeared to be positional markers within the village. The degree to which these residential blocks corresponded to other bounded social groups must be explored, however.

Two other facts pertaining to the positioning of houses in the village must be mentioned which have to do with *fengshui* (geomancy). First of all, regardless of what direction the door of a house faced, there were in all cases a front and rear of the village, and this was defined by where the entrance of the ancestral hall sat and in which direction it faced. In essence, the direction which directly faced the entrance to the ancestral hall was the front of the village, and no house could be built in front of that imaginary line drawn along the front of the ancestral hall. Secondly, no house could be built higher than the one behind it in order to avoid disrupting the geomantic disposition or obstructing the front view of those houses.

The Hakka concept of *vuk* was similar to the Cantonese *uk* in that it tended to refer to a total living unit; a *fong* (=*fang* (M)) subsequently referred to a "room" or "branch" of that house. This distinction was perhaps less distinct in Mandarin, where the term *fangzi*, for instance, meant the entire house. There were several variations of *vuk* found in this village, but the simplest type probably consisted of a one-and-a-half story structure, rectangularly shaped with an open-air atrium in the center. Houses made prior to the 20th century were almost always made out of mud brick or limestone, the latter being produced locally in many villages in the area. The entrance to the house was situated at the small end of the rectangle, and the door was set several inches inside the threshold of the main entrance. The door itself was usually made out of wood and consisted of right-handed and left-handed halves which could be opened and closed at the center. After entering the main door, one would find a cooking stove and a place for washing or bathing on opposite walls. An image of the kitchen god (*tso-kun* (H), =*zaojün*) would be pasted near the stove. The front end of the interior of a house was always covered by a roof. The adjoining part of the house situated in the center, however, was often not. In the absence of adequate window space in many houses, this roofless part of the house enabled fumes and hot air to ventilate outward. The rear of the house usually consisted of a two-story structure covered by a roof and connected by a ladder leading from bottom to top. The lower half adjoining the center of the house was called a *gan-to* (H) ("trunk-belly"), which for all intents and purposes was considered to be the seat of the house, not unlike a parlor. In the center of the rear wall on the floor, one would find an image of the tutelary earth-god (*to-pak* (H)) along with an incense pot. The upstairs room was called a *pang-diang* (H) ("top of the hut") and was used as a bedroom. Under the roof of the *pang-diang* would rest the central beam upon which one would hang the various ceremonial objects symbolizing the *vuk*, namely a red cloth, red ruler and cloth pouches filled with rice and coins. Some *pang-diang* had a balcony opening (*tien-jiang*) in front.

In addition to the aforementioned one-and-a-half story limestone house with open-air atrium in the center, one could find other variations on the basic style. Many limestone houses and most of the later red brick and concrete houses were two-story buildings. Although the basic design of front kitchen, rear parlor and upstairs bedroom was largely preserved, the extension of a full story effectively replaced the open-air atrium and expanded the upstairs to facilitate more bedroom space and in some cases a balcony for drying clothes. In other cases, a separate kitchen, bathroom, or master bedroom would be moved to the back and the parlor moved to the front, while in larger houses the kitchen and double-story bedrooms would be situated on separate sides of the house, leaving a large two-story high parlor in the center of the house leading directly from the main door. In modern 2–3 story houses built in the postwar era, the front parlor and rear kitchen on the ground floor would lead to one or more floors of bedrooms, followed by a flat roof. This roof for the most part replaced the traditional roof with the ceremonial house beam in the center, while the top of the roof became a place for drying clothes.

Given these rudiments of a village house or *vuk*, juxtaposed in village space, one can begin to describe how the *vuk-ka* was defined in symbolic terms. By and large, the majority of houses in Wo Hang tended to be living units of a rectangular shape (1 1/2, 2 or 3 story construction) consisting of a *gan-to*, kitchen, *pang-diang* (or bedrooms), single set of kitchen and earth deities, and ceremonial roof beam (at least where traditional roofs were concerned). A living unit having the above characteristics would be referred to as a *vuk*, and the persons living in this *vuk* whose relationship to each other could be seen as identifying with or belonging to a *ka* ("common livelihood", "common worship", etc.) thus constituted a *vuk-ka*.

Having thus established in what sense the *vuk-ka* is a concrete social fact with clearly definable features, one can now begin to describe the distribution and composition of *vuk-ka* both in the village and over time as well as understand how size or generational complexity reveals anything meaningful about the constitution of *ka-tin* and *vuk-ka*. Without presupposing whether "smallness" or "largeness" is a relevant issue, one must first acknowledge that household composition of a *vuk-ka* or *ka-tin* at any point in time is perpetually in flux. This flux no doubt has much to do with exigencies of a socio-economic, political and environmental nature that individually affect each household. But underlying this process of flux, there are other basic considerations pertaining to the nature of a *vuk-ka*, its reasons for being and the set of values invoked by its existence. Unless one simply assumes that one establishes a *vuk* solely for the purpose of replacing an old, dilapidated or dysfunctional dwelling, then questions like why a new *vuk* is built, whether an old *vuk* is really a nonfunctional entity, when an old *vuk* becomes an abandoned *vuk* instead of just an empty one, and how living members of a *ka* choose to locate themselves within one or another *vuk* can all be taken to be meaningful inquiries that not only reflect upon the relationship between members of a *ka* sharing a *vuk* (as opposed to living next to each other and in separate *vuk*, for instance). It now remains to see how one can decipher the principles of a *vuk-ka* in the context of actual change over time and its diversity "on the ground" at any given time.

With regard to historical flux, it is impossible to describe the complexity of changes in composition of individual *ka* over generational time and from *vuk* to *vuk*, so to speak, without being excessively tedious. Nonetheless, beginning from about the latter half of the 19th century to the present, for which there is reliable data based upon informant knowledge of the displacement of people and houses in this village, one can see a wide diversity in case histories ranging from minimal changes in the status of a *vuk-ka* (little displacement of people from *vuk* to *vuk* over time) to extreme fluctuation in the displacement of persons from one *vuk* to another. The following example perhaps displays a little of both extremes.

Vuk #8N: a pre-1900 two-story unit registered in the name of two brothers, Hoi-yu (A) and Hoi-wang (B). This was an "ancestral house" (*ah-kung-vuk* (H), =*zuwu*) built by and inherited from the father of these two brothers, who died in 1955. One of the two brothers, Hoi-yu (A), married and built a new house at #50. This new head of household (A) was a cultivator, and his wife (A1) gave birth to a son (A1S) before dying at the young age of 35 in 1950. Hoi-yu (A) remarried, and his second wife (A2) bore one daughter (A2D) and one son (A2S). All three children from the two marriages were raised in the new house at #50 along with Hoi-yu (A) and his second wife (A2). The son of the first wife (A1S) married, and his wife (A1S1) bore three grandchildren. They all continued live in the house at #50. Shortly after the birth of his third child, the son (A1S) migrated to the U.K. to find work, leaving behind his own wife (A1S1), children, brother (A2S), sister (A2D) and parents (A, A2) in #50. A few years after going to the U.K., he (A1S) married a second wife (A1S2) there, who in turn bore two daughters. All four of them continued to live in the U.K.. Meanwhile, in 1970 Hoi-yu's first son (A1S) from his first wife, with money that he earned while working in the U.K., built a new house in Wo Hang at #80C. Although he (A1S), his second wife (A1S2) and the two daughters of the second marriage continued to live in the U.K., his first wife (A1S1), whom he had left behind in the village and his three children by the first marriage, moved into the new house at #80C. His (A1S) three children later migrated to the U.K.. The daughter then married out, and the two sons now live in separate places, distinct from their father's U.K. residence as well. After the first son's first wife (A1S1) and three children moved to #80C, the members of the original household left at #50 consisted of Hoi-yu's (A) second wife (A2), and Hoi-yu's other son (A2S) and daughter (A2D). Hoi-yu (A) passed away just few years before his first son (A1S) built his new house at #80C. The remaining daughter (A2D) then married out to a nearby village, and the remaining son (A2S) likewise married. This second son (A2S) and his wife (A2S1) bore three grandchildren, all of whom continued to live in the house at #50. Shortly after the birth of his (A2S) third child, the second son's wife (A2S1) ran away from the village and eventually remarried, never to return again. The second son (A2S) also remarried, then emigrated to the U.K. along with his second wife (A2S2), where they later gave birth to and raised another son. This left the second son's (A2S) two daughters by his first wife (A2S1), both of whom went to live under the caretakership of a close relative in the village (A2's FaBrSoSo), and a son by his first wife (A2S1), who went to live along with his mother (A2, Hoi-yu's second wife), as occupants of the house at #50.

As for Hoi-wang (B), the brother of Hoi-yu (A), the history of his *vuk-ka* is less eventful. Shortly after his marriage, he built a house at #45, not far away from that of his brother at #50. Hoi-wang (B), like his brother, was a cultivator. He and his wife (B1) raised four sons (B1Sa, B1Sb, B1Sc, B1Sd) and one daughter (B1D) in the house at #45. His daughter (B1D) married out in 1970 into a nearby village. His first son (B1Sa) got married and continued to live in the house at #45 along with his wife and two young grandchildren before migrating to the U.K. in 1970 to seek a living. He was joined by his wife and two children few years later. The departure of the first son (B1Sa) to the U.K. was followed by the second son (B1Sb) in 1973. There, he (B1Sb) eventually got married and had three children. The third and fourth sons (B1Sc, B1Sd) emigrated in 1978 to seek a living, after their older brothers. The third son (B1Sc) eventually got married, while the fourth son (B1Sd) remained single. All four sons and their respective families continued to live in the U.K., and with exception of the brief period prior to settling down there each had lived in separate households. The departure of Hoi-wang's (B) five children due to marriage and emigration in turn left him and his wife (B1) as the only remaining occupants of #45. In 1981, with remittances from the four sons living abroad, a new house was built upon the same lot, replacing the old house. Hoi-wang (B) and his wife (B1) continued to live there ever since to the present.

The abovementioned example is by no means statistically representative of the life history of a typical *vuk-ka*. Nonetheless, one can from the variations found in this example abstract certain factors relevant to a conceptual discussion of the *vuk-ka*. The contrasting histories of brothers Hoi-yu (A) and Hoi-wang (B) covered four generations (starting from their ancestral house) as well as radically different periods and different circumstances "on the land". The first thing worth noting with regard to this example was that the two houses, #50 and #45, that were built and occupied by each of the brothers after marriage were registered jointly in the name of the two brothers. Prior to being owned in the name of the two brothers, they were both owned in name by their father Li San-Tseuk. Both houses were registered as property in the name of the father throughout the time the father remained *jiazhang* (family head), in other words, as long as he was alive. Only after his death did this and other property become succeeded by the two brothers. Property "ownership" in this instance reflected the fact that each house belonged to a single *jiazhang* representing the entire *jia*, which included his sons and other descendants. In other words, the status of the two houses (and other property) as family possession in the name of the *jiazhang* (which remained so until the latter's death and succession by his sons) was analytically distinct from the actual purpose for which each house was destined (i.e., one house for each son) and irrelevant to however the house was built (which could have been the sole responsibility of the father or either of his sons). The assumption that the houses essentially belonged to the entire *jia* and in the name of a single *jiazhang* more or less remained intact when the property was held jointly by the two brothers. The two brothers could have at any time following the death of their father negotiated a division of that property to reflect actual usage by each of the two new *jia*, but such a negotiation would have been analytically distinct from the situation that made the two houses common property of a preceding *jia*. Historically speaking, the construction by a *jiazhang* of separate *vuk* for each of his unmarried or newly married sons was a frequent occurrence in the village and as can be illustrated later had important ramifications for understanding the symbolic constitution of the *vuk-ka*.

In any event, by looking further at the history of the abovementioned *vuk-ka*, one can find contrasting examples which represent permutations of this same principle, namely the *vuk* at #80C and #45. The new *vuk* at #80C was built by the first son (A1S) of Hoi-yu (A) at a time when Hoi-yu had just passed away. There would have been no reason why this particular house should be viewed as joint property shared with the second son (A2S), and this had less to do with the fact that the first son (A1S) was the major financial contributor to the building of the house. One can contrast this with the case of the sons of Hoi-wang (B) who lived in #45. This new house there was put up largely by the efforts of two of the three sons living in the U.K., who were in much better financial standing than the third son. From the subjective understanding of people in that *jia* as well as from the perspective of ownership, the house was considered to be the shared possession of the entire *jia*, as represented by the *jiazhang* at the time, namely Hoi-wang (B). Thus, it would probably not be incorrect to refer to the house simply as being Hoi-wang's (B) *vuk* or from the perspective of the sons after the death of the father, as being their "ancestral house" (*ah-kung vuk*). Regarding the specifics of house construction, the new house was built ideally to accommodate each member of that *jia* with its five bedrooms. In essence, it was a large *vuk-ka* that accommodated a large *ka-tin*, and in the absence of other houses to be built in the future the sons and their respective family members viewed it as their village (ancestral) home.

In short, clear cut rules existed upon which the house was defined as family property, that is, either by members of an existing *jia(zu)* or as represented by the *jiazhang*, but these rules on the other hand did not really sufficiently account for the conditions under which a *vuk-ka* could be built and for whom a *vuk-ka* was meant to exist. The complex generational history of the brothers Hoi-yu (A) and Hoi-wang (B) exemplified in their own way certain analytical distinctions outlined here. From the perspective of *vuk*, one can clearly mark the stages of transition from one *vuk-ka* to another in time. The first was the formation of two separate *vuk-ka* at #50 and #45, one belonging to each of the two brothers, from the *vuk-ka* of their father, San-tseuk. The *vuk-ka* represented by Hoi-yu (A) at #50 then gave way to those of his two sons, each of whom maintained separate *vuk*, with the first son living in the U.K., then later building a new *vuk* at #80C, and the second son living in the same *vuk* at #50. The *vuk-ka* represented by Hoi-wang (B) at #45 on the other hand gave way to those of two of his sons, each of whom had separate *vuk* in the U.K.. The third son remained single, and although he could have been living in a *vuk* of his own, there would be no reasonable basis for referring to his *vuk* of one as a *vuk-ka*, except as part of the *vuk-ka* epitomized by the father living in #45, of which he was a dependent family member. In essence, as can be seen from this description of a *vuk-ka* and in contrast to the status of the various *vuk* as family property or possession, the definition of a *vuk-ka* had to simultaneously meet two explicit conditions, namely those of *vuk* and *ka*. Moreover, when viewed from the perspective of *vuk* (its "house") rather than *ka* (its "people"), the building of new or separate houses took on a certain significance in relation to the creation of a *vuk-ka* that was incompatible with functionalist notions of family property.

The creation of separate *vuk-ka* (at #45 and #50) by the two sons (A1S, A2S) of Hoi-yu (A) is a good case in point. From the perspective of the occupants of the two *vuk*, there was little question that the two *vuk* represented separate *vuk-ka*, and in this regard authority over the destiny of each *vuk* was not subject to "joint negotiation" of the kind reflected by their "joint ownership" status. That is to say, for all intents and purposes, each *vuk-ka* it occupied acted as if it was a domain unto itself; members of one *vuk-ka* had no say over the conduct of the other regardless of whether the *vuk* involved was jointly or separately "owned". An extension of the same kind of behavior was found to exist in the case of the new house built at #45 by the sons of Hoi-wang (B). Despite being jointly owned by Hoi-yu (A) and Hoi-wang (B), its occupants were at the same time clear in voicing the opinion that the new *vuk* existed solely for the benefit of the *vuk-ka* of Hoi-wang (B) (and to the exclusion of the other "joint owner"). By saying that notions of "family property" and "common livelihood" per se could not sufficiently explain the set of values that underlay the nature of a *vuk-ka* as "domain unto itself", one begs the question of what conditions precipitated the creation of a new *vuk-ka* (as opposed to living in the same large *vuk-ka*, as exemplified by the often noted "large family ideal").

In this regard, one should first ask whether there existed in this particular community an ideal trend toward either large or small *vuk-ka* (*ka-tin*). While the scholarly literature on "Chinese family size" has emphasized the existence of a "large family" ideal, in Wo Hang since the 19th century extended households of any kind had been rare. Statistically or ideally, there had always been a definite trend toward the formation of separate *vuk-ka* and small *ka-tin*. Certainly prior to World War II, wealthy families would eventually give way to separate *vuk* for different sons and different wives (especially in the case of polygynous marriages). The situation in the postwar era is another matter, however, as will be shown later.

This trend toward separate *vuk-ka* and small *ka-tin* is difficult to document satisfactorily without tediously analyzing individual case histories and when the composition of any particular *vuk-ka* over a long period of time is continuously in flux. Nonetheless, one can identify certain kinds of situations where the trend toward separate *vuk-ka* is most evident. The first may be referred to as "separate *vuk* for different wives". Although polygyny is by no means a statistically frequent occurrence in this village, where one finds different wives married to the same male, all living in the village at the same time, each wife would almost certainly be living in separate and nearby *vuk*, as in the following case.

Vuk #41Z: An early 20th century two-story mud brick house originally built by the father of Li San-wong, the latter being the sole son in the family. San-wong's parents died when he was little. After marriage, San-wong (W) and his wife (W1) built a house at #56Z. His wife (W1) gave birth to one son (W1S) before dying in 1950 at the age of 40. San-wong (W) remarried, and he and his second wife (W2) continued to live in the *vuk* at #56Z. His second wife (W2) failed to bear any children, and San-wong (W) married a third wife (W3), who bore two children, both raised in San-wong's (W) ancestral (father's) house at #41Z. As for San-wong (W), he built another *vuk* for himself at #56X. San-wong's son (W1S) from his first wife (W1) married few years later. He (W1S), his wife (W1S1), their son (W1S1S) and his stepmother (San-wong's second wife (W2)), whom he (W1S) addressed in Hakka as *shim-mei* (=*a shen*, literally "father's younger sister"), all continued to live in the *vuk* at #56Z. Shortly after the birth of a grandson, San-wong's first son (W1S) migrated to the U.K. in the early 1960s to seek a living. There he (W1S) eventually married a second wife (W1S2S) who bore two sons, and all four of them continued to live in the U.K.. Meanwhile, the son (W1S1S) of San-wong's first son (W1S) from the latter's first wife (W1S1) moved out to work in Tai Po market town, where he got married in 1975. After marriage, he (W1S1S) settled down to raise a family of three children and was eventually joined by his mother (W1S1). The departure of two people (W1S1 and W1S1S) from the *vuk* at #56Z left San-wong's second wife (W2) as sole occupant of the house. In the *vuk* at #41Z, occupied by San-wong's third wife (W3) and two children by the latter, the history of this *vuk-ka* was less complex, comparatively speaking. The daughter (W3D) of San-wong (W) from his third wife (W3) married out to nearby Sheung Shui district in 1970, while the son (W3S) on the other hand continued to reside in the present house (#41Z). He remained single and worked for few years in the Netherlands before returning home, where he eventually died of illness in 1981. This left San-wong's third wife (W3) as the sole occupant of #41Z. San-wong (W) himself passed away in 1980, and his house at #56X has remained unoccupied ever since then.

The above example illustrates several interesting points with regard to the nature and significance of separate *vuk-ka*. The death of San-wong's (W) first wife (W1) left him with one son, and the desire to produce more sons provided a valid reason to marry a second wife. The failure of the second wife in this regard then led to a third marriage. The second and third wives lived in separate *vuk*, as did the children of the different mothers. Although the relationship between the two wives was not very amicable, the fact that they lived in separate *vuk* was probably not a necessary condition of polygynous marriages. After all, the idealtypical large Chinese family as depicted in the prevailing literature often included several wives living under the same roof. Moreover, the fact of living in separate *vuk* did not affect at all the status of the women as wives to the same husband nor did it affect the relationship of siblings to each other as children of the same father. Yet on the other hand, biological attachment to one's mother was probably of secondary importance to the relationship between a parent and child in separate *vuk* than the relative burden of responsibility undertaken by one parent *vis-a-vis* another over the care of a particular child. In Hakka, one called one's biological mother "mother" (*ah-mei*) and father's other wives "father's older sister" (*ah-nyong*) or "father's younger sister" (*shim-mei*) depending on their age (relative to one's own mother), as if to accent the relationship between wives as one of equals ("sisters") separated by a difference in age. In all these houses, the relationship between father, wives, and children was that of a single *ka*. More importantly, at the same time, this single *ka* existed in parallel with separate *vuk-ka* and different *ka-tin*.

The *vuk-ka* composed of San-wong's third wife (W3) and his children (W3D, W3S) constituted a single *vuk-ka*, but so did the *vuk-ka* composed of San-wong's second wife (W2) and son (W1S) from San-wong's first wife (W1), even though they shared no biological relationship. The latter *vuk-ka* was a *vuk-ka* for precisely the same reasons that made a father and unmarried son living in different houses (or different countries, as in the earlier case of Hoi-wang and his fourth son) part of the same *vuk-ka*, namely their shared status by virtue of a native definition of *ka*. Yet on the other hand, the fact that each wife and her respective children chose, for whatever reasons, to live in separate *vuk* meant that there was something very significant about the set of values which contributed to their identity as separate *vuk-ka*. How this set of values can be articulated is a topic of later discussion.

Vuk #94X: Lived in by Li To-chun, an inhabitant of the village during the late 19th and early 20th centuries (died in 1935). What remains of *vuk* #94X now is just a vacant lot littered with mud bricks and situated in the Lau Wai section of the village. To-chun was a wealthy person in his lifetime, and even before his three sons (A, B, C) were of marriageable age he built a house for each of them (#90A, #90B, #90C) near his house in Lau Wai. Each of the three houses (#90A, #90B, #90C) constituted a separate *vuk* (i.e., a separate *gan-to, pang-*

diang, etc.) and was constructed adjacent to each other in a straight row. From the day the three houses were built, ownership of all three houses was in the name of Li To-chun. After To-chun's death, this and other property was set up as an ancestral trust in the name of Li To-chun Tso, and ownership of the three houses remained unchanged ever since. After the three houses were built and prior to the actual marriage of the three sons, the entire *ka* consisting of To-chun, his wife, sons (A, B, C) and two daughters lived in the new house complex. Moreover, at that time (prior to the actual marriage of the three sons), each of the three units was joined by a door that linked the adjacent units. Only after each son had married and set up his own *ka-tin* in one of the three *vuk-ka* were the units physically separated.

The eldest son, Yam-cheong (A), was a cultivator. In 1935 he emigrated to Jamaica to work, leaving behind a wife (A1), daughter (A1D) and two sons (A1Sa, A1Sb), all of whom continued to live in #90A. The elder son (A1Sa) was adopted and lived as part of that *ka*. While in Jamaica, Yam-cheong (A) married a second wife (A2), who then bore one son (A2S). Meanwhile, Yam-cheong's daughter (A1S) married into a nearby village, and his elder (adopted) son (A1Sa) went to Jamaica in 1940 along with the latter's wife and infant son to work and live with his father (A). Sometime during the war, Yam-cheong's other son (A1Sb) went to live with another relative in the village. Upon Yam-cheong's return to Wo Hang in 1950, he (A) built two new *vuk* at #91A and #91B. Like the older house at #90A, #91A and #91B were separate units built next to each other, and both were at the outset linked by an adjoining door. Yam-cheong (A), his second wife (A2), and the two sons from different mothers (A1Sb, A2S) lived in the new house. Yam-cheong's second son (A1Sb) from his first wife (A1) later married and moved into #91A as well as his wife (A1Sb1), while the rest of the family remained in #91B. Sometime later, #91A and #91B became physically separated, and the residential situation stabilized with Yam-cheong (A), his second wife (A2) and third son (A2S) living in #91B, Yam-cheong's second son (A1Sb) and the latter's wife (A1Sb1) living in #91A, and Yam-cheong's first son (A1Sa) living in Jamaica along with his wife (A1Sa1) and son (A1Sa1S). The wife (A1Sb1) of Yam-cheong's second son (A1Sb) bore a son (A1Sb1S) in #91A. In 1960, Yam-cheong's second son (A1Sb) emigrated to the U.K. to seek a living, leaving behind his wife (A1Sb1) and son (A1Sb1S). While in the U.K., he (A1Sb) married a second wife (A1Sb2) who eventually bore two daughters. The four of them continued to live in the U.K. to the present day, returning only rarely to Wo Hang to visit. Around 1980, the second son (A1Sb) petitioned for his son (A1Sb1S) born by his first wife (A1Sb1) to emigrate to the U.K.. This son (A1Sb1S) lived with his father (A1Sb) for a short while, before he too married out, then set up his own household elsewhere in the U.K.. This left Yam-cheong's second son's (A1Sb) first wife (A1Sb1) as the sole occupant of #91A.

In #91B, Yam-cheong (A) lived happily with his second wife (A2) and third son (A2S), until he died at a ripe old age of 90 in 1960. His third son (A2S) went to the U.K. to seek a living three years after his father's death, which occurred about the same time Yam-cheong's grandson (A1Sa1S) from his first (adopted) son (A1Sa) emigrated to the U.K. (from Jamaica). This left Yam-cheong's second wife (A2) as the sole occupant of #91B. When Yam-cheong's first son (A1Sa) and wife (A1Sa1) returned from Jamaica to live in 1970, they moved into #91B while Yam-cheong's second wife (A2) moved from #91B into #91A to live along with the first wife (A1Sb1) of Yam-cheong's second son (A1Sb), the latter having already gone to the U.K.. Yam-cheong's third son (A2S) later married and settled down in the U.K. not long after emigrating there, eventually raising two children of his own. In 1980, Yam-cheong's second wife (A2) also emigrated to live with her son (A2S) in the U.K.. This left the first wife (A1Sb1) of Yam-cheong's second son (A1Sb) as the sole occupant of #91A, a situation that has remained unchanged to this day.

The second son of To-chun and younger brother of Yam-cheong (A), Yam-wan (B), had a simpler family history. After marriage, he moved into #90B, one of the three adjacent units built by his father, To-chun. His wife (B1) gave birth to one son (B1S). Along with his two other brothers, he (B) went to Jamaica in 1935 to seek a living, leaving behind his wife and son in #90B. During Yam-wan's (B) sojourn in Jamaica, his son (B1S) married and continued to live in the *vuk* at #90B along with his mother (B1) and wife (B1S1). Upon his return to the village in 1950, Yam-wan (B), using wealth that he and his two brothers had amassed while living in Jamaica, built two new *vuk* at

#92A and #92B, both next to each other and near those built by his elder brother, Yam-cheong (A). Upon vacating his old house at #90B, Yam-wan (B) moved into #92A along with his wife (B1); #92B on the other hand became occupied by his son (B1S) and daughter-in-law (B1S1), who eventually raised a total of three grandsons and two granddaughters in the latter *vuk*. The eldest grandson (B1S1Sa) emigrated to the U.K. in 1955 to seek a living. There he (B1S1Sa) married and settled down. However, few years later, he (B1S1Sa) left his wife (B1S1Sa1) and married a second wife (B1S1Sa2). His first wife (B1S1Sa1) eventually returned to Hong Kong and remarried. In the meantime, both he (B1S1Sa) and his second wife (B1S1Sa2) continued to live in the U.K., raising two sons of their own before eventually divorcing in 1977. The two sons continued in the aftermath to live with their father (B1S1Sa) to this day. The second grandson (B1S1Sb) of Yam-wan (B) emigrated to the U.K. in 1960 and lived for a time with his elder brother (B1S1Sa) until he too married and settled down. He (B1S1Sb) and his wife (B1S1Sb1) established a household elsewhere in the U.K., eventually raising two sons and two daughters of their own. The third grandson (B1S1Sc) of Yam-wan (B) emigrated to Holland in 1970 to seek a living. There he (B1S1Sc) married and raised one son. Although he continued to live and work in Holland, his wife (B1S1Sc1) and young son (B1S1Sc1S) later returned to Hong Kong, where they moved to a flat in New Kowloon. The two granddaughters of Yam-wan (B) for their part married out in 1965, and both have continued to live in the U.K. with their respective husbands and children to the present.

The son (B1S) of Yam-wan (B) died in 1962, and this was followed in 1967 by the deaths of Yam-wan (B) and his wife (B1). When Yam-wan's son (B1S) died, #92B was occupied by his wife (B1S1), two unmarried daughters and third son (B1S1Sc), the other two sons having already emigrated to the U.K.. The death of the patriarch Yam-wan (B) and his wife (B1) left #92A temporarily unoccupied. The occupants of #92B (descendants of Yam-wan) later joined the two units, #92A and #92B, through a connecting door between the two *vuk* and effectively occupied the two *vuk* as a single "residential unit". Yet in all other respects, especially on ritual occasions, the two *vuk* continued to be viewed as separate units. The later departure of the two daughters in marriage and the third son (B1S1Sc) to Holland left the mother

(B1S1) (or Yam-wan's son's (B1S) wife) as the sole occupant of the (two) *vuk*, #92A and #92B. This has remained unchanged to the present day.

The youngest of the three brothers and youngest son of To-chun, Yam-lun (C), moved into *vuk* #90C after marrying. Yam-lun (C) and his wife (C1) raised a son (C1S) and a daughter (C1D) in this *vuk*. In 1935, Yam-lun (C) migrated to Jamaica along with his two brothers (A&B). In 1940, he (C) was joined by his son (C1S). Afterward, Yam-wan's (C) daughter (C1D) married out to a nearby village, leaving his wife (C1) as the only remaining occupant in #90C. In 1943, Yam-lun's wife (C1) passed away, and Yam-lun (C) eventually married a second wife (C2). When Yam-lun (C) built his new house at #93, next to his brother's *vuk* at #92A and #92B, both he (C) and his second wife (C2) moved into the new house to live. There they raised two sons (C2Sa, C2Sb). After having been raised in the new *vuk* at #93, both of these sons eventually married and settled elsewhere, the older one (C2Sa) in the market town of Luen Wo Hui and the younger one (C2Sb) in town. Meanwhile, Yam-lun's (C) first son (C1S) continued to live in Jamaica, where he married and settled down with his wife, raising five children. Unlike his wife and children he (C1S) returns often to Wo Hang to visit, living in the house at #93.

From the perspective of *ka*, the descendants of Li To-chun, as seen from their long and complex history, comprised at any one time many persons covering many generations. On the whole, they were a cohesive group of people who shared close intimate relations in everyday life and often banded together during ritual occasions involving the group-at-large. The three brothers Yam-cheong (A), Yam-wan (B) and Yam-lun (C) migrated to Jamaica, worked and lived together, then returned to Wo Hang from abroad at the same time and even constructed new *vuk* at the same time, each next to one other. Descendants of more recent generations have also managed to maintain the same level of solidarity despite their growing largeness in numbers, geographical separation and diversity of personal experience and background. Most of the landed property that they owned, including the *vuk* property mentioned above, all remained registered in the name of Li To-chun *tso*. On the other hand, each of the three brothers, Yam-cheong (A), Yam-wan (B) and Yam-lun (C), had sizeable private holdings in property which each person acquired on his own after the death of their father. In addition to and separate from these two kinds of holdings, few of the brothers, namely Yam-cheong's first son (A1Sa) and the three sons of Yam-lun (C1S, C2Sa, C2Sb) established a group called Tung Hing Tong through which they used to buy and sell land, mostly in Wo Hang.

From the perspective of *vuk*, the formation of new *vuk-ka* from previous ones was one that closely followed the successive segmentation in each generation of a previous *ka* (*jiazu*) into separate *fong* ("segments"), each represented by a newly married son. This is another way of saying that there was a definite trend toward the formation of small "nuclear" households, a trend which, as illustrated by the history of To-chun and his descendants, began long before the actual death of the *jiazhang* ("family elder") and was often initiated by the *jiazhang* himself. Thus, To-chun built #90A, #90B and #90C for each of his three sons, Yam-cheong (A), Yam-wan (B) and Yam-lun (C), while each son in turn built separate *vuk* for his own sons at #91A/B, #92A/B and #93. The *jiazhang* in each of the above cases then moved into the new *vuk* after abandoning the previous *vuk*. The older *vuk* then became referred to as their *ah kung-vuk* or "ancestral house" belonging to or associated with a previous *jiazhang*. Here again, as in all previous examples, one must emphasize that the question of which *vuk* was associated with, belonged to or intended for use by whom was quite distinct from property considerations in the legal sense of "ownership". All of the houses occupied by the living descendants of To-chun were in fact registered in the ownership of Li To-chun *tso*. This itself could be attributed to the fact that the land upon which each of the houses rested originally belonged to the *tso*, and even if the status of land ownership had not been so, the *vuk* would still have been registered in the name of the father (actual *jiazhang* at the time) instead of the sons (intended users or occupants).

Within this given framework of *vuk-ka* (separate *vuk* for different *ka*), one may find variations in living scenarios. In the case of Yam-cheong's (A) new *vuk* at #91A and #91B, the two *vuk* were joined together by a connecting door, and prior to the marriage of the second son (A1Sb), the occupants living there could not properly be referred to as different *ka-tin* nor as separate *vuk-ka*. However, after the marriage of the second son (A1Sb), they began to live as separate units, and the sealing of the adjoining door more or less concretized this separation. In the case of Yam-wan's (B) new *vuk* at #92A and #92B, each *vuk* was at the outset physically separated, with the parents living in one unit and married son living in the other. The death of the father followed by the subsequent emigration of its younger occupants inevitably led to the installation of an inside door connecting the two units. The case of Yam-lun (C) and his new *vuk* at #93 appears to be an exception to the preceding two in that only one *vuk* instead of several was built. Nonetheless, at the time of its building Yam-lun's eldest son (C1S) was married and living in Jamaica with his family while the other two sons (C2Sa, C2Sb) were living in #92 and were either just born or not yet born. Later on, the eldest son continued to live abroad, returning home occasionally for brief visits, while the other two sons, now in their 30s, eventually married then moved into the city to work. Despite these more recent transitions, the *vuk* at #93 remains undivided.

The case of Li To-chun and his descendants can be seen as representative of an idealtypical trend toward small *ka-tin* and separate *vuk-ka* observed in Wo Hang, not because it constituted the most usual or frequently observed pattern of organization at any time but because it constituted the most frequent pattern seen in all those cases where there was no lack of means to the ends. However, when one looks at actual household composition in Wo Hang either synchronically (by looking at the village as a whole) or diachronically (by tracing the history of any particular *ka* over a span of generations), one finds some variation. This variation is also significant in its own right, because there is a clearly marked transition in "household size" (of *ka-tin*, taking *vuk-ka* as a unit) from the prewar "traditional" era through the great period of outmigration in the 60s and 70s to the present. Contrary to expectation, the transition found in Wo Hang as well as other villages in the Shataukok area has been from a prevalence of small ("nuclear") *ka-tin* to large ("extended") *ka-tin* rather than the other way around. During the period before and during the war, the statistical prevalence of small *ka-tin* stemmed in part from a preference toward it and in part from the combination of low fertility and high mortality rates from poverty and war. The outmigration of villagers in the postwar years no doubt exacerbated the normally small *ka-tin* composition of houses in the village to a point where villagers living abroad outnumbered those living at home by a ratio of 2: 1, but this changed during the period of the late 70s to the present. Almost without exception, the trend was toward the building of large village houses, first two-story then three-story ones, as was as permissible under the New Territories Building Ordinance. Several factors were involved. First of all, as a result of emigration abroad, villagers began to make money, most of which was remitted to family members at home and saved for the purpose of building a new house, among other things. Some of those abroad returned to live at home, but the demographic balance of villagers abroad to villagers at home still remained in favor of the former. These considerations aside, changes in housing and land policy in recent decades that came about as a result of population growth in Hong Kong had an important if not decisive influence on household composition in the more traditional villages. The residents of Wo Hang as well as Shataukok in general were slow to respond to the drastic sociopolitical and economic changes occurring elsewhere. While villagers elsewhere had chosen to rent their land and houses to outsiders, residents here were on the whole resistant to such changes. When villagers elsewhere were selling their indigenous rights to the land *en masse* to town developers in return for cash profit, residents here began to hoard existing plots of land, adding to the growing sense of insecurity.[19] This and other changes in New Territories Small House Policy, which placed severe restrictions on house building and land conversion, resulted in a situation of increasing land scarcity in the village. Residents of the village protested their inability to build houses where and as they pleased, while residents abroad complained about being deprived of rights to reside in their natal village by a government policy which viewed them as overseas residents. The only alternative under these conditions was to build whenever possible and wherever permissible. The trend toward the building of large *vuk* for a potentially large *ka* thus represented a "rational" local response, given their means to attain limited ends and in light of irrational conditions.

The significance of a traditionally small *ka-tin* or separate *vuk-ka* ideal in Wo Hang raises theoretically more important issues that shed light on the nature and meaning of the "Chinese family". In one respect, one may read the concept of *vuk-ka* literally by saying that it is an entity bound by *vuk* occupied by people who identify themselves as being part of a *ka*. By showing that there is a trend toward the creation of separate *vuk-ka* for different wives and different sons, one must see how *ka-tin* formed on the basis of different wives and sons overlap with notions of *ka* based on common worship (through common *xianghuo* ("incense fire") of a family altar), reproduction (through marriage and symbolic unity of various ceremonial objects hanging from the roof beam of the house), subsistence (through creation of a separate kitchen god, separate *gan-to* and separate *pang-diang*), etc.. In short, the *vuk-ka*, its establishment and distinctiveness from other *vuk-ka*, and its succession in later generations can mean many things. The statistical features of residence per se appear to explain very little about the actual constitution of *vuk-ka*. But if the conditions under which *vuk-ka* displace previous ones are more relevant to the formation of *vuk-ka* and their reasons for being than the number of people that live in them, one may in turn ask if there is indeed any importance to where people live or what ramifications may result from conditions of physical proximity. In this regard, by distinguishing the discrete nature of groups ranging from ritual families and households to the lineage-village (as *jiaxiang*), one can see then how they constitute the selective synthesis of *zong*, *jia* and *qin*.

KIN RELATIVITY (*Qin*) AS A PRINCIPLE OF SOCIAL DISTANCE AND SOLIDARITY

On my arrival in the village of Sheung Wo Hang, the whole place appeared at first glance to be little more than a collectivity of anonymous individuals and indistinguishable houses. Having been initially led to Wo Hang precisely because it claimed to be a typical single-lineage village, the pervasiveness of the agnatic principle appeared to be reason enough to believe that it could constitute as well a territorial imperative that ordered patterns of residence and all relationships to land. One of the first questions I asked naturally was whether there were rules that specified that members of a particular *fong* (segment) should live together or in distinct clusters *vis-a-vis* members of different *fong*. Informants invariably and unambiguously replied that there were no such "rules of residence" in the village and that people were free to live wherever they pleased in the village.

The absence of explicit rules suggested that actual patterns of settlement must have been random and that one could not expect to find any corresponding relationship between residence and agnation. However on closer inspection, it appeared that settlement patterns in the village were not all that random either. Paradoxically, one could even say that, on the surface of things, it would be easy to "view" the entire village as a collectivity of highly nucleated units, each occupied by members of distinct ancestral segments (*fong*).

This apparent pattern of residence can conceivably be seen as a function of the territorial ramifications of genealogical segmentation. The Wo Hang genealogy writes that their predecessors represented one offshoot of a larger wave of Hakkas migrating from central to south China during the Ming dynasty several centuries ago. They moved into Guangdong province from Fujian before settling into Xinan county. Branches stemming from their common ancestor, Li Duk-wa, spread out (in territorial terms) into several adjoining villages in the Shataukok area in ways that certainly resembled a segmentary pattern. In this regard, the first split occurred during the third generation when the grandson of Duk-wa and second son of three brothers, moved into the valley below to establish the village of Ha Wo Hang ("lower Wo Hang"). The descendants of this second son, referred to locally as members of the second *fong* constructed their own ancestral hall for members of their own *fang* (*erfang ci*) and continued to live in Ha Wo Hang in succeeding generations. This left members of the first and third *fong* (descendants of the first and third brothers, respectively) in Sheung Wo Hang (upper village). One family in Ha Wo Hang of the fifth or sixth generation moved out to an another settlement further down toward the coast and directly facing Ha Wo Hang to establish the village of Tai Long. Here, several generations passed before another family in Tai Long moved still further down the coast to establish the village of Mukmintau.

Outmigration of this sort followed a "segmentary" pattern in the sense that there appeared to be an ordered movement of people between related villages over generations. In each case, usually no more than one family, hence a segment, moved out to establish a new settlement, and persons of succeeding generations continued to settle and expand accordingly, unless of course one of them decided to move out, thus starting another chain of migration. In this kind of migrational settlement, one rarely if ever found cases of reverse migration, for example, from Mukmintau to Tai Long, Tai Long to Ha Wo Hang or Ha Wo Hang to Sheung Wo Hang. Reverse migration was possible in principle and would not be unacceptable to those living in all these villages, where everyone still regarded each other as a "brother", however, such incidents were in fact unusual.

Within the village, although one did not find the kind of strict territorial division along ("genealogically") segmentary lines that one apparently found in the case of intervillage migration, one nonetheless could see the existence of the same kind of nucleation within the village, each occupied almost exclusively by members of a distinct lower level *fong*. Excluding from consideration all new houses built on Crown Land (whose sites were marked off by the government in purposes of future development), most other clusters of houses in the village could be been as being occupied by persons of close ancestral affiliation. Moreover, one can say that those persons in the village sharing the closest ancestral links were most likely to live next to each other or in the same vicinity. Thus, for example, in Lau Wai (the old village), one found that all living members of Li Chiu-tung Tso (part of the third *fong*), with exception of one family that moved to the nearby village of San Tin two generations ago, happened to reside in the neighborhood of the Li ancestral hall. Further down near the village school in Lau Wai lived the descendants of Li To-chun, all of whom lived in adjacent buildings divided into two rows, one in back of the other. Their closest relations in a genealogical sense were members of Li Chiu-ju Tso (also part of the third *fong*), and almost all of them lived in the block of houses locally referred to as Tiu Kok and part of a row of houses in the adjacent section of Ha Mun Piang. A block of three houses located in a remote corner of the village called Ti Mui Sak was also occupied by members of this *tso*. As for Ha Mun Piang, almost all those living in this block were close relatives belonging to Li Kam-hoi Tso (part of the first *fong*). Their closest higher order agnatic relatives lived in another section of the village and belonged to Li To-kam Tso. They lived at one extreme northern end of the village in a block called Wo Tang Tiu along a single row of tightly built houses. The other half of the houses in Wo Tang Tiu were also occupied by closely related families belonging to the first *fong*, but they were genealogically more distant from Li To-kam Tso than Li Kam-hoi Tso. Their closest relations outside of their immediate community lived in two rows of houses at the top of the village in a large block of houses called San Diang. On the whole, this section of Wo Hang was somewhat more heterogenous than other sections of the village as it included several families belonging to Li Kam-hoi Tso who were closely related to those living in Ha Mun Piang as well as families belonging to Li Chiu-leong Tso (part of the third *fong*), also called Pui Man Tong. The members of Pui Man Tong apparently were many and occupied several niches in the village. Some lived in the uppermost row of houses in San Diang, while the others were found to occupy the entire section of houses in the two adjoining blocks, Siu Wuk Hong and Shu Fong Jai, near the main entrance to the village as well as the block of houses called Tai Mun Liu, situated to the left of Tiu Kok and Ha Mun Piang. About half of the living members of Pui Man Tong belonged to Li Ting-kwong Tso, Ting-kwong being one of the three sons of Chiu-leong (self-styled Pui-man). They occupied part of San Diang, all of Shu Fong-jai and most of Tai Mun-liu. Most of the residents in Siu Wuk Hong were descendants of Li Ting-yung, while a small group of families descended from Li Ting-hung lived in Tai Mun Liu.

The "observable" facts of the situation thus seemed to dictate that there was a strong correlation between genealogical segmentation and residential settlement patterns. However, after being confronted with these facts, many villagers pointed to the relationship between "residence" and "agnation" as just being coincidental. People were still free to live anywhere they pleased in the village without being restrained by strict "genealogical" rules. The fact that people still tended to live near close agnates, even though there was no such rule, requires explanation.

Upon serious reflection, I came to the conclusion that they were correct and I was wrong after all. In this regard, people resided in a place not because it was occupied or owned by their own *fong* but rather because they also happened to be their closest (*qin* (H,M)) relation or what they called "one's own people" (*ji-ga nyin* (H), = *ziji ren*). Thus, instead of viewing the village as nuclei of territorially based ancestral segments (*fong*), one should view it as being composed of nuclei of closely related people (*chin-nyin* (H), =*qinren*). When asked why they chose to live in a particular place, people often replied that they preferred to live with *ji-ga chin-nyin* and that they were less "familiar" (*um-suk* (M), =*bushou*) with others whom they viewed as being distant kinsmen. In this regard, it would probably be more accurate to say that the principle of segmentation here clearly served the principle of relativity rather than the other way around. The fact that this happened to be a single lineage-village was just coincidental. The principle of relativity should be seen as working in multi-lineage communities as well. The closeness so cultivated should follow from the exchange relationships constitutive of any kin relationship.

This difference between *fong* and *qin* also has important ramifications for how one should understand the nature of a "single-lineage" village, of which Wo Hang is not an unusual example. In essence, descent, as expressed by the concept of *zong* and reflected in the term *fong*, serves only as a marker of personal status. Its conceptual validity cannot be enhanced nor diminished by virtue of where and how people of common *zong* reside. The meaning of *zong* is constant for everyone regardless of whether he owns property or not, lives in China or abroad or resides in a single or multisurname village. The transmission of *zong* from father to son, as aptly reflected in the phrase *chuanzong jiedai* ("to transmit the *zong*, to link the generations"), merely says that a particular "son" derives common substance or shared values from a particular "father" such that they may seen to be linked by generations. But if *zong* per se cannot explain the existence of single-surname villages or why people of common *zong* choose to live together as part of the same settlement, then this peculiar state of affairs must be attributable to other factors. A symbolic definition of marriage is certainly one step in this direction.

As was pointed out in the section on Chinese marriage as exchange relation between two *jia* and its ritual implications over time, patrilocal residence is to an extent already implicit in the nature of the two terms used to signify the act of "marrying", namely *qu* and *jia* (the latter being different from the *jia* of "family"). *Qu* signifies the act of a man "marrying" a woman and is made up of the root word *qu*, which means to acquire or take, followed by the radical *nü*, for woman. *Qu* is an active verb that assumes a male as subject and female as direct object. Thus, *qu* denotes the acquisition of a woman by man, and as reflected in the verb-object compound *quqin* depicts the act of marriage (from a male perspective) as one of acquiring a woman to be *qin* (one's close relation). *Jia* on the other hand signifies the act of a woman "marrying" a man and is made up of the root word *jia*, as in "family", preceded by the radical *nü*, for woman. *Jia* is always used as a passive verb and assumes a female as subject and male as indirect object. The compound expression *jianü* then denotes the act of a woman crossing over to another family, namely that of her husband. In light of these etymological meanings, the notion of "patrilocal residence" is built into both terms for marriage, especially if one views the crossing of the woman from one *jia* to another as evidence of a change in residence. Moreover, such a symbolic definition of marriage can only explain why a single-surname village such as Wo Hang remains a single-surname village instead of one regularly infiltrated by newly married son-in-laws, each presumably of a different surname; it does not sufficiently explain on the other hand why people of the same surname chose to live with each other in the first place. That is to say, rules of postmarriage virilocal residence work equally well in a single or multisurname community environment, hence are analytically distinct from those rules that define the surname composition of a particular community. The latter on the other hand is largely a function of how a "community" or "village" is defined in a changing sociopolitical environment. As was pointed out in a previous section, there is a basic difference between a village (*xiangcun* or *jiaxiang*) as a kind of moral community and an assembly of village houses in a purely residential sense. The difference is one of different holistic environments and the particular kind of world ethos associated with it. Strictly speaking, the ongoing agnatic makeup of Chinese villages is a function of a rule of marriage residence rather than descent per se, while its origin as single or multi-lineage village is a result of sociopolitical forces affecting the region as a whole. The residential settlement patterns within a village is, however, a function of rules constitutive of that moral community.

In short, the effectiveness of *qin* assumes the prior existence of institutions or contexts of social practice such as *zong* ("descent"), *jia* ("family") and *xiangcun* ("village") within which its meaning is properly embedded. The agnatic relativity of *zong* (as reflected in ancestral rights and ritual obligations) is different from the egocentric kin relativity of *jia* (as engendered through exchange relations, both symbolic and economic) which is turn different from the relativity of communal life relationships (that unifies and separates people residentially based on perceived closeness or propinquity). With regard to a single lineage-village, where there is overlap between lineage and family as units of common worship and subsistence on the land as well as between lineage and village as kin and local community, its privileged status is largely the result of the projection of a descent model.

Within the village, residence is a product on the one hand of the uninhibited status of house land and on the other hand rules or norms affecting the formation of a social community, which in the case of Wo Hang has enabled the clustering of close kinsmen. At the level of individual households, the solidary sentiments and structural tensions that pull families together or apart play a significant part in determining patterns of residential density and distance within the village that can be reflected also in other aspects of everyday living arrangements, including eating and cooking.[20] In this regard, separate households included families living separately but not necessarily eating separately as well as households split apart by people living overseas. Needless to say, variations in such arrangements were responses to complex decisions pertaining to everyday livelihood for which there was no fixed customary "law". The problem of village residence aside, one can now begin to see how various kinds of relationships form on the basis of *qin* solidarity in ways that have ramifications for understanding the constitution of the village community, kinship networks and relationships to property. In single and multi-lineage-villages, *qin(qi)* relations always cut both ways, agnatic and affinal.

Relations between kindred (*qinqi*) seem to be almost universal. In Hakka, kindred are called "one's own people" (*ji-ga-nyin*). The existence of similar terms in other dialects of Chinese suggest, moreover, that such egocentric family based relationships are a prevalent feature of Chinese kin life. In single lineage-villages such as Wo Hang, it is perhaps not unusual for one to assume that in the life of any family, all else being equal, kinship relations on the father's side tend to be more solidary than those on the mother's side. Frequency of interaction among kinsmen who are not only related to each other but live closely and intimately, not to mention the intense ritualization of communal lineage activity, would without doubt contribute to a patrilineal bias in everyday kin relations. This bias has been amplified as well by the theoretical ambiguity of descent models that tend not to distinguish sufficiently or at all between those factors contributing to the clarity of a descent ideology as opposed to the strength of descent or kin solidarity.

In terms of Chinese descent principles, it is not obvious why relations on the father's side should be any more privileged than those on mother's side (or through marriage). The focus of patrilineality is on the ancestral rites and obligations that define one's personal identity and are equally effective whether such worship is conducted by individual families or a community. The communal bias that is the focus of lineage theory is a consequence first of all of the conditions that create the estate (as willed by an ancestral founder) and secondly the values of village society that make communal worship an acceptable public activity or desirable practice.

In principle, the patrilineal sentiments that contribute to the solidarity of the village as a moral community should be analytically distinct from overlapping sentiments of kin closeness that emanate from individual families and contribute to kindred solidarity. Although they do not conflict directly, there are situations where one can contrast the relative strength of these solidary sentiments in regard to the importance of specific social relationships and even to land and property. In other words, despite the unambiguous nature of ancestral transmission of land and property within a family, that defines the continuity and livelihood of a *jia*, this should not prejudice the relative strength of patrilateral *vis-a-vis* matrilateral bonds in regard to anything else, which may be a result of other complex factors. It is necessary thus to show what relations of *ji-ga-nyin* (one's own people) entail.

Vuk #43: The *ka* (family) currently living in this *vuk* is composed of a father, who is its *jiazhang*, aged 58, named Li Tin-sou, a mother, aged 54, three sons aged 33, 30 and 27, and one daughter, aged 24. This *vuk* was built in 1974 by Tin-sou (A) with earnings accumulated while living and working in the U.K. over the past 25 years. The new house replaced an older house which stood on the same lot and was occupied by the same family. Tin-sou (A) moved into the older house shortly after getting married. His own "ancestral house" was located just two doors away at #41 on an adjacent alley. This was the house in which Tin-sou (A), his younger brother (B) and younger sister (C) were brought up. While Tin-sou settled into the *vuk* at #43, his younger brother (B) continued to live in #41 after getting married until 1978, when he and his wife and four sons emigrated to the U.K.. Tin-sou's sister (C) married out in 1960 into the city, where she and her family still live.

Members of Tin-sou's *ka* included Tin-sou (A), who had been living in the U.K. for over 25 years, his wife (A1), who during his absence overseas continued to live at #43, two sons (A1Sa, A1Sb), who for the last 15 years had been living and working in the U.K., an unmarried son (A1Sc), who lived at home (#43), and a daughter (A1D), who for the past few years after getting married was living in #43 along with her husband and infant son. By strict definition of having married out (*chujia*), the daughter (A1D) should have moved out to live with her husband elsewhere, thus one might ask whether they were considered part of that *ka-tin* living in #43 or just temporary sojourners. Nonetheless, few villagers objected to the daughter's husband living there, despite his obvious status as an "outsider", which apparently had to do with his working nearby and not having other housing anywhere. In any case, the children of Tin-sou were brought up in #43, and the primary *qinqi* relationships extending outside his immediate *ka-tin* included the family of Tin-sou's younger brother, Man-choi (B), his wife (B1) and their four sons (B1Sa, B1sb, B1Sc, B1Sd). Man-choi (B) was ten years younger than Tin-sou, and the age differential between the children of the two brothers averaged about 15 years. Until his emigration to the U.K. in 1978, Man-choi (B) continued to live at #41, where he, his brother and sister had been brought up. His wife (B1) followed him to the U.K. a year later and in the 2-3 years after that, his four children were looked after by his brother's wife (A1). Relations between the *ka-tin* of Tin-sou (A) and Man-choi (B) on the one hand and that of their sister (C) on the other hand remained close despite the physical separation. After her marriage in 1960, their sister (C) and her children returned to the village only periodically for brief visits.

Tin-sou's parents passed away before the war. In the absence of a unifying *jiazhang*, Tin-sou's household served as a focal point upon which *qinqi* relations revolved. Within this circle of intimacy, the families of Tin-sou (A), his brother and sister (C) formed a kind of primary nucleus upon which relations of mutual help and interdependence were based and from which further *qinqi* relations with mother's relatives (mother's parents, brothers, sisters and their families) turned.

Ritual cycles such as New Year and birthday celebrations were occasions where participation of *qinqi* could be clearly seen. Customarily, the first day of the New Year was a focal point for members of the immediate *jia*, which started the day by eating a vegetarian meal, then partaking in a lunch that featured pork and salted vegetables (*ham-choi* (H)), the same as that eaten on other occasions involving ancestral worship. On the second day of the New Year, daughters (and their families) would come back to their natal home for a visit. Birthdays were an individual rite of passage but according to Chinese were an event that typically involved the participation of relatives on both sides. In a recent birthday for Tin-sou's youngest son (A1Sc), his mother (A1) arranged a lunch at home that invited 20 guests. The first table was, in addition to the birthday boy himself, occupied by various relatives living outside the village, that included father's sister (C), her husband and one of her married daughters, mother's eldest sister, mother's second sister and her husband, mother's youngest sister and her married daughter, and sister's husband's (A1Sc's brother-in-law) father's sister. Father's sister gave as birthday gift a platinum ring (valued at HKD$700, =USD$100), while her married daughter brought along a birthday cake. Mother's eldest sister gave a *lai-see* (C) (cash gift) of HKD$60 and bought a small box of pastries. Mother's second sister gave a *lai-see* of HKD$100, while the birthday boy's brother-in-law's aunt gave a box of cookies. The second table was made up of other members of the immediate family and village neighbors. One village neighbor (a distant agnate) who helped with the cooking preparations gave a *lai-see* of HKD$60 and a shirt, a village aunt (distant agnate) who came with her two children gave a *lai-see* of HKD$40, and two of A1Sc's village brothers came along for free lunch and each gave HKD$20.

Perhaps unlike the exclusivity of *fang* and inclusivity of *tang* that signified the concept of *jia*, the intensity of *qin* relationships was easily measured in terms of gradation. Intensity of gift giving was a function of relative kin distance per se. It may be argued that such exchanges were largely ceremonial in nature, but the same principle of reciprocity extended to other domains of everyday life as well. The bilateral nature of overseas remittances clearly exemplified the role of *qinqi* relationships. Despite the emphasis on lineage ties in the process of emigration, given by anthropologists writing on the New Territories, kin interdependence and exchange has always been bilateral in nature. In an early era of emigration, when working males left their family behind to seek employment abroad, they relied on connections between village brothers, and income earned in this regard became the primary source of subsistence for households living in the village. In later years, as families grew abroad and income expanded beyond minimum subsistence, the nature of remittances and exchange became correspondingly more diverse. During his more than 25 years of working abroad, Tin-sou (A) had been remitting money on a regular basis to his wife, first as laborer then as owner of his own restaurant. He was joined by his two sons after they became of working age. The third son (A1Sc) who stayed behind worked in the city and also contributed to the family income at large. After Tin-sou's daughter (A1D) married out but remained in her parents' house to live, she also remitted a portion of her husband's income to her mother to contribute to the expenses of living and eating at home. Even overseas remittances were not limited to sons.[21] It was not unusual for married daughters living abroad, whether they themselves were actually working, to send monetary support to their natal families. This was always on a case by case basis and was a function of the relative need of the recipient (especially if, for example, the latter did not receive support from other family members) and the financial disposition of the giver (the primary obligation of a married woman was always to her own family first, then to her own natal relatives). The solidarity of *qinqi* relationships was thus different, analytically speaking, from that constitutive of *jia* as a unit of social livelihood, and both overlapped in practice. Their reliance on exchange has led people to confuse them; their flexibility makes them hard to define by custom.

As extension of *ji-ga-nyin*, relations of closeness (*qin*) shed a different light on the nature of Chinese kin solidarity in general. In contrast to a notion of *zong*, with its emphasis on the transmission of ancestral rights and continuity of estate within the patriline, or a notion of *jia*, with its emphasis on familial incorporation or exclusion in the contexts of ritual-cum-biological reproduction and the livelihood of a household economy, *qin* is in the first instance a direct barometer of solidary sentiment that arises from relations of propinquity. The sociological concerns of anthropologists and local historians have tended to discount the significance of *qinqi* relations, since they do not in themselves lead to the rise of institutions that have wider sociopolitical ramifications. However, it is possible to view the nature of *qinqi* relations as a social fact sui generis, then show in what kinds of contexts they conflict with, overlap or transcend with other existing principles based upon custom, descent, locality or the practice of competing institutions.

In the context of everyday kin relationships at the local level, bilateral *qinqi* relations appear to overlap with cultural constructions of *jia* insofar as both are based on the maintenance of ongoing exchange. Even in the constitution of *ka-tin* (households), there is a fine and sometimes ambiguous line that separates priority on patrilineal notions of shared livelihood, with its ties to land and property, from unrestricted influence of bilateral kin ties. The traditional village withstanding, where the existence of a moral community tied to a social livelihood on the land enhances the agnatic appearance of a patrilocal rule of residence, the *ka-tin* is in essence a flexible kin group that cannot be fixed by any rigid rule of descent. It is not unusual, in the city, for example, to find households that include a married daughter along with her husband and children. If it is not statistically common, it is certainly acceptable in practice, for it accents the criterion of shared livelihood that constitutes the basis of a *ka-tin*. In this regard, the factors that necessitate or invoke a situation of shared livelihood do not conflict with "descent" principles that stipulate transmission of ownership in a house through the male line. One Wo Hang villager living in the U.K. with his wife and children also accommodated in his household his younger unmarried brother and his wife's mother, the total genealogical picture of which makes no sense in normal social structural terms. Without doubt, his brother was a legitimate member of the family, and his living there was clearly a result of strategic considerations pertaining to life needs. His wife's mother on the other hand had been living alone in her home village after the death of her own husband. The strategic considerations made to support his mother-in-law by taking her in as part of the household was no different in kind from those that induced his brother to live there, but the likelihood of his mother-in-law living there would probably have diminished greatly if his own parents had been living there or were alive. Thus, *qinqi* relationships can be seen in their own terms as primary and solidary, but they always had to be sensitive to its specific context, which defined their relevance to competing values and relationships.

Even in the context of a single-lineage village, there is no reason why *qinqi* relations could not outweigh (distant) agnatic relations in situations where they did not conflict with the existence of other agnatic rules, such as those pertaining to ownership of land, the village order or the constitution of descent groups. *Qinqi* relations often extended to realms of interpersonal trust and prevailed over diffuse bonds of agnatic solidarity seen to tie village "brothers". Similarly, the residential closeness of agnatic villagers attested strictly speaking to principles of *qin*, not to *zong* or *fong* per se. On the other hand, in a regional context, relations based on *qin* closeness were translatable best as broad metaphors for common local interest that frequently overrode ties of common surname or ethnicity. In the vicinity of Wo Hang, for instance, there were other villages surnamed Li as well, but this did not necessarily accord them any special privilege *vis-a-vis* other villages.

This notion of *qin* as kin closeness or relativity has been distorted by the more often cited notion of Chinese "familism" and its extension into various non-kin contexts such as the economy and the phenomenon of family based enterprises. In this regard, familism is a clear distortion of *jia* but is an appropriate rendition of *qin* solidarity. Perhaps unlike Eurocentric notions of a consanguineal family on the other hand, *qin* has no underlying assertion of biological tie that restricts its applicability to kindred per se. Its literal meaning of "closeness" can be extended to friends and other non-kinsmen in a way that can be summed up neatly by the term *guanxi* ("connection"). In short, *qin* should be an important concept in its own right, perhaps even more so in a "kin" context. However, it can be properly understood only by carefully articulating its differences with other core concepts.

ZONG, JIA AND QIN IN THE DOMESTIC PROCESS: A SECONDARY SYNTHESIS

Our attempt to understand the dynamics of Chinese domestic process has been distorted in part by the tendency to view households, families and lineages simply as different levels of kinship organization, when they are in fact distinct sociological entities. This is compounded by the polysemic and multivalent nature of what should be the most basic entity, namely the family. Kulp's (1925: 142–50) functional differentiation of the Chinese family (what he calls "sex groups" as well as the "sib") into the "natural family", "conventional family", "religious family" and "economic family" is, to be sure, an indication of how the Chinese family crosscuts many aspects of social life, but it is necessary to show how it serves as a fulcrum for different cultural concepts, as represented by the morphemes *zong, jia* and *qin*.

As I have tried to show, the *jia* is a complex construction in its own right that must be seen in the context of marriage and ongoing affinal exchange. More than just a unit for biological reproduction, the *jia* is a ritual construction that ties together relatives of the husband and wife into an egocentric community of "one's own people", which in turn becomes the primordial basis of relative kin solidarity. This community of "one's own people" overlaps but does not interfere with agnatic bonds that tie together village "brothers", as magnified by the dichotomy between village insiders and outsiders. The creation of a *jia* is also tied to the maintenance of common subsistence for a family so formed by exchange through notions such as *tongjü gongcai* (literally "common living, communal wealth"). As Shiga Shuzo (1978: 111–13) has rightly pointed out from cases in the Tang Code, the concept of common living (*tongjü*) has nothing to do with physical residence per se and more with the existence of a common account, the sharing of all living expenditures by its members and the distribution of equal, indivisible shares to common property among its members (Shiga 1967: 69–85).[22] In this regard, the phrase "the creation of a *jia*, (thus) the establishment of a way of life" (*xingjia liye*) is more to the point in tying the notion of common family subsistence to shared livelihood on the land. Without doubt, shared subsistence and transmission of property from father to son are parallel processes, but the *jia* (as a group of people or *jiazu*) differs from an ancestral group in one important respect, namely that it and the property that it shares survives only as long as the family head himself, after which the estate is either divided or memorialized as an ancestral trust in perpetuity. The ancestral group and its estate on the other hand depend on the inclusion of both living and dead, which is perpetuated by ongoing acts of veneration and memory. The focus on common subsistence has even more relevance to a notion of household (*jiating*). Unlike family (*jiazu*), which is a group of all people tied together by a single head (*jiazhang*), a household is a familial unit that defines itself in addition as living in a single house. Of course, the symbolic definition of that household depends in part on the local customary definition of a house as well as complex considerations pertaining to the feasibility and desirability of common residence. Ironically, the often discussed phenomenon of large/small family size in the sinological literature is a misnomer that refers more accurately to household size. Anthropologists such as Chuang (1972) have attempted to minutely subdivide Chinese household types into "nuclear" (*hexin jiating*), "stem" (*zhugan jiating*) and "federated" (*lianbang jiating*) households but without delving much into the dynamics of family fusion and fission. Yet it should be clear that the kinds of strains that plague household composition should arise out of relations of propinquity, such as strained relations between mother and daughter-in-law (*poxi*), as described by Yao Ciai (1933), or between brothers, brother's wives, daughter-in-law and father's sisters, husband and wife, as well as parents and children, as Lei Chijing (1936: 598–99) has shown. These are analytically distinct from property conflicts intrinsic to *jiazu* per se.[23]

The symbolic construction of *jiazu* has important ramifications not only for understanding the nature of social exchange that drives kinship (including affinal) relations at an everyday level but also for showing how ritual obligations of a *jia* differ from those that engender ancestral worship per se. In many respects, *jia* (rather than *zu*) constitutes the proper primordial unit of both marriage exchange and ancestral worship, but the rites and beliefs invoked by both are nonetheless distinct. As a unit of ancestral worship, the *jia* is the nucleus for memorializing and venerating the dead. The scope of its practice (whether it be for five or more generations) and the content of its prescriptive rites (whether it be at a shrine or at the gravesite) have been the subject of intense political and intellectual debate throughout Chinese history, but they are analytically distinct from the symbolic constitution of *jia* and its ritual maintenance. No ancestral worship would exist without the participation of individual *jia*, but the appropriate conditions by which ancestral rites are carried out by individual families or higher-order agnatic units, such as a lineage segment or entire village, are determined by factors external to *jia*. On the other hand, the exchange process that engenders *jia* and maintains ongoing relations between *jia* is less concerned with descent relations than with cultivating ties with close kindred that cross-cut agnatic or even village solidarity.

With an egocentric definition of kindred, relations between close agnates can be cultivated by the same kinds of gift exchange, hence can overlap, but they are nonetheless analytically distinct, hence often compete with close affinal relations. Land, as part of the family property that is inherited after the death of the family head (*jiazhang*) and divided among succeeding *jia*, is also relevant to the symbolic constitution of a *jia*, since it provides the social basis for subsistence in the form of agriculture, whose sedentary nature is also related to the sedentary notion of village as *jiaxiang*. However, land's relationship to the sedentary nature of a *jia* is less relevant to the colonial imagination of land in its regulation of village social and territorial organization. As an abstract concept about inclusivity (which is not even limited to kinship) whose relativity and boundedness is effectively defined by symbolic exchange, the primordial notion of *jia* can be seen in many cognate terms such as *jiazu* (kin group), *jiaxiang* (natal village) or *jiating* (household), but these latter entities are bounded by other functionally distinct and incompatible criteria.

Distinct from the family per se, the dynamics of household formation in the village have important ramifications for land insofar as they impinge on occupancy of the house. Even more than in the case of *jiazu*, household fusion and fission are sensitive to concrete matters of everyday subsistence, in addition to structural conflicts mentioned above. The trend in Wo Hang toward the building of separate houses for individual families has created a certain pattern of residential mobility and expansion that parallels the course of village growth and development. The concentric pattern of lived village space reflects here a tendency to aggregate along relations of kin closeness. Radiating from individual households, it is possible to replicate in the end the "segmentary" structure of the lineage-village, but this is an outgrowth of the same principles of *qin* that regulate kin relations in general.

Seen as assemblage of households, the village as *jiaxiang* is on the one hand a community of people whose primary identification to land invokes reference to "one's own people". The locus of activity is centered on the "house", which is both the source of its livelihood and the basis of its social relationships. One's view of the world is relativistic, hence hierarchical from an egocentric perspective. Within the village, relationships of kin closeness and solidarity are thus inevitably and unceasingly differentiated. They can account for fissions at the level of household organization as well as spatial mobility at a higher level of residential structure.

Seen as a distinctive kind of moral universe on the other hand, the village as *jiaxiang* is a community of people whose identification to land invokes reference to a different set of symbols that pits one's village *vis-a-vis* other like sedentary communities. In the context of a single-lineage village, the ancestral hall becomes a primary locus of the community's public identity and within which all men are viewed as "brothers". In a multi-lineage community, however, the village is not just the sum of its constituent surname groups. It must be grounded in a broader sense of fate that incorporates all inhabitants as insiders, in contrast to outsiders. In both single and multi-lineage villages, the very definition of who a resident is and who can have access to land is subject to an overarching moral authority that usually transcends strict legal definitions. This is another example that illustrates the traditional moral autonomy of the village *vis-a-vis* the state or outside world.

One's subjective attachment to the village as *jiaxiang* is also a flexible set of conditions that cannot be defined by hard and fast rules of residence. People who are born there but later work or live elsewhere still, if they so choose, remain "residents" of the village, as may their descendants who have never actually lived there. This is less a matter of rights of ownership than a function of the intention itself to identify. The peculiar sense of attachment that binds one to his *jiaxiang* makes it unlikely that one will identify in this way with more than one village or an overseas or city residence. This is another way of suggesting that the kind of community engendered by notions of *jiaxiang* is regulated by its own set of rules. In its encounter with colonialism and modernity, the village confronts in the final analysis a system of moral regulation that conflicts with its own basic practices that has ramifications for various aspects of community in its relation to land.

THE NEW FACE OF TRADITION: EMPTY FIELDS AND VACANT HOUSES

Generally speaking, Shataukok coped hesitantly with material growth in the early 20th century. Rice continued to be a staple production despite the fact that vegetable cultivation practiced by immigrant farmers had begun to displace padi cultivation in other traditional agricultural regions. Unlike those living in rural communities closely adjoining the urban-industrial center, few villagers chose to take up wage labor in the city. Instead, indigenous males preferred to go abroad, either to Southeast Asia or the Americas, which was a trend that actually began in the latter half of the 19th century. While such overseas migration was far from being a universal phenomenon, some villages near the northern frontier had been depleted greatly by villagers who signed on *en masse* as laborers to go abroad.

The influx of refugees from mainland China after 1945 brought about much chaos in many parts of the New Territories. Cash-rich refugees looking to invest in some form of local enterprise began to buy up land in the countryside, leading to a rapid changeover in existing patterns of land use. In addition to the general trend toward vegetable cultivation, entrepreneurs ventured heavily into poultry and pig raising in particular. The demand for land in the midst of a burgeoning population, a large influx of capital and the speculative energies of entrepreneurs on the land quickly forced up the market value of land, driving many landlords to replace existing tenancy relationships with short term cash contracts. The areas most affected by these changes were rapidly developing areas of New Kowloon like Tuen Mun and the area surrounding the new market town of Fanling. Traditional rice producing areas such as Ping Shan reacted most sharply to the radical trend toward cash cropping and destruction of fertile padi land for animal domestication. In the long run, while the remaining padi farmers began to pay higher rent with a larger percentage of their crops, the trend in this regard was definitely toward short-term leases. As for vegetable cultivation and pig and poultry raising, short-term leases on the basis of cash rent gradually became a standard practice. By 1961, the percentage of vegetable cultivators among all farmers in Tuen Mun and Fanling approached 50% and 68%, respectively, with about 33% and 79% engaged in poultry or pig domestication (HKCSD 1961 III: 56). This set the overall tone.

The Shataukok area encountered a large number of refugees and immigrant cultivators in the immediate post-war period, but unlike most other remote areas, such as the neighboring district of Ta Kwu Ling, residents of indigenous villages there on the whole resisted the influx of outsiders into their own villages. Many villages rented out land for vegetable cultivation to tenants in areas outside their own village per se, and tenants were left to build squatter huts on their own fields. These tenants were in most cases Hakka, but despite the price of admission they were consciously isolated from the mainstream of traditional village life there. By 1961, Ping Shan, Shataukok and Sai Kung North remained the only major rice-producing areas in the territory, with the ratio of rice to vegetable cultivation in Shataukok exceeding 11: 1 (HKCSD 1961 III: 59). Animal domestication accounted for a sizeable percentage (22%) of all farming enterprises in Shataukok, but unlike elsewhere 85% was owned by indigenous villagers to the exclusion of outsiders.

Thus in the face of changing times, one can detect in Shataukok a rather headstrong attempt to maintain its traditional livelihood on the land amidst the growing economic irrationality of such practices (*vis-a-vis* cash-cropping) as well as a strong resistance to outside intrusion and change which, as compared to other areas, apparently constituted a threat to the functioning of existing relationships. In a sense, their attempt to maintain their traditional mode of livelihood on the land represented less a throwback to an idealistic past for the sake of preservation itself than a reflection of their fragile economic condition within a larger societal framework, which was in large part due to its poverty of natural resources (for production on the land). Moreover, the general hostility of indigenous residents to outsiders was less a product of a natural fear of the unknown or the provincial character of their world ethos per se than a pragmatic assessment of the value of traditional social relationships in light of economic degradation and other factors relevant to their sense of security as a community "against the world". In the long run, the fate of the Shataukok region in this global context first led to increasing poverty on the land followed by total abandonment of traditional agriculture, then intensified their traditional commitment toward the indigenous community.

In Wo Hang, as in neighboring villages of Shataukok district, the 1950s saw a gradual deterioration of local livelihood and a hardening of indigenous resistance toward the ravages of the outside world. Starting in the early 60s, male villagers emigrated *en masse* to seek a living (*wen-sik* (C), literally "to find eat") in the U.K., then later on in other places in Europe. This outmigration followed the pattern of other villages in the New Territories earlier hit by emigration. Initially, young male villagers, mostly of prime working age, went out first, usually in father-son, brother-brother or village brother-village brother (*qun xiongdi*) groups. On arrival at their destination, they would be aided by other village brothers who arranged lodging and employment. Work found under such conditions were usually arduous in nature, long in hours, and low in pay. Typically, sacrifices had to be made in personal lifestyle, since even under these conditions they were eventually able to accumulate and save their earnings to a point where other village brothers, family members (usually in the order of wife, then children, then grandparents) and close relatives (brothers-in-law, sister's son, etc.) could be accommodated in this manner. Those emigrant laborers who were able to save enough usually went into business on their own, opening a restaurant, store or other small business.

Within the village, the radical changeover to a new mode of livelihood and rapid depopulation combined with fierce resistance to the outside produced two phenomena representative of the times, namely empty fields and vacant houses. The complete abandonment of padi fields and terraces was replaced by occasional vegetable cultivation for personal consumption, otherwise padi stalks everywhere gave way to weeds and tall grass. Most of the day, groups of unemployed youths would be sitting about idly along with similar groups of elderly men and women in various popular hangouts in the village. By 1983, 68 of the 137 total residential structures in Wo Hang were physically vacant (in various states of use/nonuse), and of the 69 houses that were found to be occupied only 38 of the houses were literally occupied by a "household" (i.e., two or more persons related in any way). The other 31 (69-38) houses were thus occupied by a single resident, most of the time an elderly man or woman and, in few instances, a youth working in town but living at home while all other members of the family were living abroad. Whether one considers the number of occupied houses in the village to be 69 (50% of total), 38 (28%) or less, it is clear that outmigration had taken a heavy demographic toll, while depletion of productive human resources had taken an even greater toll.[24]

A brief breakdown of village household composition following recent decades of outmigration, based on my own survey in 1983, highlights the extent to which villagers have been affected by changing household structure, extended family ties and increasing dependence on overseas remittances. Of the total 137 residential structures in Wo Hang, 69 were found to be physically occupied, and 68 vacant. Of the 68 vacant houses, 39 were considered to be residences of villagers who had migrated abroad or were living and working in the city, while the other 29 units were either older ancestral houses replaced by newer ones or extra buildings used actually for non-residential purposes (such as storage). Thus, of the 137, only 108 (69+39) were actively claimed to be village residences. A total of 175 persons were found to be living in Wo Hang at the time, but if one were to count up for these houses the total number of extended family members who emigrated or were living in the city (but still claimed ties to their natal home (*jiaxiang*)), it would produce a very different picture of the village community. A significant number (80) were living elsewhere in Hong Kong, while 472 persons (and their descendants, which excluded married out daughters and divorced wives who remarried) could claim to be Wo Hang villagers as well. The 472 total included 385 who went to the U.K., 55 to continental Europe (mostly Holland), 27 to North America, 1 to mainland China and 4 to the Caribbean. The inclusion of extended family members into the "living" population of Wo Hang would no doubt change the "household" structure of the village considerably, especially if they were all to return to their natal home to live. In this regard, of 108 total residences, there would be 11 single-generation households, 50 two-generation households, 45 three-generation households and 2 four-generation households. While sociologists dealing with actual populations would consider this a hypothetical fiction, made real only by the assumption that all residents would return to their natal village, the strains of inadequate housing already appear in the number of houses physically occupied by people who were not the actual owners of the house, namely 16 (or 23% of all occupied households). In almost all of these cases, the occupant of the house was a close agnatic relation to the actual owner who did not own a house of his own. The number of overseas residents who still claim "residence" to the village added to the number of villagers who do not own a house acutely epitomizes in effect the extent of land scarcity.

In demographic terms alone, most observers would simply conclude that Wo Hang was an economically depressed village suffering the same aftereffects of poor resources, depleted manpower and remoteness from the core that afflicted the less developed areas. It was one among the first to be devastated by the onslaught of traditional padi cultivation by the global economy and refugee influx, thus among the first to emigrate on a large scale. However, the decision to accept extreme degradation in lifestyle, when less radical options for development were available, namely by abandoning the fields totally (and not renting to tenants) and to let the houses remain unoccupied (thus resisting the temptation to sell off the land), seem to be "irrational" responses to the market that contrast with those seen elsewhere.

In input-output terms, the process of outmigration without doubt intensified mass depopulation and abandonment of local production, while economic success of villagers overseas without doubt institutionalized a pattern of dependence on remittances from abroad as a primary source of livelihood. However despite this increase in economic dependence, the tendency to hold on even more to the land reflected, if anything, an affirmation of existing values, while the very reliance on remittances, if anything, intensified even more the necessity of solidary family ties (linking male head of household, wife, children and, if applicable, grandparents) in the household economy. In other words, there is more here than meets the eye.

The abandonment of traditional agriculture could be understood in the same economic terms that linked Shataukok to other areas of the New Territories in the global sphere. Yet this did not stop villagers from reinvesting their remittances into the land, as many of them continued to do. In this regard, the step-by-step process of outmigration demonstrated the role of traditional family relationships and the implicit priority placed on certain kinds of relationships, insofar as mutual obligations toward maintenance of a common livelihood were concerned. Finally, the process of change resulting in the abandonment of production on the land did not necessarily imply in the case of Wo Hang any loss of social solidarity among fellow villagers with whom one shared a traditional relationship to the land.[25]

Economic degradation offset by the benefits of overseas migration and new forms of economic production that appears to reinforce an even higher degree of traditional familism may seem like a plausible explanation of why villages such as Wo Hang seem to accept the abandonment of their previous form of livelihood with seemingly little adverse consequences, but this is not the whole story. Casual observers and well-meaning scholars have on the other hand tended to romanticize the situation altogether by downplaying the economic irrationality of villagers and by asserting simply that villages such as Wo Hang have happily chosen tradition over progress. Above all, they have remained single-lineage villages.

Alternative rationality and nostalgic traditionalism aside, it is necessary to point out certain meaningful characteristics of Wo Hang's experience not only as a peculiar example of village community in the New Territories but in ways that reflect (in concrete terms) various intrinsic relationships between land (as a social fact), village (as a territorial community) and *zu* (as an agnatic community) that underlay the process of change in the postwar era. To a trained social scientific observer scrutinizing the ubiquitous scene of empty fields and vacant houses that epitomized the state of land in Wo Hang, as in most of Shataukok district, such phenomena constitute obvious signs of a village in the process of dissolution or defiantly resisting progress. However, contrary to what might be expected, I argue that such conclusions are basically misleading if not erroneous. These errors stem less from our incomplete knowledge of the facts than from the way observers have confused the various meanings of land and consistently misinterpreted the values which indigenous villagers attach to their village and kin community.

Thus before passing judgment on its apparent "irrationality" or "tradition", it is necessary first of all to explore the perceptions of the inhabitants themselves and the definitions by which their village constitutes a moral community. More than just legal definitions of land, hard and fast rules regarding the boundedness of people, and notions of agnatic omnipotence in matters of property and village, I suspect that the principles that define the village and its community are more complex than has been portrayed by anthropologists interested in the application of kinship principles to local society and historians interested in the development of the village predominantly in terms of its tangible events and institutions. This cultural construction of the village can then be contrasted with other domestic institutions, such as ancestral worship groups, families and households. Far from being a kin institution, the village is itself a meaningful nexus for kin relations.

LAND IS TO LIVE, OR A VILLAGE IN SUSPENDED ANIMATION

In utilitarian terms, the villagers of Wo Hang appear downright irrational. That they suffer from geographic remoteness from centers of activity and poverty of natural resources on the land is, of course, no fault of their own. However, in midst of total abandonment of their fields and the proliferation of vacant houses in the village, one has to wonder why they do not rent out village land to others for cultivation or residence in response to what they admit to be rampant poverty. Scholars and other local observers have usually explained this state of affairs by pointing to the lack of demand for land in such a remote, impoverished area or a basic reluctance on the part of villagers there to accept innovation in any form. But like other areas of the territory, Wo Hang had been inundated by offers of refugee tenants to rent land for purposes of cultivation and animal domestication, most of which, especially land within the boundaries of the village, were rebuffed. Again during the 1970s, when speculative fever on the land affected the property market in other areas and outmigration from Shataukok escalated to its current point, villagers rejected rational choices to conditions of material deprivation.

Yet to the villagers of Wo Hang, there are no empty fields or vacant houses. It is true that the fields had been left uncultivated, but the decision of whether to rent them out to outside cultivators was a matter for villagers as a whole to settle. First of all, the renting out of agricultural land in the village did not and never affected the rights of villagers to rent out land to cultivators on the periphery of their village or in other villages. In other areas of Shataukok, tenant cultivators were tilling vegetable patches outside the traditional villages. Some of this land was owned by Wo Hang ancestral estates. There was also little if any change in the ownership of land by various Wo Hang ancestral estates in Shataukok district. Few sales of ancestral land took place. The only noticeable change in the postwar period was the collection of rent in cash from vegetable cultivators.

What made the status of agricultural land in the village unique was not the ownership status of the land itself, but rather the sanctity of the village and the community of persons it represented. Ownership and/or use of land in the village was always subject to interests of the community as a whole, and it entailed more than just the economics of subsistence. In strictly legal terms, there was nothing to prevent the sale of village land to outsiders. On the other hand, the collective conscience of the community was much stronger insofar as the moral constitution of the village and its perceived security were at stake. By letting tenants onto village land, one was dealing essentially with a social problem and the possible conflicts of interest that might involve them either as individuals or as a group.

Moreover, the decision not to rent out village land to tenants seemed to be less attributable to the fact that Wo Hang happened to be a "single-lineage village" than the fact that it simply did not want to accept outsiders (strangers) into their community. This response was consistent with that of other villages in the region, many of whom were multi-surname villages. In this regard, its agnatic origin was less important than the socio-historical specificity which conditioned it.

When I first inquired into the possibility of renting a house in the village, I was told by different persons on different occasions in a matter of fact tone that there were no houses for rent and that there were people living in all the houses, even though upon later inspection it was obvious that many of them were boarded up by occupants who emigrated to work abroad many years ago. As in the case of agricultural land, the ownership status of the house was less of an issue than people's definition of *residence* or what was meant by people "living" there.

First of all, it is worth distinguishing between the terms *hu* (*wu* (C), *fu* (H), "household"), *jia* (*ga* (C), *ka* (H), "family") and *wu* (*uk* (C), *vuk* (H), "house"). The term *hu*, literally meaning "door", has a long history of bureaucratic usage and refers to a group of people living in a definable residential structure. While it is similar to the colloquial term *jiating* (*ka-tin* (H), *ga-ting* (C)), its broader meaning is reflected in Chinese words for "population" (*hukou*, "number of mouths residing in households") and "residential family" (*jiahu*, households whose members belong to a single family). The term *jia* on the other hand refers in essence to a group of related persons. In some dialects, such as Mandarin and Hakka, it can refer to the physical unit that a family lives in, as in "home", but in other dialects, such as Cantonese, it never refers to an actual house. Finally, the term *wu* explicitly refers to a residential unit. In Mandarin, it means a "room", while in Cantonese and Hakka, it refers to the entire "house". The above terms give an approximation of the various senses of "residence" or "living" in a local village context.

Residence by strict census definition of actual occupancy would probably correspond most closely to *hu* in Chinese, although it might be debatable whether the Chinese concept of household registration (*huji*) in administrative practice ever meant actual occupancy. In any case, it was clear from people's usage of the term living (*zhu*) that they were referring to a definition of permanent residency *for the purpose of being a villager*. This definition was relevant insofar as it reflected ultimately what for them constituted a *village* (as *jiaxiang* or *xiangcun*). In short, a village was an assemblage of houses like no other. As a permanent residence, it rooted one's identity to a home and source of livelihood on the land. Although villagers recognized that most of their fellow villagers worked (*wen-sik* (C), "find eat" or seek subsistence) abroad, they nonetheless continued to live or reside in the village where their house (*wu*) in the village stood. To rent out one's house to outsiders would not only infringe upon the identity of villagers but also undermine the nature of the village as a moral community. On the other hand, in matters pertaining to management of the house, the owner was free to do as he wished.

Insofar as residents of a house (as *vuk-ka*) constituted a peculiar community of persons (*ka-tin*) that had symbolic associations also with the creation of a family and continuity of rights to worship and estate, one must ask in what sense their presence as active residents in the village was marked and whom the house was meant to include as members of that family. Especially as physical presence did not appear to be a major criterion for village residence, one might also ask to what extent it included people who never lived there but could claim by other kind of (kin) filiation to be part of that *ka* (such as in the case of dependents born abroad).

In Wo Hang, there were in physical terms three kinds of houses: unlivable (abandoned) houses, unlived-in (vacant) houses, and lived-in houses. Of a total of 137 livable houses, there were 69 units that were actually occupied by at least one person and 68 units that were physically vacant (not physically occupied). Of the 68 units, 51 were attended to by fellow villagers or relatives of the vacant house. Of the 51 houses, 17 were attended to by family members or lineal descendants of the original household (excluding married out daughters and adopted out sons) currently living elsewhere in the village. In other words, these 17 houses could be considered ancestral houses (*ah-kung vuk* (H)) that had been vacated after the building of a new house. Most of these ancestral houses were used for storage, and they were potentially livable in the sense that the owners had not yet given them up as abandoned. One (1) of the 51 houses was attended to by the absentee household head's grandfather, and another one (1) by the mother of the household head, both of whom were still living in the village. Another six (6) of the houses were attended to by actual brothers (or brother's wives) of the household head, and another thirteen (13) were attended to by actual patrilineal uncles (FaBr) or close agnatic cousins (FaBrSo) (or their wives) of the household head, all of whom were living in the village. In other words, of the 51 vacant houses where there was a caretaker, 17 of them were attended to by members of that family who had simply moved to a new house in the village (or in one case, into the city). Another 21 of them were attended to by close agnatic kinsmen living in the village for household members who were residing abroad (or in one case, living in the city). This left thirteen (13) whose caretakers were other than family members or close agnates.

One (1) of the remaining thirteen involved a married-out daughter living in an adjacent district in the absence of household members living abroad. Another five (5) were attended to by affinal relatives living outside the village. Two (2) of these cases involved the mother-in-law of the household head, two (2) involved an unspecified relative on the wife's (or mother's) side, and one (1) other involved a son-in-law's nephew. The remaining seven (7) houses were attended to by village brothers or neighbors of convenience with whom (absentee) household members had no close agnatic relationship. On the whole, the latter 13 (of 51) cases were noteworthy, since in each case none of the households originally had close agnatic kinsmen in the village. The fact that affines could be called upon to manage and take responsibility over one's village house property in preference to fellow agnates in the village implied that, in matters of personal trust, even those involving land, relative closeness in principle took precedence over agnation per se and that this did not impinge upon questions of villager identity or the moral authority of that community. In the seven (7) cases where distantly related village brothers had been attending to the vacant houses, only three (3) of these absentee households could be said to have any kind of close kin (including affinal) relationship there. One had an actual brother living in the village, but both of them were not on good speaking terms. One (1) other had a niece (BrDa) who married out to an adjacent village over 25 years ago; she rarely returned, nor did household members, who were living abroad. One (1) other former resident, a widower, left the village after her husband's death to live with her only daughter, who had married out and lived in the city. None of them ever returned to the village to live. Apart from these three, one (1) household was not survived by descendants, and its house was lent to its present user by its previous owner, both of whom were on amicable terms. The remaining three (3) households had few relatives in the Hong Kong area, went overseas long ago and rarely returned to their natal village to visit.

Some general remarks can be made with regard to the 51 (of 78) absentee households where there was a caretaker. In the overwhelming majority of cases, the former occupants were living and working abroad. There were in addition only a handful of cases where previous residents had moved to the city and two cases where previous residents failed to be succeeded by any descendants, in which case responsibility for the house was handed over to the closest agnates in accordance with custom. Many of the emigrant households, not to mention those partially depleted ones belonging to physically lived-in houses of the villages, initially left the village decades ago. Some emigrated as a group, while others gradually moved out over a long period of time. Some returned regularly to visit, others rarely or never. Moreover, there was no simple correlation between the existence of close kin relations on the one hand and length of stay abroad or frequency of return on the other, the strength of solidarity with the natal village being subject to many factors. One could only say for certain that the high percentage of such links was reflective of *preexisting* social bonds which contributed to the maintenance of the community, bonds that could not have been deduced from material circumstances.

Of the 68 total vacant households in Wo Hang, 17 houses had no caretakers. The 68 did not include 12 other houses abandoned beyond repair but left standing. Of the 17 without caretakers, some were old ancestral houses, while others were vacated by their former occupants. Durkheim would have called them instances of anomie, and reasons for their neglect should be viewed in contrast to the other 51 cases. The dispositions of the 17 cases can be briefly summarized as follows:

(1) Household consisted of a sole son who left the village in the early 1940s. *No other close kin in the village,* has never returned to his natal village to live. Present whereabouts unknown.

(2) Household consisted of a sole son who was raised by his grandmother after the early death of his mother and his father's departure to mainland China to fight during the Sino-Japanese war (never returned). After the death of his grandfather in 1960, occupant went to U.K. to make a living. He has since married and raised two children.

Returned to natal village only once in 1973 and has since sold off most of his property in the village. *No other close kin in the village.*

(3)   Household consisted of two parents, one son and one daughter. Father died in 1950. Son left for Holland in 1965 to seek work, has since married and raised two children. Never returned to natal village to live. Daughter married out around 1955 to nearby village. Mother had lived here until her death in 1980. *No other close kin in the village.*

(4)   *Old ancestral house* from two generations back belonging to current village headman. Occupants have since moved twice to new houses in the village, in 1936 and in 1974.

(5)   *Old ancestral house* from two generations back. Occupants have since built new houses in the village, in 1930 and in 1974.

(6)   Ancestral house once inhabited by two parents, concubine and one son. They moved to a new house in 1955. Concubine remained in the old house until she left the village in 1975 due to friction with fellow villagers, current whereabouts unknown. Main wife died in 1960 and was followed by death of the husband in 1965. Son migrated to U.K. in 1970, has since married and never returned to the village. *No other close kin in the village.*

(7)   House once inhabited by two parents, one son and one daughter. Mother died in 1950, and father died in the same house in 1975. Son moved to the city in 1960, has since married and raised three children. Returns to the village once every few years. Two of his daughters married out and living now in U.K.. *No other close kin in the village.*

(8)   *Old ancestral house* that appears to be used but in unlivable condition. Previous occupants moved to a new house in the village in 1940.

(9)   Household consisted of two parents, one son and one daughter. Father died around 1950. Daughter married out to nearby village in 1955. Son emigrated to U.K. in 1957 to make a living, has since married and settled. Current

whereabouts unclear. Has never returned to village. Mother went to live with son in 1965. Several close agnates (FaBr) live in the village, but *nature of their relationship not particularly close.*

(10) Relatively new village house built in 1975. Household head left for U.K. in 1960 to seek a living; was joined by wife and five children in 1973. Has rarely returned to the village, the last time being in 1983. Has one brother living in the village, but *relations reportedly not amicable.*

(11) *Old ancestral house* from two generations back. Moved to new house around 1925. Previous household survived by grandchildren.

(12) *Old ancestral house* of a generation preceding that described in #10. Members of the household also the same.

(13) Household once consisted of two parents, two sons and one daughter. After the death of father in 1973, mother remarried and moved to the town of Tai Po, accompanied by the children, two of whom have since married. Parents of former household head still living in the village. *Relations between remarried woman and villagers described as antagonistic.* After moving out, they never returned and sold off their land in the village.

(14) Household formerly inhabited by two parents and three sons. Parents died before 1950. The three sons migrated to U.K. in 1965, two of whom have since married. One of the three returns to the village every year to pass the New Year; the other two returns only occasionally, the last time being in 1983. *No other close kin in the village.*

(15–17) Three separate *old ancestral houses* belonging to three brothers. The three brothers built a large new house in 1950, where they and their descendants have lived since then. Ancestral house at present appears to be used but in generally unlivable condition.

In the large majority of cases, matters of trust and responsibility pertaining to maintenance of the house had much to do with the nature of social relationships between the emigrant household and natal villagers. The presence of the house (recognition by villagers of its social existence) subsequently had much to do with recognition of its occupants as being resident members of that community. With exception of the eight ancestral houses that had fallen into disuse, in most of the nine instances of neglect (absence of caretakership), the emigrant household had no close agnatic relation within the village. In the two instances where there was a close relation within the village, one was clearly marked by "bad blood" between brothers. Thus, as in the preceding fifty-one absentee households where there was a formal caretaker, kin closeness (*qin*) rather than agnation per se served as the primary basis of interpersonal solidarity. These relationships radiated out of the *jia* as a focal point, were maintained by ongoing reciprocity and exchange, both ceremonial and material, hence prone to shifts in sentiment. Amicable relations that stemmed from propinquity were analytically distinct from rules of "descent" that tied people through common worship or people within the village as members of an imagined moral community. In this regard, there should have been nothing privileged about the solidarity of the "single-lineage village", all else being equal.

The symbolic presence of the village as a living community was most clearly manifested during the passing of Lunar New Year, when business accounts were settled. The first week of the New Year was a time when people returned to their home village. One elder remarked that in the old days some Wo Hang villagers would make New Year pilgrimages to their old ancestral hall in Bolo county in Guangdong; few even went as far as Fujian province. Nonetheless, most people simply returned to their natal village. Of course, overseas residents returned less frequently and, when they did, usually stayed for several months at a time.

It was a custom in Wo Hang for villagers to open their porch, parlor and bedroom lights on the evening of New Year's Eve and continue to keep them open 24 hours a day through the first five days (in some cases fifteen days) of the New Year. A house-to-house survey conducted one year showed, that, with exception of two houses, all of the vacant houses where there was a known caretaker were lighted up. As with other lived-in houses, the doorways of the houses were also decorated with the pasting of long red sheets of paper bearing auspicious sayings on the sides and the pasting of red colored talismans over the top. The red paper shrines for the earth god and kitchen god were replaced with new ones, and on the morning of the first day of the New Year incense was burnt in front of the shrines, on each side of the door and on the ground (or wall) at a distance of about six feet from the front door. In almost all 51 cases of absentee households attended to by a caretaker, the caretaker was responsible for ritually decorating the house. The two instances where the house was not ritually decorated, despite the existence of a caretaker, were both households which had not been survived by descendants.

In all seventeen absentee households where there was no formal caretaker, there was correspondingly no sign of ritual decoration on the houses. Unanimity of neglect in these cases appeared to suggest that, at least from a native point of view, these people were not included among the resident community of the village. Their "non-existence" did not necessarily mean that they had no strict legal rights to land ownership or village membership in any other regard. The "identity" being invoked here was a highly subjective one that was not definable in hard and fast terms. To the contrary, it was a negociable product of mutual recognition of moral belonging. In the long run, these sentiments and memories had to be maintained.

The nature of the village as a moral instead of just territorial community has important ramifications for how understands its relationship to people, land and the wider society. It can be argued that the cultural constellation that viewed the amalgamation of lineage and village organization or the resurgence of village solidarity through mobilization of agnatic ideology and the practice of ancestral rites and beliefs that tied the social existence of a village to the land and its ritual legitimacy to a mythical past was the peculiar product of complex ideological and sociological transformations culminating only in the last 200-300 years. Without doubt, there were distinctive differences between the kind of local society that existed in the pristine evolution of descent groups and village settlements in the era of the so-called "Five Great Clans of the New Territories" and the more recent role of ancestral halls in galvanizing village autonomy, leading to the omnipotent appearance of lineage-villages. However, this goes beyond the scope of the present study. It suffices here to say that the cultural construction of those communities are also complex configurations in their own right that defy explanation in terms of Eurocentric notions of land and rights in rem that initially guided the colonial government in their admin- istration of the New Territories and that are implicitly coded, albeit more abstractly so, in certain anthropological models of descent and social structure. Contrary to the enduring sense of boundedness in- voked by such models, the factors contributing to village solidarity were quite distinct from the solidary relations that tied individuals to their place and livelihood in the village. The latter were not easily discernible from the overt kin constitution of the village, and in practice the scope for negotiation of sentiment and memory that ultimately impinged upon underlying notions of identity and attachment was quite large. In fact, the village community as a whole had no authority to determine or influence one's ties to the village. Even in obvious cases where house and land had both degenerated to a point of neglect and abandon and that their former residents had no intention of returning or disappeared completely, few interfered with them, as though to emphasize their chosen fate. Those who chose to disengage completely rarely had any reason to reclaim their ties. Rare examples of distant genealogical kinsmen from other villages wanting to live in Wo Hang were almost always taken in on the basis of personal acquaintance and not agnation per se.

HOUSEHOLD AND VILLAGE IN THE COLONIAL ENCOUNTER: A TERTIARY SYNTHESIS

By most accounts, Wo Hang epitomizes the vestiges of a "tra- ditional" village caught in the midst of a rapidly growing, modernizing society. According to such accounts, tradition is represented by the continued existence of a "single-lineage village" community, the main- tenance of old ancestral customs and practices, the unchanging appearance of limestone and brick houses, the failure of its residents to be enticed by the "attractions" of an urban-industrial society, and hesitance of villagers to give in to pressure to cash in on an escalating property market. The persistence of tradition has moreover been rein- forced by British colonial policy and its efficacy in preserving the rule of indigenous custom.

Part of the problem with the above characterization involves our definition of "tradition". That we tend to view the traditional village as being synonymous with a single-lineage community is almost entirely the influence of lineage theory, as propagated only recently by anthropologists and widely adopted by sinologists as a whole in their study of local Chinese society. Yet as I have argued, it is far from evident what the underlying principles of Chinese lineage organization are, not to mention those of the family, household and village, despite "appearances" to the contrary. Similarly, when we see the tranquillity of old row houses amidst a spacious countryside, it is perhaps easier to imagine a kind of rural utopia than to comprehend why inhabitants complain about the severity of the housing crisis, not to mention a condition of extreme land scarcity. The rural utopia in large part is an illusion of naive urbanites that is hardly shared by those already unable to maintain subsistence on the land. The very real problem of land scarcity is on the other hand a consequence of legal fictions perpetrated by official policy which in the process of "preserving" tradition has to the contrary introduced restrictions on land use that have not only subverted the essential practice of custom but also in the long run petrified it to the extent where the only avenue for change, especially under conditions of material deprivation, is a radical break with tradition.

The characterization of "tradition" in the above senses not only reflects our narrowness of definition but also their assumed value-free objectivity. Particularly as "custom", tradition has the illusion of being a pristine phenomenon untainted by the vissitudes of society-at-large (and the powers that be) whose history is for the most part sui generis, if not self-regulating. The fiction of Wo Hang (and the Shataukok region) in the historical past is that it was not affected by global events and developments reverberating throughout society-at-large. Yet contrary to being just another idealtypical single-lineage village, the settlement history of the village shows instead that the village form itself (along with its appropriation of lineage organization) is a creation of recent history. Similarly, its formative events cannot be divorced from the conditions that set the staple for the region as a whole and contributed to its ongoing socio-political climate. Seen from this perspective, the colonial presence was merely another phase in this ongoing global history.

The irony of Wo Hang in the ethnographic present is that it is not so much the victim of British colonialism (the usual fall guys) but rather the excesses of other indigenous Chinese who were inculcated by the system to emulate the self-interested values of the system. One such case in point is the Small House Policy and its subsequent revision, given the claims of indigenous rights. Abuses of the Small House Policy by overseas residents during the heyday of the speculative 70s that attempted deliberately to take advantage of the government's concession to custom by profiting from the booming property market subsequently led to its abolition by the government. The turn of events apparently showed, contrary to initial assumption, that overseas residents really had no intention of returning to their natal village or had broken off ties together. If one can take seriously the contention of Wo Hang villagers that, despite the appearance of vacant houses and a declining standard of life, people were still living there, then it should change our perception of who the villagers are, in what sense the village is still a relevant social entity for those people who continue to identify with it and what meaning land holds for these people. More than just a contest of power, the entire history of colonial administration in Hong Kong has been an ongoing interpretation at the level of mind of the nature of indigenous values and institutions. The subsequent exclusion of overseas villagers from concessionary grants on the assumption that they were after all only motivated by profit maximization is then justifiable only to the extent that it accurately perceived the values and goals of the "traditional" villager. In the case of Wo Hang, however, the traditional villager still loses out.

In retrospect if tradition, as it has been narrowly defined and systematically misunderstood by scholars and through application of our models, is simply our distortion of what actually is by being unwitting reflections of our own subjective biases, then one might more accurately conclude that our definitions of tradition have meaning only in a progressive society. That is to say, they are essentially defined relative to progress as the default. Tradition is simply that which is different from the present or that which has been forsaken by the present (i.e., the past as bygone). From the perspective of those who have chosen not to change on the other hand, progress is simply a set of values that is espoused by others. There is no break between the past, present and future, just an ongoing struggle for existence.

From a sociocentric perspective, the local history of Wo Hang is in the first instance a global history within which the entire social landscape of Hong Kong's New Territories has been radically transformed over the past decades through its incorporation and marginalization into different world systems, the dynamics of which one has only begun to adequately comprehend. It is not just a narrative of lineage-villages "on the ground", as has been coolly described by anthropologists and historians. Whether one calls these experiences "colonial" or "modern" is less important than how one decodes the symbolic mechanisms by which these various underlying regimes of power define, put into practice and regulate a certain life situation. These regimes engender a certain civilizing ethos as well as moral order that necessarily reflect back on the cultural influences of their respective time and place. One need not characterize the interactions between government and people as a clash of civilizations, but the events themselves clearly manifest a discrepancy in cultural perceptions that has serious ramifications for the ongoing creation and survival of those life situations. How these cultural interactions work themselves out in history and become ideologically and institutionally incorporated into these changing life situations is one problem; how these situations on the ground give rise to discourses and rationalizations that form the basis of making sense of the past in the present (once removed, so to speak) is another problem. One cannot hope to unpack the history of events and institutions on the ground without at the same time recognizing its embeddedness in discourses and rationalizations that have been produced by those actual situations of power and contestation.

The history of large-scale lineage-villages in southeastern China is without doubt a seminal part of the constitution of local society in the New Territories of Hong Kong as well, a point that has been reiterated in almost every ethnography and local history. Because of the colonial government's policy of non-interference with indigenous "custom", lineage institutions, ancestral rites or beliefs, and kin notions pertaining to descent per se were seen as elements of tradition that tended to be preserved. Yet despite the obvious survival of these phenomena into the present, from the perspective of those people who live in "traditional" villages, one gets a different sense of how important these institutions are to contemporary life. When economic conditions changed radically, people proved willing to change their relationship to land, to the point of abandoning traditional relationships to tenants to accommodate new ones or just abandon agriculture altogether. Lineage halls and their accompanying ritual accoutrements were actually relics of a bygone era, and they probably were dependent aspects of village organization rather than the backbone of its existence, as scholars have made them out to be. One gets little sense from local inhabitants themselves that the survival of their lineage, symbolic or otherwise, was a necessary condition for ongoing existence. On the other hand, colonial land and housing policy seemed to directly affect the survivability of the village community in ways that overshadowed all other aspects of traditional local society. Its threat on the land affected above all the tangible aspects of an already fragile economic livelihood as well as a disintegrating sense of moral community, but its effects were mostly intangible. By threatening concepts of village space rather than expropriating land per se and by introducing legal distinctions based on equally fictive notions of the Lease that removed it even further from the rest of changing social reality, the conflict had to explode, when pushed to the extreme. Rather than embodying different structural dispositions (from the perspective of any preconceived model of kinship), different villages clearly displayed different perceptual stategies to deal with changing socio-political conditions that impinged in the first instance on indigenous definitions of that community and secondly on the power geometry that defined one's position to land (and village) *vis-a-vis* other people. The postwar crisis was complicated not only by artificial distinctions of traditional and modern but also internal class divisions across and within villages.

At a deeper level, an anthropological analysis of local village history must simultaneously proceed at two levels or in two directions. First of all, the larger situation of power within which local life is constantly embedded and remade must be viewed as an entity in itself with a view toward the interaction of discourse and practice. The colonial-cum-modern experience of Hong Kong's New Territories has origins both in the cultural-political sociology of the state as well as in the space created by this regime of power within which various agents constantly negotiate. On the other hand, the institutions at the local level also have their own lineage of ideologies and practices that are the consequence of different cultural-political forces. The difficulty of analyzing them is attributable to our embeddedness in modern institutions and their derivative concepts in the former instance and our removal from the cultural experiences of local society in the latter.

From an egocentric perspective, the local history of Wo Hang should be by necessity a narrative that takes into account the subjective constitution of their village as a living community and not just a territorial entity whose nature and relevance is defined by reference to our definitions of "local society". It is evident from an indigenous point of view that the meaningful composition of the household and the village does not just include those physically residing there but also those who work in the city and live overseas. A narrative of the village that includes all those who still identify with the place and whose kin interactions incorporate this wider community, albeit transcending actual cartographic boundaries, would no doubt contribute a very different picture of local society. There is no reason why such a narrative could not, from a different vantage point, enlighten our attempt to understand inherent relationships between people and to land that have been the focus of the present investigation. In this regard, one must in effect transcend the appearance of vacant houses and the economically depressed village to inquire into the sources of its new livelihood and the possibility of future change. Even the dependence on overseas remittances that in sociocentric terms has been taken as evidence of its peripheralization in the global order should be effectively turned around to show how it has become the staple of something quite different, even if the foci of kin life have shifted away from the village center. Only in this way can one really begin to understand that underlying life situation "in its own terms".

NOTES

[1]   In actuality, lineage-village organization displayed a large degree of variation. Sometimes, a single descent group would envelope a cluster of aggregate villages while in other cases it would occupy distinct niches in a village. One can contrast, for example, the percentage of single-surname villages in central China (86.85% of a total of 1291 villages in western Jiangsi) reported by Hu Hsien-chin (1948: 14) with the percentage (12.5%) of such villages in a county in

north China studied by Niida Noboru (1952: 60–61), where 87.5% of villages contained up to 3–12 surnames.

2 See also the discussion by Wang Sung-hsing (1991) on the word *jia*.

3 For a more comprehensive discussion of these three concepts, see Chun (1996a).

4 For an argument regarding the ramifications of the neo-Confucian revival of the agnatic ideal (*zongfa*) for the emergence of the lineage-village, see Chun (1996b).

5 Cases of village abandonment for *fengshui* reasons were common throughout the Hong Kong region, as in the rest of China. In most instances, even in those where there is reliable historical data, it is difficult to ascertain whether *fengshui* is the cause to which one usually attributes bad fortune or the consequence of known or repeated instances of bad fortune. Geomancy is a serious consideration in matters pertaining to the siting of villages, position of houses, and influences of the natural environment on the human world. The first Li settlers in the area were led to Wo Hang by a geomancer named Li Sanyou (no relation to Wo Hang Lis). Subsequent generations of Wo Hang Lis memorialized Sanyou by placing a tablet within their ancestral hall directly to the right of their own ancestors to honor him. To the left is a tablet in honor of Guanyin, "the Goddess of Mercy", whom villagers claim to worship. Wo Hang villagers attribute their gradual decline in later history to the building of Shataukok Road by the British in 1910. Archival records show that there were differences of opinion between residents and government officials over the initial building of the road. Hayes (1967: 25–27) notes similar instances in the past where government engineers tried to build over places that villagers claimed to cause bad *fengshui*. The fact that it caused mysterious deaths of cows in the end was for most people proof enough of *fengshui* influence. In another instance reported by Hayes (1963), an entire village moved because residents claimed that buildings in an adjacent village inexorably damaged the fortune of their village. In another instance, a typhoon which blew over many features of the surrounding landscape of one village was said to cause gradual depopulation (Hayes 1969: 157).

6 According to the 1905 Block Crown Lease for Sheung Wo Hang (upper village), no less than 36 different ancestral estates owned land (mostly agricultural rather than house) in the village. Some of these were *tso* belonging to descendants living in Ha Wo Hang (lower village), that formed one of the three major segments (*fong*) in Wo Hang. Members of the first and third *fong* resided in the upper village. Also excluded from this list were other ancestral estates that owned and collected rent from land outside Wo Hang. In contrast to village agricultural land, which was cultivated in rotation by members of the respective *tso* for their own purposes, ancestral land owned outside the village was a real source of revenue on the land. The 36 ancestral estates can be broken up as follows: one (1) to a 2nd generation ancestor, one (1) to 3rd generation ancestor, ten (10) to 4th generation ancestors, nine (9) to 5th generation ancestors, nine (9) to 6th generation ancestors, four (4) to 7th generation ancestors, and two (2) to

8th generation ancestors. Needless to say, the village at the time was probably inhabited by members of the 7th, 8th and 9th generations. Few of the more memorable ancestors made their riches directly from the land (as tillers of the soil), although this cannot be fully determined for the 36 or more ancestors in Wo Hang (who have left behind estates). Some made their wealth in business or enterprise, while most others remain unclear. In each case, wealth was plowed back into land as a form of permanent trust for future generations instead of reinvested as capital, as would be the case in the case of a modern enterprise. In this sense, what was being transmitted then was a mode of livelihood; ancestor worship thus memorialized the contribution of the trust's creator to the reproduction of the livelihood of future generations to the land.

7   The pattern of outside land ownership by Wo Hang ancestral estates resembled the carving of a pie. Instead of randomly scattering their holdings over a broad area, land owned by a particular *tso* tended to be clustered in a few specific areas so that one could easily point out which areas of land were controlled by which *tso* and where a particular *tso* tended to have its holdings. In general, Wo Hang *tso* owned large patches of land in villages north of Wo Hang surrounding Shataukok, portions of the market town itself and much of the valley past Shataukok on the Chinese side of the border. To the south, it owned numerous but smaller plots of land past the adjoining villages of Man Uk Pin and Loi Tung and in the Ping Che valley around Ma Mei Ha, which was a mixed Hakka-Cantonese speaking area.

8   Winston Hsieh's research on mulberry cultivation in the Canton Delta region and David Faure's work on rice markets and production in Guangdong in the 19th century have dealt explicitly with the overall economic decline of traditional padi agriculture in south China and its replacement by other forms of subsistence. In Xinan county, mulberry was grown occasionally in between crops of padi, but it is unclear how long ago such a practice was adopted or what the extent of its production was. Postwar surveys tended to subsume mulberry cultivation under padi, which was reported to be the primary crop produced under such conditions, but the territory was never known for its mulberry cultivation in any case.

9   In this regard, two examples stand out. Wiest (1976) in a study of conversion patterns to Catholicism in rural Guangdong during the 19th century describes the function of what he calls "Catholic lineages". These lineages were initially families which had been rejected by their own lineages because of their Catholicism, then proceeded to establish "agnatic" communities based upon Christianity. While the question of how they could reject ancestor worship and remain at the same time "agnatic" communities based on Catholicism was not explained, Wiest nonetheless argues that ideology was the essential criterion upon which they could maintain themselves as a tight knit kin community while at the same time regulating ties of intermarriage with other "like" lineages then expanding to convert others. So-called "slave lineages" (*ximin, toukau*) in the historical and

ethnographic literature are a similar case in point. As a group, not only did individuals lack any kind of kin identity, more importantly they lacked at the same time the ideological basis (of ancestor worship) upon which they could construct an identity and its intrinsic relationships (to others) (see, for example, Watson 1976, Hsieh 1932, Fu 1961: 83). Watson (1980) also cites an interesting example where descendants of such slaves attempted to construct such an identity complete with (fictitious) ancestral tablets and communal shrine only to be discovered and ridiculed by others.

10 From the point of view of worship, however, there is nothing privileged about the status of communal *vis-a-vis* private land, at least in principle. In each case, the status of both the ancestor and ancestral obligations remain the same.

11 Faure (1989) has pointed to the purely political nature of Ming family shrines in southeastern China that contrasted with lineage halls in the Qing era. For an account of the historical emergence of the lineage-village, see Chun (1996b).

12 In all the cases of land inheritance by outsiders cited by Ahern (1973: 130, 152, 246) and (Wolf 1976), they fail to mention who those individuals were or why they might want to give away property. Most likely, the deceased were army veterans who came from the mainland after the war, were not survived by relatives locally, and had no way of returning to the mainland. The fact that the recipients of that land also cared for the ancestral tablet of the deceased does not mean, of course, that they worshipped more than one "agnatic" kinsman and thus claimed "descent" from more than one person but rather that the deceased and his ascendants had left their fates in the hands of outsiders. Responsibility for negligence by the recipient to carry through in his ritual duties would still fall upon the deceased as a consequence of his inability to be attended by his own descendants. Moreover, Wolf and Ahern neglect to cite instances of worship by "outsiders" in the absence of prior land inheritances, which were equally numerous, if not more so.

13 Shao (1935: 279) argues that *jia* means "unity of man and woman", adding, "*hai* is the fact of a man and a woman producing a child; if this is not *jia*, then what?".

14 This particular stipulation is taken from a handwritten manual on customary practice copied and edited by a village elder, Li Nganling. On the meaning of the candles, he added the following commentary: "Ancestral incense, a thousand sons" (*zuxiang chianzi*), "ancestral candles, double luminescence" (*zuzhu shuanghui*), "ancestral money, 10,000 strings (of cash)" (*zuchian wanguan*), "the guiding of the candle, the making of luminescence" (*yinzhu chihuang*). Another village handbook in the possession of Li Geng also recorded the same kinds of gifts exchanged.

15 The list of gifts given varies slightly from one informant to another and one customary handbook to another, however the giving of meat by the groom's family to the bride's family appears to be a standard item on each list. One may contrast this with the following list from a Cantonese customary handbook in

Tai Po Uk Tou Village. Here, gifts given by the groom's family to the bride's family on this day include pork, salted fish, abalone, shark's fin, dried oysters, sea cucumber, duck eggs, ten chickens, wine, brideswealth, a set of gold earrings and a pair of scissors. Gifts reciprocated by the bride's family include a colored cap and shoes for the groom, shoes for the groom's parents and grandmother, fan, brush pen, ink and paper, a silk belt, cloth purse, a roll of fine quality cloth, one pair of chickens (returned to the groom's family), a box of peanuts, sweets, tea, onions and garlic.

16 One customary handbook on marriage etiquette (JL: 36–38), dated 1923 but of unknown origin, cites different rules of etiquette for mother's eldest brother (*dajiu*) and her younger brother (*xiaojiu*). Most villagers, however, are unfamiliar with the specific role of mother's brother on wedding occasions, while elders say that he is simply a representative of the bride's family.

17 Wilson (1954) has noted the following things attached to the roof beam of a Cantonese house: a piece of red cloth, a big taro with many small ones around it (symbolizing a mother with many children), two small bags of red cloth, one with millet (*gu*) and the other rice (*mi*) (representing subsistence), a red bamboo sieve (the numerous holes representing mouths of a large family), two bundles of red chopsticks (the Cantonese term for chopsticks (*fai-ji*) being a pun on "quick to have sons"), several onions (the Cantonese term for onions being a pun on "intelligence" (*chung-ming*)), several garlic bulbs (the Cantonese term for garlic (*suen-tou*) being a pun on "calculating ingenuity"), a pair of black trousers (the Cantonese term for trousers being a pun on "wealth and prestige" (*fu-kwai*)), and two paper lanterns (the Cantonese term for lantern (*tang*) being a pun on "getting a son" (*tim-ting*)).

18 In a recent example in the village, an elderly man apparently suffering from stomach ailments and believing that he was nearing death insisted on being sent home from the hospital so that he could die at home. He also had his family move him to his ancestral house, which had been used for storage purposes, where he could die in peace and dignity. Wilson (1960) also described various other customs observed in the New Territories pertaining to the handling of a corpse as well as the plight of 10,000 coffins and urns deposited in the Tung Wah Hospital awaiting transfer to the mainland so that they could be buried in their ancestral village.

19 Sales of private house land between kinsmen in the village for purposes of building was a common occurrence in the prewar era, and memorials to the Block Crown Lease averaged about three conveyances per year. Curiously, however, the last such transaction was in 1948, and the absence of house land sales in the postwar era is perhaps one indication of a growing awareness of land scarcity.

20 Anthropologists in Taiwan such as Hsieh (1982) have pointed to the practice of "meal rotation" (*lun huotou*) as one way sons resolved the problem of sharing responsibility for the care of aging parents, namely by having parents eat with

each son on specified days of the week. In Wo Hang, there was a tendency toward separate household residences but eating arrangements varied with each case.

21 Watson's (1974) study of Chinese restaurant workers in London neglected the role of married-out daughters as well. In the 1970s, when the emigration of entire families increased in comparison to migration of male workers, and as immigration laws began to stiffen, one found an increasing diversity in household composition, where mothers-in-law, cousins or other *qinqi* could be living in the same house and where exchange of money and services constituted a staple aspect of life.

22 Japanese scholarly interest in Chinese customary law and family property was inspired largely by the writings of Nakata Kaoru (1926), Tai Yen-hui (1934) and Niida Noboru (1942) on Chinese "family communism" (*kazoku kyosan sei*). Their attention, however, focused mostly on determining the extent of the family head's (*jiazhang*) authority *vis-a-vis* male siblings in the management of family property.

23 Cohen (1970: 29-30) cites an example of a large *jiazu* as follows:

> In May 1965, the group of which Lin Shang-yung was *jiazhang* consisted of forty-two (42) persons. In the oldest generation only Lin himself survived. In the second generation the marriage of each of his three sons had led to the formation of as many *fang*. The first of these had twenty-two members: in addition to a father and mother it included five sons and two daughters, the wife and seven children of the first son, and the wife and four children of the second. The second *fang*, twelve persons in all, consisted of a father, a mother, four sons, four daughters, and the wife and child of the first son. In the third *fang*, with a father and mother there were five young children. The Lin *jia* had established four households, each associated with a part of the estate. There were the buildings and fields that had been obtained (and later expanded) by Shang-yung when he separated from his brother. In an adjoining village (Yen-liao) the *jia* owned a rice mill, and in another nearby settlement it operated a shop selling fertilizers and animal feed. Twenty-five miles to the south, additional land and buildings had been purchased. *In the management of all these holdings, a common budget was maintained.*

24 In my household survey of January 1983, I considered only structures used for human habitation, as opposed to grain storage houses, latrines, houses for animal domestication, etc.. The statistical results of the survey differ slightly from official census reports, due perhaps to differences in demarcating the borderline between livable and unlivable (abandoned) houses. According to

village cluster tabulations for Sheung Wo Hang, the census department reported a total of 223 people (97 male, 126 female) living in the village and a total of 135 residential units, 101 of which were simple stone buildings, with the other 34 being modern village houses. Of the 135 households, 74 were occupied at the time of census enumeration (only 1 of which was a joint family household), and 61 were vacant (HKCSD 1981: 120).

[25] Of all the ancestral estates in Wo Hang, the poorest one was the maximal *tso* of Wo Hang memorialized in the name of its apical ancestor. He had little wealth, thus left behind little in terms of any communal estate. There were no communal pilgrimages to his grave and no division of pork during *Chong Yang*, and many villagers did not know which day was designated to worship him. Village elders nonetheless made yearly offerings at his grave. The lack of wealth held by the maximal *tso* did not appear to detract from agnatic solidarity as a whole, however.

CHAPTER FIVE

Culture's Colonialism: The Future of Method

'**W**hen Sir John Bremridge came to see me about the [Chinese] banks he was in a rage'.

'I've told them', he spluttered, 'they've got to toe the line, otherwise. . . otherwise, we'll *nationalise* them'!

'Oh, no, Sir John', I said, 'you *can't* say 'nationalise'— we're not a nation'.

'Well, we're a colony, aren't we'? he said, 'So we'll *colonise* them'!

'Oh, *no*, Sir John', I explained, 'you *can't* say that, we *never* refer to Hong Kong as a "colony" these days'.

'Well then, what *are* we called then'?

'Well', I explained, 'these days we call ourselves a "territory".

'Right, then', said Sir John, 'we'll *terrorise* them'!

(Anecdote recounted by Sir Philip Haddon Cave, Hong Kong, May 30, 1985)

In a recent book on Hong Kong's colonial experience, Abbas (1997: 7) sees a change in Hong Kong culture "from reverse halluci-nation, which sees only desert, to a culture of disappearance, whose appearance is posited on the imminence of its disappearance". More than just the often repeated "borrowed time, borrowed place", Hong Kong had no precolonial past to speak of, according to Abbas. Joined by common ethnicity but divorced culturally and intellectually from the mainland, this genealogy of culture had evolved out of its colonial history. Moreover in the double demise of an earlier capitalism and colonialism, the rise of transnational globalism had made this cultural space even more paradoxical. Caught between the tensions of a floating identity that saw itself essentially as the product of a cultural desert and the need to construct a more definite identity under conditions of political uncertainty, Hong Kong then saw "an expansion of culture throughout the social realm", amounting to an "explosion". A culture of disappearance implied not absence per se but a misrecognition or pathology of presence. Ephemerality, speed and abstraction became tools for confounding the senses as a precondition for replacement and relocation. All this problematized representation as well as the self-invented subjectivity that was at the apex of this symbolic production. It was as if, through a deliberate space of disappearance, one tried to transcend the colonial condition and its various temptations of local, marginal and cosmopolitan.

Disappearance, seminal as it is for Abbas' narrative of the changing cultural spaces in film, architecture and writing, was not just a symbolic representation of late colonial modernity in Hong Kong but also a discursive embodiment of colonial practice that spanned the entirety of Hong Kong's sociopolitical history. Subjective effacement, institutional codification and political sublimation became tools with which the colonial government systematically downplayed or silenced the existence of conflict, rationalized their own actions, then negotiated the many contradictions in practice that afflicted their experience of ruling on the basis of native custom, in accordance with the myth of "the lease". At the level of policy, colonialism was itself a series of overlapping and congruent spaces that was determined at times by principles of trade mercantilism-cum-expansionism, legal administration-cum-pacification and utilitarian maximization-cum-rationalization. Concrete actions and conscious intentions then engendered larger unconscious forces that were set within a sociological or institutional framework of power, forces that were products themselves of historically grounded cultural values, civilizing ethos and ritualized behaviors or institutions. Thus, culture was not just limited to privileged domains such as art, architecture and literature or archivalizing industries such as travel or museums but also fundamentally linked to everyday regimes and practices. In this sense could one then see how events at the level of high politics eventually had reverberating effects on the routine conduct of normative life. More than just a battle of ideologies or clash of civilizations, this conflict of culture was fought on many fronts, conscious and unconscious, between individuals as well as between institutional forces or systemic lifestyles. The constitution of culture and cultural spaces was a seminal aspect of the colonial experience, since its underlying conflict was as much a contest (or interpretation) of meaning as it was a contest between individuals, institutions or polities. The unraveling of historical events showed that misinterpretation was more a norm than exception. But this did not prevent the government from rationalizing their own actions and implementing a system that it thought mirrored native reality. The codification and institutionalization of this system in routine practice, backed by the government's undying conviction to preserve tradition (as though never changing), ended up in the long run making reality on the ground increasingly convoluted and survival even more problematic. In short, the history of colonialism in Hong Kong begins not with its *discourses* of disappearance but rather with its changing *realities*. It had to be a clash of cultures in the first instance, played out between conscious agents as well as by unconscious institutions and embedded within a larger ongoing global politics.

The evolution of colonial rule can be traced from the late nineteenth century imperial archive to the advent of a modern world system that incorporated market capitalism and social structuration as parallel and mutually reinforcing processes that radically transformed the fabric of society. In the earlier era, the spectacle of empire was maintained by a politics of ethnic difference that depended upon the ongoing narrative or knowledge of the native other as a precondition for effective rule. In effect, indirect rule was in conscious terms a ritualistic mimicry of native form (such as in the way the District Officer personified the paternal benevolence of the mandarin in his explicit actions) and represented in unconscious terms the practical instrumentality of state domination (through village land registration, fiscal administration and legal codification). The inscription of colonial experience was based not only on compilations of clerical-administrative knowledge of native society (in the form of cartographic surveys, census reports and social statistics, among others) but also the writing of imperial histories that typically started with founding events, were sanitized with narratives of local pacification and structured in a way that reproduced the unilineality of and embeddedness in the global order. The expansion of the empire was to be sure a function of its ability to overcome the physical challenges of achieving global domination, invoking Cell (1970: 220–53) to emphasize the seminal role of communications. Nonetheless, the enforcement of colonial hegemony, given the mantle of indirect rule and collusion of global-*cum*-local interests, eventually became in the long run a practice that relied on a varied mixture of force, legitimation and assuagement, as Low (1991: 4) phrased it.

This intrinsic ambivalence of indirect rule, which on the one hand relied on the spectacle of brute force, buffered by a regime of knowledge, surveillance and contiguity at all levels of administration, yet on the other hand actively promoted indigenous interests as a means of galvanizing local recognition of its own political legitimacy in the broader view of things was probably uniformly coherent in theory but mutated in actual practice to accommodate changing global conditions. As a colonial society, the British administered Hong Kong in accordance with their own judicial conventions, as a colony. Yet in spite of its colonial status, there was no question as to the cultural identity of its ethnically Chinese inhabitants. Before 1950, most people just called themselves Chinese; there was no notion of being Hong Kongers. The border between Hong Kong and China was open, and there was little to differentiate Hong Kong from foreign enclaves in other treaty ports. The dualistic nature of Hong Kong's colonial society was then a function of the way in which the British demarcated the public and private spheres. There was a strict separation between official spheres, which was carried out in the medium of English, and indigenous spheres, which were rooted in Chinese tradition. Social intercourse was segregated along ethnic lines, and the government did little to cultivate among the populace any sense of national affinity to Britain. In this era characterized by the split between the two Chinas from 1949–67, Hong Kong was transformed into a battleground for contesting "national" identities. Polarization of sentiment along ideological lines peaked in the Cultural Revolution of 1966–67 and erupted in fierce riots. Separation of the private sphere along ethnic strata made the New Territories no different from Hong Kong according to the general principle of indirect rule, but the special status of the leased territory should have distinguished the institutional nature of political rule. From the very beginning, rule of custom was difficult enough to achieve; rule of law made sure discrepancies in practice became institutionalized. Later, pressures of urban-industrialization and expansion of the colony proper into the New Territories, which accelerated to its peak in the postwar era, created new tensions of administrative uniformity that exacerbated legal entanglements already taking place on the ground, which made any real difference between colony and lease increasingly untenable in any case.

In general, the evolution of a market society and the structural changes that took place in local level administration were parallel processes that could be seen in part as a deliberate policy initiative by the colonial government, but this action was itself made possible by other changes in the global political order, epitomized by the contraction of the British empire elsewhere and the nationalist civil strife that turned Hong Kong into a liminal political and cultural space *vis-a-vis* the two Chinas. Thus, the autonomy of an emergent Hong Kong society in the succeeding decades was in effect an illusion that took shape initially with its marginalization from the Chinese mainstream. Divisions of class and education produced by the market system fractionalized the social or public sphere in a way that replicated itself in the diverse responses to land witnessed in different regions of the New Territories. In short, utilitarian capitalism and social structuration actively incorporated local society into the new global order as a precondition for further fractionalizing it and introducing new social tensions that shook the heart of the existing community. In the process, the sociology of state hegemony mutated too.

Subjective effacement of the colonizer and of Hong Kong's status as colony in official discourse accompanied the creation of these new public spheres in a way that attempted to mask the hegemonic aspects of the state's moral regulation in all aspects of the social body. Economic windfall from Hong Kong's transformation into a free market port and development of its local political infrastructure made possible and desirable the colonial government's new function as a modern welfare state, and the effacement of the colonial self in the writing and admin- istration of the "territory" not only attempted to sublimate the politics of ethnic difference that underpinned an earlier colonial rule but also brought about deeper integration and tighter discipline in the state's moral regulation of society. In the culture of public spheres, new forms of identity consciousness and culture industries mimicked the rise of new social mentalities and the waning of preexisting ones. The utili- tarian, politically indifferent ethos of "Hong Kong Man" was a combination of Hong Kong's liminal status *vis-a-vis* the two Chinas and the colonial sublimation of politics. All this contributed to the rise of a peculiar kind of Hong Kong culture, one that saw the flourishing of a media oriented popular culture, which was financed by large capitalist interests, not unlike Horkheimer and Adorno's (1944) culture industry. The emergence of artistic genres like kung fu movies and absurdist comedies also had roots in this self-propelled culture industry, which was insulated from and indifferent to the politics of identity (Chan 1992). The promotion of utilitarianism as a way of life also broke down rigid distinctions between Chinese and Western culture but at the same time fractured perceptions of identity along lines of class and education. Hong Kong's hybrid culture, which seemed to effortlessly fuse East and West, was thus brought about oddly by unrestrained capitalism's wholesale demystification of an ethnic stratification inculcated by an earlier "colonialism". Cosmopolitan syncretism disrupted fixed norms of identity in much the same way absorption of natives into the system created new patterns of institutional rule.

In sum, the breakdown of this politics of ethnic difference had both positive and negative effects. The fiction of an autonomous Hong Kong identity in various forms was actually created in a vacuous social space made liminal by its uneasy existence *vis-a-vis* existing cultural-political mainstreams. Its depoliticized nature was a consequence of its being relegated to residual status as a matter of colonial policy. While this mass media, on the one hand populist and on the other nihilist, became a common public space linking all Hong Kong people, its intellectual and political poverty represented a source of culture that fractionalized different niches of the polity. In the political domain, increasing absorption of natives within the official administration as well as the replacement of magisterial authoritarianism with increased reliance on local level communication and systemic integration gave illusions of self-regulating government, even though policy at the executive level continued to be made in the Home Office. Ironically, the more it appeared (as a discursive fiction) that there was a distinct Hong Kong society (instead of regional appendage to China) made up of people who identified (through representations of a common media) as Hong Kongers sharing a common ethos as well, the more it became obvious that the basis of people's identification was in reality fractured along lines of class and education, in other words as a result of market situation. The social tensions that fractured the public in this regard were not irrelevant to the kind of changes affecting land and community in the New Territories and were in fact the source of ongoing debates over the fate of the community.

The Sino-British Joint Declaration of 1984 to return Hong Kong to Chinese sovereignty in 1997 precipitated another crisis of identity by suddenly killing that false sense of autonomy, thus calling into question what Wilson (1990) termed Hong Kong's "gathering identity". Actually, there was nothing wrong with this gathering identity itself. What became suddenly apparent was that Hong Kongers really had no identity *as a people* in the sense of being bound by shared values and assumptions. The free market institution which gave rise to illusions of an autonomous culture industry also gave rise to mentalities and lifestyles that were a product of one's differential access to culture. Youth brought up in Hong Kong's apolitical culture were also now forced to ask how they were Chinese. This post-1984 crisis of identity is the real preamble for Abbas' narrative of disappearance.

It is necessary thus to recognize the existence of colonialism's culture, and as the history of Hong Kong's cultural experience has amply demonstrated, culture can take many forms, conscious and unconscious. Cultural representations and discourses engendered within a concrete setting of colonialism are not just neutral mediating agents but rather tools by which interests of individuals, communities and institutions can both be meaningfully articulated and strategically disguised. Contrary to the way Abbas depicts culture, through architectural style and media representation, largely as floating signifiers, the representations and discourses of colonialism's culture in Hong Kong were all ultimately embedded in the flow of social formations and the construction of pragmatic interests. They tended less to be abstract inventions of high priests of culture than the unconscious *mentalités* of actors and institutions entangled in an everyday contest of political survival.

The subjective effacement of a colonialism that now began to see Hong Kong as a territory in an era of progressive modernization also made utilitarian notions of culture so engendered doubly removed from the source of state hegemony. But instead of the colonial project being incorporated into modernity, it appeared more the case that colonial hegemony transformed itself by appropriating the language and practices of modernity. Laissez-faire economy and social structuration were in effect modes of socio-political control that were initially strategic responses to nationalist instability and the breakdown of an older system of colonial authority. The cultural narratives of hedonistic progress and social order that appeared as celebrations of this era of modernity were thus not *ipso facto* value free but rather something intrinsically or potentially colonial, whether or not their ulterior motives or interests were actually decipherable on surface reading. First-order narratives of modernity based on such depictions of prosperity and stability were probably not unlike structuralist or functionalist theories by actually being consequences of what Asad (1973: 115) called a situation of routine colonialism, and the structural-functionalist logic that underscored these versions of modernization theory more importantly served a hegemonic function by politically sublimating the intrinsic violence of rule in the colonial state's project of moral regulation. King's (1975) focus on the "administrative absorption of politics" and Lau's (1981) notion on "utilitarian familism" have been typical of efforts by sociologists in Hong Kong to interpret the nature of indigenous culture and society. King's attempt to attribute Hong Kong's postwar political stability to the importance of cooptation as a grassroots political strategy was at one level the result of the growth of local administration during the postwar era and the government's effort to transfer the authority of official-mandarins to a routine clerical-managerial level. At a deeper level of analysis, the posthoc rationalization of cooptation as a traditional Chinese adaptive strategy within a colonial context of rule can be read too as an attempt to gloss over, hence sublimate, the actual existence of resistance and conflict in the system. In other words, differences between colonizer and colonized or ruler and ruled may have persisted in theory, but cooptation in practice managed to "absorb" or internalize them in ways that resulted largely in long term stability. Similarly, Lau's characterization of Hong Kong Chinese social relationships as an extension of utilitarian familism was at one level an attempted explanation of the successful adaptation of Hong Kong's people to modernization, but (erroneously) by reference to an essentialized notion of Hong Kong Chineseness that was clearly the product of a commoditized, cosmopolitan lifestyle which came about only in the 1970s. It is easy to see how these second-order abstractions of modernity reproduced various narratives of progress that characterized Hong Kong's postwar history, but these discourses theoretically implied (by their uncritical nature) a basically harmonious relationship between ruler and ruled and traditional and modern, thus served to divert attention away from the initial setting of power by downplaying the politics of social control and exploitation of the market. As posthoc rationalization of a routine situation of stability and prosperity, they unconsciously and hygienically purged the system of its underlying repressive and divisive elements. By refining the colonial *mentalité*, they domesticated its very source of institutional violence.

The postwar history of Hong Kong may be called the triumph of modernity, and it is in the culmination of its rewriting of factual history that it becomes the triumph of colonialism as well (by its effective disappearance). The irony of the New Territories in this re-gional-cum-global history is that, contrary to its ongoing archivalization as "traditional" society, it has become irrevocably incorporated into that larger history and society. The government's petrification of "tradition" and the defense by "natives" of their land rights that led instead to the wholesale and radical transformation of their existing community rep-resented two extremes that had as the same frame of reference this history of modernity. Yet, ethnographies of the present continue to be written as though the present does not exist or that it has to be filtered through reference to a tradition that has been imposed in fact from the outside (by government policy) and disseminated in discourse through the dual orthodoxies of historical (cum-imperial) writing and social (scientific) theory.

Far from being a simple phenomenon, the intertwined relation-ship between the political processes of colonial rule, their underlying cultural constructions and the embeddedness of both in specific his-torical and local contexts has scarcely been systematically or rigorously analyzed. Without even extensively interrogating the nature of what constitutes nationalism or modernity, I think the question of what constitutes colonial rule in Hong Kong is problematic enough. It is necessary first of all to view colonialism, not as an abstract force but as the interplay of concrete discourses and practices. As a specific

historical imagination, it shares common features with British colonialism elsewhere. It is important to see, at each point in time, how it
is a product of global political forces, while invoking a global vision,
as a precondition of its imposition in a specific cultural context. Yet
despite the common conceptual and institutional framework, British
colonial rule everywhere differed widely in its actual deployment.
Uniqueness of experience was the result less of its confrontation with
different cultures in different contexts but rather the specificity of
different situations of practice, within which cultural perception was
one of many relevant factors. In theory, for example, the explicit nature
of the lease should have made Hong Kong's New Territories no different
from Weihaiwei. Comparisons with imperialist or extraterritorial situations in other parts of China likewise made the Chinese cultural factor
per se a poor constant in explaining the nature of this colonial experience. On the other hand, the role played by various agents in their
specific interpretations of the situation on the ground underscored even
more the negotiable and oftentimes negotiated quality of the events that
have contributed in the long run to the manifest contradictions, deep
seated ambiguities and cumulative systematicity that eventually became
institutionalized in everyday practice. Over history, in light of the
peculiarity of the system so engendered and confronted with new global
conditions, it becomes impossible to isolate colonialism from other
processes, not to mention contrast it with other experiences elsewhere.

The historical irony of Hong Kong's handover to China on July
1, 1997 (or "return to the motherland", depending on one's point of
view) was that the future of Hong Kong, which was supposedly a cession
in perpetuity, was made to coincide with the end of the 99-year lease
of the New Territories (a larger land mass to which Kowloon Peninsula
was attached), which was originally ceded to Britain by China for
purposes of defending Hong Kong. In practice, despite the legal status
of the New Territories as a leased territory and the government's policy
of ruling it on the basis of local custom, it was administered for all
effective purposes as an extension of the colony. To this heap of contradictions, one might add the mystery of why Chinese government on
the other hand continued to play along with the reality of the lease,
all the while denying the validity of Hong Kong's status as a ceded
colony (being the result of a treaty signed under duress). It not only

made Handover Day a Chinese national holiday, whose media hype became an industry in itself, but the coincidence of Hong Kong's celebration of the Queen's Birthday on the eve of the handover canonized the five-day weekend into an event of unreal proportions many times over. The reality of Hong Kong's colonial existence, no doubt already mystified by its official "disappearance", was suddenly resurrected then by the fiction of a lease that had already been meaningless and long dead.

Much more than just the fact of economic exploitation or product of ethnic discrimination, not to mention the imagination of postcolonial theory, the concept and practice of colonialism must first be viewed literally, as a historical and social manifestation of a peculiar, ongoing global order, whose mentalities and strategies are the end product of negotiated and culturally constituted actions. Yet despite the real violence characteristic of such rule (as though backed by the appearance or threat of force), even less has been said regarding its efficacy of governance, not only as a mode of subjection but also social and moral regulation. It would appear that, at some point in the long run, these implicit contradictions of politics and culture should have sown the seeds of its own self-destruction. In addition to the dubious process of cultural translation, it is not entirely clear why colonial rule relied on the maintenance (if not invention) of tradition as a condition for its own success. To say the least, the uniqueness of the Hong Kong experience stems in part from the mutation of colonial rule and its appropriation of modernity in many senses. The evolution of the state apparatus altered the essential character of rule by replacing the spectacle of power with a system of local, routine control that was supposedly self-regulating in nature. The emergence of a market society radically transformed the intrinsic contradictions of a system built on political difference by supplanting it with class struggles based upon differential access to economic and cultural capital. The discursive effacement that followed these mutations of the colonial system both in terms of official policy and intellectual writing, epitomized by self-congradulatory imperial histories that essentially reproduced narratives of pacification or unbroken unilineal progress and sanitized ethnographies extolling the pristine structures of local society, represented the final stage of "colonialism".

Colonialism does not explain the whole of Hong Kong's history and society, but its power and presence is much more pervasive than scholars have previously recognized. In terms of the evolution of power, it is difficult at times to separate the colonial regime itself from the process of state hegemony, since both overlap historically and conceptually. Both have as its point of application society itself, and both have necessitated the construction of knowledge as an intricate feature of political control. But it is clear that the politics and culture of difference that nurtured an earlier era of colonialism increasingly gave way to a new sociology of power, especially with the waning of Britain's imperial power in the postwar era. Hong Kong's fragility as a colony in the midst of nationalist crossfire between the two Chinas may have accelerated its transition to a market economy, but this was accompanied by structural changes in the nature of political administration, which had to do also with the breakdown of an earlier civilizational ethos that buttressed the rigidity of ethnic stratification. The nationalist tensions that marked the Cold War era had a direct impact on routine administration of the colony in ways that perpetuated an autocratic, albeit socially disinterested, bureaucracy well into the era of free market capitalism. The "apolitical" ethos of Hong Kong Man cultivated in that later era effectively diverted one's attention from the increasingly political, moral regulation of state policy. In the transition from coloniality to modernity, one can see a metamorphosis in knowledge from the imperial archive and imperial histories that tend to inscribe the continuity of (imperial) self and other within an unfolding spectacle of civilizational progress to different narratives of progress and order. At every level of transition, culture serves a seminal purpose in reinforcing underlying frameworks of power. The collusion of colonialism and culture stems in part from the origins of the latter from the former, but culture's status in high theory has subsequently made it the object of further refinement (reification) that then becomes a model for the concrete study of social institutions. In the final analysis, the kinds of theoretical models of society being perpetrated here as social science are not unlike Orientalism. They are historically the product of a colonial contest and epistemologically the refinement of a cultural narrative.

In the context of the New Territories, the impact of colonial rule has been most heavily felt on the land and with reference to the village community. It is difficult to downplay the consequences of colonial land policy, whose ongoing prime directive was tied to the principle of the Lease and defense of indigenous custom (or deference to indigenous rights) but whose institutionalization of this directive created in practice an increasingly convoluted set of legal, political and conceptual entanglements. The rhetorical and cultural underpinnings of this policy set the stage upon which relations with indigenous inhabitants of the territory (or agents thereof) were defined and policy discourse continued to develop, even as interests, values and intentions on both sides were changing subtly yet radically. It not only dualized colonizer and colonized but also divided and pitted indigenous interests against each other according to class relativity in a market situation. The crisis on the land so engendered went beyond the destruction of an economic livelihood, the artificially induced scarcity of land and the inequities that marginalized and impoverished those already on the fringe of rural society. The crisis was one that ultimately struck at the heart of the village community by raising anxieties and uncertainties in its existing way of life and by stripping it of its traditional moral autonomy. Social structuration was in this sense the end point of a long, ongoing history of incorporation into a wider global order, first as an object of the imperial gaze, then as a disciplined subject in the state's project of moral regulation.

The origin of social structuration in a Hong Kong colonial context does not infer, of course, that it should be a necessary consequence of any colonial regime. Nonetheless, the specificity of its formative process and the concurrence of parallel events and cultural influences strongly suggest that it is hardly a general theory, much less natural science, of society, as has been the accepted wisdom in certain circles of mainstream anthropology. Even if it is not a product specific to colonial experience, it almost certainly mirrors the cultural logic of modernity in general. Its application to a non-modern situation, such as the traditional New Territories, where the village's relationship to land and community was based on incompatible cultural rules, posed an implicit threat to the survival and operation of the village. This perceived crisis was exacerbated by the cumulative entanglements of "indirect rule", then by the radical disruptions brought about by incorporation of the village and its livelihood into the global market. The economic peripheralization suffered in the process made life choices pertaining to the viability and moral solidarity of the community anything but free. Even for those who played the market and sold their land, hence following the path of progress, only to be exploited by capitalist interests, the sense of emancipation turned out to be shortsighted. The ultimate incompatibility between such utilitarian logic (which buttressed Freedman's theory of Chinese lineage organization) and traditional social organization was attested by the fact that the former led directly to the dissolution of traditional community rather than its expansion. From "tradition" to "modernity", there was a diverse range of responses to the general market situation, but the systemic injuries and incongruencies were mostly hidden or internal rather than externally visible.

In retrospect, the crisis of modernity that afflicted the village landscape in the New Territories could have taken place with or without colonial intervention, but it is important to note that its cultural specificity and degree of intensity were unique elements of that historical experience. In problematizing colonialism, one need not romanticize the pristine and ideal qualities of indigenous reality either. It suffices to say that, as a product of different cultural values and social practices, the latter must be seen firstly in terms of its own potentialities and contradictions. In light of expanding urbanization, industrialization and globalization, tradition without doubt has its own limitations and flaws, but it is impossible to assess this hypothetically. Thus, it would be inappropriate to compare the plight of land and village here directly with developments in other Chinese ethnographic venues.

Even without the colonial interregnum, it would be erroneous to view the lineage-village in a local historical or ethnographic vacuum. As I have argued at length elsewhere (Chun 1996b), the lineage-village complex in southeastern China was the result of a peculiar interplay between ideological and political forces that coalesced during the 17th century, then precipitated a rapid diffusion of lineage institutions throughout southeastern China. The systematic differences between lineage types found in north and south China that can be traced to this ideological diffusion make it unlikely that such organizations were homegrown developments that took place in local or regional isolation. Moreover, the forces that contributed to its particular evolution as symbolic or sociological form should be analytically distinct from those factors that enabled the lineage-village to become the locally entrenched, self-regulating system that it was during its heyday. Needless to say, lineages played an important role in the life of many villages at that time. Temple alliance systems in many regions served as the foci for collective activity and social organization. However, their significance in broader terms has to be understood in relationship to other mitigating factors, cultural, economic as well as political. By the early 20th century, even in light of the colonial government's lack of direct involvement in matters of local government, the ritual effervescence that appeared to characterize activities of lineage-villages and temple-alliance cults in an earlier heyday paled considerably, according to many villagers. Thus, the mere existence of surviving institutions in the ethnographic present offers us little to assess their underlying sociological significance or ongoing political permanence.

The hidden injuries of "tradition" in contemporary rural Hong Kong also do not seem to resolve the question of single-lineage villages there and their future survivability. Curiously however, the status of the lineage seems to be less of a cause for concern among traditional villagers themselves than for anthropologists and local historians of Chinese society. That these kin institutions still exist and do not seem to have been a direct target of colonial or state regulation raises the question of to what extent the villagers themselves perceive the relevance of these institutions to be with respect to the social solidarity and meaningful existence of the village as a moral community. The abolition of the dual landlord system by the colonial government may have indeed undermined the considerable economic and political basis that the large, established lineage-villages in particular once enjoyed, but the complexity of local functions that the lineage probably had in the village and wider regional context as a self-regulating public body was already in the process of being supplanted by the expanding disciplinary reach of the colonial state. The lineage's historical specificity underscored its social acceptability and functional importance in an earlier era when various related factors contributed to its complex organizational development. But the presence of such a tradition at that time hardly guarantees their continued survival in situations characterized by changes in their local supporting institutions and socio-political infrastructures.

The historical ephemerality of the lineage-village complex in southeastern China contrasts with the sociological generality that descent theory has accorded to it. Moreover, its historicity suggests that the theoretical focus of anthropology should shift instead to a consideration of other factors that contribute generally to the emergence and maintenance of local society. I for one do not believe that there is a "structure" of Chinese society from time immemorial that contributes to the stability of local social organization, articulated most eloquently in the work of Kuhn (1970), as though immune from cultural, economic and political factors that tie it to society-at-large. Faure (1986) has also developed Freedman's bottom-up model of Chinese society to a higher pitch by showing how the making of "real" lineage society is an extension of "rights of settlement" grounded in descent terms. While the mythical omnipotence of the "Five Great Clans" of the New Territories, a term coined by Baker (1966), deserves deflating, the territorial exclusivity that coalesced with the appearance of lineage halls in the last 300 years and effectively galvanized the rise of autonomous villages was only one of many factors, the least of which was a fictive descent right of settlement, that among other things cannot explain the non-applicability of this territorial imperative in other places of China characterized by heterogenous village settlement patterns and the same ideology of descent. The "conservatism" of Chinese peasant values toward the land, which was alluded to by Gallin (1967), then led to various forms of local myopia among sinologists, does appear to have a cultural basis, but it has been badly understood. As Schurmann (1956) noted in a significant paper on Chinese notions of property, beliefs and practices intrinsic to ancestor worship and folk religion tied notions of inalienability and productivity of land to the continuity of agriculture as a valued mode of social livelihood that explained why China was unable to develop a system of *Freies Eigentum*, which played a key role in the rise of capitalism in the West in ways that also point to the existence of cultural conceptions of the village as moral community. Lineage organization and territorial exclusivity were not necessary aspects of that moral universe, thus had to be the consequence of factors traceable ultimately to the complex interplay between ideological discourse, local politics and their embeddedness in the wider practice and constitution of the polity. However, this is a topic that deserves detailed and systematic attention in a separate study.

Deconstructing colonialism or decolonizing social structure in its various guises cannot directly reconstruct what traditional customary reality is or should be, but it offers several clear indications of what it is not. In this regard, there is still room for reinterpreting the nature of Chinese kinship both inside and outside the context of lineage organization. First of all, it should be clear that the lineage and village are two distinct cultural constellations that have by force of historical dynamics come together and mutually reinforced each other. All else being equal, the existence of a village does not necessitate the creation of a lineage and vice versa. In other words, the formation of a territorial community can adopt as its recruitment criteria any number of factors, agnation being only one, which should follow from a native definition of what a village, instead of agnation per se, is. On the other hand, the existence of ancestral rites and beliefs is not dependent on the institution of a lineage for its symbolic effectiveness. To be sure, part of the mystique of the lineage derives from its power to magnify ancestor worship, which in a Chinese context has been typically carried out at the level of individual *jiazu*, into a collective phenomenon, presumably of greater social significance. I argue that this collective power is a function less of the lineage's internal dynamics than of its appropriation by the village, whose renaissance in late imperial China must be viewed in a larger intellectual, social and political context. Moreover, ancestral worship is distinct from the system of rites and ideas that constitute a *jia*. Unlike ancestor worship, which is based on *zong*, the obligation to maintain generational continuity through ritual acts of veneration, the *jia* is an entity that exists only from the time of its creation (through marriage) until the death of the family head. The ties of relative closeness (*qin*) that are cultivated through ongoing exchange make *jia* a quintessentially egocentric notion whose domestic cycle can be viewed as both a process of kin exclusivity (*fang*) and inclusivity (*tang*). This relational flexibility makes *jia* less a sociological group per se than an assumption of shared substance whose sociological nature is a function of its appropriation by other morphemes in compound terms such as *jiazu* ("family") and *jiating* ("household").

The conception and operation of the village as a moral community (*jiaxiang*, literally "home-country") rather than territorial community per se (*cun*) resides at the core of the lineage-village complex. Contrary to the hard and fast rules that scholars have relied upon to define the boundedness of the village, either through reference to common land or agnatic rights of settlement, I argue that the nature of the village community has always been subjectively defined, prone to changing conditions and subject to negotiation within limits. In contrast to north China, for example, where it is sometimes difficult to definitively mark the end of one village and the beginning of another, there are perhaps in a south Chinese context valid socio-political reasons for the boundedness of the village and the degree of one's subjective attachment to them, that often transcend the facts of actual residence. With regard to the galvanization of the local village in south China, the concurrent development of sedentary lineages based on a "first migrant", the construction of village based ancestral halls and the widespread writing of genealogies could not have been isolated incidents. They had to be to some extent cultural (ritual and discursive) phenomena that had intellectual or other roots in the larger social flow of things which could at the same time be accommodated by the politics of place.

In this sense, the higher order lineage was a symbolic place marker for the aggrandizement of the village rather than the other way around. Instead of being the vehicle for a more efficient practice of ancestor worship, the lineage functioned simply to make worship a collective institution that had clear roots and identity in the village. In a New Territories context, if not elsewhere as well, the temple cults that allied a network of neighboring villages for defense purposes and mutual aid paralleled in many ways the function of collective ancestor worship in lineage-villages. The boundaries that distinguished insiders from outsiders were loose in times of relative tranquillity and hardened in an environment characterized by instability and regional hostility in ways that had little to do with kin ties per se.

The cult of the ancestral hall, which may be an accurate characterization of the lineage, was only a privileged subset of an entire structure of genealogical relations. If one were to look at all the ancestral estates created within a lineage-village, such as in Wo Hang, one would find many genealogically identical estates created under different names and different conditions. Moreover, wealthy estates did not necessarily establish ancestral halls. In fact, it was rare to find more than one hall for any surname group in any one village. Ancestral estates were thus markers of individual wealth created for the benefit of succeeding generations, but they were not related to the conditions that invoked the creation of ancestral halls (asymmetric segmentation, as Freedman defined it). Contrary also to the process of higher order aggregation that Freedman regarded to be the building blocks for the formation of large-scale lineage organization, ancestral estates rarely combined to form higher level units. This was inconsistent with the purpose for which they tended to be formed, namely for the continued livelihood of succeeding generations. Thus, with increasing numbers of descendants sharing per stirpes rights to this common estate, its fractioned wealth could be seen to gradually dissipate with the passage of time, instead of accumulating. This did not mean, however, that per capita wealth of individuals would decline, since people in succeeding generations would naturally have access to more sources of wealth. To the contrary, it would be more difficult to find instances of lineage-villages in the New Territories, if not elsewhere, being founded as a result of gradual accumulation of communal wealth, which is the logical outcome of Freedman's model, than to find instances where the creation of lineage hall was part of the early settlement history of the village.

Distinct from the processes of ritual transmission that characterize the *zong* of ancestor worship, the *jia* is characterized by a different set of dynamics. In contrast to the tendency of many scholars to see household, family and compound as different levels of family organization, I argue that the *jia* is a dual process of segmentation (*fang*) and incorporation (*tang*). Its existence as living group (*jiazu*) underscores the social importance of ongoing gift exchange that marks its rites of passage from marriage through childbirth to the death of its family head. Kindred solidarity overlaps with but does not conflict with agnatic solidarity, and, as the caretaker relationships in Wo Hang tend to reflect, it often supercedes the latter.

Despite the shared notion of *jia* in terms for "family" (*jiazu*) and "household" (*jiating*), not to mention "village" (*jiaxiang*), the others are functionally distinct entities whose assumption of shared substance linking members within the group is conditioned as well by its root morpheme. In the case of *jiating* or household, the local customary definition of a "house" has been shown to strongly determine indigenous conceptions of household membership. Moreover, property associated with the household is analytically distinct from that of the family (*jiazu*) as well as various ancestral estates that an individual may have per stirpes rights to. The difference between family and household as sociological entities show that they are maintained by different functional criteria. The household is very much a unit of social and economic livelihood. The conditions that influence whether it should maintain itself as a multi-generational community, headed by its family patriarch, or split up into independent households, each headed by separate sons, usually have little to do with the principles of *jia* but rather matters affecting the viability of one's livelihood. Unlike the strict definition of a *jiazu*, which is a familial group that includes all descendants of a living patriarch, regardless of actual residence, the *jiating* has no such rigid "genealogical" rules. It would not be unusual for two brothers and their respective families to occupy a single household, even after they have already formed separate *jiazu* (upon the death of their father). This was a common occurrence in Wo Hang, which increased with the crisis of housing policy in the early postwar era. The loose genealogical definition of a household explains also the common occurrence and cultural acceptability of mother-in-laws (WiMo) living in urban households. While there is a limit by cultural definition to which a household can include non-family members, factors affecting its livelihood and setting appear to override genealogical ones per se. Similarly, the notion of village as *jiaxiang* (home country) has deep resonances of common moral ethos indicative of *jia* that differs from the more value-neutral notion of *cun* as residential village. The notion of *jiaxiang* is the same, whether one is dealing with a single lineage-village or mixed community. It invokes above all one's rootedness to a house and a source of (agricultural) livelihood on the land. Like the familial notion in *jiating*, the *jiaxiang* is not, strictly speaking, a kin group or lineage. The factors that have contributed to the appropriation of lineage to the constitution of villages in late imperial China, as I have already argued, was a result of the complex interplay between various intellectual and socio-political factors peculiar to the times. Even the genealogical rights that members of a household presumably have as members of the village as well are probably less important than knowing what affects the constitution of a village at any time or under particular socio-political conditions.

In light of such a "native" or symbolic understanding of the various notions of Chinese kinship and its customary institutions, it should be clear in retrospect why the advent of colonial rule brought about disastrous consequences upon the village and household in particular and why the inhabitants viewed government policy as a threat to the viability of that community, despite repeated assurances by the state of preserving "tradition" and not interfering with "custom". These were not threats to the lineage per se, but it is doubtful whether in the minds of inhabitants themselves the lineage acquired the status of all-powerful symbol that characterized its veneration by anthropologists and local historians obsessed with the sacredness of descent theory and its various permutations. If anything, the subjective nature of the village as a moral community is a complicated issue that can only understood "locally" (from the inside out), thus deserves further scrutiny in its own right. Moreover by understanding the household and village locally and egocentrically, one gets a very different sense of community that transcends both its agnatic and territorial boundaries, not to mention of the outside "world" itself. Anthropological research of this kind should be theoretically seminal rather than marginal. Contrary to expectation, it has also hardly begun.

In sum, if it is necessary to deconstruct "colonialism" in order to reconstruct "tradition", it is only because colonialism-cum-modernity has already obscured the contemporary nature of society in ways that reflect generally on the embeddedness of culture in power. In the long term, "colonialism" will prove to be an ephemeral episode in Hong Kong's history, but this should not detract us from the broader need to view local society in the practice of culture, discourse and global politics.

Bibliography

Abbas, Ackbar
1997   *Hong Kong: Culture and the Politics of Disappearance.*
        Minneapolis: University of Minnesota Press.

Ahern, Emily
1973   *The Cult of the Dead in a Chinese Village.* Stanford: Stanford
        University Press.

Aijmer, L. Goran
1972   A Note on Agricultural Change in Hong Kong. *Journal of
        the Hong Kong Branch of the Royal Asiatic Society* 12:
        201–06.
1973   Migrants into Hong Kong's New Territories: On the Back-
        ground of Outsider Vegetable Farmers. *Ethnos* 38(1–4): 57–70
        (Stockholm).
1975   An Enquiry into Chinese Settlement Patterns: The Rural
        Squatters of Hong Kong. *Man* 10(4): 559–70.
1980   *Economic Man in Shatin: Vegetable Gardeners in a Hong Kong
        Valley.* London: Curzon Press.
1986   *Atomistic Society in Shatin: Immigrants in a Hong Kong Valley.*
        Gothenburg: Acta Universitatus Gothoburgensis.

Airlie, Shiona
1989   *Thistle and Bamboo: The Life and Times of Sir James Stewart
        Lockhart.* Hong Kong: Oxford University Press.

Asad, Talal
1973   Two European Images of Non-European Rule. In *Anthro-
        pology and the Colonial Encounter.* London: Ithaca Press.

Atwell, Pamela

1985   *British Mandarins and Chinese Reformers: British Administration of Weihaiwei (1898–1930) and the Territory's Return to Chinese Rule.* Hong Kong: Oxford University Press.

Baker, Hugh D.R.

1966   The Five Great Clans of the New Territories. *Journal of the Hong Kong Branch of the Royal Asiatic Society* 6: 25–47.

1968   *A Chinese Lineage Village: Sheung Shui.* Stanford: Stanford University Press.

Balfour, S.F.

1970   Hong Kong before the British: Being a Local History of the Region of Hong Kong and the New Territories before the British Occupation. (originally T'ien Hsia Monthly 11–12, Shanghai, 1940–41.) Reprinted in *Journal of the Hong Kong Branch of the Royal Asiatic Society* 10: 150–79.

Barnett, K.M.A.

1957   The Peoples of the New Territories. In *Hong Kong Business Symposium,* J.H. Braga ed.. Hong Kong: South China Morning Post.

Bennett, Tony

1988   The Exhibitionary Complex. *New Formations* 4: 73–102.

Blackie, William John

1954   *Agriculture in Hong Kong with Policy Recommendations.* Hong Kong: Government Printer.

Brim, John A.

1970   *Local Systems and Modernizing Change in the New Territories of Hong Kong.* Ph.D. thesis, Stanford University.

Burrow, J.W.

1966   *Evolution and Society: A Study in Victorian Social Theory.* Cambridge: Cambridge University Press.

Cell, John W.
1970   *British Colonial Administration in the Mid-Nineteenth Century: The Policy-Making Process.* New Haven: Yale University Press.

Chan, Kit-ching Lau
1990   *China, Britain and Hong Kong, 1895–1945.* Hong Kong: Chinese University of Hong Kong Press.

Chan, Ming K.
1983   Stability and Prosperity in Hong Kong: The Twilight of Laissez-Faire Colonialism? A Review Article. *Journal of Asian Studies* 42(3): 589–97.

Chan Hoi-man
1992   Comedy and Mediation: Charting the Cultural Mentality of Hong Kong. Paper presented at Conference on Cultural Criticism 1992. Chinese University of Hong Kong, Hong Kong, 12/29/91–1/9/92.

Chatterjee, Partha
1993   *The Nation and Its Fragments: Colonial and Postcolonial Histories.* Princeton: Princeton University Press.

Chen, Edward K.Y.
1984   The Economic Setting. In *The Business Environment in Hong Kong,* 2nd ed., D. Lethridge ed.. Hong Kong: Oxford University Press.

Cheng, Kwong Chi
1978   *The Heung Yee Kuk and the New Territories of Hong Kong, a Case Study in Urban Political Geography.* B.A. thesis, University of Hong Kong.

Chiu, Stephen W.K. and Hung Ho-fung
1997   The Colonial State and Rural Protests in Hong Kong. Hong Kong Institute of Asia-Pacific Studies Occasional Paper no.59, Chinese University of Hong Kong (Hong Kong).

Chow, Steven Chi Man

1977   *Economic Growth and Income Distribution in Hong Kong*, 2 vols.. Ph.D. thesis, Boston University.

Chuang Ying-chang

1972   *Taiwan nongcun jiazu dui xiandaihua de shiying – yige tianye diaocha shili de fenxi* (The Adaptation of Taiwan Rural Families to Modernization – An Analysis of Field Survey Cases). *Zhongyang Yanjiuyuan Minzuxue Yanjiusuo Jikan* 34: 85–98 (Nankang).

1973   *Taiwan hanren zongzu fazhan de ruogan wenti – shimiao zongci yu Zhushan de kenzhi xing tai* (Some Problems with Respect to Lineage Formation of the Han Chinese in Taiwan – The Developmental Pattern of Temples, Ancestral Shrines and Chushan). *Zhongyang Yanjiuyuan Minzuxue Yanjiusuo Jikan* 36: 113–40 (Nankang).

Chun, Allen J.

1988   Is There a Structure of Chinese Rural Society? *Journal of the Hong Kong Branch of the Royal Asiatic Society* no.28: 240–61.

1996a   Chinese Kinship 'From the Native's Point of View' (in Chinese). *Bulletin of the Institute of Ethnology, Academia Sinica, Taiwan* 81: 1–18 (Nankang).

1996b   The Lineage-Village Complex in Southeastern China: A Long Footnote in the Anthropology of Kinship. *Current Anthropology* 37(3): 429–50.

Clammer, John

1973   Colonialism and the Perception of Tradition in Fiji. In *Anthropology and the Colonial Encounter*, T. Asad ed.. London: Ithaca Press.

CO 129: Colonial Office Correspondence

Correspondence Respecting the Extension of the Boundaries of the Colony

1900   Hong Kong, Correspondence (June 20, 1898 to August 20, 1900) Respecting the Extension of the Boundaries of the Colony. *Eastern* no. 66. Colonial Office, London.

Cohen, Myron L.
1970   Developmental Process in the Chinese Domestic Group. In *Family and Kinship in Chinese Society*, M. Freedman ed.. Stanford: Stanford University Press.
1976   *House Divided, House United: The Chinese Family in Taiwan.* New York: Columbia University Press.

Cohn, Bernard S.
1984   The Census, Social Structure and Objectification in South Asia. *Folk* 26: 25–49.
1988   The Anthropology of a Colonial State and Its Forms of Knowledge. Paper presented at Wenner Gren Conference "Tensions of Empire", Mijas, Spain, May 5–12.

Comaroff, Jean and John
1991   *Of Revelation and Revolution: Christianity, Colonialism and Consciousness in South Africa.* Chicago: University of Chicago Press.

Cooper, Eugene
1982   Karl Marx's Other Island: The Evolution of Peripheral Capitalism in Hong Kong. *Bulletin of Concerned Asian Scholars* 14(1): 25–31.

Corrigan, Philip
1990   *Social Forms/Human Capacities: Essays in Authority and Difference.* London: Routledge.

Corrigan, Philip and Derek Sayer
1985   *The Great Arch: English State Formation as Cultural Revolution.* Oxford: Blackwell.

CSO: Colonial Secretary Office Files

Davis, S.G.
1964 Rural-Urban Migration in Hong Kong and the New Territories. In *Symposium on Land Use and Mineral Deposits, Hong Kong*, S.G. Davis ed.. Hong Kong: Hong Kong University Press.

Dirks, Nicholas B.
1986 From Little King to Landlord: Colonial Discourse and Colonial Rule. *Contemporary Studies in Society and History* 28: 307–33.
1992a Castes of Mind. *Representations* 37: 56–78.
1992b Introduction to *Colonialism and Culture*, N.B. Dirks ed.. Ann Arbor: University of Michigan Press.

Emrys-Evans, D.M.
1971 Common Law in a Chinese Setting – The Kernel or the Nut? *Hong Kong Law Journal* 1(1): 9–32.

Endacott, G.B.
1958 *A History of Hong Kong*. London: Oxford University Press.

England, Joe and John Rear
1975 *Chinese Labor under British Rule: A Critical Study of Labor Relations and Law in Hong Kong*. Hong Kong: Oxford University Press.

Fabian, Johannes
1986 *Language and Colonial Power: The Appropriation of Swahili in the Former Belgian Congo, 1880–1938*. Cambridge: Cambridge University Press.

Faure, David
1986 *The Structure of Chinese Rural Society: Lineage and Village in the Eastern New Territories*. Hong Kong: Oxford University Press.

1988   Custom in the Legal Process: The Inheritance of Land and
              Houses in South China. *Proceedings of the Tenth Interna-
              tional Symposium on Asian Studies,* Vol.1, pp.477–97. Hong
              Kong: Asian Research Service.
1989   The Lineage as a Cultural Invention: The Case of the Pearl
              River Delta. *Modern China* 15(1): 4–36.

FEER: Far Eastern Economic Review
1980a   Land Policy Vital to Diversification. (March 21)
1980b   Those Police 'Squatters' on Elegant Shouson Hill.
              (March 21)
1982a   The Debtor's Dilemma. (February 19)
1982b   Sons of the Qing Dynasty. (February 19)
1982c   Down to Earth. (June 25)

Fei Xiaotong (Fei Hsiao-t'ung)
1939   *Peasant Life in China: A Field Study of Country Life in the
              Yangtze Valley.* London: Routledge and Kegan Paul.
1945   *Earthbound China: A Study of Rural Economy in Yunnan.*
              Chicago: University of Chicago Press.
1947   *Shengyu Zhidu* (The System of Fertility). Shanghai: *Shangwu.*

FO: Foreign Office Correspondence

Fortes, Meyer
1953   The Structure of Unilineal Descent Groups. *American
              Anthropologist* 55: 17–41.

France, Peter
1969   *The Charter of the Land: Custom and Colonization in Fiji.*
              Melbourne: Oxford University Press.

Freedman, Maurice
1958   *Lineage Organization in Southeastern China.* London:
              Athlone Press.
1966   *Chinese Lineage and Society.* London: Athlone Press.

Fu Yiling

1961   *Ming-Qing Nongcun Shehui Jingji* (Rural Society and Economy during the Ming and Qing Dynasties). Beijing: *Sanlian.*

Gallin, Bernard

1967   Chinese Peasant Values toward the Land. In *Peasant Society: A Reader*, J. Potter et al eds.. Boston: Little, Brown and Co..

Gates, Louis Henry, Jr.

1991   Critical Fanonism. *Critical Inquiry* 17: 457–70.

Groves, R.G.

1969   Militia, Market and Lineage: Chinese Resistance to the Occupation of Hong Kong's New Territories in 1899. *Journal of the Hong Kong Branch of the Royal Asiatic Society* 9: 31–64.

Guo Songyi

1980   *Qingchu fengjian guojia kenhuang zhengce fenxi* (An Analysis of the State Policy of Land Reclamation during the Early Qing Dynasty). *Qing Shi Lun Cong* 2: 111–38.

Hadland, B.J.

1978   Land Policies in Hong Kong. In *Housing in Hong Kong: A Multi-Disciplinary Study*, L.S.K. Wong ed.. Hong Kong: Heinemann.

Halliday, Jon

1974   Hong Kong: Britain's Chinese Colony. *New Left Review* 87–88: 92–112.

Hambro, Edvard

1955   *The Problem of Chinese Refugees in Hong Kong.* Report to the United Nations High Commissioner for Refugees. Leiden: A.W. Sijthoff.

Han Henggyu
1979   *Shilun Qingdai qianqi diannong yongdianquan de youlai ji
            qi xingzhi* (An Examination of the Nature and Origins of
            Perpetual Tenancy Lease Rights during the Early Qing
            Dynasty). *Qing Shi Lun Cong* 1: 37–53.

Han, Daniel W.T.
1978   Social Background of Housing in Hong Kong. In *Housing
            in Hong Kong: A Multi-Disciplinary Study*, L.S.K. Wong ed..
            Hong Kong: Heinemann.

Hayes, James W.
1963   Movement of Villages on Lantau Island for Fengshui Rea-
            sons. *Journal of the Hong Kong Branch of the Royal Asiatic
            Society* 3: 143–44.
1967   Geomancy and the Village. In *Some Traditional Chinese Ideas
            and Conceptions in Hong Kong Social Life Today*, M. Topley
            ed.. Hong Kong: Hong Kong Branch of the Royal Asiatic
            Society.
1969   Removal of Villages for Fengshui Reasons: Another Example
            from Lantau Island, Hong Kong. *Journal of the Hong Kong
            Branch of the Royal Asiatic Society* 9: 156–58.
1974   The Hong Kong Region: Its Place in Traditional Chinese
            Historiography and Principal Events since the Establish-
            ment of Hsin-an County in 1573. *Journal of the Hong Kong
            Branch of the Royal Asiatic Society* 14: 108–35.
1976   Rural Society and Economy in late Ch'ing: A Case Study
            of the New Territories of Hong Kong (Guangdong). *Ch'ing-
            shih Wen-t'i* 3(5): 33–71.
1977   *The Hong Kong Region, 1850–1911: Institutions and Lead-
            ership in Town and Countryside*. Hamden: Shoe String Press.
1988   Customary Law in the New Territories of Hong Kong.
            *Proceedings of the Tenth International Symposium on Asian
            Studies*, Vol.1, pp.455–76. Hong Kong: Asian Research
            Service.

1991   Chinese Customary Law in the New Territories of Hong
            Kong: The Background to the Operation of the New Ter-
            ritories Ordinance, 1899–1987. *Asian Profile* 19(2): 97–136.

Heung Yee Kuk
1977   *The New Territories Community of Hong Kong under Colonial
            Administration* (pamphlet).

HKCSD: Hong Kong Census and Statistics Department
1961   *Hong Kong 1961 Census*. vols. I-III.
1969   *Hong Kong Statistics, 1947–67.*
1971   *Hong Kong 1971 Census.*
1981   *Hong Kong 1981 Census: Street Block/Village Cluster Tabu-
            lations, Tai Po and Fanling.*

HKRP: Hong Kong Research Project
1974   *Hong Kong: A Case to Answer.* Hong Kong: Spokesman
            Books.

Hoang, Pierre
1888   A Practical Treatise on Legal Ownership. Translated and
            excerpted in Tenure of Land in China and the Condition
            of the Rural Population, by George Jamieson. *Journal of the
            North China Branch of the Royal Asiatic Society* 23: 118–74.

Horkheimer, Max and Theodor W. Adorno
1944   The Culture Industry. In *The Dialectic of Enlightenment*, M.
            Horkheimer and T.W. Adorno eds.. New York: Continuum.

Hsieh Jih-chang
1982   *Lunhuotou zhidu chutan* (A Preliminary Examination of the
            Rotating Meal System). Paper presented for Symposium on
            "Chinese Family and Its Ritual Behavior", Institute of Eth-
            nology, Academia Sinica, Nankang, June 17–19.

Hsieh Guozhen

1932   *Mingching zhi ji Huizhou nubian kao* (An Analysis of Slave Rebellions in Huizhou at the Turn of the Qing Dynasty). *Xuefeng* 7(5): 1–27. (Beijing)

Hsieh Kuo-ching

1931–32 Removal of Coastal Population in Early Tsing (Qing) Period. *The Chinese Social and Political Science Review* 15: 559–96.

Hsu Chia-ming

1973   *Zhanghua pingyuan fulaoke de diyu zuzhi* (Territorial Organization of the Hoklo on the Changhua Plains). *Zhongyang Yanjiuyuan Minzuxue Yanjiusuo Jikan* 36: 165–90.

Hu, Hsien-chin

1948   *The Common Descent Group in China and Its Functions.* New York: The Viking Fund, Inc..

Huang, Shu-min

1980   The Development of Regionalism in Ta-chia, Taiwan: A Non-Kinship View of Chinese Rural Social Organization. *Ethnohistory* 27: 243–65.

1982   Hong Kong's Colonial Administration and the Land Tenure System. In *Rural Hong Kong: The Anthropological Perspectives*, Shu-min Huang ed.. Papers in Anthropology no. 6. Ames: Iowa State University Department of Sociology and Anthropology.

JL: *Jili Lu*

1923   (Record of Marriage Rites). (handwritten manuscript)

Jolly, Margaret

1992   Custom and the Way of the Land: Past and Present in Vanuatu and Fiji. *Oceania* 62: 330–54.

Jones, G.W.E.
1978   Rural Housing in Hong Kong. In *Housing in Hong Kong: A Multi-Disciplinary Study*, L.S.K. Wong ed.. Hong Kong: Heinemann.

Kamm, John
1977   Two Essays on the Ch'ing Economy of Hsin-an, Kwangtung. *Journal of the Hong Kong Branch of the Royal Asiatic Society* 17: 55–83.

King, Ambrose
1975   Administrative Absorption of Politics in Hong Kong: Emphasis on the Grass Roots Level. *Asian Survey* 15(5): 422–39.

Krause, Lawrence B.
1988   Hong Kong and Singapore: Twins or Kissing Cousins? *Economic Development and Cultural Change* 36(3): S45–S66.

Kuan Hsin-chi and Lau Siu-kai
1979   Development and the Resuscitation of Rural Leadership in Hong Kong: The Case of Neo-Indirect Rule. Chinese University of Hong Kong Social Research Centre Occasional Paper No.81 (Hong Kong).

Kuhn, Philip A.
1970   *Rebellion and its Enemies in Late Imperial China: Militarization and Social Structure, 1796–1864.* Cambridge: Harvard University Press.

Kulp, Daniel Harrison II
1925   *Country Life in South China.* New York: Columbia University Press.

Lam, Eric Cheong-yee

1986   An Assessment of the Role of the Heung Yee Kuk in the Formulation of Rural Policies in the New Territories, M.Soc.Sci. thesis in Public Administration, University of Hong Kong.

Lau, Siu-kai

1981   Utilitarianistic Familism. In *Social Life and Development in Hong Kong*, A.Y.C. King and R.P.L. Lee eds.. Hong Kong: Chinese University Press.

Lee, Ming-kwan

1984   The Evolution of the Heung Yee Kuk as a Political Institution. In *From Village to City: Studies in the Traditional Roots of Hong Kong Society*, A. Birch et al eds.. University of Hong Kong, Centre of Asian Studies Monograph.

Lee, Rance P.L.

1981   The Fading of Earthbound Compulsion in a Chinese Village: Population Mobility and Its Economic Implications. In *Social Life and Development in Hong Kong*, A.Y.C. King and R.P.L. Lee eds.. Hong Kong: Chinese University Press.

Leeming, Frank

1975   The Earlier Industrialization of Hong Kong. *Modern Asian Studies* 9(3): 337–42.

Lei Chijing

1936   *Zhongguo jiating wenti yanjiu* (A Study of Problems in the Chinese Household). *Shehui yanjiu* 125: 575–601 (Beijing).

Liu Han

1976   *Xinjie shih* (A History of the New Territories Part 1). *Xinjie Nianjian* (New Territories Annual Mirror) 1976.

1977   *Xinjie shih* (A History of the New Territories, Part 2). *Xinjie Nianjian* (New Territories Annual Mirror) 1977.

1988   *Tangzu wenti* (Problems of *Tso* and *Tang*). *Zhongli Bao*, no.196–98.

Liu Qunkuan ed.
1995   *Zhujie Xinjie* (Leasing of the New Territories). Hong Kong: Sanlian.

Lo, C.P.
1968   Changing Population Distribution in the Hong Kong New Territories. *Annals of the Association of American Geographers* 58(2): 273–84.

Lo Hsiang-lin
1933   *Kejia yanjiu taolun* (Introduction to Hakka Research). Taipei: Guting Shuwu (1975) reprint.
1963   *Hong Kong and Its External Communications before 1842.* Hong Kong: Institute of Chinese Culture.

Low, D.A.
1991   *Eclipse of Empire.* Cambridge: Cambridge University Press.

Lu Ge
1975   *Guangjiaojing xia de xianggang nungmin* (A Broad Overview of Hong Kong's Rural People). *Guangjiaojing* 28: 11–18; 29: 30–49 (Hong Kong).

Mason, R.R. et al
1968   A Review of Pig Farming in Hong Kong and Factors Limiting Expansion. *Agricultural Science* 1: 29–48.

Miners, Norman J.
1977   *The Government and Politics of Hong Kong,* 2nd edition. Hong Kong: Oxford University Press.

Mitchell, Timothy
1988   *Colonizing Egypt.* Cambridge: Cambridge University Press.

Morris, Jan
1988   *Hong Kong: Epilogue to an Empire.* London: Penguin.

Nakata Kaoru
1926   *To So jidai no kazoku kyosansei* (Family Communism during Tang and Sung Times). *Kotsuka Gakukai Zasshi* 40: 7,8 (Tokyo).

Nelson, Howard G.H.
1969   British Land Administration in the New Territories of Hong Kong and its Effects on Chinese Social Organization. Unpublished paper given at the London-Cornell Project for East and Southeast Asian Studies Conference, Adele en Haut, France, August 24–30, 1969.

Ng, Peter Y.L.
1983   *New Peace County: A Chinese Gazetteer of the Hong Kong Region.* Hong Kong: Hong Kong University Press.

Niida Noboru
1942   *Shina Mibunhoshi* (History of Personal Law in China). Tokyo: Tokyo University Press.
1946   *Shina no ichi-den ryo-shu kanko to sono seiritsu* (The One-Field, Two-Lord Practice in China and its Establishment). *Hogaku Kyokai Zasshi* 64(3): 129–54, 64(4): 241–61.
1952   *Chugoku no Noson Kazoku* (The Chinese Rural Family). Tokyo: Tokyo University Press.

NTA: New Territories Administration
1972a   Small Houses in the New Territories. Unpublished report.
1972b   Small House Policy Instructions. Unpublished documents.

Owen, Nicholas
1971   Economic Policy. In *Hong Kong: The Industrial Colony: A Political, Social and Economic Survey*, K. Hopkins ed.. Hong Kong: Oxford University Press.

Palmer, Michael J.E.
1987   The Surface-Subsoil Form of Divided Ownership in Late
          Imperial China: Some Examples from the New Territories
          of Hong Kong. *Modern Asian Studies* 21(1): 1–119.

Pasternak, Burton
1972   *Kinship and Community in Two Chinese Villages.* Stanford:
          Stanford University Press.
1973   Chinese Tale-Telling Tombs. *Ethnology* 7(3): 259–73.

PMOH: Principal Medical Officer of Health
1972   Village Type House Survey (New Territories). Unpublished
          report.

Polanyi, Karl
1944   *The Great Transformation.* Boston: Beacon Press.

Potter, Jack
1968   *Capitalism and the Chinese Peasant: Social and Economic
          Change in a Hong Kong Village.* Berkeley: University of
          California Press.
1970   Land and Lineage in Traditional China. In *Family and Kinship
          in Chinese Society*, M. Freedman ed.. Stanford: Stanford
          University Press.

Pratt, Mary Louise
1991   *Through Imperial Eyes: Travel Writing and Transculturalism.*
          New York: Routledge.

Rabushka, Alvin
1976   *Value for Money: The Hong Kong Budgetary Process.* Stanford:
          Hoover Institute Press.
1979   *Hong Kong: A Study in Economic Freedom.* Chicago: Univer-
          sity of Chicago Press.

Radcliffe-Brown, A.R.
1935   Patrilineal and Matrilineal Succession. *Iowa Review of Law* 20: 2. Reprinted in Structure and Function in Primitive Society (1952).
1950   Introduction to *African Systems of Kinship and Marriage*, A.R. Radcliffe-Brown and D. Forde eds.. London: Oxford University Press.

Rawski, Evelyn S.
1972   *Agricultural Change and the Peasant Economy of South China.* Cambridge: Harvard University Press.

Rear, John
1971   One Brand of Politics. In *Hong Kong: The Industrial Colony*, K. Hopkins ed.. Hong Kong: Oxford University Press.

Richards, Thomas
1994   *The Imperial Archive: Knowledge and the Fantasy of Empire.* London: Verso.

Riedel, James Charles
1972   *The Industrialization of Hong Kong.* Ph.D. thesis, University of California, Davis.

RLC: Report on the Land Court
1901   compiled by H.H.J. Gompertz. *Hong Kong Sessional Papers 1900.*
1902   compiled by H.H.J. Gompertz. *Hong Kong Sessional Papers 1901.*
1905   compiled by Cecil Clementi. *Hong Kong Sessional Papers 1900–05.*

RNT: Report on the New Territories
1899   compiled by J.H.S. Lockhart. *Hong Kong Sessional Papers 1898.*

1900   compiled by J.H.S. Lockhart. *Hong Kong Sessional Papers* 1899.

1901   compiled by J.H.S. Lockhart. *Hong Kong Sessional Papers* 1900.

1902   compiled by J.H.S. Lockhart. *Hong Kong Sessional Papers* 1901.

1903   *Hong Kong Sessional Papers* 1903.

Report on the Possibilities of Agricultural Extension in the Colony

1940   *Hong Kong: Report on the Possibilities of Agricultural Extension in the Colony.* Hong Kong: Colonial Secretariat Library.

Rutz, Henry J.

1987   Capitalizing on Culture: Moral Ironies in Urban Fiji. *Comparative Studies in Society and History* 29(3): 533–57.

Said, Edward W.

1978   *Orientalism.* New York: Vintage.

Salaff, Janet

1974   'Modern Times' in Hong Kong. *Bulletin of Concerned Asian Scholars* 6(1).

Schurmann, H. Franz

1956   Traditional Property Concepts in China. *Far Eastern Quarterly* 15(4): 507–16.

SCMP: South China Morning Post

Scott, David

1994   Colonial Governmentality. *Social Text* 12(4): 191–220.

Scott, Ian

1980   Administrative Growth and Change in the New Territories. In *Hong Kong: Dilemmas of Growth*, Leung Chi-keung et al eds.. Research School of Pacific Studies, Australian National University and Centre of Asian Studies, University of Hong Kong joint publication.

1989   *Political Change and the Crisis of Legitimacy in Hong Kong.* Honolulu: University of Hawaii Press.

See Chinben
1973   *Jisiquan yu shehui zuzhi – Zhanghua pingyuan juluo fazhan moshi de tantao* (Temple-alliance Religious Spheres and Social Organization – An Investigation into the Pattern of Community Development on the Changhua Plains). *Zhongyang Yanjiuyuan Minzuxue Yanjiusuo Jikan* 36: 191–208 (Nankang).

Shao Chün-p'u
1935   *Shi jia* (An Interpretation of *jia*). *Zhongyang Yanjiuyuan Lishiyuyan Yanjiuso Jikan* 5(2): 279–81 (Nankang).

Shiga Shuzo
1967   *Chugoku Kazokuho No Genri* (Principles of Chinese Family Law). Tokyo: *Sogensha.*
1978   Family Property and the Law of Inheritance in Traditional China. In *Chinese Family Law and Social Change*, D.G. Buxhaum ed.. Seattle: University of Washington Press.

Sihombing, Judith
1984   The Torrens System in the New Territories. *Hong Kong Law Journal* 14: 291–305.

Siu Kwok-kin
1982a   *Xianggang xinjie zhi wudazu* (The Five Great Clans of the New Territories). In *Zupu yu Xianggang Difang Yanjiu,* by Siu Kwok-kin and Siu Kwok-kwan. Hong Kong: Hin Chiu Institute.
1982b   *Pudie zhong suo jian Ming-Qing zhi ji lai gang zhi kezu* (The Arrival of the Hakkas into Hong Kong between the Ming-Qing Periods as Seen in Genealogies). In *Zupu yu Xianggang Difang Yanjiu,* by Siu Kwok-kin and Siu Kwok-kwan. Hong Kong: Hin Chiu Institute.

1982c   *Yingren zujie xinjie chian zhi dizhu chuan chuan shuo i ze*
(A Mythical Account of Land Rights in the Pre-British Era).
In *Zupu yu Xianggang Difang Yanjiu,* by Siu Kwok-kin and
Siu Kwok-kwan. Hong Kong: Hin Chiu Institute.

Smith, Henry
1966   *John Stuart Mill's Other Island.* London: Institute of Economic Affairs publication.

Smith, Richard Saumarez
1985   Rule-by-Records and Rule-by-Reports: Complementary
Aspects of the British Imperial Rule of Law. *Contributions
to Indian Sociology* (n.s.) 19(1): 153–75.

Stocking, George W.
1968   *Race, Culture and Evolution: Essays in the History of Anthropology.* New York: Free Press.
1987   *Victorian Anthropology.* New York: Free Press.

Stocking, George W. ed.
1992   *Colonial Situations: Essays on the Contextualization of Ethnographic Knowledge.* Madison: University of Wisconsin Press.

Stoler, Ann Laura
1989   Rethinking Colonial Categories: European Communities
and the Boundaries of Rule. *Contemporary Studies in Society
and History* 31(1): 134–61.

Strauch, Judith
1983   Community and Kinship in Southeastern China: The View
from the Multilineage Villages of Hong Kong. *Journal of
Asian Studies* 43(1): 21–50.

Sung Hok-p'ang
1938   *Ts'in Fuk* (being an account of how part of the coast of South
China was cleared of inhabitants from the 1st year of Hong
Hei (K'ang Hsi) 1662 to the 8th year of Hong Hei 1669).
The Hong Kong Naturalist 9(1–2): 37–42.

Tai Yen-hui

1934   *Kinsei Shina oyobi Taiwan no kazoku kyosansei* (Family Communism in Modern China and Taiwan). *Hogaku Kyokai Zasshi* 52(10): 1852–69, 2083–2107 (Tokyo).

Tang, James T.H.

1994   From Empire Defence to Imperial Retreat: Britain's Postwar China Policy and the Decolonization of Hong Kong. *Modern Asian Studies* 28(2): 317–37.

Tribe, Keith

1978   *Land, Labour and Economic Discourse.* London: Routledge and Kegan Paul.

Thomas, Nicholas

1990   Sanitation and Seeing: The Creation of State Power in Early Colonial Fiji. *Contemporary Studies in Society and History* 32: 149–70.

1994   *Colonialism's Culture: Anthropology, Travel and Government.* Princeton: Princeton University Press.

Tsang, Steve Yui-sang

1988   *Democracy Shelved: Great Britain, China and Attempts at Constitutional Reform in Hong Kong, 1945–52.* Hong Kong: Oxford University Press.

Viswanathan, Gauri

1989   *Masks of Conquest: Literary Study and British Rule in India.* New York: Columbia University Press.

Walker, J.

1972   *Under the Whitewash.* Hong Kong: The 70s Biweekly.

Wang Sung-hsing

1981   *Lun diyuan yu xieyuan* (On Locality and Descent). In *Zhongguo de Minzu, Shehui yu Wenhua,* Li Yih-yuan and Chiao Chien eds.. Taipei: *Shihuo Chubanshe.*

1991   *Zhongguo ren de "jia" zhidu yu xiandaihua* (The Chinese Family (*jia*) System and its Modernization). In *Zhongguo Jiating ji qi Bianqian* (The Chinese Household and its Transformation), Chiao Chien ed.. Hong Kong: Chinese University of Hong Kong Asia-Pacific Institute.

Watson, James L.

1974   Restaurants and Remittances: Chinese Emigrant Workers in London. In *Anthropologists in Cities*, G.M. Foster and R.V. Kemper eds.. Boston: Little, Brown and Co..

1975   *Emigration and the Chinese Lineage: The Mans in Hong Kong and London.* Berkeley: University of California Press.

1976   Chattel Slavery in Chinese Peasant Society. *Ethnology* 15: 361–75.

1980   Transactions in People: The Chinese Market in Heirs, Servants and Slaves". In *Asian and African Systems of Slavery*, J.L. Watson ed.. Berkeley: University of California Press.

Watson, Rubie

1985   *Inequality among Brothers: Class and Kinship in South China.* Cambridge: Cambridge University Press.

Wesley-Smith, Peter

1979   Diplomatic, Political and Legal Factors in Early Administration of the New Territories. Paper presented at the Annual Meeting of the American Anthropological Association.

1980   *Unequal Treaty, 1898–1997: China, Great Britain and Hong Kong's New Territories.* Hong Kong: Oxford University Press.

1982   Some Legal Problems Relating to Land in the New Territories. In *The New Territories and Its Future*, A. Birch ed.. Hong Kong: The Royal Asiatic Society.

Wiest, Jean-Paul

1976   Lineage and Patterns of Conversion in Guangdong. *Ch'ing-shih Wen-t'i* 4(1): 3–31.

Wilson, B.D.

1954   Chinese Customs in the New Territories. Hong Kong Records Series 119, Deposit 1, Serial 92.

1960   Chinese Burial Customs in Hong Kong. *Journal of the Hong Kong Branch of the Royal Asiatic Society* 1: 115–23.

Wilson, Dick

1990   *Hong Kong! Hong Kong!* London: Unwin Hyman.

Wolf, Arthur P.

1970   Chinese Kinship and Mourning Dress. In *Family and Kinship in Chinese Society*, M. Freedman ed.. Stanford: Stanford University Press.

1976   Aspects of Ancestor Worship in Northern Taiwan. In *Ancestors*, W.H. Newell ed.. The Hague: Mouton.

Wolf, Eric R.

1959   *Sons of the Shaking Earth.* Chicago: University of Chicago Press.

Wolf, Margery

1972   *Women and the Family in Rural Taiwan.* Stanford: Stanford University Press.

Wong, C.T.

1964   Changes in Agricultural Land Use in Hong Kong. *Symposium on Land Use and Mineral Deposits.* Hong Kong: University of Hong Kong Press.

1971   Uses of Agricultural Land: Some Changes in New Territories Farming Patterns. In *The Changing Face of Hong Kong*, D.J. Dwyer ed.. Hong Kong: *Hong Kong Branch of the Royal Asiatic Society.*

Wong, John

1972   Hong Kong's Food Supply from China: Dependence or Interdependence? *Economic Journal*, University of Hong Kong.

XG: *Xinjie Gailan*

1954   (New Territories General Report), Volume 1.

XN: *Xinjie Nianjian* (New Territories Annual Mirror)

1970–1a *Cong Yingguo de tudi zhidu tan dao xianggang de tudi zhengce* (Hong Kong Land Policy from the Perspective of the English Land System).

1970–1b *Xinjie de chiantu* (The Future of the New Territories). by Yuan Mei.

1970–1c *Xinjie zhi guoqu he xianzai yu jianglai* (The Past, Present and Future of the New Territories).

1976   *Zhengqu Xinjie renmin heli quanyi* (Fighting for Rational Rights of the People of the New Territories).

1977a   *Xinjie shi* (A History of the New Territories). by Liu Han.

1977b   *Tan gangfu de nongye zhengce* (On the Hong Kong Government's Agricultural Policies). by Jian Liang.

1977c   *Zhengfu zai xinjie fazhan so yinchi zhi bushang yu anzhi wenti* (The Problems of Security and Compensation Engendered by the Government in the Development of the New Territories).

1977d   *Xinjie chiaobao liu ying xu zhi* (Necessary Facts for New Territories Compatriots Emigrating to England).

1977e   Methods to Improve the Relation between the Government and N.T. People. Published statement dated 15 November 1973.

1977f   New Territories Land Problems by New Territories Heung Yee Kuk. Published statement, n.d..

1977g   Letter to the Hon. District Commissioner of the New Territories from Chan Yat-san, Chairman, N.T.H.Y.K., dated 2 January 1974.

1978a   *Huifu banli xingjian cunwu shenqing* (Restoration of the Small House Application Policy).

1978b   *Xinjie shoudi bujia zaici tiaozheng tigao* (New Territories Land Reclamation Premiums to be Revised Upward Again).

1980–1 *Xinjie shoudi bushang zaiyu tigao* (New Territories Land Premiums to be Raised Upward Again).

1982   *Xinjie yuanjumin lizheng de dingwu yu huandi chuanyi* (House
            and Land Conversion Rights Fought for by New Territories
            Inhabitants).

XXG: *Xinjie Xiangyiju Gongbao* (Heung Yee Kuk Official Gazette)
1976a   Memorandum Tabled at the Meeting of the Working Party
            on Land Matters Held on 3rd March, 1976. no. 13.
1976b   Clearance of Structures on Private Agricultural Land in
            Shatin for Development of New Town (letter to Secretary
            for the New Territories, dated 26 November 1975). no. 13.
1976c   Compulsory Removal of Residents and Demolition of Struc-
            tures at Shatin Satellite Town (letter to Secretary for the New
            Territories, dated 29 April 1976). no. 13.

XXN: *Xinjie Xiangyiju Nianpao* (Heung Yee Kuk Annual Report)
1964–6a   *Juwu baogao*, 1964–66 (Report of Kuk Affairs, 1964–66).
            by Wen Zhushi et al. no. 16.
1964–6b   *Tudi bujia wenti de shangjiao he heli de zhengchu* (A Discus-
            sion of Land Compensation Problems and Their Resolution).
            no. 16.
1966–7a   *Xinjie gaikuang* (Situation of the New Territories). no. 17.
1966–7b   *Juwu baogao: i nian lai gongzuo baogao* (Report of Kuk
            Affairs: A Report of Work Done in the Past Year). by Peng
            Fuhua et al. no. 17.
1967–8   *Zhengfu fali: jianzhu fa (shi yung yu shinjie) tiao-li* (Govern-
            ment Regulations: Building Ordinance Statutes (with
            Applicability to the New Territories)). no. 17.
1970–2   *Gongzuo baogao zongwu* (General Work Status Report). no.
            19.
1974–6   *Gean cailu* (A Summary Record of Individual Cases). no. 21.

XZ: *Xinjie Zhanwang* (New Territories Observer)
1971a   *Xinjie tudi wenti* (New Territories Land Problems), 4 parts.
            Vols. 1–4.
1971b   *Xinjie fazhan de zhangai* (Obstacles to Development in the
            New Territories), by Gao Yuan. vol. 3.

1971c   *Fan lun xinjie wenti* (Speaking in General about Problems in the New Territories), by Liu Jing. vol. 3.

1971d   *Xinjie tudi wenti jingwei* (New Territories Land Problems in Broad Perspective), by Gao Yuan. vol. 4.

1971e   *Jiantao xianggang zhengfu shoudi bushang zhengce* (Analyzing the Compensation Policy for Land Resumption of the Hong Kong Government), by Yang Baisha. vol. 5.

Xu Tiantai

1941   *Fujian zudian zhidu yanjiu* (A Study of Tenancy Systems in Fujian). *Fujian wenhua jikan* 1(1): 59–80.

Yang Ch'ing-kun

1925   *Jiangsu Sheng Nongye Diaocha Lu* (Agricultural Survey of Jiangsu). Department of Agriculture, Nantung University.

Yang Guozhen

1981   *Shilun Qingdai Minbei minjian de tudi maimai* (An Investigation of Customary Transactions in Land in Northern Fujian during the Qing Dynasty). *Zhongguo Shi Yanjiu* 1: 29–41.

Yao Ciai

1933   *Poxi chongtu de zhuyao yuanyin* (Major Causes of Conflict between Mother-in-law and Daughter-in-law). *Shehuixue Jie* 6 (Beijing).

ZB: *Zhongli Bao* (The Neutral Post)

1979   *Xinjie xiaoxing xiangcunwu zhengci* (New Territories Small House Policy), January 15. by Zheng Yungcai.

1989   *Tudi wenti yuanyuan benben* (The Origins of (the New Territories) Land Problems), 2 parts, January 31, March 31. by Deng Guanghua.

ZYWHZS: *Zhongyuan Wenhua Zongshu*

1969   *Kejia chianru gangjiu xinjie de shihua* (Historical Notes on the Migration of the Hakkas into the Hong Kong Region), Vol.3: 64–65.

Wo Hang 'Extended Families' by Household Unit, 1983

Unit	WH	HK	PRC	UK	EC	NA	CA	LivingGens	Own/Occ
01	2			4				3	Own
02	5	2		5				3	Own
03	0			5				2	N/A
04	5			1	3			2	Occ
05	0			9				3	N/A
06	2							2	Occ
07	1			8				3	Own
08	0			4				2	N/A
09	1			3				2	Occ
10	1	2		2				2	Own
11	0	4			4			2	N/A
12	2					2	2	3	Own
13	1	3		1				2	Occ
14	2			5		6		3	Occ
15	1			10	6			3	Own
16	5							3	Own
17	0			6				3	N/A
18	0		1	3				2	N/A
19	2			4	1			3	Own
20	1			4	7		2	4	Own
21	3				1			3	Own
22	1					5		3	Own
23	6				1			2	Occ
24	6			2				3	Own
25	0			4				2	N/A
26	7			1				2	Own
27	5	1		8				2	Own
28	5			2				2	Occ
29	0				5			3	N/A
30	5							2	Own
31	0	1			3			2	N/A

32	1		4			3	Own
33	6	1				2	Own
34	1			8		3	Own
35	0		5			2	N/A
36	0		9			3	N/A
37	1					1	Own
38	0			4		2	N/A
39	1					1	Occ
40	0		6			2	N/A
41	1	4				2	Own
42	1					1	Own
43	1					1	Own
44	4		5			2	Occ
45	0		2			1	N/A
46	2		12			3	Own
47	0		4			2	N/A
48	0	2	12			3	N/A
49	0	1	2			1	N/A
50	4		3			3	Own
51	0	2	11			3	N/A
52	2		3			2	Own
53	0		8			3	N/A
54	1				5	3	Own
55	2					2	Occ
56	0	5				2	N/A
57	1	5	3			3	Own
58	3			3		2	Own
59	0		2			1	N/A
60	0	6	8			3	N/A
61	1					1	Own
62	1	5				3	Own
63	4		4			2	Own
64	3		4			3	Own
65	1		3			3	Own
66	0		4			2	N/A
67	3		4			2	Own
68	0		3			2	N/A
69	0		5			3	N/A
70	7	3				3	Own
71	2	3	8			3	Own
72	6	4	2			3	Own
73	0		8			3	N/A
74	4		1			2	Own

75	0			3				2	N/A
76	0	6		2				2	N/A
77	0			4				2	N/A
78	1			4	2			3	Own
79	0			9				3	N/A
80	0			9				3	N/A
81	1			7				2	Occ
82	0			9				3	N/A
83	0			8				3	N/A
84	1			3				3	Own
85	6			6				3	Own
86	1			4				2	Own
87	2			3				2	Occ
88	5			1				2	Own
89	0			7				2	N/A
90	4				2			2	Own
91	0			6				2	N/A
92	1			4				3	Own
93	0	1						1	N/A
94	0			3				2	N/A
95	0				4			2	N/A
96	4			1				2	Own
97	1	1						1	Occ
98	1			5				3	Occ
99	0	6						2	N/A
100	1	1		4				2	Occ
101	3							2	Own
102	2							1	Own
103	2							2	Own
104	1			16				3	Own
105	1	3		10	1			3	Own
106	1	9				9		4	Own
107	1			6				2	Occ
108	2			15				3	Own

Totals	175	80	1	385	55	27	4		
								1G	11
								2G	50
								3G	45
								4G	2

Own	53
Occ	16
N/A	39

Abbreviations:

WH	Wo Hang	*LivingGens*	Number of Generations in "Family"
HK	Hong Kong Area	*1G*	Total of One Living Generation
PRC	Mainland China	*2G*	Total of Two Living Generations
UK	United Kingdom	*3G*	Total of Three Living Generations
EC	Continental Europe	*Own*	Owner-Occupant
NA	North America	*Occ*	Non-Owner Occupant
CA	Caribbean Islands	*N/A*	Not Applicable (Unoccupied)

Explanation of Statistical Totals:

Of the total of 108 active residential households in Wo Hang, they totalled (by my survey of 1983) 175 "villagers" residing locally, 80 living elsewhere in Hong Kong, 1 living in China, 385 living in the U.K., 55 living in continental Europe, 27 living in North America, and 4 living in the Caribbean. Taking into account both local and overseas residents who identified with these households, 11 of the households constituted a single generation, 50 were composed of two generations, 45 spanned three generations and 2 stretched over four generations. Of the total households, 53 were occupied by people who also owned the house, 16 were occupied by those who did not own it (but were close agnates) and 39 were unoccupied at the time (or occupied by absentee landlords). Although not shown above, 100 of the total households occupied land that belonged to the same owner (while the remaining 8 did not). Moreover, 95 of the households were taken care of by the occupants themselves or close agnates, while the remaining 13 were taken care of by non-agnatic relatives of the owner (who had no other relations with villagers overall).

INDEX

347